Homo americanus

Homo americanus

Ernest Hemingway, Tennessee Williams, and Queer Masculinities

John S. Bak

Madison • Teaneck
Fairleigh Dickinson University Press

© 2010 by Rosemont Publishing & Printing Corp.

All rights reserved. Authorization to photocopy items for internal or personal use, or the internal or personal use of specific clients, is granted by the copyright owner, provided that a base fee of $10.00, plus eight cents per page, per copy is paid directly to the Copyright Clearance Center, 222 Rosewood Drive, Danvers, Massachusetts 01923. [978-0-8386-4254-2/10 $10.00 + 8¢ pp, pc.]

Associated University Presses
2010 Eastpark Boulevard
Cranbury, NJ 08512

The paper used in this publication meets the requirements of the American National Standard for Permanence of Paper for Printed Library Materials Z39.48-1984.

Library of Congress Cataloging-in-Publication Data

Bak, John S.
  Homo americanus : Ernest Hemingway, Tennessee Williams, and queer masculinities / John S. Bak.
     p. cm.
  Includes bibliographical references and index.
  ISBN 978-0-8386-4254-2 (alk. paper)
  1. Hemingway, Ernest, 1899–1961. 2. Williams, Tennessee, 1911–1983. 3. Homosexuality and literature—United States—History—20th century. I. Title.
PS3515.E37Z574 2010
813'.52—dc22
[B]
                                                    2009017185

PRINTED IN THE UNITED STATES OF AMERICA

*In memory of my father, Joseph Martin Bak, Jr.,
and of my mother, Patricia Ann Koziol Bak*

A hotel is no good when you have to put the glass on the floor because there's no table by the bed. (a Hemingway type sentence)
— Tennessee Williams, personal notebook entry, December 7, 1953

Thurs. A.M. — A bright day without the weight of Roman summer. I woke too early, about 6:30, and applied medication and sat in hot water (bidet) to relieve rectal trouble, which is not serious, so far, except as an apprehension. Read "Death In the Afternoon" by Hemingway with ever increasing respect for it as a great piece of prose, and honest acknowledgment of a lust which is nearly always concealed. H's great quality, aside from his prose style, which is matchless, is this fearless expression of brute nature, his naively candid braggadocia. If he drew pictures of pricks, he could not more totally confess his innate sexual inversion, despite the probability that his relations have been exclusively (almost?) with women. He has no real interest in women and shows no true heterosexual eroticism in any of his work.

(I don't think this is just the usual desire to implicate others in one's own "vice".)

Hemingway calls El Greco, whom he greatly admires, "El Rey de Maricones" — perhaps in literature H. deserves the same crown.
— Tennessee Williams, personal notebook entry, August 5, 1954

Contents

List of Illustrations	9
Acknowledgments	11
Introduction	17
1. Williams's *Cat* and Hemingway's *Sun:* Queerly Masculine	32
2. *The Sun Also* Sets: Jake Barnes, Impotence, and Sexual Existenialism	53
3. "A Dying Gaul": The Signifying Phallus and Williams's "Three Players of a Summer Game"	101
4. "sneakin' an' spyin'" from Broadway to the Beltway: Cold War Masculinity, Brick, and Homosexual Existentialism	130
5. The Impotence of Being Ernest: Scott and Hemingway's "Gender Trouble" in Williams's *Clothes for a Summer Hotel*	160
Conclusion	208
Notes	224
Bibliography	280
Index	294

Illustrations

1. Hy Roth illustration of Williams and Hemingway at the Floridita bar in Havana, *Playboy*, May, 1964.   19

2. Antonio Ordóñez, with inscriptions to Tennessee Williams, 1955.   26

3. Williams with Maria Britneva at the Floridita bar in Havana, 1956.   27

4. Al Hirschfeld cartoon of Hemingway with Truman Capote on the Left Bank in Paris, with Williams sitting on the left, August 13, 1950.   102

5. Pierce Arrow touring car, ca. 1925.   110

6. Williams and Marion Vaccaro with Jean-Paul Sartre and Simone de Beauvoir at the Hotel Nacional in Havana, October, 1960.   134

Acknowledgments

AS ANY RESEARCHER KNOWS, A BOOK INVOLVES THE EFFORTS OF more than one writer, and there is no exception here.

Though this book began back in 1999 as a conference paper at the Université de Metz on homosexual identities, it developed over the years into a study of considerable length through the help of many friends and colleagues, notably André Kaenel and R. Barton Palmer. Several Williams scholars and aficionados, including Philip C. Kolin, Robert Bray, W. Kenneth Holditch, Allean Hale, George Crandell, Michael Paller, Annette Saddik, Jacqueline O'Connor, Brian Parker, Nancy Tischler, Albert J. Devlin, Thomas P. Adler, Fred Todd, and Thomas Keith, have at one time or another improved the contents of this book. I owe all of them a debt of gratitude.

I would like to thank the staffs of the various Williams archives. At the Rare Book and Manuscript Library, Columbia University, Director Michael T. Ryan and Jennifer B. Lee were instrumental in locating Williams's photos of Antonio Ordóñez, and Jane R. Siegel tracked down and annotated for me the list of Hemingway's works found in Williams's Key West home at the time of his death. Siva Blake and Mark Cave of the Williams Research Center of Historic New Orleans Collection were always available to answer my requests for various manuscripts. Richard Workman, Associate Librarian at the Harry Ransom Humanities Research Center, University of Texas (Austin) — the Mecca of Williams studies — provided copies of invaluable manuscripts and letters.

As for permission rights, I would also like to thank again Thomas Keith, Kate Johnson, Lydia Zelaya, The University of the South, and the Tennessee Williams and Ernest Hemingway Estates for allowing me to cite from both writers' published and unpublished works. Natasha Grenfell kindly allowed me to reproduce a photo from her mother's collection of letters, *Five O'Clock Angel*. W. Kenneth Holditch, who is currently editing the second edition of Richard F. Leavitt's *The World of Tennessee Williams*, and Elizabeth Dunham, research librarian at the University of Tennessee Special Collections Library, helped me procure a copy of the photo of Williams with Jean-Paul Sartre that first appeared in Leavitt's book. Daria Enrick and the Margo Feiden Galleries granted me permission to use the Al Hirschfeld cartoon of Hemingway and Williams that first appeared in the *New York Times*. Tracy Roth-Myers, daughter of celebrated Chicago artist Hy Roth, permitted the use of her father's illustration for the cover of this book. In addition, I would also like thank Kelly Rogers and Noel Polk at *Theatre Journal* and *Mississippi Quarterly* for allowing me to reproduce material in chapters 3 and 4 of this book that first appeared in their pages.

Special thanks are also due to the editorial and production staffs of Fairleigh Dickinson University Press and Associated University Presses, in particular Harry Keyishian and Christine A. Retz, and to the research group *Interdisciplinarité Dans les Études Anglophones* (I.D.E.A.) at Nancy-Université for financial support in the publication of this book.

Finally, I would like to thank my wife Nathalie, whose keen critical eye and loving patience saw me through to the end of this travail, and my daughter and son, Margaux and James, for teaching me that there is more to life than a computer screen and a musty library.

Despite all of their sagacious advice, any error still present in this work is solely of my own making.

※ ※ ※

Quotations from published material by Tennessee Williams are taken from the following sources:

Excerpts from *Cat on a Hot Tin Roof*, by Tennessee Williams, copyright © 1954, 1955 by The University of the South, copyright renewed 1982, 1983 The University of the South. Reprinted with the permission of New Directions Publishing Corporation.

Excerpts from *Clothes for a Summer Hotel*, by Tennessee Williams, copyright © 1980, 1981, 1983 by The University of the South. Reprinted with the permission of New Directions Publishing Corporation.

Excerpt from *A Streetcar Named Desire*, by Tennessee Williams, copyright © 1947 by The University of the South, copyright renewed 1957 by The University of the South. Reprinted with the permission of New Directions Publishing Corporation.

Excerpts from "Three Players of a Summer Game," from *The Collected Stories of Tennessee Williams* by Tennessee Williams, copyright © 1952, 1985 by The University of the South. Reprinted with the permission of New Directions Publishing Corporation.

Excerpts from "Critic Says 'Evasion,' Writer Says 'Mystery,'" "A Writer's Quest for a Parnassus," "Introduction to *Reflections in a Golden Eye*," "Something Wild . . ." "Let Me Hang It All Out," and "A Festival Night in Paris," from *New Selected Essays: Where I Live*, copyright ©

ACKNOWLEDGMENTS

1948, 1950, 1955, 1973, 2009 by The University of the South. Reprinted with the permission of New Directions Publishing Corporation.

Excerpts from *The Selected Letters of Tennessee Williams, Volume I: 1920–1945*, copyright © 2000 by The University of the South. Reprinted with the permission of New Directions Publishing Corporation.

Excerpts from *The Selected Letters of Tennessee Williams, Volume II: 1946–1957*, copyright © 2004 by The University of the South. Reprinted with the permission of New Directions Publishing Corporation.

Quotations from published material by Ernest Hemingway are taken from the following sources:

Excerpts from *Under Kilimanjaro*, by Ernest Hemingway, copyright © 2005 by The Ernest Hemingway Foundation. Reprinted with the permission of The Ernest Hemingway Foundation.

Excerpts from *The Dangerous Summer*, by Ernest Hemingway, copyright © 1960 by Ernest Hemingway. Copyright renewed © 1988 by John Hemingway, Patrick Hemingway, and Gregory Hemingway. Reprinted with the permission of The Ernest Hemingway Foundation.

Excerpts from *Death in the Afternoon*, by Ernest Hemingway, copyright © 1932 by Charles Scribner's Sons. Copyright renewed © 1960 by Ernest Hemingway. Reprinted with the permission of The Ernest Hemingway Foundation.

Excerpts from *The Garden of Eden*, by Ernest Hemingway, copyright © 1986 by Mary Hemingway, John Hemingway, Patrick Hemingway, and Gregory Hemingway. Reprinted with the permission of The Ernest Hemingway Foundation.

Excerpts from *A Moveable Feast*, by Ernest Hemingway, copyright © 1964 by Mary Hemingway. Copyright renewed © 1992 by John H. Hemingway, Patrick Hemingway, and Gregory Hemingway. Reprinted with the permission of Scribner, a Division of Simon & Schuster, Inc., and The Ernest Hemingway Foundation.

Excerpts from *The Sun Also Rises*, by Ernest Hemingway, copyright © 1926 by Charles Scribner's Sons. Copyright renewed 1954 by Ernest Hemingway. Reprinted with the permission of Scribner, a Division of Simon & Schuster, Inc., and The Ernest Hemingway Foundation.

Excerpts from *Islands in the Stream*, by Ernest Hemingway, copyright © 1970 by Mary Hemingway. Copyright renewed © 1998 by John Hemingway, Patrick Hemingway, and Gregory Hemingway. Reprinted with the permission of Scribner, a Division of Simon & Schuster, Inc., and The Ernest Hemingway Foundation.

Excerpts from *Ernest Hemingway: Selected Letters, 1917–1961*, by Ernest Hemingway, edited by Carlos Baker, copyright © 1981 by The Ernest Hemingway Foundation. Reprinted with the permission of Scribner, a Division of Simon & Schuster, Inc., and The Ernest Hemingway Foundation.

Homo americanus

Introduction

"The best I can say for myself is that I worked like hell."
—Tennessee Williams, *Notebooks*

"Perversion's dull and old-fashioned."
—Ernest Hemingway, *The Garden of Eden*

"Tennessee has never met Castro since; and he never saw Hemingway again after this account of two accidental meetings simply because they happened. Artistically, nothing came of them; but they may contribute, to future histories of American literature, a bizarre and frivolous footnote."
—Kenneth Tynan, "Papa and the Playwright"

ERNEST HEMINGWAY AND TENNESSEE WILLIAMS SURELY MAKE strange bedfellows. What, if anything, could the heteromasculine novelist and the homoeffeminate playwright have in common beyond a mutual distrust bordering on acrimony? British theater critic Kenneth Tynan asked a similar question in 1959: "I often play the game ["Imaginary Conversations"] in my mind, and one of the pairings with which I have often toyed is that of Ernest Hemingway and Tennessee Williams. How would the great extrovert react to the great introvert, the big-game hunter to the hot-house plant, the virility symbol to the student of deviation?"[1]

This book is an attempt to answer that question.

Though separated by only eleven years of age, Hemingway and Williams are a literary generation apart—Hemingway, the modernist, World War I writer, and Williams, the (post)modernist playwright more closely aligned with World War II. To be sure, Hemingway's career reached its summit with his novels of the 1920s and 1930s, whereas Williams's fame came with his plays of the 1940s and 1950s. But Williams was already writing at the time Hemingway had achieved his fame, just as Hemingway continued writing throughout the 1950s when Williams reigned on Broadway. In short, while a world seemingly separates them in time and space, Hemingway and Williams had more in common than either publicly admitted or perhaps would have ever admitted. If there were ever a sense of literary camaraderie between them, however, it surely emerged from Williams more than from Hemingway, though their work, particularly in how they challenged sex/gender roles and identity politics of their day, does demonstrate a literary tradition worth exploring.

They met only once, in Castro's Havana back on April 7, 1959.[2] Hemingway's career was in its twilight, or so it seemed to the literary world, and he was just a couple years away from committing suicide. Williams's was gradually waning, with the success of *Cat on a Hot Tin Roof*, for which Castro and Hemingway had known him, already a few years behind him. Hemingway, the Nobel safely in his pocket, could still hold court; Williams, among the practicing elite of American playwrights, nonetheless struggled with each new play to win back doubting critics and dwindling audiences. In March of 1959, just weeks prior to that meeting, Williams's *Sweet Bird of Youth* was enjoying a successful premier on Broadway despite its lukewarm reviews. Among those critics who panned the play was Tynan himself, who felt "dismayed and alarmed" by it.[3] Just like the play's heroine, Alexandra Del Largo, who flees Hollywood in anticipation of her latest film's critical panning, Williams ditched the Great White Way for safer havens. After brief stays in Miami and Key West, Williams flew to Havana where, through the help of Tynan, he met and lunched with Ernest Hemingway at El Floridita.

Hemingway had just arrived in Havana himself, having fled Ketchum, Idaho, where he had just buried his friend Taylor Williams. Not long after the funeral, Hemingway rented a car and, with wife Mary and Ed Hotchner (a Washington University alum, with whom Williams had worked on the staff of *The Eliot* in 1936–1937), drove to Key West via Phoenix, Tucson, and New Orleans, where Hotchner had left them.[4] On Easter Sunday March 29, 1959 — just four days after Tennessee Williams's forty-eighth birthday — Hemingway and Mary flew to a Havana fresh from a revolution that had just ousted the corrupt Batista regime.[5]

In his *Memoirs*, Williams recalls in detail this brief but momentous meeting with Hemingway and, later, with Castro. His version of the story depicts a kind and soft-spoken Hemingway, which may have been more the way Williams had wanted to remember him than the way he actually was that day. As Williams writes,

> Before Castro took over Cuba, Marion [Vaccaro] and I used to have riotous weekends in Havana. Marion just as much enjoyed the frolicsome night life in Havana as I did and we would go to the same places to enjoy it. We even went back after Castro came in. The first time I went back to Havana after

Hy Roth illustration of Williams and Hemingway at the Floridita bar in Havana, *Playboy*, May, 1964. Courtesy of Tracy Roth-Myers and the Hy Roth Estate.

Castro's triumph, I was introduced to him by Ernest Hemingway, whom I met through the British theatre critic Kenneth Tynan. Tynan called me—I was staying at the Hotel Nacional in Havana—and he said, "Would you like to meet Ernest Hemingway?" and I said, "I don't think that's advisable, do you? I understand that he can be very unpleasant to people of my particular temperament." And Tynan said, "Well, I will be there to lend you what support I can. I think you ought to meet him because he is one of the great writers of your time and mine." I said, "Okay, I'll take a chance on it." So we went down to the Floridita, which was Hemingway's nighttime and daytime hangout, when he wasn't at sea, and he couldn't have been more charming. He was exactly the opposite of what I'd expected. I had expected a very manly, super-macho sort of guy, very bullying and coarse spoken. On the contrary, Hemingway struck me as a gentleman who seemed to have a very touchingly shy quality about him.[6]

The truth behind Williams's recollections are worth calling into question (it was, for example, his and Vaccaro's second trip back to Havana since the revolution), given that several people were there to witness the meeting, and each recorded varying, at times contradictory, resposes to the situation. What this may suggest is that Williams had unintentionally recalled the meeting differently (after all, it had been nearly fifteen years when he finally penned his versions of the story). Or, he may have been heavily under the influence of the works by and about Hemingway that he was reading at that time while preparing his final Broadway play, *Clothes for a Summer Hotel*. Whatever the reasons, there are several versions of their meeting, and Williams's is at odds with others who have attempted to capture the story with some accuracy.

The first discrepancy is Tynan's own account, published in two separate essays for the magazines *Holiday* and *Playboy*, later to be reprinted in his collection, *Right and Left*.[7] According to Tynan, Williams was at first apprehensive about meeting Hemingway: "'But won't he kick me?' said Tennessee, stricken with unease. 'They tell me that Mr. Hemingway usually kicks people like me in the crotch.'"[8] To be sure, Tynan's quote not only differs from Williams's version ("very unpleasant to people of my particular temperament"), but it also belies the playwright's famed Southern manners, which would have kept him from speaking so frankly in an interview, particularly in 1959 when his homosexuality was not yet made public. But, Tynan adds, Hemingway was "delighted" to have met him (or at least to have had the opportunity), which Williams validates to a certain extent with his own recollections.[9]

During their meeting, Tynan continues, the two writers talked about Williams's appreciation of Hemingway's "care about honour among men," to which Hemingway curtly replied: "'What kind of men, Mr Williams,' he said, 'did you have in mind? . . . People who have honour never talk about it. They know it, and they confer immortality on each other.'"[10] They also spoke of the bullfighter Antonio Ordóñez—a very close friend of Hemingway's and the son of Cateyano Ordóñez (Nino de la Palma), after whom Jake Barnes was fashioned—and of his *cogidas*:[11] "'I was in Spain last year for the bullfights,' Williams said, 'I go every year. I get so disturbed I have to leave after the third bull . . . .

Last summer I met one the matadors on the beach,' Tennessee went on, 'a lovely boy, very friendly.'"[12] Tynan describes an "all deadpan" Hemingway to Williams's attempts to strike up a conversation, one obviously slanted more toward Hemingway's work and interests than Williams's.

After a short exchange on William Faulkner and just before another one on kidneys and livers in which they exchanged their doctors' names and addresses, they continued their conversation on the death of Hemingway's second wife, Pauline, in 1951: "'I used to know your second wife, Mr Hemingway. . . . I believe her name was Pauline. I knew her in Key West when I was young. She was very kind to me when I was poor—a lovely lady, a most hospitable lady. I often wondered what happened to her. They tell me she died. Did she die in great pain?'"[13] It was rather a sore subject for Hemingway, who replied sharply to Williams: "'She died like everybody else . . . and after that she was dead.'"[14] All in all, the two-hour luncheon was not a very fruitful encounter, Tynan concludes, with a suffering Hemingway remaining typically distant and sardonic, which the tipsy Williams may or may not have detected.

Having read Tynan's version of the meeting, Williams would later recall in his *Memoirs* that "Tynan has reported this first encounter humorously but not accurately" (*M* 67), and then sets out to put the record straight. Williams admits that he was "naturally awkward" and had said "some *gauche* things" about Pauline Hemingway's death: "Hemingway didn't seem to take it amiss, but he said (sort of a struggle), 'Well, she died, and then she was dead,' and went on drinking" (*M* 67). Next, and fully in line with what Tynan had written, Williams describes how he and Hemingway talked about bullfighting: "I was not an *aficionado* of bullfighting, not somebody who knew the fine technique, the fine points of bullfighting, but one who enjoyed the spectacle of it and I had become, the previous summer, a good friend of Antonio Ordóñez, who was, you might almost say, an idol of Ernest Hemingway's. I mentioned to Hemingway that I knew Antonio Ordóñez. Hemingway was pleased, I thought, and he was also pleased that I shared his interest in bullfighting" (*M* 67–68).

If Tynan had intimated that Hemingway was being ironic in his responses to Williams about bullfighting or about Ordóñez, Williams felt that he was being in earnest. To be sure, Williams may not have detected any irony in Hemingway's voice, or perhaps there simply wasn't any there to detect, and Tynan was guilty of reading too far into the responses, disingenuously or otherwise.

From there, Williams and Hemingway had turned to the revolution, which, according to Williams, Hemingway saw as having been "good" for Cuba, with which Williams agreed: "Well, I knew that it was a good revolution, because I had been to Cuba when Batista was in power and he had a charming habit of torturing young students. . . . He would sometimes even emasculate them. He was a horrifying sadist" (*M* 68). Williams next describes in some detail his subsequent meeting with Castro. He verifies that "Hemingway wrote [him] a letter of introduction to Castro," and that Tynan and he had visited the Palacio, the seat of the Cuban government:

> Castro was having a cabinet session at the time. His cabinet session lasted quite long. We waited it out, sitting on the steps outside the room in which the session was being held. After about a three-hour wait, the door was thrown open and we were ushered in. Castro greeted us both very warmly. When Kenneth Tynan introduced me, the Generalissimo said, "Oh, that cat," meaning *Cat on a Hot Tin Roof*, which surprised me—delighted me, of course. I couldn't imagine the generalissimo knowing anything about a play of mine. Then he proceeded to introduce us to all of his cabinet ministers. We were given coffee and liqueurs and it was a lovely occasion, well worth the three-hour wait. (*M* 68)[15]

Williams, in fact, would often repeat this version of his meeting with Hemingway in several interviews he made during the late 1970s when *Clothes for a Summer Hotel* was nearing completion. As John Hicks recalls in 1979, "Though Key West is renowned as the city of Ernest Hemingway, Papa had left town by the time Williams arrived on the scene. 'I only met him for one afternoon and that was in Havana at a bar-restaurant called the Floridita. We had a nice friendly conversation, and he gave me a letter of introduction to Fidel Castro. I was with the English critic Kenneth Tynan, and he gave both of us the letter, and we met Fidel Castro.'"[16] Dotson Rader, in his essay "The Art of Theatre V: Tennessee Williams," would confirm Williams's comment that he had "a very pleasant meeting" with Hemingway (*CTW* 348). All in all, then, while Williams's side of the story provides information that Tynan's version does not, it does raise questions about whose version is most accurate—the self-aggrandizing critic's or the self-effacing (and probably drunk) playwright's?

Elaine Dundy, Tynan's wife, was also present at that meeting and has recently added a third version where she tries to separate truth from myth, the colorful from the colored.[17] In a chapter entitled "Hem and Tenn" in her memoirs, *Life Itself!*, Dundy intimates that while her husband's version is perhaps most accurate in detail (despite its sardonic tone), Williams's story better captures the mood of this meeting of literature's "twin peaks."[18] Dundy was actually on assignment with Tynan for *Holiday* magazine to cover the recent revolution in Cuba and recalls how Tynan had contacted Hemingway, whom he had previously met in Spain and again in New York, and how Hemingway had then invited them out to his suburban *finca* for lunch. She and Tynan then ran into Williams by accident at the Hotel Nacional, where the invitation to meet Hemingway had been made.

Dundy had known both writers beforehand, describing them as the "yang and the yin of American letters": "Heart-wrenchingly, Hemingway wrote of grace under pressure; heartbreakingly, Tennessee wrote of *dis*grace under pressure."[19] "They seemed poles apart," Dundy writes, "[b]ut were they?"[20] To a certain extent, they were "arrestingly alike": both had "literary" homes in Key West; both were consummate writers who worked daily at their craft (systematically in the small hours of the morning until noontime); both had a passion for Italy and for Spain and were strongly influenced by Latin culture; both were attracted to and tormented by their Christian faiths (passing from Protestantism to Catholicism to finally something akin to liberal humanism); both had domineering mothers and alcoholic fathers; both were second children with older sisters; and both had grandfathers of whom they were proud and fathers for whom they felt ashamed.[21] To this list, I would add that both were avid writers of letters, using the epistle as a form of psychotherapy and daily literary training; both were hypochondriacs; both suffered bouts of depression after a decade of critical onslaughts; both were paranoid later in life; both were gregarious and required company but virulently protected their need to be left alone; both were advocates for the rights of society's pariahs, be it Hemingway's "outlyers" or Williams's "Fugitive Kind"; and both were voracious readers, which included each others' work. Williams even admitted to Dundy his admiration for Hemingway's fiction: "'He writes about the quest of honour among men,' he said in my presence. 'I know of no quest more dangerous than that.'"[22] And while "Hemingway did not give me his assessment of Tennessee's work," Dundy notes, "he was certainly, by any standards, a harsh critic of his contemporaries."[23] That no criticism was ever leveled directly or indirectly against Williams or his work, she writes, was a sign of Papa's unspoken respect for the playwright.

And, as if providentially, they finally met that April in Havana. Unlike her predecessors' work on the subject, Dundy attempts not to let reputation trump truth, and balances the various versions through her own recollections: "Ken and Tenn and George Plimpton (also in Havana as the time) have all written about it, each seeing it from his point of view."[24] Williams, she writes, told her and Tynan that Plimpton was arranging for him to meet Hemingway, but that he was also a bit nervous: "'I—ah—gather he is not overfond of people of my persuasion,' he said, then with that upward inflection, 'but I hear he's very courteous?' "[25] In recalling certain remarks Hemingway had made to her earlier in Spain that "could definitely be construed as homophobic," Dundy suggests that Williams's fear was not entirely unfounded: "Specifically Hemingway had told me of an incident that took place on an ocean liner when a famous actor, Frank Vosper, a homosexual, went over to Hemingway's table with the idea of joining him for a drink and Hemingway smashed his glass "to indicate that [he] did not wish to drink with a pederast."[26]

That was then, and this was now. Hemingway, who had just "completed" the manuscript for the novel that would be published posthumously as *The Garden of Eden*—an unorthodox Hemingway novel to be sure, given David Bourne and his young wife Catherine's exploration of the hetero-/homosexual divide—was perhaps more tolerant now toward sexual "perversion" than ever. He told Dundy that he was "'for normalcy and against homosexuality'" but only because "'sexually there are infinite variations for the normal person but none for the homosexual one,'" a thesis that this study will explore more fully.[27] Dundy felt that Hemingway's comment implied he would meet Williams without similar incident.

As for the meeting itself, Dundy admits that "Ken and Tenn's stories d[o] not tally," at first preferring but now despising Tynan's version because it "turned Tenn into a buffoon while Hem deadpanned caustic monosyllables and elaborately pulled his leg."[28] Dundy, for example, refutes Tynan's description of Williams as having worn "a yachting jacket with silver buttons" to show Hemingway that "although he might be a decadent, he was at least an *outdoor* decadent";[29] she writes instead that Williams wore a simple navy blue blazer that she had seen him wear several times before.[30] Plimpton, who suggests that it was he and not Tynan behind the writers' introduction, took Tynan's mockery one step further, even equating Williams's yachting cap and white flannel trousers as evidence of his posturing to the sea-worthy Hemingway: "'Papa and I sat at the bar at La Floridita waiting for Tennessee. . . . An hour late, Tennessee came in wearing an all-white sailor's outfit, complete with the hat and gold piping. I introduced the two, then Papa turned around, looked Tennessee over from head to toe, and said just three words: 'Not even close.' With that, Hemingway turned back to the bar and Tennessee melted away in embarrassment."[31] For Dundy, Williams's outfit represented more his sign of respect for Hemingway than some premeditated, sporty drag performance.

She also dismisses Tynan's version of the story about Williams's encounter with Antonio Ordóñez. In his version, Tynan has Hemingway mocking an innocent reply to Williams's comment that he befriended the famous bullfighter: "'Do you think he would talk to us and show us his *cogidas?*'"[32] Tynan's implication here is that Hemingway thought Williams did not really know Ordóñez that well, nor that the bullfighter and Hemingway were very close friends at the time, which Dundy plainly refutes by pointing out that their friendship was widely reported in the press and that Williams was an avid reader of the gossip columns. Though Hemingway was suspicious of Williams's statement about Ordóñez, Williams corroborates his story in the July 29, 1955 entry of his personal notebooks: "This P.M. drove out to a lovely hotel on a beach between here and Sitges with Carlos and the great Torero Antonio Ordonez [*sic*], a charming 'chico' but not a perfect model for Swim trunks. He showed us his six 'cogidas' two of which were grave ones."[33] Columbia University has in its Rare Book and Manuscript Library two photos of Antonio Ordóñez from 1955, one of which is inscribed "Para Williams du un amigo y admirator" ("For Williams from a friend and admirer").[34] Williams even mentions Antonio Ordóñez in his *Memoirs* while reminiscing about the opening of *A Streetcar Named Desire*: "Kazan and I were standing in the lobby of the Philadelphia theatre before curtain time and the crowd was pressing like *aficionados* of the bull ring about to see the great Ordóñez" (*M* 137). Thus, if Williams mentioned Ordóñez at all to Hemingway, it was intended to find a topic of mutual interest.[35]

Furthermore, Dundy suggests that Hemingway would not have written such praise for Williams in his letter of introduction to Castro if he had just spent the afternoon mocking him. To be sure, Dundy's point is well taken, for after the meeting, Hemingway "scribbled to Castro his introduction to 'the English journalist Kenneth Tynan' and 'the great North American playwright, Tennessee Williams'. Reading that must have told Tenn something."[36] George Plimpton validates this compliment when he writes that, after Tynan, Dundy, and Williams had left to go and visit Castro, Hemingway commented humorously upon Williams's regalia but admitted that, though "unpredictable," Williams was a "[d]amn good playwright."[37] The compliment is noteworthy if we take into consideration Hemingway's own failed attempt years earlier at writing and producing a Broadway play, *The Fifth Column* (1937), which he later admitted was the worse thing he had ever written.[38] Whatever he had thought about Williams the man before or after their encounter in Cuba, one thing is for certain: Hemingway at least respected Williams the artist.

This first and final encounter between the two writers has been well documented, not only among the journalists present there that day, but also among a few Hemingway and Williams scholars. Most comparisons made between the two men, however, end with their lunch at the

Antonio Ordóñez, with inscriptions to Tennessee Williams, 1955. Courtesy of the Tennessee Williams Papers, Rare Book and Manuscript Library, Columbia University.

Floridita. Carlos Baker, for example, describes the meeting as having been amiable, with the "novelist and the playwright then part[ing] in amity, linked at last, as Tynan said, by 'by medicine and mortality.'"[39] Perhaps tellingly, though, none of Hemingway's more recent biographers, including Kenneth S. Lynn, James R. Mellow, and Michael S. Reynolds, ever felt the need to build upon Baker's single paragraph devoted to their encounter.[40] Jeffrey Meyers even dismisses the meeting entirely with one factual sentence that demonstrates how little Williams figures among Hemingway scholars: "That same month, after Hemingway returned to Havana, he met Tennessee Williams and the drama critic Kenneth Tynan at the Floridita."[41] Williams appears in Hemingway criticism, if at all, as a mere biographical footnote.

In Williams's biographies, Hemingway fares much better, though again little is amended to the existing knowledge of their encounter provided earlier by Tynan. What several Williams scholars have overlooked is that Williams had hoped to meet Hemingway in Havana as early as spring 1955, while he was preparing *Cat on a Hot Tin Roof* for publication. Williams had even sent Hemingway a telegram, but "after two days of waiting on the island, they [he and Carson McCullers] returned to Key West: Hemingway had never received the advance telegram, and was not there."[42] In her biography of McCullers (for which

Williams wrote the foreword), Virginia Spenser Carr corroborates this trip to Havana to see Hemingway but suggests that Mary Hemingway screened her husband's mail out of "a spirit of overprotectiveness" and thus Williams's telegram never got through to him.[43]

Spoto, however, fails to mention that Williams met Hemingway while in Havana with Marion Vaccaro that April 1959.[44] Philip C.

Williams with Maria Britneva at the Floridita bar in Havana, 1956. Courtesy of Natasha Grenfell and the Maria St. Just Estate.

Kolin, in "Tennessee Williams, Ernest Hemingway, and Fidel Castro," translates portions of an article in *Revolución* (April 8, 1959) about Williams's meeting with Castro and notes that Williams was such a "big fan" of Hemingway that he even echoes Papa's comment about Castro's revolution as not only being "good" for Cuba but "the most beautiful one I have ever seen" (*"revolución mas linda que he visto"*).[45] Drawing upon Meade Roberts's comment to Spoto that Williams had a "crush on Castro,"[46] Kolin concludes: "Papa and Tennessee both liked the Cuban revolution and Fidel, though their admiration for the latter stemmed from different sexual orientation."[47] Just as with Hemingway's critics and scholars, then, Papa's meeting with Williams remains for the playwright's in the realm of the gossipy, the ephemeral, and the apocryphal.

To be sure, if Hemingway has received more serious treatment in Williams studies than Williams has in Hemingway studies, it is because Hemingway was more senior than Williams, and not just in age. Hemingway was the acknowledged master, and no matter how good a writer was in his presence—and Williams was by 1959 *the* leading American playwright—he would still pale in comparison. As such, for Hemingway scholars, Williams was little more than a passing oddity in the master's life, and this one meeting in Havana seems to justify that conclusion. For Williams scholars, Hemingway was a literary giant whom Williams was lucky enough to have met, and little more is said. And yet Hemingway remained a source of profound literary inspiration for Williams throughout his career, and Margaret Thornton's recent editing of Williams's *Notebooks* has begun documenting to just what extent that admiration can be seen.[48] What that one encounter in Havana revealed years ago, then, is that there is much more to talk about with Hemingway and Williams than what Hemingway felt about Williams's inquiring after Pauline's death or his "overdressing" for the occasion.

This book begins, theoretically speaking, where that first meeting in Havana ends. In other words, it is interested less in the biographical history of the two artists, brief as it is, that other critics and biographers have repeatedly concentrated on, and more in the literary history that Hemingway and Williams shared. That is not to say their chance encounter in Havana should be slighted in a study dedicated to the two men's work. To a large extent, biography and autobiography underpin hermeneutics here. To claim a literary affinity between their work to the extent that this books does requires a firm sense of historicizing, not just in terms of how the two artists viewed their own work as engaging with and commenting upon their respective times, but also in how they understood their art with respect to the other's sociopolitical agenda. As such, I return time and again to Williams's passion for Hemingway the artist. From unpublished essays and journal entries he wrote during his college days at Washington University in the mid-1930s to the interviews he gave in the 1970s about the posthumous works he was reading, Williams never stopped talking about Hemingway, never ceased finding in his work a prose style and a bitter sense of irony that Williams had not only respected but had also wanted to reproduce in his own writing. And yet, as fascinating as their shared history may be and as illuminating as these details are in framing a particular reading of a literary work, the drive of the book remains analytical in nature and intertextual in design.

Because this book looks at Hemingway's art as it relates to Williams's, it is not intended to be a book about Hemingway per se, and as such will not likely be of great interest to Hemingway scholars beyond those concerned with the effects Papa had on a generation of writers after him. Rather, this book is written for a Williams audience by a Williams scholar who uses Hemingway as a means to examine Williams's evolving relationship with the heterosexual community at the height of the Cold War and with the homosexual community of post-Stonewall gay liberation. Williams's own complex relationship to the hetero-/homosexual binary of both periods is explored in his admiration for and frustration with Hemingway, whom he saw as the greatest American writer of the twentieth century and perhaps its most disingenuous one, too, given the gaping inconsistencies in Hemingway's public image and the private one evoked in the (semi-autobiographical) posthumous novels that spoke more to Williams's efforts to derail existing identity politics in America than Hemingway's earlier, more signature works.

This study examines, therefore, the literary affinity between the two writers, specifically between Hemingway's novel *The Sun Also Rises* and Williams's *Cat on a Hot Tin Roof* as discussed in chapter 1. The premise of this chapter is that there exists an intentional link between the two works, notably in their ironic endings, which Williams used to help challenge the Cold War's sexual politics in America as Hemingway's novel had done with the gender politics of the postwar "flapper" 1920s. While it seems, then, that I am returning to well-worn material in both writers' criticism, I do so not only with a new critical eye but also with the intention of showing how Hemingway perhaps influenced Williams in ways not otherwise known. Though that relationship was essentially unilateral—that is, Hemingway's influence on Williams is more recognizable than Williams's on Hemingway—the polemical subtext of this study suggests that Hemingway was aware of Williams's work in sexual identity politics and perhaps was partly influenced by it in the writing of his later fiction (as Williams was by Hemingway's), a period which saw the writing of some rather atypical Hemingway novels, including

Islands in the Stream, The Garden of Eden, and *True at First Light/Under Kilimanjaro.*[49]

Since problems of masculinity directly lead to problems of sexuality and thus sexual identity, chapter 2 focuses more closely on the problems of America's gender and sexual wars as explored in *The Sun Also Rises*, particularly in how the novel's ambiguous closing lines reflect more than Jake and Brett's sexual existentialism alone, but also Hemingway's construction of the queer Jake Barnes as a representation of the dysfunctional post-World War I American male. Chapter 3 begins turning toward Brick Pollitt, examining Williams's early treatment of the protagonist's masculine existentialism and the narrator's sexual initiation as they are worked through in "Three Players of a Summer Game," the short story on which *Cat on a Hot Tin Roof* was partly based, as well as through the intertextual references (in particular, the bullfight as a heterosexual metonymy) that begin establishing Brick as a Cold War reincarnation of Hemingway's Jake.

Stating that the American male has undergone a sexual identity crisis in the twentieth century is not to say anything new today, nor that male characters in American literature mirror such a crisis, though that is certainly more virgin territory in literary scholarship. To understand Brick, though, we first need to understand where Brick acquired his queer homophobia, and, to understand that, we need to reconstruct Brick's life *before* the action that constitutes the three-plus hours we see him onstage. In short, we need to see what social influences had worked, for good or for bad, to construct Brick's personal and political self as it is revealed to us, just as they had worked to shape the sexual epistemologies of generations of men like Brick who felt and expressed much the same sexual anxiety as he. As no psychiatrist would expect to unmask the psychosexual problems of a patient in one three-hour session, no literary critic should expect anything said within the limited scope of the play's Aristotelian timeframe to unveil Brick's "mystery." Only through literary reconstruction are we able to navigate our way through that mystery in *Cat on a Hot Tin Roof,* a mystery that has left its impression firmly etched on the history of American masculinity in crisis. Chapter 4, then, studies Brick more fully in *Cat on a Hot Tin Roof,* arguing the case that through Brick's homosexual existentialism Williams is speaking against national containment ideologies that foster inappropriate and frequently damaging identity politics.

During the 1970s, Williams returned to Hemingway's novel to heal old wounds, not those he had suffered at the hands of the homophobic community whom Hemingway represented for the most part, but those that were dealt now from the gay community itself, who frequently attacked Williams with the same acidity for not having served the gay cause that the heterosexual community had attacked him in the 1960s for having served it up too well in plays like *Suddenly Last Summer*. Chapter 5, then, examines a post-Stonewall version of Brick in *Clothes for a Summer Hotel* to show how the historical male and his literary counterpart cross paths in Hemingway and Williams, and where Williams narrows the gap between modernist fiction and postmodern biography by making his Hemingway both victim and victimizer of the masculine stereotyping that he had empathized with in Jake but had practiced in real life.

It is my hope that, in exploring the sociohistorical, sociopolitical, literary, and intertextual relations between Hemingway and Williams, this study will turn what Tynan once called "a bizarre and frivolous footnote"[50] of American literary history into one of its more defining moments. That simple afternoon luncheon in Havana brought together two of America's greatest, if not entirely dissimilar, writers of the twentieth century to discuss issues that, as insignificant as they may have seemed at first, were essential to both men's literary productions—honor, bullfighting, alcoholism, revolution, death and, implicitly, homosexuality.

1
Williams's *Cat* and Hemingway's *Sun*: Queerly Masculine

"The poetic mystery of BRICK is the poem of the play, not its story but the poem of the story, and must not be dispelled by any dishonestly oracular conclusions about him: I don't know him any better than I know my closest relative or dearest friend which isn't well at all: the only people we think we know well are those who mean little to us."
—Tennessee Williams, manuscript fragment, n.d., HRHRC

"an unfrocked priest, a professional ex-communist, or a retired nonpracticing pederast are figures of blinding interest and charm."
—Ernest Hemingway, *Under Kilimanjaro*

"The homosexual male and the man who was insufficiently manly were understood in the same figure of speech.... The longer the association lasted between the homosexual and the unmanly man, the greater the power of the homosexual label to stigmatize any man.... The more he feared he might be one of the stigmatized group, the more he needed to prove himself a man or what was more difficult come to terms with what was not manly about himself. Romantic friendship disappeared, as the sharp line was drawn between homosexual and heterosexual.... The creation of the homosexual image produced a deadly new weapon for maintaining the boundaries of manhood."
—E. Anthony Rotundo, *American Manhood*

At the end of the third act of the Broadway version of Williams's *Cat on a Hot Tin Roof* (1955), Brick and Maggie exchange the following sentiments:

> *Brick.* I admire you, Maggie....
> *Margaret.* Oh, you weak, beautiful people who give up with such grace. What you need is someone to take hold of you—gently, with love, and hand your life back to you, like something gold you let go of—and I can!

I'm determined to do it—and nothing's more determined than a cat on a hot tin roof—is there? Is there, baby?[1]

These were not, we well know, the final words of the play that Williams had originally intended back in 1955. Instead, Williams had wanted the following lines to conclude his play:

> *Margaret.* Oh, you weak people, you weak, beautiful people!—who give up.—What you want is someone to—. . .—take hold of you.—Gently, gently, with love! And—. . . . I *do* love you, Brick, I *do!*
> *Brick.* Wouldn't it be funny if that was true?
>
> (*C* 3:165–66)[2]

Brick's final words to Maggie in Williams's original ending are, to be sure, an exact copy of Big Daddy's reply to Big Mama's earlier declaration of love to him:

> *Big Mama.* And *I did, I did so much, I did love you!*—I even loved your hate and hardness, Big Daddy!
> *Big Daddy.* [*to himself*] *Wouldn't it be funny if that was true.* . . .
>
> (*C* 3:78)

Given Brick's echo of Big Daddy's repudiation of love here, it would appear that Williams's original intention was to underscore the circularity of generational mendacity at the heart of the play's conflict for at least one of two reasons: either to show how inbred mendacity can be within a sociopolitical system like the Pollitt family, where women are instruments of fecundity to uphold the patriarchy and their children bargaining chips within that sexual economy; or to display two views of how to live within that system of mendacity that Big Daddy champions but that Brick ultimately negates.

Both probing interpretations effectively became moot, however, when in 1955 *Cat*'s first director, Elia Kazan, requested that Williams rewrite the original ending for the play's Broadway debut, and, for reasons Williams would later regret, he did. This history between accommodating playwright and domineering director is, of course, well known, and has frequently been the focus of much of the play's secondary literature. Initiated first by Williams himself in his "Note of Explanation," which he published along with these two versions of act 3, then taken up again more than thirty years later by Kazan in his autobiography *A Life*, *Cat*gate (as theater history might well remember it over time) has continually enjoyed wide currency among the theatric and academic communities, and the queries show no sign of slowing down.[3] Whereas some critics have defended Williams and his justification for having accepted Kazan's alterations because, in his own words, a "failure reaches fewer people, and touches fewer, than does a play that succeeds" (*C* 3:168), Brenda Murphy notes that several others "have condemned Williams for violating his artistic integrity by giving in to what they see as a manipulation of his artistic vision for profit."[4] One such critic is Marian Price, who finds that Maggie and Brick in the first two endings of the play demonstrate the struggle Williams was undergoing to find commercial success without betraying his idealism and his homosexual truth, which Price feels he ultimately did; for her, Brick's guilt in the play over abandoning Skipper is akin to Williams's for leaving Frank Merlo.[5]

Williams would repeatedly deny any wrongdoing on his part and for years resented the fact that he did not or could not perform his original third act to the play. In a letter to *New York Times* theater critic J. Brooks Atkinson, dated March 25, 1955—one day after the play's premiere at the Morosco Theatre—Williams had this say about the two endings:

> Some time I would like you to read the original (first) version of Cat before I re-wrote Act III for production purposes. Both versions will be published and, confidentially, I do mean confidentially, I still much prefer the original. It was harder and purer: a blacker play but one that cut closer to the bone of truth I believe. I doubt that it would have had the chance of success that the present version has and since I had so desperate a need of success, and reassurance about my work, I think all in all Kazan was right in persuading me to shape Act III about the return of Big Daddy—in the original the family conference was interrupted not by a storm but by his off-stage cry when pain struck.[6]

By November 1955, after New Directions had published the two endings, Williams told Audrey Wood, "Almost everybody of taste that I have talked to about 'Cat' are disturbed and thrown off somewhat by a sense of falsity, in the ending, and I don't want this to ever happen again, even if it means giving up the top-rank names as co-workers" (*SL II* 594).

Notwithstanding the bipartisanship that has subsequently emerged in Williams studies surrounding *Cat*'s third-act controversy, most critics and scholars finally side with Williams's original ending for its artistic coherence, though nearly all agree that Kazan was essentially right in requesting certain changes for dramatic effect, a truism Williams himself would later acknowledge in a 1972 interview with Jim Gaines: "I still prefer the one that I wrote first. But the thing is, I worked longer on the third act as Kazan wanted it, and, consequently, it is texturally the better written of the two, the more fullbodied. . . . But still I think I prefer the original ending, though I doubt that the play would have been successful with it" (*CTW* 216–17).

Williams would later attempt to resolve this quandary for good when he returned to the third act of *Cat* for the American Shakespeare Theatre's 1974 revival (based on a 1973 version Williams produced at Stage/West, a regional theater in Springfield, Massachusetts) and revised it once again, now incorporating the best from both his original version of the third act and the Broadway version of 1955—namely, in keeping Brick's original curtain-line and resilience to Maggie's charms and machinations but in allowing Big Daddy to return to the stage to deliver his symbolic elephant joke (whose reference to an erection is intended to underscore Brick's impotence) and bear false witness to Maggie's proclaimed pregnancy.[7] By definitively installing Big Daddy onstage in the play's final act, Williams, too, was effectively deferring to Kazan's earlier dramatic vision of play, but in maintaining his original curtain-line, Williams was unquestionably privileging his own version's thematic unity.[8]

Surely, there must have been something particularly significant in Brick's echoing his father in his final words to Maggie for Williams to have felt the need to restore them to their rightful place twenty years after the play's initial Broadway run in 1955 and even later admit that "the published version of *Cat on a Hot Tin Roof*" was his "favorite among the plays [he had] written" (*M* 168). And surely that *something* remains elusive to us still, for nearly half a century has passed, and Williams scholars are no closer to putting the issue of Brick and the third act to rest than they were when Williams had first made it a cause célèbre with his "Note of Explanation." While we have moved beyond the school-yard finger pointing that had dominated early studies of the play's third-act controversy, we have not satisfactorily addressed what, precisely, these two (now three, or four if we count the Dramatists Play Service's edition) third acts achieve—or do not—with respect to the play's message. As Mark Royden Winchell writes, "Most observers have been troubled by the playwright's difficulty in achieving a convincing sense of closure at the end of the play. Both the original and the Broadway versions of the third act leave questions unanswered and an uneasy sense that the answers suggested are willed and artificial. . . . If the ending of the play (in either version) is willed, what exactly has the playwright willed?"[9]

One reason for this critical impasse no doubt lies in the collective belief that, questions of artistic refinement and dramatic structure aside, none of the third acts appears coherent with the rest of the play because of Brick's cool detachment from the action in each, and yet it is precisely his *in*action that precipitately touches the frenetic lives of each character at the end.

Each, in fact, depends on Brick to do or *say* something resolute: Maggie, to confirm her pregnancy—in word, then in deed—and thus inherit the plantation; Big Daddy, to *reaffirm* his earlier affirmation of that pregnancy and thus transfer his patriarchal lineage onto Brick; Big Mama, to return to the womb and thus petrify her delusional past; Mae, to reject Maggie's sexuality and thus ensure her the role as fertility goddess; and finally Gooper, to remain an emasculated drunk and thus mitigate his Esauian plot to usurp his brother's birthright of "twenty-eight thousand acres of the richest land this side of the Valley Nile!" (*C* 3:86). *Cat on a Hot Tin Roof*'s ambiguity, simply put, *remains* Brick's ambiguity, and without a clearer explanation as to what motivates Brick in any of the third acts, no version of the play will ever be definitively revelatory.

Cat and the Hetero/Homo Matrix

The key to unlocking *Cat*'s mystery, then, must begin with Brick and his role in the third acts, but to understand *what* prompts Brick toward action or inaction in any of them, we need to know *why* he responds the way he does to everyone, and therein lies the play's essential problem. For none of the three thirds acts apparently provides us with the necessary information to discern his motivations for inaction, something Charles May had observed years earlier: ". . . even those critics who consult Williams' original third act, included in the published version of the play, complain that the meaning of Brick's tragedy remains obscure."[10]

More recently, in his study of the third-act controversy from the original to the Broadway to finally the Hollywood ending in Richard Brooks's 1958 film, James Gilbert concludes that all versions underline the essential theme that "[l]ife is a lie" and therefore "the exact ending does not matter, nor indeed does Brick's purported homosexuality."[11] Thus, for all that Brick does or does not do, says or does not say, the mystery surrounding his relationship with his best friend Skipper, and the residue that that has left on his marriage to Maggie, remains as shrouded for the audience as it does for each character in the play. The audience is ultimately denied its privileged fourth-wall omniscience and left at the end asking the same question Maggie and Big Daddy address in the first and second acts: why does Brick drink? Consequently, Williams has cleverly hidden that critical skeleton key, negligently misplaced it, or, as Walter Kerr had polemically charged in 1955, intentionally discarded it altogether.[12]

Despite all the historical commentaries and value judgments made over the years as to which ending is finally superior, and which most *honest*, three intrinsic problems to all three of the third acts remain unresolved: what, exactly, *is* that system of mendacity that Brick sardonically repudiates in the original (and 1974) version and comes to "admire" in the Kazan rewrite; how are we to understand his relationship to it in either ending; and what does that relationship's resultant ambiguity reveal about Williams's artistic or sociopolitical intentions? Brick is an alcoholic and refuses to make love to his seductive wife, that we know, but for exactly *what* reasons we do not: because he no longer loves her? Because he is seeking purity amid all the liars of the world, most notably his wife and family? Because he is still devastated by the death of his best friend, for which he feels directly responsible? Because his best friend's homosexuality has destroyed his faith in male companionship, a bond that is at the heart of his family's patriarchy itself? In sum, Brick's alcoholism has led him to be repeatedly diagnosed over the years as either a pre- or closeted homosexual, a homophobe, a guilt-ridden basket-case, a misogynist, a mama's boy, a Circean swine, a boy-man, a modern-day Narcissus, and a host of other seemingly inclusive psychological portraits-cum-epithets.

These inquiries—all critical isotopes of Walter Kerr's initial foray into the subject in 1955—have nearly unilaterally unmasked Brick's "mendacity" as a pseudonym for "homosexuality" and its sociopolitical component "homophobia," though not all are even in concert as to what *that* signifies. Is Brick's salient homophobia, for instance, a socially-constructed default setting engineered to protect his male privileges, of which his relationship with Skipper was one?[13] Or is it simply a ruse to misdirect suspicion away from the gender-exclusiveness of that friendship or of some secret, "illicit" desire he might have harbored, as was the case with his concurrent historical brethren—namely, J. Edgar Hoover, Roy Cohn, and quite possibly the demagogue par excellence, Joseph McCarthy, himself? In other words, does Brick resort to wholesale repulsion of male desire out of his knee-jerk reaction to his times' entrenched homophobia, out of his rising fears that he too might be homosexual at a time when it was not only dangerous but unAmerican to be so (especially given his archetypal, masculine role as the all-American football hero), or out of the simple fact that he does not understand the social rules that define the male friendship that separates homosociality from homosexuality? As James Gilbert explains,

> The unresolved problem that Williams posed for the play is Brick's sexuality. If he is gay, if he understands that his relationship with Skipper had been a loving one—whatever they did or didn't do physically—then there

can probably be no reconciliation with Maggie, no truth possibly to come from her fabricated pregnancy. In a way, this problematic is closest to the original version of the script. If, on the other hand, Brick is really as straight as his horror at the accusation of "unnatural" love suggests, then his initial alienation from Maggie is harder to understand, although much easier to overcome, as the film version suggests. Quite clearly, Williams struggled with this issue and, in the end, left it an open question, probably even in his own mind.[14]

To be sure, if any certainty about Brick's disgust in sleeping with Maggie remains elusive, any final understanding of his attitude toward that disgust will surely remain ambiguous, for critics and audiences alike, something Michael Paller and Michael Bibler were also to recently confirm.[15]

Because we are never given that definitive portrait of Brick's response to homosexuality in any version of the third act of the play (of which Williams was certainly well aware), save for the fact that his first social instinct in all three is to reject it, recent theater critics and scholars have repeatedly taken Williams to task for the apparent ambiguities that his imprecision engenders or his silence entertains.[16] Is Williams's equivocation, they have leveled, the result of his adopting the mores of his times and thus denouncing homosexuality as destructive or, at least, as wrong?[17] Or of his playing up to popular prejudices of the 1950s, so as to assure himself a Broadway hit, only to subvert them in the end?[18] Or even of his displaying his own flawed uncertainty over Brick's objective correlative?[19] In short, the critical consensus concerning the play's treatment of homosexuality echoes either Foster Hirsch's vituperative attack on *Cat* for its "shifty and evasive treatment of Brick's possible homosexuality,"[20] or Dean Shackelford's sympathetic assessment of how the play "confront[s] the taboo subject of homosexuality directly and without apology."[21] Perhaps Dennis Allen articulates the problem best when he asks why *Cat on a Hot Tin Roof* should attack "conventional mores only to recapitulate them?"[22]

For over half a century, then, Williams has either been castigated for his disingenuousness or revered for his suggestiveness in obfuscating both Brick's motivations and *Cat*'s raison d'être, and we seem no closer today in bridging the gap between these two critical extremes than we have been since the play's first production. Williams would only complicate the issue himself when he repeatedly said in interviews and letters that Brick was heterosexual, albeit problematically so: "Here's the conclusion I've come to. Brick *did* love Skipper, 'the one great good thing in his life which was true'. He identified Skipper with sports, the romantic world of adolescence which he couldn't go past. Further: to reverse my original (somewhat tentative) premise, I now believe that, in the deeper sense, not the literal sense, Brick *is* homosexual with a heterosexual adjustment . . ." (*SL II* 555–56).[23] To be sure, these comments, as well as the changes Williams made over the twenty years from his original third act to the Broadway version then to some hybrid of the two for his 1975 New Directions edition, have all helped to compound the problem. But, as we have just seen, the seeds of contentious ambiguity were sewn from the start.

With this critical impasse hinging upon rhetorical ambivalence, traditional hermeneutics alone appear incapable of delivering Brick and *Cat* from a sexual miasmas where fertility—the play's dominant theme, strophe, and leitmotif—is opposed to sterility as poignantly as life is to death.[24] To look upon *Cat* only in New Critical isolation, then, is to forever mire the play and its authorial uncertainties, its poetic unspokenness, and its Machiavellian half-truths because nothing within its dramatic three walls harbors the truth that both Brick's family and Williams's audience finally demand. Perhaps its impregnable ambiguity and hallmark irony have helped to establish the play as one of the pillars of modernist America drama. To study the play analogically with the story from which it evolved, as several critics, including Charles May and Brenda Murphy, have already done, is to begin recognizing that only external sources can shed light on Brick's and *Cat*'s mysteries; but since Brick in the story is as nebulous as his namesake in the play, little has been revealed as to why both Bricks drink and have turned frigid toward to their wives. Other critics such as David Savran and Robert Corber have looked further outside the text for answers, viewing the play through the contextual kaleidoscope of the Cold War era, challenging us to recognize the play not only as a hermetic allegory of the fall of Southern hegemony but also, and if not more so, as a political "rejoinder to the violently homophobic discourses and social practices that prevailed during the so-called domestic revival of the 1950s."[25] But since Brick in "Three Players of a Summer Game" and Brick in *Cat on a Hot Tin Roof* are haunted by different periods in American history, Savran's and Corber's impressive advances in our understanding of the play today fail to account for the heroes' varying responses to their respective troubled times.

To study the play even further outside the text, using literary *re*constructionism via cotextuality (that is, studying the playtexts and their various contexts as co-texts equally involved in contributing to the making of meaning) to broaden out the play and its characters' relationship to the concerns of modernist American literature (and culture) on the whole—which is what this book attempts to do—is finally to recognize *Cat*'s socioartistic coherency. For Brick's (and by extension *Cat*'s) ambiguity concerning his perceived and self-perceived homosexuality reflects a much larger sociopolitical problem in America than simply one man's struggle to hide or understand the inconsistencies of his sexual nature and its resulting social identity. Simply put, both Bricks were not born in a vacuum, and to equate them in their struggles is to ignore their roles in the continuum of modern America's obsession with questions surrounding notions of masculinity, sexuality, and sexual identification per the *Homo americanus*, and also to miss Williams's wider interests in the play, something he was to uphold from the start in his rejoinder to Walter Kerr and to reassert later with his restoration of Brick's ironic curtain-line.[26] The ambiguities surrounding both Bricks' sexual identities are, in fact, as much the result of their epistemological confusion in understanding the rules governing sexual identification in their respective postwar Americas as they are of the two Bricks' reticence in satisfying their societies' contagious hunger to root out and expel its miscreants—political, social, and sexual alike. Both Bricks' internal and external battles are essentially twofold: first, with the manufacturing and the controlling of the production of truth concerning their relationship with others—be it Margaret and Isabel in the story, or Maggie and Skipper in the play; and second, with their families' needs to "normalize" those relationships for various social, metaphysical, and economic reasons. Thus, *Cat* represents more than the Cold War era's struggle to contain homosexuality as it had tried to communism; it captures instead the then-culmination of a nation's half-century struggle to find, define, and refine its weakened sense of masculinity, one that perhaps peaks with Brick and the Jazz Age/Cold War worlds they occupy, but which certainly does not start, nor end, with one or the other.

To be sure, the pages of modernist American culture, like those of its literary history, are filled with figures representing the two postwar paradigm shifts in gender and sexual identification, where the Freudian phallus as penis of World War I evolved into the Lacanian Phallus as signifier after World War II. The red menace of the 1920s, with its emphasis on the effeminacy of communists and their suspected fellow-travelers, inside and outside of the State Department, moved inevitably toward the pink "panic on the Potomoc" of the 1950s, which stuffed gay men and social reformists in the same pigeonhole.[27] From the gender-splitting Josephine Baker and Mata Hari of the post-World War I era (feminine guile masculinely wrapped in spy clothes) to the delicately-featured "spy" Ethel Rosenberg of the post-World War II era (the feminine anathema of Jane Wyatt if only in her political leanings), evidence that danger could be found in any shard of American ideology filled the chauvinistic rhetoric and the political dockets of eager writers and politicians hoping to secure their places in high school history books.

Whether it was the xenophobic scribblings of Owen Wister in the 1920s, or the demagogic ramblings of Joseph McCarthy in the 1950s, the struggle to rid the country of its potential malefactors made masculinity a de facto litmus test for national identity, and sexuality one means to validate its measures. Both of Williams's Bricks demonstrate, then, how at two different periods of American history masculinity first worked to establish one's social status, and how sexual ambiguity later trumped whatever gender was able to construct. Reading both characters with respect to their sociocultural timeframes in terms of masculine and queer studies equally demonstrates how neither is an isolated example of social constructionism gone amok, but rather how both were only one case among many, revealing how America's postwar(s) struggle to signify its masculinity was (and perhaps still is) entirely endemic.

As in real life, so too in art, for the road to sexual/gender identification is virtually littered with the fallen heroes of modernist literature like Brick, incontestably heterosexual men stripped of their phallus by an ill-fated piece of shrapnel, by an emancipating woman, or by a society ill-equipped or indifferent to securing staid gender identities after World War I. The Jay Gatsbys, Joe Christmases, Lawrence Seldens, Frederick Winterbournes, Ethan Fromes, Charley Andersons, Will Kennicotts, and George Hurstwoods are all celebrated literary representations of dysfunctional masculinity countered not only by the strong-willed Daisy Bunchanans, Joanna Burdens, Lily Barts, Daisy Millers, Zeena Fromes, Mary Frenchs, Carol Kennicotts, and Carrie Meebers of their days, but also by the sexually-thawing mores that had precipitated the advancement of (white) middle-class women in the wake of a Victorian crisis of masculinity sparked by the lethal cocktail of corporate capitalism, fattening middle-management, and rapidly closing frontiers. While fin de siècle sexual politics, championed by Teddy Roosevelt's rough-riding push to reinvigorate flabby manhood, saw American men through the dark years of Victorian sexual repression and into the European arena of the "Great Adventure" of World War I, the stark, modern realities of a mustard-gas ethos and howitzer shell-shock were more convincing than any Roosevelt bull-moose propaganda that masculinity was *not* to be found on or proven in the dank trenches of la Somme. And for those lucky enough to have escaped a European burial, returning home to a nation on the eve of a gender revolution — sponsored, ironically enough, by Sears, Roebuck, and Ford — meant that their masculinity would become nothing more than can(n)on fodder for embattled psychoanalysts.

Perhaps the naive idealism that accompanied the doughboys across the sea in the first place was in many ways responsible for the wounded manhood that limped home, of which both Bricks in Williams's texts are exemplary. Lost indulgently in the dizzying haze of the laissez-faire-corrupted, sexually liberated, Tayloresque mass-produced, bathtubgin-sipping, speakeasy consumer culture of the 1920s, Jazz Age America could not be bothered with the party-ending realities of George Campton's death in Edith Wharton's *A Son at the Front* (1923) or Claude Wheeler's in Willa Cather's *One of Ours* (1922). What self-respecting Trotskyite or flapper would concern him/her/self with that "old bitch gone in the teeth," Pound's poetic vilification of the "botched civilization" responsible for the War? This was a new society, one bent on change, one that would have neither the time nor the whim to assimilate its wounded sons back into the masculine fold. Dos Passoss's John Andrews in *Three Soldiers* (1921), cummings's *auto*narrator in *The Enormous Room* (1922), and Hemingway's Nick Adams in *In Our Time* (1925) all suffer physical wounds from the War that result in impotence—psychological, sociological, or sexual—which they feel more poignantly *at home* than they had when they were abroad. This larger issue of impotence and sterility, expressed most singularly in T. S. Eliot's *The Waste Land*, would become the war *after* the War, establishing, in fact, a subtext to postwar American masculinity, which, though given partial reprieve at the start of the World War II, would come to haunt the (heterosexual) male American psyche throughout the twentieth century.

With the phallus becoming the nation's shibboleth, American men of the interwar years divided themselves between those who had it (heterosexuals) and those who wanted it (homosexuals). But the phallus, with its signifying penis, proved an ineffective way to categorize masculinity, let alone protect it, though that fact is perhaps more clear to us today than it was to men in 1919, 1926, or even 1955. There were those men who, for various reasons, could not ascribe to the cult of masculinity, who could not wield the phallus (either because they did not desire to, or more simply, because of castration, they could not physically do so), but who nonetheless were not gay and lived their lives as heterosexual men in every way other than the most performative one, that is, engaging in a heterosexual act and procreating. These men, whom I call in this book queer heterosexual males, were perhaps far more numerous in their day than had been first believed, and only now are they being given their sociological dues. But that is not to say that certain artists and social critics in the 1920s and 1950s had not already seen and attempted to demonstrate for the nation what the Johnny-come-lately literary critics are only now confirming—namely, that American men of the interwar years lacked the phallus.

"Men Without Women": Queer Masculinities

When Michel Foucault brazenly, if not inaccurately, fixed the birth date of the modern homosexual at 1870 with the publication of Karl Friedrich Otto Westphal's "Die Konträre Sexlempfindung," he was launching a polemic whose political aftershocks are still being felt in the humanities today.[28] In arguing that sexuality was a Victorian production, constructed to fill the exponentially expanding needs of a burgeoning capitalist society, and the homosexual a tool within that construction to control and police heterosexuality for "economically useful and politically conservative" ends,[29] Foucault would influence how we understand modern epistemes of sexual identification. Though his unfinished *History of Sexuality*, begun more than thirty years ago, has repeatedly come under attack by sexologists, gay historians, and queer theorists alike for its at-times questionable empirical research, few have in fact renounced its intuitive conclusion that homosexuality emerged as an identity entirely detached from the sexual act that gave rise to its name, passing, in effect, from an act of the body to an act of the body politic. Quite to the contrary, most scholars have accepted the basis of this Foucauldian paradigm that homosexuality in the twentieth century has very little in common with *stuprum*, the sodomite, the moll, or any other host of terms used to describe the historically variable social response to same-sex relations.[30]

Perhaps what Foucault had overlooked in his exegesis of the prevailing discourses of Victorian sexuality was that such theories of sexual inversion were widely disseminated in Europe not just because they carried with them a scientific authority lost in the penal codes that punished homosexuality, but that the men who wrote, disseminated, challenged, and defended those codes in the nineteenth century did so because Western manhood was itself imploding and therefore felt the need not just to police heterosexual society against the sexual *Other* but also to shore up its own flagging masculinity. The Cleveland Street scandal, the Oscar Wilde trials, and the Eulenburg Affair were proof enough that Victoria's England and Wilhelm's Germany understood the modern homosexual not as a sexual threat, as sodomy laws were rarely enforced, but as a social challenge to masculinity itself, which was needed to shoulder the burden of postindustrial imperialism.[31] To be sure, around the time that the modern homosexual was said to have been born, the modern heterosexual male was himself experiencing growing pains, and no doubt one had greatly influenced the other.[32]

Victorian Europe, though, was not Victorian America, despite the fact that both hemispheres experienced similar social phenomena accorded to the rise and spread of corporate consumerism. While men, just as women, in all of these protomodern societies were competing for gender privileges and constructing the sexual and social identities to insure them, Victorian America was undergoing an additional revolution that Victorian England and the Continent had only experienced vicariously through its colonialist endeavors (something postcolonial immigration is quickly reversing): integration of the cultural *Other*. Though no state is homogenous, socially, political, or sexually speaking, Victorian Europe surely enjoyed a larger base of secured mores and solidified cultural identities, for better or for worse, than did America at the turn of the twentieth century, which saw its frontiers closing and its population exploding with each postbellum year.

And since homogeny breeds hegemony, fears of the social, political or sexual *Other* actually *displacing* those traditional mores were less present (for the moment) in Europe than they were in a heterogeneously expanding America. That is not to say Western men in general were not conscious of the emancipating woman or the consolidating homosexual, for they most certainly were, but Victorian Europe's patchwork of homogenized cultures (ironically responsible for the two World Wars) did not respond to these forces with the same degree of contempt that their American cousin did. America, by contrast, saw itself rapidly becoming unsettled by the mass immigration of peoples from various, and often conflicting, cultures, particularly in terms of gender identities. Thus, the question became: if Victorian Europe could struggle over questions of sexual identities, as it had done with the scandals noted above, what would happen in an already culturally-destabilized America? The answer was simple, albeit unreasonable: avoid the need to have the struggle by eliminating sexual perversions altogether. One way to achieve this (quixotic) plan was to instill a cult of masculinity, which many believed was the gender panacea to sociosexual ills. The American crisis of social expansionism, then, which led in many ways to its own celebrated crisis of masculinity, was unique from its European model. And what it brought in its wake was a species of American men (of course white, heterosexual, and bourgeois, as their forefathers had been or, at least, had been mythologized as having been) more adamant, more virulent in securing their masculinity than any previous generation of American men had been, who considered manhood as having been measured uniquely through their success or failure in becoming self-made, as Anthony Rotundo, Michael Kimmel, and a host of other social historians have competently informed us over the years.[33]

American masculine studies, though considered a fairly recent trend, has in fact been active since the mid-1960s, prompting the Plecks to note in the introduction to their 1980 collection *The American Man* that

"The history of masculinity is a relatively new subject of inquiry with a small but growing literature."[34] Groundbreaking studies in new masculinities, like those by Myron Brenton, Marc Fasteau, Peter Filene, and Joe Dubbert,[35] had attempted to codify that crisis of American masculinity described above by exploring how the American male's sense of his gendered self has run inversely proportional to the rise of interventionist politics and laissez-faire capitalism; that these studies should have appeared concurrently with Jonathan Katz's seminal study, *Gay American History*,[36] figures well in explaining the historical schism that masculine studies has repeatedly practiced, consciously or not, over questions of sexual plurality. As Myron Brenton had noted, "Despite the fact that homosexuality in the present-day United States has been widely discussed, few contemporary cultures are as hostile to homosexuality as America's is. That there should be intense hostility is understandable both from the viewpoint of the Puritanical roots from which this nation's sexual attitudes have emanated and from the threat that the mere existence of homosexuality poses to men concerned about their adequacy."[37] To study masculinity was to parry it with those cultural phenomena that challenged, impeded, threatened, or debilitated it, and homosexuality, like effeminacy and feminism in general, was essentially considered only in its debilitating effects on American manhood.

These two competing disciplines, then, have often looked at the issue solely as one of sexuality or of masculinity, failing to consolidate masculine and gay studies' efforts to reinterpret, reconstruct, or recover the lost American *man* responsible for the pronounced rupture between heterosexuals and homosexuals at the dawn of the twentieth century. Despite the enormous advances that Rotundo and Kimmel have made in their respective histories of American man qua man to correct this historical oversight, Bryce Traister has called for a "more thorough assessment of the critical relations between heteromasculinity and gay male studies," one that would begin "picturing the 'crisis' of heteromasculinity within the framework provided by a masculinity whose agonistic construction may well be the more immediately and politically vital of the two."[38] Though Traister reads this theoretically- and historically-defined crisis with suspect eyes, and even questions whether or not there was ever a paradigmatic crisis separating transcendentalized from constructed or performative heteromasculinity in the first place,[39] he does admit that the new phallocriticism that has emerged (to some a legitimate field of unearthered history, to others an unwelcomed mimicry of Elaine Showalter's *gynocritique,* and to even others an academic manna that has opened academic doors not only to promotion and tenure but also to a stagnant and impregnable job market)[40] has begun a necessary consolidation of heteromasculine studies with gay studies:

The new complexity of the historical American male invites a reconsideration of a cultural record previously examined; we get to take another crack at Teddy Roosevelt, not to celebrate the cult of muscular manhood but rather to take it apart. The American male literary canon, while never entirely uninteresting and never entirely ignored, is now interesting again in slightly shifted terms, as hunter Hawkeye gives way to bachelor Natty, and Ahab astonishes less as political megalomaniac than as screaming queen.[41]

Despite the enormous gains made in men's and gay studies in understanding man *as* man, then, we still have a long way to go in reconciling the relationship between masculinity and sexuality.

Only until very recently have Traister's charges been answered. The academic journal *Men and Masculinities* has put together a recent collection of essays devoted to exploring the crossover between masculine and gay studies.[42] "Queer Masculinities," which merged sexed with gendered identities, attempts to theorize the sociosexual problem men (predominately, but not exclusively, gay) had (and still have) since the end of the nineteenth century, echoing in principle the notion of the "queer" male that historian George Chauncey, Jr. describes in his book *Gay New York*.[43] Issue editor Les Wright defines "queer masculinity" as a male gender type existing outside heteronormative constructions of masculinity that disrupt, or could disrupt, traditional images of heterosexual masculinity. I will use this term throughout this book to precisely confront the perceived and the lived notions of sexual identity, at one time consistent with social epistemologies of sexuality, and at other times wholly antithetical to it. One man can be masculine and still be gay, just as one can be effeminate and still be straight, but that second man will surely have more difficulties in America proving his sexual bent than the first man will have in professing or hiding his; and in a country where one's sexual identity is one's political identity, any gender sign or performative sex act speaks volumes.[44]

The Hemingway Connection

Since masculinity is a measure not just against women, with gender roles in question, but also, if not more so, against other men, with sexual identities now at stake, heterosexuality cannot legitimately be discussed outside of its relationship to homosexuality. If any writer of the modernist period who was not gay-identified best understood this phenomenon, it was Ernest Hemingway. Considered heteromasculinity incarnate of his day, even packaged and sold by *Look* magazine in the 1950s as the answer to America's waning masculine image, few readers, lay and critical alike, ever considered the queerness of his work until the publication of posthumous novels shattered the erstwhile macho image of Hemingway and his code heroes. Well read in the sexology literature of his day, notably Havelock Ellis and Alfred Kinsey, Hemingway repeatedly examined the role of the phallus (as penis, as sexual prowess, and as linguistic proficiency) in the gender wars that not only pitted men against women but also men against themselves, straight and gay alike.[45] As Debra A. Moddelmog writes, "Hemingway's struggle with the homo-hetero binarism was lifelong."[46] Hemingway even once told Elaine Dundy during an interview in Havana in 1959 just before meeting Tennessee Williams, "'I am for normalcy and against homosexuality . . . because sexually there are infinite variations for the normal person but none for the homosexual one.'"[47]

In an enlightening albeit reductive manner, his novels from *The Sun Also Rises* (1926) to *True at First Light* (1999)/*Under Kilimanjaro* (2005) can be said to have explored this credo more fully. Jake Barnes's sexual dysfunction forces him to practice sex vicariously with Brett through her relations with other men. David Bourne's sexual escapades with Catherine in *The Garden of Eden* (1986) were so unconventional for its day that even Hemingway "did not think [the novel] publishable in his lifetime."[48] Even his most recently published "fictionalized" memoir, *True at First Light* and its re-edited version, *Under Kilimanjaro*, have further advanced our appreciation of Hemingway's complexities with cross-gendered (and cross-racial) sexual appetites.[49] Written, though never completed, a few years after his second African safari in 1953–1954, "the African book" (as Hemingway referred to it) offers a more compelling portrait of his preoccupation with bi-, homo-, and interracial-sexuality than any of his previously published works: the character G.C., Mary's joke about Papa and Proust/Albertine having lived in the same hotel in Paris,[50] and Hemingway's half-serious affair with his Kamba "fiancée" Debba, by whom he had hoped to have a child.[51] Though perhaps referring to any of these characters in his comment to Dundy, Hemingway may very well have been referring to himself with his own notorious sexual experimentation with his wives.

In professing to Dundy the potentially "queer" side to his masculine identity in advocating heterosexual experimentation (which may have included a homosexual "act" such as sodomy, albeit in what Hemingway would have deemed a heterosexual context), while tacitly determining homosexuality to be a fixed "identity" regardless of the sexual acts committed, Hemingway calculating preserved his image by pre-empting any social reading into his explanation. In other words, the emancipated heterosexual could enjoy the entire spectrum of sexual acts because his identity allowed for such freedom, whereas the homosexual, by the very nature of the word, prohibited him from having access to such free sexual licence. For the "public" Hemingway at any rate, sexuality was what one *did*, while masculinity was who one *was*. They were separable components of one's identity, the former supplied by the individual and the later by society. For a homosexual like Tennessee Williams, such sex/gender differentiation was inconceivable: what you were *was* what you did (or, as the case with Brick, what you did not do). As such, if Hemingway's "masculinity" allowed for its "queer" side, Williams "effeminacy" prohibited him from having something similar in public in 1959 without fear of retribution. He did, however, manage to show it, if not with Brick in *Cat on a Hot Tin Roof*, than at least with Sebastian in the Broadway play *Suddenly Last Summer*, as well as in the successful film version released by Columbia Pictures that same year.

The "private" Hemingway was another matter altogether. And yet, it is that Hemingway who interests us today more so than the "public" Hemingway of the 1950s. It certainly interested Williams in 1959, and continued to intrigue him well into the 1970s. What Williams found most interesting in Hemingway was precisely the glaring inconsistencies between his public image and his private self, and in particular how Hemingway came to know so much about homosexuality as an identity and as a culture, and not just in its antithetical relationship to masculinity in America. With legal, scientific, and medical discourse at the turn of the century proclaiming homosexuality to be essentially congenital, and the national narrative reinforcing characteristics that would expose this "flaw" in masculinity, it was not difficult to *see* homosexuality in 1959 and therefore contain it through homophobic exclusionism. But the private Hemingway (that is, the novelist whose characters allowed him to explore ideas and voice opinions not always popular to the public of their day, or to even to the "public" Hemingway himself) demonstrated a sensibility in his homosexual characters atypical of homophobic writers of the day; it was *that* Hemingway with whom Williams (and a host of Hemingway scholars after him) was most intrigued.

Few in America during the interwar years would have mistaken the lisping, effeminate male as the stereotype of the homosexual, what George Chauncey, Jr. has documented as the historical "fairy"; few would also have been able to identify the "queer" man, Chauncey's noted term for gay men who did not fit the standard image of what a homosexual was. Reinforced in America through New York's growingly visible fairy culture that Chauncey and John D'Emilio have thoroughly documented,[52] as well as through the then-popular inversion model of sexual identity that populated American stages and movie screens before the Wales-Padlock Law and Hays Code began policing mass culture to resuscitate fading Victorian mores,[53] "the homosexual was now," in Michel Foucault's celebrated phrase, "a species."[54] Though the heterosexual male struggled to find what masculinity meant in a Freudian America, he certainly knew what it did not mean—cross-dressing, effeminacy, and, contrary to the once-prominent Attic measurements of male authority, sodomy. And yet, Hemingway's fictional world, as we will see in the next chapter, is filled with both types of homosexual characters. So why denigrate homosexuals in a public voice as a fixed social identity only to express their sociosexual fluidity in a more private, literary voice later?

To be sure, Foucault's "species" was the homosexual type that Hemingway was referring to in his response to Dundy, but it was not the homosexual that Williams believed Hemingway really knew, especially given his privileged access to the inner-circle of the Spanish matadors, several of whom were gay. During one summer in Madrid in 1961, for instance, Elaine Dundy joined Williams at a party hosted by a businessman, where an angry Williams snapped at the Japanese ambassador and several other diplomats who were there as honored guests: "'I have been trying to hold a literary conversation with you. . . . But all you want to talk to me about is which bullfighter is homosexual.'"[55] Williams knew several gay bullfighters personally, and he also knew that Hemingway knew them too; thus Williams could not accept the "public" Hemingway who denounced homosexuals repeatedly but who had gay friends. For Williams, Hemingway's relationship to the gay community was similar to the postbellum South's toward blacks, as described in James Weldon Johnson's *The Autobiography of an Ex-Colored Man:* "Southern white people despise the Negro as a race, and will do nothing to aid in his elevation as such; but for certain individuals they have strong affection, and are helpful to them in many ways."[56] Williams just wanted to know why this was the case with Hemingway, and perhaps, in their 1959 meeting in Havana, if he were one of those whom Hemingway would "help" or not.

Unlike homosexuality, heteromasculinity, such as that embodied by Hemingway, claimed to have established clear and protective gender barriers against the "predatorial" homosexual, something the Lynds effectively documented in their two landmark *Middletown* studies.[57] Or so we thought. For once Kinsey published his longitudinal study on the diversified sex habits of the American male in 1948, not only did the former rules of sexual identification prove to have been a myth all along, but also the foundational binaries distinguishing masculine heterosexuality from effeminate homosexuality.[58] If men could not trust who they were in 1948, why would there be any reason to trust who they *thought* they were in Hemingway's and Williams's 1950s? Hemingway clearly knew that, and so did Williams, but he would not discover this fact before Hemingway's posthumous novels—those he was working on when the two men met in Havana—began being published.

Though not to the extent that he would later do in *Islands in the Stream* (1970) and *The Garden of Eden*—both begun in 1946, then abandoned, only to be picked up again in the late 1950s—Hemingway had begun challenging America's epistemologies of sexed and gendered identities from very early on in his writing career. Hemingway had always had a more lucid vision of sexed identities than did his contemporaries Fitzgerald and Dos Passos, who were more interested in exploring the relatively new hetero-gendered identities afforded them by America's Jazz Age. To a large extent, Hemingway had by 1926— the years his first novel, *The Sun Also Rises*, was published—already predicted Kinsey's conclusion that the modern heterosexual/homosexual binary more closely resembled a spectrum of chromatic shades than the black and white scale that America had always understood it to be. Jake Barnes, to be sure, represents a generation's icon of falsely ritualized masculinity par excellence, whose ancestral traits find a (post)-modernist (or, at least, late-modernist) expression in Brick. Caught in a mire of sexual identification from an injury that during the war could have insured his masculinity but which now only calls it into perpetual question, Jake suffers from an existential angst that has him fight at first to preserve his identity only to acquiesce to its inevitable resolution. His only weapon against this struggle is a calculated dose of irony, which he resorts to repeatedly in his actions and comments to those he calls friends, former lovers, and enemies alike.

In the final line of *The Sun Also Rises*, upon whose interpretation the balance of the entire novel hinges, Jake offers to Lady Brett Ashley an ironic rejoinder to her veiled declaration of love that is not entirely dissimilar to the one Brick utters to Maggie at the end of Williams's original third act of *Cat on a Hot Tin Roof*:

> "Oh, Jake," Brett said, "we could have had such a damned good time together.". . . .
> "Yes," I said. "Isn't it pretty to think so?"[59]

Jake's growing awareness that all social identities are constructed around relationships with the sexual *Other* keeps him staying on in a more sexually-tolerant Europe after the War. But his inability in the novel to perform his heterosexuality—either with the equally-sick *poule* Georgette or with the libidinous Brett—forces him at the end of the novel to recognize that the only defense mechanism a childless bachelor in his thirties—that extinct Victorian species to which cruel Fortuna, the insatiable Brett, and a gossip-mongering society have irrevocably destined him—has against the encroaching *Other* is irony, and a good helping of it.

The two ironic endings, separated by more than a quarter of a century and two World Wars, reflect many of the problems that American males had in defining masculinity and framing sexual identities in the first half of the twentieth century. Hemingway's ending certainly spoke for and to many men of the Lost Generation, particularly its war-torn artists who abandoned their native lands to commiserate at Gertrude Stein's or Nathalie Barney's salons or in Sylvia Beech's Shakespeare and Co. bookstore over a failed love affair with their countries. His irony sharply offsets the conspicuous consumption, sexual and otherwise, that held the nation captive for a decade. Twenty years later, when its soldiers returned to a nation recently awakened from its economic slumber and on the eve of a collective revolution that was to establish it as half of the new world order, America was determined to shut the doors to the revolutionaries that it had earlier given berth to after the Great War. In this age of material prosperity and proscribed good feeling, personal expressions of irony, as Allan Ginsberg and William Burroughs were to discover, were now deemed anarchistic, if not entirely unAmerican. Familial expressions of irony, however, such as that of Big Daddy's to Big Mama or Brick's to Maggie, were considered self-contained and therefore unrepresentative of a generation's bitter love affair with its era. If Hemingway spoke openly for a generation's disillusionment, even for those not yet ready to admit to it (though they eventually would after October 29, 1929), Williams did not, which perhaps is as good a reason as any in explaining why no one really saw an affinity between Jake and Brick for the next twenty years.

Those critics who have recognized the similarities between the novel's and the play's final lines have done so on a very superficial level, however. In 1977, Charles May noted that Maggie's declaration and Brick's ambiguous reply "bears a striking resemblance in its hopeless ambiguity to Jake Barnes' reply to Lady Britt [*sic*] at the conclusion of Hemingway's *The Sun Also Rises*," but May does nothing more with this observation.[60] Twenty years later, Robert F. Gross, in examining the play's erotica, effectively repeats May, for he too takes note of the two endings' resemblance but like May (and Brenda Murphy)[61] says nothing significant about it: "This refrain echoes, in tone and subtext, one of the most famous conclusions in the modern American novel, that of Ernest Hemingway's *The Sun Also Rises*...."[62] Mark Royden Winchell also acknowledges May's earlier observation but only to supply one of his own, namely to point out the similarities between Brick's comment to Maggie and Nigger Jim's to Huck in *The Adventures of Huckleberry Finn:* "It's too good to be true, Honey [. . .]. It's too good to be true."[63]

To be sure, Williams's and Hemingway's conclusions are so strikingly similar that it is far more than sheer coincidence that one should be a mere echo of the other—striking not just in this expression of irony but, as we will see, more in the manner in which they both indirectly implicate their audiences' unwitting participation in the heroes' private tragedies by forcing them to recognize their culpability in engendering the social rules that initially governed the sexual identities currently troubling both protagonists. In fact, Williams was not only familiar with Hemingway's novel, as he was with *all* of his fiction[64]—in an unpublished college essay from 1936, for example, Williams writes, "With the exception of one book, 'Torrents of Spring', I have read all of Hemingway's published works [up to *Green Hills of Africa*]"[65]—but was even drafting his original third act *while* reading Hemingway in Spain,[66] which would account for the traces of Hemingway's fingerprints on the play's ending.[67] In short, the ambiguity behind Jake's response in the novel prepares us for Brick's thirty years later, and any attempt to understand the complexities of one literary effort would, in fact, be unveiling the apparent ambiguity in the other. Such an argument would also counter all existing claims, like Kerr's initial inquiry into Brick's "mystery," that chide Williams for his posturing reticence concerning Brick's "moral paralysis" (*C* 3:168).

This study, then, defends the position that Brick's apparent silence about the reasons behind his alcoholism does not constitute a theatric ruse on Williams's part to avoid admitting that Brick was gay to a Broadway audience, no more than Hemingway's uncharacteristic use of the word "pretty" at the novel's close was meant to unconditionally confirm that Jake was queer. Williams *was* in earnest where Brick is concerned, and his original ending to *Cat on a Hot Tin Roof is* much more explicit in its leveling of the homosexual implications subsequently lost in the Broadway rewrite than critics have heretofore acknowledged. Both authors were simply exploring the limits of masculine identification with respect to a nation's post-Victorian obsession with sexual identity and criticizing their societies' need "to know" someone's sexual bent, and determine from it their political identity. By suggesting to audiences the possibility of a queer Brick or a queer Jake in particular, Williams and Hemingway were both challenging the essential constructs of an American heteromasculinity in general.

2

The Sun Also Sets: Jake Barnes, Impotence, and Sexual Existentialism

> "Some mystery should be left in the revelation of character in a play, just as a great deal of mystery is always left in the revelation of character in life, even in one's own character to himself."
> —Tennessee Williams, *Cat on a Hot Tin Roof*

> "And everything the author knows
> He shows and shows and shows and shows
> His underclothes
> Are more important than the sun."
> —Ernest Hemingway, Untitled poem, 1926

> "The term 'queer' emerges as an interpellation that raises the question of the status of force and opposition, of stability and variability, *within* performativity."
> —Judith Butler, *Bodies That Matter: On the Discursive Limits of "Sex"*

UNLIKELY IS THE MARRIAGE OF HEMINGWAY AND QUEER THEORY, AND yet the latest generation of his biographers and critics have opened up what is to some a door, to others a can of worms: problematizing the intimation of Gertrude Stein and others in Hemingway's literary circle—such as Zelda Fitzgerald, Virginia Woolf, and Max Eastman, to name but a few—that Hemingway was a closeted homosexual. While biographer Kenneth Lynn calculatingly weighs the supposition, tempering numerous examples of Hemingway's notorious homophobia against the famous photo of him as a young boy dressed in girl's clothes to help explain certain inconsistencies in his sexual epistemology,[1] James Mellow unrepentantly proclaims it, exploring in some detail the curious contradiction between Hemingway the heteromasculine myth incarnate and Hemingway the sensitive writer obsessed with sexual and gender identification. As Mellow contends, "the author, until proven otherwise, is guilty of everything he intimates, imagines, or invents."[2] In spite of these probing biographical inquiries into this paradoxical portrait of Hemingway, Jeffrey Meyers conservatively concludes, "Hemingway has been suspected and even accused of being a covert homosexual because of his aggressive masculinity, his preference for exclusively male company, his occasional impotence, his sexual boasts and his hostility to inverts.... Despite all the theorizing, there is not a shred of real evidence to suggest that Hemingway ever had any covert homosexual desires or overt homosexual relations."[3]

Reconstructing/defending the male American myth built around Hemingway's heteromasculine persona inside and outside his œuvre has, in fact, proved something of a trend in Hemingway studies of late. Mark Spilka's *Hemingway's Quarrel With Androgyny* challenged scholars to conduct a whole-scale reexamination of Hemingway and his canon, which has grown larger and undeniably more complex with the posthumous publications of *Islands in the Stream*, *The Garden of Eden*, and *True at First Light/Under Kilimanjaro*. Aware of the dangers of concomitant author/character theorizing, Spilka still contends that Hemingway's exploration of failed masculinity and the androgynous resolution it precipitates in novels from *The Sun Also Rises* to *The Garden of Eden* can be attributed to his own androgynous rearing as a Victorian "girl" by his domineering mother Grace.[4]

If Spilka's reading of Hemingway's work as proof that the androgynous novelist "was wrestling furiously and secretly with devilish and adoring female versions of himself!"[5] sent shudders throughout the Hemingway camp in 1990, Nancy Comley and Robert Scholes's study a few years later, *Hemingway's Genders: Rereading the Hemingway Text*, rocked Hemingway studies to its epistemological foundation. Androgyny was, by their measures, a conservative reading at best of this new Hemingway, the *el nuevo* Hemingway, a writer whose novel *The Garden of Eden* (which his wife Mary guarded from publication) explores the transgendered, transracial, and transsexual experiments of a writer and his wife and their girlfriend, Marita. Their Hemingway was downright queer, bordering even on homosexual (or at least homoerotic). Aware of the potential fallout from their study of Hemingway's obsession with sex and gender identification, Comley and Scholes tone down their rhetoric by their conclusion: "Have we been trying to show that Hemingway was gay? No. If anything, we have been trying to show that such a question is too simple. The complexit[ies] of human sexuality... were issues that had been given a prominent place... around the turn of the century. What we have been trying to show is that Hemingway was much more interested in these matters than has been supposed— and much more sensitive and complex in his consideration of them."[6] Precisely because Hemingway promoted his own image as the macho homophobe, they contend, he was able to write more openly about homosexuality at a time when gay writers dared not do the same, though that does not implicate him as having been homosexual himself.

Several books have continued the work of Spilka, Comley and Scholes, particularly in the examination of how questions of masculinity in Hemingway's work are often fused with problems of sexuality. As Debra Moddelmog writes in *Reading Desire: In Pursuit of Ernest Hemingway*, "one quickly discovers that people have high stakes in circulating a particular image of Hemingway and in reading and teaching his work in a specific way. Some still revere him as a positive masculine icon, agreeing with the Barnes and Noble catalogue that advertises him as the 'He Man of American Literature.' Others view his masculinity as negative machismo. They consider him the worst example of a sexist, racist, homophobic man, and often refuse to read or teach Hemingway, or make apologies when they do."[7] Like Comley and Scholes, Moddelmog is "not positing a gay Hemingway," let alone a queer one, though she admits that "surely my Hemingway is both gayer and queerer than most Hemingways."[8] Rather, Moddelmog wishes only to situate Hemingway's "sexual identity in the tension between the homosexual and the heterosexual" and to read his texts via this newly constructed image of the author in order to demonstrate that "Hemingway's struggle with the homo-hetero binarism was lifelong."[9]

Carl Eby similarly explores the queer Hemingway by analyzing the novelist's fetish for hair as displayed both in his life and in his work, an obsession that relates to the "castration anxiety" implicit in several of his heroes, notably Jake Barnes.[10] For Eby, "just as one part of the fetishist's ego is hyperaware of sexual difference while a submerged part of the ego denies this difference, so the fetishist will often be overtly homophobic while covertly suspecting himself of harboring homosexual impulses."[11] Also like Comley and Scholes and Moddelmog before him, Eby is not interested in outing Hemingway but rather in exploring the *new* Hemingway of the posthumous works:

> Ever since Aaron Latham's "A Farewell to Machismo" appeared in *The New York Times* in 1977, it has become increasingly clear that Hemingway's reign as the hairy-chested icon of American masculinity in coming to an end. To be sure, this message hasn't yet filtered down to the general reading public. In the popular imagination, Ernest the monovocally masculine bullfight aficionado, boxer, hunter, deep-sea fisherman, and pitchman for Ballantine ale and khaki pants still looms over the American literary horizon like a testosterone-crazed colossus. . . .[12]

Eby feels that this once mythical Hemingway as icon of American masculinity "has now been demythologized," and "any revelation about the process by which he constructed his masculinity—and femininity—suggests something about how a multitude of men in our culture may have done the same."[13]

For Eby, opening up the Hemingway myth to include a queer Papa liberates the image of the man and of his work which the myth has restricted, offering readers of Hemingway's work insight into his grappling with problems of sex and gender identification that erstwhile criticism had labeled homophobic or chauvinistic. Stephen Clifford, however, finds such authorial readings (what he terms the "heroic 'I,'" or the need to find the author in the narrator) dangerous to literary criticism, though he agrees that in the case of Hemingway it is at times unavoidable. Positioning himself between the positivist critic who reads the Hemingway text as myth and the phenomenological critic who, in respecting Roland Barthes's theory of the "Death of the Author" (or the denial of the presence of any authorial persona), reads the Hemingway text qua text, Clifford proposes "the death of the critic-as-heroic I": "Once readers are able to move beyond the idolatry of Oedipal constructions of biographically bound narratives in the fiction of . . . Hemingway, we can begin to respond to those antagonistic readers who see only the bombast of self-centered masculine and the degradations of misogyny in their fiction."[14] Imposing the macho myth of Hemingway, which the author himself helped to fashion, onto the narrative "I" of his texts essentially mires their narrators into positions of homophobia and misogyny. We would do better, Clifford maintains, to see the masculinity expressed in the text in isolation of the Hemingway myth so as to better understand its relationship to the androgyny and the sexual transgression that are equally explored in his fiction.

Thomas Strychacz reminds us how difficult Clifford's goal in separating the Hemingway myth from the text can be in literary criticism, for *Hemingway's Theaters of Masculinity* returns to the myth as critical paradigm in Hemingway studies and reexamines the Hemingway canon via masculine studies to challenge the "stability of Hemingway's concept of manhood."[15] As Strychacz posits, "Hemingway's need for *evidencing* manhood"[16] in his texts is proof of how uncertain the writer was of his own heteromasculinity, thus all of his narrators are "constituted as men" by performing the author's masculinity not only to the other characters but to the reader as well.[17] In this respect, Strychacz examines various examples of "theatricalized masculinity in his fictional narratives of manhood-fashioning" and suggests that Hemingway's "self-dramatiz[ed]" masculine performances in life were a "powerful trope for the way his male protagonists emerge into manhood before an evaluating audience."[18] As a result, "Masculinity in Hemingway can be seen more profitably as a trope that must be negotiated into meaning by means of a changing structural relationship between character, masculine code, and legitimating audience."[19]

What these recent Hemingway biographers and critics have shown, which is what Tennessee Williams had predicted a decade earlier in his play *Clothes for a Summer Hotel* (1980), is that the Hemingway text *is* the Hemingway myth, and divorcing one from the other would somehow cast both into literary purgatory from which neither would ever return. They are inseparably fused, one the palimpsest of the other, in spite of or because of Hemingway and his several "conspirators."[20] For this reason, any Hemingway text has the potential not only to exploit the fissures in the masculine wall of the man, but also, and more importantly, to demonstrate that the macho myth itself was a sham, a celluloid copy of an already staged photo-op. Consequently, Hemingway's biographers and critics alike have been focusing much critical attention on the crises of masculinity, the struggles with femininity, and the presence of homosexuality in his work to understand, and hopefully enlarge, our view of Hemingway the writer and the man.

To be sure, curious bouts with masculinity and covert and overt homosexuality figure prominently in Hemingway's canon, from his earliest works to his late ones. Stories from the 1920s and 1930s such as "The Sea Change," "A Simple Enquiry," "The Mother of a Queen," "Mr. and Mrs. Elliot," "Che Ti Dice La Patria," "God Rest You Merry, Gentlemen," "A Pursuit Race," "The Light of the World," "The Last Good Country," "There's One in Every Town," "Portrait of Three or the Paella," and "A Lack of Passion" (the last three unpublished during his life)[21] all contain references to homosexuality that play a significant, often thematic role in the text that is treated as sympathetically as it is pejoratively. For instance, while Doc Fisher is kind and understanding to the young man frightened by his homoerotic inclinations in "God Rest You Merry, Gentlemen," Roger in "The Mother of a Queen" is vitriolic in his slander against the gay bullfighter, Paco (a fictionalized version of the bullfighter José Ortiz): "What kind of blood is it that makes a man like that?" (*CSS* 319);[22] and while the poet Hubert Elliot (presumably Hemingway's jab at T. S. Eliot) and his lesbian wife Cornelia are portrayed without hostility in "Mr. and Mrs. Elliot," Tom and the narrator of "The Light of the World" are themselves taken for "punks" (a word Hemingway uses throughout his canon to signify homosexuality)[23] and later impugn the cook at the end for actually being gay. At other times, homosexuality seems to be a simple narrative detail, as with the "smartly dressed and clean-cut looking" writer in "Che Ti Dice La Patria" (*CSS* 225), and neither the narrator nor a character in the story says or does anything that might be construed as homophobic. In short, given the varying, often contradictory perspectives toward homosexuality in Hemingway's stories, it is difficult to read any of them as projecting the viewpoint of its author.

These examples represent no small a list of stories with homosexual content or theme from an author reputed for his virulent homophobia. Moreover, similar treatments of sexual identification, and their similar problems of narrative authority, can be found in Hemingway's novels, such as *The Sun Also Rises, A Farewell to Arms, To Have and Have Not, For Whom the Bell Tolls, Islands in the Stream,* and *The Garden of Eden* (these last two novels having been started in 1946–1947, then abandoned, only to be published posthumously in 1970 and 1986, respectively), as well as in his nonfiction, *Death in the Afternoon, A Moveable Feast,* and *True at First Light/Under Kilimanjaro.* In *The Garden of Eden,* for example, David Bourne privately excoriates his wife Catherine's experimentation with lesbian sex with the dark-skinned beauty, Marita, but he is equally open to sexual experimentation himself throughout the novel, leaving the reader to question not only David's sense of sexual righteousness but Hemingway's as well. To be sure, the work of academic critics, such as Nina Schwartz, Ira Elliott, Gregory Woods, Michael S. Reynolds, Cary Wolfe, Linda Wagner-Martin, Peter Hays, Axel Nissen, and Wolfgang Rudat (to name but a few), have perhaps just begun the long and arduous task of untangling the sexual/gender mess in Hemingway's stories, novels, and memoirs.[24]

Among this not-so-insignificant list, *The Sun Also Rises* remains perhaps the most important, and certainly most intriguing, of Hemingway's sexual dysfunction novels, not only because it was his first novel to explore sexual incongruities, but because it was his most subversive. While no overtly gay *hero* appears in *The Sun Also Rises* and homosexuality is dismissed curtly in the *bal musette* passage, Hemingway is still very much playing throughout with queer politics and gay sensibilities and their relationship to the heterosexual world of the epoch, both internal and external to the novel. As such, critics have gone to great lengths either to reassure us of Jake's heterosexuality among the gay world[25] or to drag him, kicking and screaming, out of the closet.[26] The result has reinforced the critical impasse among Hemingway scholars, who have locked ideological horns between appropriating the lost Hemingway myth, and thus securing Jake's masculinity by making him the sexual victim of stolid gender classifying, or demolishing it all together, taking with it the stability not only of Jake's sexual identity but of Hemingway's as well.

What is more significant, however, both to Jake and to Hemingway and his fellow Parisian expatriates, is *precisely* Jake's sexual ambivalence, for with perhaps one foot in the closet and the other securely outside, Jake situates himself among the earliest modernist heroes in

American literature whose personal and spiritual crises of masculine identity are centered not upon their sexual dysfunction alone but also upon the relation of that dysfunction to the gendered norm and the existential angst it generates in them when they realize there is no escaping social classification. Torn between the consolidating sexual identities of the boorish Rough Rider and the effeminate Aesthete, both cultural products of fin de siècle sexual politics, Jake remains permanently fixed in that nether region wherein lays the *Homo americanus:* those modernist heterosexual American men whose "queer" masculinities belie their sexual identities socially constructed through the popular psychosexual thought of the day. Neither concomitantly gay nor determinately straight, Jake represents one of Hemingway's finest expressions and subsequent criticisms of his time's emerging construction of the sexually binary male, and nowhere is this more evident than in Jake's final line to Brett.

Queer is as Queer Does (or Does Not Do): Impotence as Sexual Existentialism

The celebrated conclusion to Hemingway's *The Sun Also Rises*, where Jake delivers his ambiguous "Isn't it pretty to think so?" line to Brett during a taxi ride through Madrid, has been the locus of critical debate among Hemingway scholars for well over thirty years now. The two widely accepted readings of the novel's conclusion are that Jake is either falling back into a pattern of sexual aberration from which he had briefly established some distance (given his earlier dependence on Brett in their first taxi ride in chapter 4), which lends the novel its pessimistic circular structure;[27] or that he is now affirming that distance by delivering the line with a calculated dosage of irony, as ironic as the "mounted" policeman's "raised" baton in the intervening lines mocks Jake's lack of an erect phallus.[28] While both readings of the conclusion are unquestionably valid, especially given Jake's own inconsistent relationship to irony throughout the novel and his hapless love for Brett, more and more critics have opted for the latter. One reason for this paradigm shift has been the spate of inquiries into the novel's sexual politics.

For instance, in that first taxi ride in chapter 4, which helps to establish the novel's framed structure, we find the crystallization of nearly all of Jake's problems that will be explored and perhaps exorcised in the novel's closing lines.[29] Here, he pursues sexual intimacy with Brett, but she rejects him: "I can't stand it.... You mustn't.... Oh, darling, please understand!" (*S* 26). She hates being physically enticed by Jake, which she undoubtedly is here, because she knows that her arousal can find no outlet, and Brett does not want "to go through that hell again" (*S* 26). What exactly "that hell again" *is* Hemingway never states in the novel, but through fragments of dialogue and sexual situations, we have come to understand that Jake is physically impotent. But impotent how? Has he in fact been castrated like the steers of the fiesta from the wound he received during the war or from the surgery to repair it, and thus his need for the prostitute Georgette's companionship early in the novel satisfies only some "vague sentimental idea" (*S* 16) of sexual intercourse? Or has he lost *only* his penis, like the self-mutilated teenage boy in "God Rest You Merry, Gentlemen," which would leave him all of the desire for that intercourse but not the tool with which to satiate it?[30] The distinction is not an insignificant one, for if Jake could feel *only* the sentimental jealousy of Brett's having sex with other men and not the physical desire itself during those sexual escapades, his trauma would not appear as severe as if the opposite were true.

In a December 1951 letter to Rinehart editor Thomas Bledsoe, and later in his comment to George Plimpton during an interview for *The Paris Review*, Hemingway put the issue to rest by insisting that Jake, despite his injury, still has all the normal sex-drives of a man:

> Every writer is in much of his work. But it is not as simple as all that. I could have told Mr. [Philip] Young the whole genesis of *The Sun Also Rises* for example. It came from a personal experience in that when I had been wounded at one time there had been an infection from pieces of wool cloth being driven in to the scrotum. Because of this I got to know other kids who had genito urinary wounds and I wondered what a man's life would have been like after that if his penis had been lost and his testicles and spermatic cord remained intact.[31]

Therefore, Jake's physical desire in the novel is left unfulfilled, and unfulfillable, torturing him emotionally, physically, and psychologically with the knowledge that he will never be able to satisfy Brett or himself sexually. His impotence, then, leaves them both in what Carlos Baker inappropriately calls a "Heloisa-Abelard relationship."[32]

Like Wolfgang Rudat, Linda Wagner-Martin and James Hinkle have explored the intricate, (a)sexual relationship (and the dark humor that accompanies it) that develops between the woman who resembles a boy but acts the Jezebel and the man who resembles a stud but plays the eunuch.[33] What all of their scholarship has been able to unearth, in fact, is that *The Sun Also Rises* is thematically centered around numerous phallic references that Hemingway uses not just for comic but also ironic effect.[34] For example, we find multiple levels of Hemingway's phallocentric punning in the following exchange between Brett and Count Mippipopolous:

"What about your little friend, *Zizi?*"
"Let me tell you. I *support* that boy, but I don't want to have him around."
"He is rather *hard.*"
"You know I think that boy's got a future. But personally *I don't want him around.*"
"Jake's *rather the same way.*"
"He gives me the *willys.*" (*S* 63, my emphasis)

The conversation loses all of its dark humor and poignant irony in describing the seriousness of Jake's condition if we do not recognize that, first, the Count is probably impotent too[35] and, second, the final pun on a "willy," which the *OED* defines as an "infantile" or "slang name for a child's penis" that dates back to 1905, echoes an earlier one with *un zizi,* which the *Dictionnaire historique de la langue francaise* notes is a childish name in French for the penis, having first appeared in print in 1920, just six years prior to *The Sun Also Rises.*[36]

All of these erect/limp penis jokes, puns, and allusions run contrapuntal to Jake's impotence and thus serve to repeatedly underscore the irony of Jake's sexuality and gender in the face of social norms, prompting him finally to adopt a feminine stance in his "pretty" rejoinder at the end of the novel. Yet this dark humor in the novel frequently draws its irony not from Jake's impotence itself but from the existential situations into which his impotence leads him, something all of these critics have overlooked: desired by a woman whom he equally desires but whose sexual appetite he must satisfy vicariously through an act of love she has with another—be it Cohn, Romero and, presumably, Mike—Jake is forced everyday into finding a truer meaning to his life, leaving him no option other than to constantly redefine his role as a man among a society that has already fashioned for itself an image to which Jake cannot ultimately ascribe.[37]

Jake's predicament between personal and social identification is an existential one to be sure, and many critics have already noted Hemingway's *nada* theory here and elsewhere as being the artistic harbinger of the philosophical theories forged by the European existentialists twenty years later.[38] Hemingway, John Killinger contends, understood the nada feeling present in modern man's fear "of nihilation by absorption into the machine, the mass, or whatever"[39] but, since he was a novelist and not a philosopher, he chose instead to capture its effects through art. It was not until Søren Kierkegaard, Martin Heidegger, Karl Jaspers, Jean-Paul Sartre, and Albert Camus could name and codify this postwar phenomenon that existentialism would obtain its currency to describe (both in art and in life) the collective anxiety of a war-torn generation. As Sartre would later confirm, "We learned from Hemingway to depict, without commentaries, without explanations, without moral judgments, the actions of our characters. The reader understands them because he sees them born and formed in a situation which has been made understandable to him. They live because they spurt suddenly as from a deep well. To analyze them would be to kill them."[40]

Though maddeningly complex in its phenomenological explanation of ontology, Sartre's own *Being and Nothingness* (*L'Être et le néant*, 1943) accurately captures the existential angst of a generation of men who, like Jake, contracted modernist nausea from having ingested the hypocrisy of sociopolitical identification consistent with their day. Accepting the premise that man is born devoid of any known or knowable essence to his life — be it a preordained (determinist) or an objectified (religious) one — Sartre posits that to avert the inevitable social typing that works to fill that void man must supply himself with his own essence (or meaning) to his existence. In defining his own individuality, he abates those fears that inevitably accompany thoughts of human meaninglessness when absorbed into the masses. Such thinking put Sartre at odds with Cartesian ontology, effectively inverting his *Cogito ergo sum* into *Sum ergo cogito* — "I am; therefore, I think."

Consciousness, Sartre maintains, "is not produced as a particular instance of an abstract possibility but that in rising to the center of being, it creates and supports its essence — that is, . . . its existence implies its essence."[41] Because it can never exist prior to Being (*l'être*), consciousness must produce nothingness (*le néant*) in order to define its limits (*l'être-pour-soi*), which is subsequently its immediate nihilation (*l'être-en-soi*). In other words, a person exists before he has knowledge of that existence, and once that knowledge begins forming, it defines the individual negatively through the recognition of what he is not. However, once knowledge establishes the self within this void in opposition to the Other (*l'être-pour-autrui*), the *pour-soi* is forever encased within its own shell of defining nothingness and thus permanently detached from its immutable *en-soi*.

Yet, the *thought* of being is not enough to satisfy the *state* of being. To define the self, one simply must act. Given that each individual is born into a particular *situation* (and necessarily so since each *pour-soi* has this inescapable engagement with the world), he is totally responsible for the choices he makes. He cannot help but be defined by the sum of his choices, which are only rendered through his actions, or, as the case may be here with Jake, his inactions. Though not itself an essence, this agency of self-determination pre-exists in him and challenges him daily with the freedom to choose how to define, and therefore give meaning to, his *authentic* existence (acting true to one's self and beliefs). To avoid choosing to act or to invoke anti-individualist axioms of determinism or of external paradigms (such as a philosophy, a religious faith, or a bourgeois morality) in order to justify one's action (or lack of it) constitutes *la mauvaise foi,* Sartrean bad faith: to live an *inauthentic* life, to escape the responsible freedom of the *pour-soi,* to accept social definition over individual epistemology. Overwhelmed by the full implication of this imposing freedom and granted little means with which to access or explicate its precise nature on him, the existentialist experiences moral anguish, absurdity, alienation, and ultimately despair.

In light of Sartre's definition, it becomes more clear how Jake Barnes, in his honest attempt to find meaning in a dehumanizing world responsible for the horrors of Verdun and la Somme, could be seen as a literary forerunner to the existential heroes of World War II. He observes his environment with a jaundiced eye and acts according to a code that places him in opposition with those who make up his immediate surroundings. Work (as he repeatedly tells us, other characters, and himself) is one way to fight against the existential angst of the postwar period; alcohol is another. And while everyone in the novel, Jake included, chooses wine, beer, and champagne to temporarily fill their spiritual vacuity, Jake opts finally for work, and writing, to quell his anxiety. As Killinger writes, "For both Hemingway and the existentialists, the choice is never made finally, but must be made again and again, as if it had never been made before. The real hero is the man who chooses this difficult way to self, who perpetually reconstitutes his *existence* by choosing to be authentic and to bear the responsibilities of personal action."[42] For this reason, Killinger notes, Jake is an existentialist who, "as a result of his wound, leads a simple, unentangled life"[43] among the mindless postwar revels of *les années folles.*

Yet, it is not some larger struggle he has with the reality responsible for his wound, as Killinger maintains, but rather the nature of Jake's wound itself which directly brings about that existential crisis in the first place and that perhaps directs him toward a socially-detached, Western equivalent of nirvana. For example, the power that the impotence initially has over him individually is clearly profound, despite the fact that he says he was "pretty well through with the subject" (*S* 27). Sitting alone in his bedroom, after having just left Brett in their first taxi encounter, Jake tries to convince himself that what happened to him during the war was "supposed to be funny" (*S* 26), but the pain behind the ironic laughter cannot be masked: "At one time or another I had probably considered it from most of its various angles, including the one that certain injuries or imperfections are a subject of merriment while remaining quite serious for the person possessing them" (*S* 27). We are clearly early in the novel here, and Jake is still entertaining thoughts of a possible "good time together" with Brett, which he will repeat three chapters later when she visits Jake again with the Count. Each sexual arousal triggers in him his existential response, one that lies unabated until he can numb it with the opiates of alcohol and sleep: "... in a little while I felt like hell again. It is awfully easy to be hard-boiled about everything in the daytime, but at night it is another thing" (*S* 34). By the end of the novel, however, Jake will realize that this longing only constitutes a pipe dream that must finally be put to rest. How he arrives at that conclusion, then, is based more on how his sexual experience with others shapes his social understanding of his injury than on any personal acceptance he has, or does not have, of it.

Judith Butler's theoretical distinction between sex and gender helps to effectively explain how Jake's trouble with masculine signification has its roots in the identity politics of existentialism.[44] If, as Butler argues, gender privileges heterosexual constructs through performativity more than through physical appearance alone (unless appearance is precisely *performed*, as with drag or camp), and Jake has lost his signifying penis in which to perform a heterosexual identity, he can no longer "exist" as a heterosexual man. One's desires remain a private affair; one's performativity a public one. In other words, to say nothing of Jake's loftier aspirations of the soul in the novel, his ready-made sexual essence can no longer serve Jake in identifying his gendered existence to others, which he must fulfill in other ways.[45] That is, on the basest level, he is at least predefined biologically at birth by his sex, where only a woman can bear children and only a man can impregnate her, regardless of whether either finally desires to do so or not. As Butler writes,

> To what extent do *regulatory practices* of gender formation and division constitute identity, the internal coherence of the subject, indeed, the self-referential status of the person? To what extent is "identity" a normative ideal rather than a descriptive feature of experience? And how do the regulatory practices that govern gender also govern culturally intelligible notions of identity? In other words, the "coherence" and "continuity" of "the person" are not logical or analytical features of personhood, but, rather, socially instituted and maintained norms of intelligibility. Inasmuch as "identity" is assured through the stabilizing concepts of sex, gender, and sexuality, the very notion of the "person" is called into question by the cultural emergence of those "incoherent" or "discontinuous" gendered beings who appear to be persons but who fail to conform to the gendered norms of cultural intelligibility by which persons are defined.[46]

Such "regulatory practices" of gender produce a "'truth' of sex" (*GT* 23), Butler adds, but for Jake—and for Brick Pollitt in Williams's *Cat on a Hot Tin Roof* as we will see in the following chapters—his "internal coherence" as a heterosexual male cannot be confirmed indefinitely since he will lack the necessary "regulatory practices" of making love with a woman to sustain that identity his gender acts attempt to express.

Unperformed heterosexuality can thus precipitate a homosexual identity over time, regardless of the nature of the "internal coherence" of individual's object-desire. For men like Jake who must confer upon themselves a heterosexual identity through expression (the act of generating a sexual identity) more so than through performativity (the process through which a sexual identity is constituted by an act) often redirect their anxiety and frustration away from sex-defining acts to those of gender-defining ones, here masculinity. As Butler notes,

> The disavowed homosexuality at the base of melancholic heterosexuality re-emerges as the self-evident anatomical facticity of sex, where "sex" designates the blurred unity of anatomy, "natural identity," and "natural desire." The loss is denied and incorporated, and the genealogy of that transmutation fully forgotten and repressed. The sexed surface of the body thus emerges as the necessary sign of a natural(ized) identity and desire. . . . In the case of the melancholic heterosexual male, he never loved another man, he *is* a man, and he can seek recourse to the empirical facts that will prove it. But the literalization of anatomy not only proves nothing, but is a literalizing restriction of pleasure in the very organ that is championed as the sign of masculine identity. (*GT* 91)

Thus a masculine essence, or gender expression which "confirms" a heterosexual identity in modern sexual epistemologies, must be enacted, and re-enacted, not just to express a sexual preference in the individual but even to help formulate one.

This distinction between gender "expression" and gender "performativity," then, becomes crucial when considering how Jake is seen and how he sees himself with respect to other men, gay and straight alike. For example, the men who accompany Brett to the *bal musette* are gay because, as Ira Elliott argues,[47] Jake (and his society) "reads" their "behavioral or performative acts," much in the same way that Brett is feminine,[48] though she looks like a boy, because she is known to sleep with several men. In short, both perform their proper genders, which society subsequently reads as a sexual identity. Jake, on the other hand, is left only with the option of posturing as a heterosexual man by performing masculinely-identified gendered acts like soliciting prostitutes and publicly parading them or flaunting his acceptance into the exclusively masculine college of the bullfighting afícionados. Since his sexual *non*essence will remain permanently fixed, denying him the ability to express his sexuality via the traditional modes of gender identification (i.e., he cannot produce children or ever satisfy the sexual appetite of the woman he desires), Jake will only appear masculine and heterosexual to others as long as he can maintain those peripheral gender performative acts which underpin that sexed identity. Lose them, and Jake's masquerade (like Henry James's at the time) falls apart. And for Jake, a childless bachelor (presumably) in his mid-thirties, time is running out, and he knows it.

Therefore, when the Italian liaison colonel says to Jake that he had "'given more than [his] life'" (*S* 31) to the cause when he was injured and lost his penis, we are to understand that he means Jake sacrificed his whole defining *essence* as a sexual being in light of his future *existence* as a gendered male.[49] As Butler explains,

> If gender attributes and acts, the various ways in which a body shows or produces its cultural signification, are performative, then there is no preexisting identity by which an act or attribute might be measured; there would be no true or false, real or distorted acts of gender, and the postulation of a true gender identity would be revealed as a regulatory fiction. That gender reality is created through sustained social performances means that the very notions of an essential sex and a true and abiding masculinity or femininity are also constituted as part of the strategy that conceals gender's performative character and the performative possibilities for proliferating gender configurations outside the restricting frames of masculinist domination and compulsory heterosexuality. (*GT* 180)

In other words, Jake's sexual dysfunction in *The Sun Also Rises* pits Freudian genital sex (we are defined by our genitalia, which Monique Wittig confronts with her postgenital sexual politics) against Saussurean "absence" or Lacanian "lack." What he now lacks in reality (that is the penis), he relocates in the symbolic gestures of masculine bravado (that is the phallus and the Phallus), and the language games that underwrite them, to signify through metonymy what should be there in reality but is not. It is not that Jake has failed to develop genitally, as Freud argues in *Three Essays on the Theory of Sexuality* is the cause of homosexuality, but that his penis is in all fact "a lack," an absence, and thus a signifier of his sexual existentialism.[50]

The need to act in order to define one's self, and the choices that go with that action, form striking similarities between Sartre's existential and Butler's gender theories. Both place particular emphasis on the manners in which man's essence is constructed internally and externally by what he does or chooses not to do. Butler insists in *Gender Trouble,* however, that her gender theory is not existential in nature:

> The foundationalist reading of identity politics tends to assume that an identity must first be in place in order for political interests to be elaborated and,

subsequently, political action to be taken. My argument is that there need not be a "doer behind the deed," but rather that the "doer" is variably constructed in and through the deed. This is not a return to an existential theory of the self as constituted through its acts, for the existential theory maintains a prediscursive structure for both the self and its acts. It is precisely the discursively variable construction of each and through the other that has interested me here. (*GT* 181)

In other words, Butler does not adhere to the existential tenet of "existence before essence" and, if any, seems to return to a Cartesian way of thinking: "I act; therefore I am." The corollary to Butler's definition, however, would seem to be that no "doer" would be constructed if no deed was ever enacted. My basic disagreement with Butler's explanation here is that a person still *does* become something or someone even though the *deed* has not been done. Sexual existentialism, then, maintains the following premise: "I did not perform; therefore I am." Existentialism precisely places significance on the *undeed* as well as on the deed, as with Jake's *not* rejecting Brett in the end of the novel, and as such any inaction unquestionably works to construct the non-doer's identity as well.

Jake's "paradox of existential philosophy," as Nina Schwartz contends, is thus inextricably tied to Leon Seltzer's paradox of impotence, where Jake's sexual incapacities, like Brick Pollitt's later, are at the core of his existential gender crisis.[51] If he could learn to redefine his new role and reject how others might perceive his androgyny, then he would, like Camus's Sisyphus, achieve to some degree a freedom from all external perceptions of his pain and reestablish primary control over his defining essence. As Schwartz wryly puts it, ". . . if he could cancel the determinacy of the inscribed meaning of castration to achieve a certain skepticism toward it—he might be able to effect a transformation of the significations of the phallus in Western culture, which would be a radical revision indeed."[52]

Whether or not Jake has come to accept fully his injury and its consequences in the novel is debatable and, in the aims of this study, insignificant. I do not wish to make light of the future implications Hemingway raises in the novel; on the contrary, Jake's uncertain future is precisely what lends the novel its final tragic dimension.[53] Nor do I want to prescribe some literary analgesic with which to deaden our response to his private and generational plight. Rather, I wish now to focus theoretically on how Hemingway combines these two central concerns of the novel—Jake's impotence and his existential struggle to understand its consequences in light of his heteromasculine identity—and externalizes Jake's internal conflict by, in addition to the numerous penis references already uncovered, placing his hero in various social situations that clarify for Jake how his impotence, though concealed from society, unconditionally defines him among those in it. As Wendy Martin suggests, "His sexual impotence is a sign of loss of masculine power and authority and the axiomatic right to exercise social control."[54] In short, Jake's lack of a fixed sexual identity defines his social identity by default—as poststructuralists from Althusser to Lacan, from de Saussure to Foucault have informed us—for one's *social* being is solely contingent upon how *others* perceive us and our gender-performative acts or lack of them, and Jake is or will soon be perceived as a queer heterosexual. The hero, then, is not just struggling to come to some separate peace with himself, as Killinger posits, but also, because of the nature of his wound, with his unique relationship to those in the novel who make up his society.[55] Proof of his response to that emerging identity is revealed in his uncharacteristic use of the word "pretty."

"Pretty" as Pink: The Language of Homophobia

No single word has arguably caused so much consternation in all of American literary scholarship. Why would a character, whose unflinching masculinity has been repeatedly underscored throughout the novel and whose adjectival arsenal is limited to a few appropriately *neutered* terms like "nice" or "good," suddenly, and unexpectedly, come out with the word "pretty," a word unconditionally signifying feminine beauty in the past century or more? No doubt it is used to signal a change in Jake in the end, as Louise R. Achuff suggests,[56] but what kind of change exactly? Wolfgang Rudat, echoing Mimi Reisel Gladstein, has argued that this reversal of gendered language reflects Jake's final acceptance of the sterility of his relationship with Brett, for while Brett retains her masculine identity through to the end (her titled name, Ashley, is after all in the "stud-book" [*S* 76]), Jake consciously feminizes himself here and "meets Brett's psychological-castration attempt by verbally withdrawing into the safe position of the homosexual on whom she could not and would not make any sexual demands": "In an earlier version Jake had replied, 'Yes. . . . It's nice as hell to think so'. . . . [thus] he had tried to out-macho the masculinely aggressive Brett. In the final version, however, Hemingway chose the opposite course. . . . When he adopts the pose of a homosexual, he shows her that for him their relationship has now become as meaningless as the relationship between her and the homosexuals, a relationship whose inaneness the narrator had taken pains to point out."[57]

But such a change, it must be conceded, is fairly radical, even if we consider Jake's earlier display of rabid homophobia as precisely delineating that change. Sexual chauvinism, like social mores, are not changed with so much insouciance, especially not in Hemingway's world. Something more political must be at stake here than simply Jake's wanting to have the last word—or the last laugh. What those stakes are, in fact, has more to do with Jake's understanding of himself through the eyes of others than through his own emerging vision of who he is, though the one is undeniably influenced by the other. In other words, Jake's feminized "pretty" and his initial response to homosexuality do not combine to show how Jake suddenly queers himself in his unexpected affiliation with the gay community as much as they establish his bitter recognition of how society is queering him, forcing upon him a consolidating sexual identity by situating him along their nonnegotiable gender lines.

In *Epistemology of the Closet,* Eve Sedgwick argues that homosexuality as a social identity grew out of Western society's bourgeois definition of what heterosexuality was, and anything not meeting those requirements immediately became queer. Homosexuality thus emerged "precisely from the inexplicitness or denial of the gaps *between* long-coexisting minoritizing and universalizing, or gender-transitive and gender-intransitive, understandings of same-sex relations."[58] The result of this "inexplicitness," Sedgwick maintains, was a modern brand of homophobia that has led all kinds of men, particular gay ones themselves, to openly and privately excoriate homosexuality more as a social identity than as a sexual act. In short, running contrary to the traditional means of assessing and condemning sexual incongruities, homophobic assessments in this century have determined someone's sexual nature based not on any proof of a homosexual *act* committed but rather by the presumption of that act based uniquely on a non-heterosexual *identity* resulting from the lack of heteromasculinity, thus ensuring "the fundamental incoherence of modern constitutions of homosexuality."[59] Since sociosexual rules were difficult to ascertain among heterosexual men who needed to cultivate this space between homosexual desire and their homosocial need to protect masculinity, Sedgwick concludes, "paranoia in men result[ed] from the repression of their homosexual desire" and left in its wake "a widespread, endemic male homosexual panic as a post-Romantic phenomenon."[60]

Specifically in America, homosexual panic of the type Sedgwick describes here emerged on the national scene at the turn of the twentieth century, when homosexuality began to coalesce as a social identity and heterosexual American men were experiencing a crisis of masculinity ignited by significant changes in the social fabric during the Gilded Age. With the bisexual theories of William James, Havelock Ellis, and

Freud having largely been framed around the time that the Aesthete Oscar Wilde was on trial in London for sodomy and the President-to-be Theodore Roosevelt (with whom Hemingway repeatedly identified) rode with the Rough Riders through southern Cuba to assure victory in the Spanish-American War, the popular image of the American male was becoming feverishly binarized, with gender often substituting for sexuality, and homophobia marking that distinction.

Donald Yacovone explains that Republican America had not problematized male-male desire within its definitions of manhood since men could share between them a passionate, *agape* love with intimacy and physical contact just short of intercourse. It was not even uncommon, for instance, for men to share a bed or exchange passionate love letters. As such, pre-Victorian friendships between men should not be misinterpreted by modern standards as having been homoerotic because "mid-nineteenth century social attitudes permitted great liberty in personal relations, largely untainted by homophobia."[61] As Yacovone concluded, "The nineteenth century understood and rejected what we would call homosexual acts but had no consciousness of a homosexual persona. . . ."[62] One could *be* masculine despite his same-sex desire, just as one would later *become* homosexual despite never having *acted* upon any desire. However, by the turn of the century, the growing legal, medical, and scientific literature on sexual inversion in Europe raised the "specter of femininity" in American men, prompting them to protect their gender space by closing off sexual borders from the encroaching other and redefining for themselves what it meant to a man within that determined space.[63]

In the opening pages of the novel, just prior to Brett and Jake's first taxi ride, Jake finds her in the company of a group of gay men at the *bal musette*. Jake's response to these men is, as one would expect from a character whose affiliations with Hemingway are so seamless (Jake was even called "Hem" in the early drafts), an admixture of disgust and hostility: "I was very angry. Somehow they always made me angry. I know they are supposed to be amusing, and you should be tolerant, but I wanted to swing on one, any one, anything to shatter that superior, simpering composure" (*S* 20). While it first seems that Jake hates the gay men because of their superior "composure," in the same way he dislikes Cohn for flaunting his superior Jewishness, Jake soon dispels this reading when he begins hating Cohn *only after* Cohn has hurt him (either with the Brett affair or with the assault in Pamplona) and not before, though Cohn's "superiority" has been with him from the opening pages of the novel. Jake may not like something or someone, be it Cohn or his fiancée Frances Clyne, but he clearly understands why and never passes condemnation unduly. Thus it would appear that Jake here, like Hemingway, simply cannot tolerate gay culture, as Hinkle and Wagner-Martin both suggest,[64] or that Hemingway is using homosexuality only to intensify the novel's "atmosphere of sterility," as Philip Young contends.[65]

In their assessment of Hemingway's and Jake's homophobia here, however, these critics miss one essential point: why would Jake even feel the need to be "tolerant" toward gay men in the first place if he were unabashedly homophobic? After all, Jake does tolerate his friend Bill, whom many critics believe to be closeted, and he knowingly places himself in social milieus where he will repeatedly confront homosexuality, such as the *bal de la Montagne Sainte Geneviève,* a known gay Parisian nightspot in the 1920s.[66] What, then, in 1925 would make Jake as an American male even question his gut-reaction toward homosexuality? One answer lies in his, and Hemingway's own, "homosexual education" in Paris of the 1920s.

Like Jake, Hemingway frequently encountered gay individuals in Paris, not the least of whom were expatriate writers that he met at Gertrude Stein's literary salons. Because Hemingway "probably never met a homosexual" growing up in Oak Park, Michael Reynolds writes, his "initial response of anger or disgust" when he did meet them in Paris "was a knee jerk reaction, a part of his essentially conservative nature." But, Reynolds adds, as an honest writer, Hemingway could not dismiss aspects of human nature without having studied them extensively in books as in life experiences. Stein, like Ezra Pound, influenced what he read, and Reynolds informs us that "Hemingway knew his Freudian theory and had also read extensively Havelock Ellis, an English sexual psychologist whose theories fascinated him."[67] In reading homocentric works like Ellis's *Studies in the Psychology of Sex* (co-authored with John Addington Symonds), which he first encountered in Sylvia Beech's Shakespeare and Co. bookstore since it was banned in the United States (he later purchased his own copies, which Reynolds lists among his reading inventory),[68] as well as being exposed to a gay public unlike any he had encountered in America before the War, Hemingway encountered European theories on sexuality that challenged his prior prejudices and opened him up to the idea that American sexual mores were ostensibly locked in a strangling Puritan past.

Echoing many of the German sexologists before him, Havelock Ellis argues in *Studies in the Psychology of Sex* that homosexuality was neither a disease nor a crime and thus should be tolerated by society, or at least decriminalized: "That [homosexual] impetus, in a well-bred individual who leads the normal life of his fellow-men and who feels the ordinary degree of respect for the social feeling surrounding him, can only be supplied by a fundamental—usually, it is probable, inborn—perversion of the sexual instinct, rendering the individual organically abnormal. It is with this fundamental abnormality, usually called sexual inversion, that we shall here be concerned."[69] Though there is disagreement among scholars as to how much of the legal, medical, and scientific literature on the sexual "invert" produced at the turn of the century had affected lay society (gay and straight alike), one fact agreed upon is that heteromasculine men in America began denigrating homosexuality as a sexual identity as much as they had before deplored it as a sexual act. As George Chauncey, Jr. writes, "the changing focus of medical inquiry into sexual deviance . . . can be analyzed as a response to particular changes in and challenges to the Victorian sex/gender system such as the women's movement, the growing visibility of urban gay male subcultures, and the changing gender structure of the economy."[70] Victorian men, who had already been engaged in a gender war on the signifier front against women and immigrant men in America (discussed in the next section) now looked to appropriate sexuality as well. Anthony Rotundo explains that the more the heteromasculine American male "feared he might be one of the stigmatized group, the more he needed to prove himself a man or—what was more difficult—come to terms with what was not manly about himself. . . . The creation of the homosexual image produced a deadly new weapon for maintaining the boundaries of manhood."[71]

Despite the increasing antagonism in America toward sexual inversion at the turn of the century, the effeminate male and the homosexual-as-person would be fused only by World War I. As Chauncey points out in his study of the Newport Naval Training Center in 1919, where "a series of disputes over the boundaries between homosociality and homosexuality in the relations of men and over the standards by which their masculinity would be judged":

> While many straight men took the sexual advances of gay men in stride, most engaged in certain ritual behavior designed to reinforce the distinction between themselves and the "queers." Most importantly, they played only "masculine" sex roles in their encounters with gay men—or at least they claimed that they did—and observed the norms of masculinity in their own demeanor. They also ridiculed gay men and sometimes beat them up after sexual encounters. Other men, who feared it brought their manhood into question simply to be approached by a "pervert," were even more like to attack gay men.[72]

Chauncey points out elsewhere in *Gay New York* that the process

> by which the normal world defined itself in opposition to the queer world was manifest in countless social interactions, for in its policing of the gay

subculture the dominant culture sought above all to police its own boundaries. Given the centrality of gender nonconformity to the definition of the queer, the excoriation of queer served primarily to set the boundaries for how normal men could dress, walk, talk, and relate to women and to each other.... Indeed, the policing of queer ways, and thus of normal ways, was most commonly effected through the informal policing of the streets, in gossip and in the jeers and manhandling visited on men whom other men regarded as queer.[73]

Though gay subcultures existed in America's larger cities, their visibility grew less and less as the century pressed forward, forcing most gay enclaves underground by the end of World War II.

Even in Jake's (and Hemingway's) postwar Paris, we can find similar forms of overt homophobia, but nothing to the extent that the gay community in America, particularly in New York, experienced at the time. French playwright Edouard Bourdet's play, *La Prisonnière*, best captures these differences in social climate concerning the limits of accepted homosexuality in France and in America during the Jazz Age. The play opened to critical acclaim at the Théâtre Femina in Paris on March 1926, around the same time that Hemingway was completing the second draft of *The Sun Also Rises*. A play that treats in earnest the lesbian tendencies of an older woman who successfully captures the sexual curiosities of a young bourgeois girl, *La Prisonnière* met with scandal when it opened in New York on September 30, 1926 as *The Captive*, which J. Brooks Atkinson of the *New York Times* condemned as potentially degenerating "into a commercial exploitation of a revolting theme."[74] A year later, Mae West's gay play, *The Drag*, which was first billed as "The Male Version of *The Captive*," was found to be so repugnant (and titillating) to Broadway audiences and New York law enforcement that it would even earn the playwright brief jail time. According to theater historian Kaier Curtin, West had wanted *The Drag* "to dramatize her theories about gay male sexual predilections, which she likened to a contagious social cancer," that is, what she saw as a "tragedy of 'born inverts' and the threat of gay 'perverts.'"[75]

Though homophobia was still endemic in early twentieth-century Europe, as Jeffrey Weeks and James Steakley have informed us,[76] its visibility brought homosexuality more into the pan-national discourse and thus subsequently desensitized Europe on the whole to it much more quickly than in America, which censored homosexuality at all levels, religious, social, and political alike, despite the existence of the 1924–1925 charter of the Chicago Society for Human Rights, whose nonprofit organization in Hemingway's own home town was chartered "to ameliorate the plight of homosexuals."[77] For these reasons, a homosexual subculture was allowed to flourish in European cities like Paris and Berlin. But legal tolerance and social disdain were entirely separate issues, and homosexuality nonetheless carried a certain amount of stigma that many gay men and women were willing to avoid. In writing about homosexuality in France around the time of Wilde's trials, for instance, Havelock Ellis notes that it "has been untouched by the law for a century, yet it abounds . . . ," and "although the law is silent social feeling is strong. . . ."[78]

By Jake's (and Hemingway's) 1925, little had in fact changed. As Gilles Barbedette and Michel Carassou demonstrate, repression had lessened to the point where a gay subculture could not only exist but flourish in Paris, evidenced in part by the popularity of the gay magazine *Inversions* (1924–1925) and by the many gay and lesbian expatriate writers at the time—Gertrude Stein, H.D., Djuna Barnes, to name but a few. But same-sex erotic acts remained stigmatized, and men were still sent to jail for participating in homosexual acts in public toilets.[79] This Parisian paradox of tolerance and revulsion—which Hemingway suggests in the "Café des Deux Magots" (1932) episode in *Death in the Afternoon*, as well as in the stories "Mr. and Mrs. Elliot" (1924), "A Lack of Passion" (ca. 1924–1927), "A Simple Enquiry" (1927), "The Sea Change" (1931), and "There's One in Every Town" (1933), actually creates homosexuals out of erstwhile heterosexuals[80]—is summed up best by Shari Benstock: "The laws of normative sexuality were very much in place in Paris, protected by both church and state, and 'deviancy' was tolerated provided it was discreet."[81]

At the time he was writing *The Sun Also Rises*, Hemingway was clearly familiar with the scientific conclusions on sexual inversion and the social latitudes afforded to it in Europe and, moreover, interested in exploring it in detail in his fiction, as in stories (in addition to those listed above) such as "Che Ti Dice La Patria" (1927), "The Mother of a Queen" (ca. 1931–1932), "God Rest You Merry, Gentlemen" (1933). That he also had the opportunity to study it for himself in daily encounters with Paris's Left Bank artists, several of whom he counted as friends, no doubt influenced Hemingway's portrayal of Jake's disgust/tolerance dialectic, as it no doubt reflected his own struggle to negotiate his American prejudices with European standards toward sexuality in general, and homosexuality in particular.

Later, Hemingway even wrote about his epistemological growth concerning homosexuality during these years in an early chapter on Gertrude Stein in *A Moveable Feast*, which could also explain in part Jake's "tolerant" response here. After admitting his "prejudices against homosexuality" to "Miss Stein," the narrative voice (I hesitate to say Hemingway explicitly here since this memoir is fictional to a certain extent) describes the reasons for his present homophobia: "I knew it was why you carried a knife and would use it when you were in the company of tramps when you were a boy in the days when wolves was not a slang term for men obsessed by the pursuit of women."[82] Another "wolf" with "beautiful manners" (like "punk," a recurrent Hemingway signifier for homosexuality) attempted to "corrupt" him while he lay injured in a Italian hospital during World War I: ". . . never to let that man [Mr. Englefield] into the room again" (*MF* 19). And while Hemingway had certainly held disdain for other homosexual men he had met at Stein's salons, he could not come to persuade himself to attack Stein's open lesbian relationship with Alice B. Toklas.

In a November 1952 letter to Edmund Wilson, for example, Hemingway writes:

> In the matter of homo-sexuality in Stein I wish you had mainstreamed your position rather than qualify it. I will give you all the material you will need on that if you wish to back up the position you took in the review of the early book. She talked to me once for three hours telling me why she was a lesbian, the mechanics of it, why the act did not disgust those who performed it (she was at the time against male homosexuality but changed later out of patriotism) and why it was not degrading to either participant. Three hours is a long time with Gertrude crowding you and I was so sold on her theory that I went out that night and fucked a lesbian with magnificent results; ie we slept well afterwards. It was this knowledge, gained from G.S., that enabled me to write A Sea Change, which is a good story, with authenticity. This conversation, in which Toklas left the room, was one of the reasons for her later malice. At one time it reached the proportions of, "You give up the friendship of Hemingstein or you give up me." Toklas used to be quite wicked to Gertrude but Gertrude's ego grew vaster than that thing Andrew Marvell described and finally it was all she needed. But her whole attitude toward life and toward the practice of letters changed with menopause. It was the year she had the menopause that she broke with all her old and good friends. (*SL* 794–95)

Yet, when he does denounce her later in *A Moveable Feast*, Hemingway's anger is directed less at her homosexuality and more at her literary snobbishness — she calls him "yellow," "fragile," and "ninety percent Rotarian" in *The Autobiography of Alice B. Toklas*, for example, and claims that he learned from her the craft of writing "without understanding it."[83] The reason for Hemingway's tolerance toward Stein lies in her distinction between gay men as "criminals and perverts" (*MF* 19) and those, like herself, who lead respectable, bourgeois lives: "The main thing is that the act male homosexuals commit is ugly and repugnant and afterwards they are disgusted with themselves. They drink and take drugs, to palliate this, but they are disgusted with the act and they are always changing partners and cannot be really happy" (*MF* 20).

This subdivision of gay men between those who lead corruptible (or decadent, a term Hemingway frequently uses in *Death in the Afternoon* in reference to homosexuality) lives and those who lead normal, respectable lives (and perhaps even marry) without ever making one's same-sex desire a social issue or incident explains Jake's hostile response to the decadent gay men at the *bal musette*. Being homosexual is one thing for Jake and Hemingway; flaunting it publicly, as these gay men do, is something entirely different—and repugnant. This decadent type of homosexual appears frequently in the Hemingway canon, and he is always the object of ridicule: the "sad clerk with plucked eyebrows" in *Islands in the Stream*,[84] "Hal" in the chapter "Birth of a New School" in *A Moveable Feast*, or even the "impotent" and emasculated Informer in *True at First Light/Under Kilimanjaro* (*UK* 108, 145). In this last example, there are even further cultural subdivisions between acceptable and unacceptable homosexual love. No one, for example, in *True at First Light/Under Kilimanjaro*, in particular the Hemingway persona, can tolerate the Informer, a tribal snitch who is always dressed in his paisley shawl and porkpie hat. It is only later in the book, however, that we learn the reason why:

> Keiti hated the Informer, with considerable cause, since he had served under Keiti in the old days and they had many old unresolved things dating from when the Informer had served as a lorry driver and offended Keiti with his, then, youthful insolence and with his treasonable frankness about the great nobleman who was, by other accounts than his, a backward man. Keiti had loved Pop ever since he had taken service under him and with the Kamba hatred of homosexuality he could not tolerate a Masai lorry driver impugning a white man and especially one of such renown.... (*UK* 356)[85]

Like the pedophile culture of ancient Greece, there are established tribal rules to practicing homosocial and homosexual love, and those who transgress those rules are subjected more to social ostracism than simply those who practice one form of love over the other. Neglecting to recognize this subtle distinction in Hemingway's sexual code oversimplifies his reaction to homosexuality as being purely homophobia, which it is not in both his fiction and nonfiction alike.

It is not, then, simply homosexuality that bothers Jake (or Hemingway) in the *bal musette* passage, but rather the effeminate gender that the gay men affect in the scene. As David Greenberg notes, "The literature is divided on the question of whether effeminate homosexual men evoke a stronger hostile response from heterosexuals than gay men whose gender is conventional." One example Greenberg cites that is relevant to Jake (and to Hemingway) both in France and later in Spain is the distinction between the masculine *guarrones* and the effeminate *maricas*: "The latter were pitied but not feared; boys could look at them and say with reassurance, 'I'm not like that, therefore I'm okay.' The former resembled them more. . . . If they could be homosexual then so could anyone." The fear was that the "*guarrones* would turn them into *maricas*."[86] For Hemingway, and for his work, there is little doubt on which side of Greenberg's divide he situated himself. To be sure, the gay men's performed homosexuality via their affected effeminacy at the *bal musette* preserves Jake's heteromasculine identity, for he would never be considered gay as long as he did not look or act like them in public. As such, any public display of homophobia he may have enacted, such as his shared smile of disdain for the gay men with the policeman serving as bouncer (*S* 20), could readily be interpreted as an act of heteronormative bravado aimed to protect his homosocial privileges with other men.

In wanting at first to tolerate the gay men at the *bal musette* but instead disparaging their "simpering" behavior, Jake is responding the way most enlightened heteromasculine men like Hemingway would have done in Paris during the 1920s. That is, he defines who they are (i.e., their existence) by what they are (i.e., their essence), namely feminized men who do not eroticize the female body or, as Ira Elliott writes, "'femininity' expressed through the 'wrong' body": "Gender-crossing is what troubles Jake; the rupture between a culturally-determined signifier (the male body) and signified (the female gender) disrupts the male/female binary."[87] As the Davidsons conclude about this passage of the novel, the "terrifying ambiguity of [Jake's] own sexual limitations and gender preferences may well be one source of his anger (it usually is) with Brett's companions, and another reason why he articulates his anger and hatred for them before he reveals his love for her."[88]

But a more complex problem arises when we consider the fact that Jake is not like all homophobic heteromasculine males: with Brett, the sole object of Jake's heterosexual desire, the gay men represent multiple versions of Jake himself—unmanned men sexually (and potentially psychologically as well) impotent with regards to feminine sexuality—and function ironically in the end to define Jake sexually, a point Brett undiplomatically makes clear when she says to Jake, "And when one's with the crowd I'm with, one can drink in such safety, too" (*S* 22).[89] The implication that he is like the "pretty" homosexuals since he too is *safe to drink with* is not lost on Jake. For Jake, what is most important for him in the novel is the *now* of his existence, sexual and social alike, because it is linked to his essence more fully than it is for any non-impotent man, gay or straight. And since Jake is incapable of ultimately proving his heterosexuality to others through any normalized or naturalized performative act, he opens himself up to this type of homosexual identification.[90] As Ira Elliott posits, "Inasmuch as Jake considers himself to be heterosexual, the novel posits the site of sexuality in gendered desire rather than in sexual behavior. What distinguishes Jake from the homosexual men is gender performance and erotic object choice. By this logic, it follows that sexuality is determined by gender identification rather than sexual activity. . . . Sexual identity issues not from the sex act but from covert desire or overt social behavior."[91]

If queer inquiries attempt to demonstrate "how gender functions in licensing heterosexuality as normative"[92] and how, when gender identification is no longer functional, all standard models of sexual identity begin to deconstruct, what is left for Jake is the recognition that he will never be completely at ease with himself because society will always be ready, as *he* was ready at the *bal musette,* to "read" others. But this is still early on in the novel, and Hemingway uses this scene, as he had Jake and Brett's first taxi ride, to help demonstrate Jake's epistemological development concerning sex and gender identification. In short, in queering the men early on in the novel, Jake is essentially queering himself, though he only comes to realize this during his final taxi ride with Brett through Madrid.

Jake's overtly homophobic remarks about the gay community, then, do not finally reflect any sexist chauvinism in him (or, more significantly, in Hemingway, as it has often been leveled) as much as they are used to help establish his growth by the end of the novel, where his original contempt for the gay men later shapes his understanding of the fact that he is *physically* their equivalent by social definition. In defining them, Jake is caught in a homosexual panic, essentially defining himself in opposition to their gender and sexual natures. Jake may not like homosexuals any more by the end than he did at the beginning, but not to assimilate himself within their society and thus maintain his homophobia would be to write off his own emerging identity: to assert *who* he is, he must first accept *what* he is, no matter how averse he might have been or still could be to that reality. And what he is is a "pretty" eunuch; who he is, however, remains to be determined in the novel.

"A Strange Enough Ending": The Fin-de-Siècle "Cult of Masculinity"

The Sun Also Rises could be read, then, not just as a book about Jake's bitter acceptance of his injury with regards to his relationship with

Brett, but also as his (homo)sexual Bildungsroman, or more specifically his acceptance that his prior understanding of sexual identification now needs reconsidering. But in any novel of education, there are those defining moments which the protagonist undergoes that irrevocably alter his vision of himself or of others, as we have seen in the *bal musette* episode. But what, for example, helped Jake through this process from being blatantly homophobic in the beginning to feminizing himself in the end? The answer brings us once again back to the novel's closing lines, ones that have a precedent in an earlier exchange between Brett and Jake that has repeatedly been overlooked in the novel's criticism, but that deliberately shows how Jake's "pretty" was not so uncharacteristic after all and that, if anything, proves how the entire novel was building precisely just towards its utterance. In the middle of book 2, just three weeks into the novel from when Brett *trompe* Jake (and Mike) with Cohn, and now only moments before she will do the same with Romero, we encounter the following dialogue:

"Don't be difficult. You're the only person I've got, and I feel rather awful to-night."
"You've got Mike."
"Yes, Mike. Hasn't he been *pretty?*"
"Well," I said, "it's been *damned* hard on Mike, having Cohn around and seeing him with you." (*S* 181, my emphasis)

Echoing Brett's two earlier comments about her feeling "so miserable"—the first occurring in their initial taxi ride (*S* 24), which helps to establish Jake's existentialism, and the second one inside Zelli's in Montmartre, which prompts Jake to recognize the "nightmare of it all being something repeated, something I had been through and that now I must go through again" (*S* 64)—this passage prepares us for their final taxi ride where Jake is reminded once again that his injury with Brett will always present a "pretty" nightmare. It is a key moment in the novel, a sexual fulcrum that balances two of Jake's social experiences after Brett's affair with Cohn that help him to formulate his sociosexual education: first, his fishing trip with Bill, which momentarily relieves him of his angst (though not without its own problematics), and second, his time alone after the fiesta in San Sebastián, where he discovers that sexual equilibrium is purchased only at the cost of one's social isolation.

The fishing-trip on the Irati in Burguete has often been seen as the most idyllic movement of the novel in contrast to the helter-skelter lifestyle that Jake and the others lead in Paris and then in Pamplona during the Feria. James Mellow even calls the trip "one of Hemingway's unabashed paeans to male camaraderie."[93] Here, in the mountains with his "preacher" Bill, Jake can renew his soul, his artistic sensibilities, and his faith in the truth of clean and pure male-bonding. Though not as homosexually explicit as Jim Willard and Bob Ford's camping trip in Gore Vidal's *The City and the Pillar* (1948), it is a camaraderie that Leslie Fiedler, in his essay "Come Back to the Raft Ag'in, Huck Honey!," suggests is at the heart of the American myth whose representations offer "a chaste male love as the ultimate emotional experience": "the camaraderie of the locker room and ball park, the good fellowship of the poker game and fishing trip, a kind of passionless passion, at once gross and delicate, homoerotic in the boy's sense, possessing an innocence above suspicion. . . . To doubt for a moment this innocence . . . would destroy our stubborn belief in a relationship simple, utterly satisfying, yet immune to lust; physical as the handshake is physical, this side of copulation."[94]

Indeed, Jake and Bill, and later Wilson-Harris, profit nearly a week's respite in the mountains fishing, drinking, "utilizing," talking, and playing three-handed bridge. They have "such a jolly good time" (*S* 129) that Wilson-Harris is near-tearfully sentimental at their departure: "You don't know what this all means to me" (*S* 129). What seems like healthy male-bonding in Burguete, however, could be subtlety questioned for its motives by those outside of their hermetic circle, for surely Jake is no normal heterosexual male, and Bill's sexual credentials do not instill much confidence in many. For that reason, we should look also at the problems ideal male companionship brings to Jake, and there are a few.

Eve Sedgwick posits in her other seminal queer study, *Between Men: English Literature and Male Homosocial Desire*, that the male-male bond Fiedler describes indeed differentiates itself from a homosexual one, but that the *desire* for male company exists in both. In fact, homosociality, Sedgwick contends, describes male-male relationships precisely analogous to homosexuality and has since classical times formed "the potential unbrokenness of a continuum between homosocial and homosexual—a continuum whose visibility, for men, in our society, is radically disrupted."[95] Thus, when Hemingway establishes Jake's heterosexuality early on in the novel with, in addition to his homosexual panic at the *bal musette*, having him tell Brett that he loves her and admitting *to himself* (bearing in mind that he is conscious of the reader from the start in telling this story) that he is jealous of her affair with Cohn, we are to feel reassured from the start that Jake fits our understanding of what the masculine (that is, the heterosexual-type of the epoch) American male is and that we can use him as a sexual barometer by which to measure the various gender *types* encountered in the novel:

"Why I felt that impulse to devil him I do not know. Of course I do know. I was blind, unforgivingly jealous of what had happened to him" (*S* 99).

And yet, in addition to all of these signs of heterosexuality, Jake can equally display some rather unconventional ones, most notably in the fact that he can equally speak admiringly of other men, and not just in social but in physical terms as well. Jake can admit to himself (and to us), for instance, that he admires Cohn's body: "He was nice to watch on the tennis-court, he had a good body, and he kept it in shape . . ." (*S* 45). So too does he find Pedro good-looking, and again is neither ashamed nor embarrassed to admit it to others: "He was the best-looking boy I have ever seen. . . . 'He's a good-looking kid,' I said" (*S* 163); "'He's a damned good-looking boy. . . . When we were up in his room I never saw a better-looking kid'" (*S* 167); and "'He's nice to look at,' I said" (*S* 184).

What could be concluded from all of this is that Jake is seemingly so assured of his heteromasculinity that he can admire another man, physically or otherwise, without the fear of being labeled a queer by society, or even thinking himself gay for having made the remark in the first place (notwithstanding the fact that modern American sexual mores unconditionally prohibited such public declarations among men). The question remains, though, is how *aware* is Jake as a first-person narrator of the limits of his own homosexual inklings, or of his homosocial desires, or of his homosexual panic? In other words, can he, like the Hemingway narrator in "Portrait of Three or the Paella" (ca. 1931), Ernesto, who "describes the [naked] bodies of the two Spanish bullfighters in loving detail,"[96] distance himself intellectually in his personal reflections on sexuality from his era's own unconditional prejudicing of Freud's heteromasculine paradigm over Ellis's homoeffeminate one? Perhaps an even more probing question is, could Hemingway? While he publicly disparaged Jean Cocteau and belittled Gertrude Stein in print, he also admired them both for their intellectual capacities and artistic commitments (Glenway Wescott was readily dismissed in the novel because Hemingway liked neither his image nor his writing). What Hemingway could not tolerate about either of them, however—or about any of the openly gay literati in Paris—was how their public personas made them exhibitionists of what Hemingway considered to be a private affair.

The greatest of all Hemingway paradoxes here is that he, too, was the exhibitionist par excellence, using a masculine persona to project a heterosexual bent that sanctified his writing admiringly about men he knew. About his Kamba cook in *Under Kilimanjaro*, for instance, Hemingway writes, "He was very good looking, almost as good looking as a girl without being at all effeminate, and G.C. used to tease him and ask him if he plucked his eyebrows. He may very well have since one of the great amusements of primitive people is to arrange and rearrange their appearance and it has nothing to do with homosexuality" (*UK* 78).[97] About the naked bullfighter Antonio Ordóñez in *The Dangerous Summer*, Hemingway has this to say: "Antonio lay naked on the bed except for a hand towel as a fig leaf. I noticed the eyes first; the darkest, brightest, merriest eyes anybody ever looked into and the mischief urchin grin, and could not help seeing the scar welts on his right thigh."[98] To a great extent, Jake's education in homosexuality in the novel *is* Hemingway's, as we saw in the previous section, and it is one informed as much, if not more, by gender performance as by sexual preference alone. For that reason, masculinity, and not homosexuality, defines the model Hemingway male here and elsewhere in his canon.

To be sure, Jake (like Hemingway) was raised during a time in America that witnessed a conscious fin de siècle thrust to reinvigorate American masculinity only partly in response to the increased visibility of homosexuality in the larger cities. Surviving their bout with Victorian repression and feminization, American sexual mores gradually began to thaw at the turn of the century—spurned on in part from the current medical discourse that slowly began diffusing throughout the popular conscience—and with them emerged a largely refashioned concept of masculinity and homosociality by the century's end. Evidence of this "cult of masculinity" is often cited through the increased membership in social fraternities, the popularization of "Muscular Christianity," the mythologizing of Theodore Roosevelt's Rough Riders, and the founding of the Boy Scouts. All represented physical, social, moral, and metaphysical havens for men to rediscover their lost masculinity among men, ones which were passed down to their sons to insure that American masculinity would see the country safely through its colonist endeavors.

It is surely not coincidental that most of the influential philanthropic clubs in America, like the Moose and the Knights of Columbus, were created initially to facilitate Christian humanism and reinvigorate "Christian Muscularity" in a nation growing increasingly areligious due to its capitalistic growth. These predominantly, if not exclusively, all white male clubs equally underpinned the domestic male's sense of a masculine ego and political networking.[99] As with the founding of other men's clubs (the Elks in 1868, the Eagles in 1898, and the Sons of the American Revolution in 1889), these fraternal organizations, created for the most part after 1830, saw a yearly increased population, with the last third of the nineteenth century being dubbed "The Golden Age of Fraternity." By 1897, America had "over three hundred different fraternal orders" which boasted "a total membership of 5.5 million American men out of a total population of about nineteen million."[100] While work in the Gilded Age required from men cutthroat competition and aggressiveness before Progressivist reforms, and the home made them feel innerved and feminized, "Fraternal orders filled that gap, re-creating the artisan brotherhood, the masculine parish, and the patriarchal family that had virtually disappeared from men's lives."[101]

Similarly, Theodore Roosevelt, a favorite icon of Hemingway's, had himself campaigned for a recovered masculinity as much at the time of the Spanish-American War as he did later during his presidency. F. Scott Fitzgerald had even written to Hemingway in 1927 from the Hotel Roosevelt, which he called "formerly the warehouse where Theodore Roosevelt kept his jock straps—you remember, of course, how balls kept growing on him after the Spanish-American war. . . ."[102] In fact, Roosevelt's enacting the heroic codes of his Rough Riders' ascent up San Juan Hill on the national level was the stuff the young Hemingway dreamed of:

> the rougher, manlier virtues, and above all the virtue of personal courage, physical as well as moral. If we wish to do good work for our country we must be unselfish, disinterested . . . but in addition we must be vigorous in mind and body, able to hold our own in rough conflict with our fellows, able to suffer punishment without flinching, and at need, to repay it in kind with full interest. A peaceful and commercial civilization is always in danger of suffering the loss of virile fighting qualities without which no nation, however cultured, however refined, however thrifty and prosperous, can ever mount to anything.[103]

To be sure, imperialism would become one way for Roosevelt to perform the masculinity he preached. The dominant image of masculinity supplied by colonialization, for example, was at first bolstered by the socialist trade unions during the Progressive Era, which reflected in its domestic attacks against the corporate behemoths what the rugged Teddy Roosevelt had had adopted abroad as his foreign policy: to reign in the excesses of corporate capitalism by wielding a "big stick" form of diplomacy.[104]

One of the focuses on failing masculinity turned, of course, to Victorian boys (which Hemingway, Jake, and Williams's Big Daddy were at this time), who were the torchbearers of this new-found masculine identity. Since they were the sons of Gilded Age fathers suffering from masculine withdraw, they inherited a weak image of men, and a nation mobilized under Teddy Roosevelt to insure that flabby Victorian masculinity would not affect them as well. As Michael Kimmel notes in

Manhood in America, "The fin de siècle mission to thwart feminization and revirilize boyhood—and by extension, manhood—reached its symbolic apotheosis in Theodore Roosevelt."[105] Thus, Roosevelt's fulminations on the "doctrine of the strenuous life" were seen as a way for men to recover their lost masculinity and for boys to instill it: "We need . . . the iron qualities that must go with true manhood. We need the positive virtues of resolution, of courage, of indomitable will, of power to do without shrinking the rough work that must always be done, and to preserve through the long days of slow progress or seeming failure which always comes before any triumph, no matter how brilliant."[106] With four of five elementary school teachers by 1910 being women, up from two-thirds in 1870, the specter of the sissy had emerged, brought on by the increasing visibility of the gay male subculture in the big cities; so that by 1900 boys would do whatever was necessary to appear masculine, including partaking in the health and sports crazes that were sweeping the nation, from cycling, to boxing, to even bodybuilding, all of which are used in *The Sun Also Rises* as signs of masculinity.[107]

Finally, Scouting became another means to realize Roosevelt's "strenuous" life. Daniel Carter Beard, the spirit of the Boy Scouts of America founded in 1910 by William D. Boyce (a Chicago publisher who had based his ideas on masculinating boys from General Lord Robert Baden-Powell's earlier Scouting movement in England), had seen the great outdoors as the only place to make real men. Following Roosevelt's lead, Beard would repeat in the title of his autobiography, *Hardly a Man Is Now Alive* (1939), what he had earlier espoused in the Boy Scout Manual, *Scouting* (1914): "The Wilderness is gone, the Buckskin Man is gone, the painted Indian has hit the trail over the Great Divide, the hardships and privations of pioneer life which did so much to develop sterling manhood are now but a legend in history, and we must depend upon the Boy Scout Movement to produce the MEN of the future."[108]

As Jeffrey P. Hantover writes, "At the end of its first decade, the Boy Scouts was the largest male youth organization in American history with 358,537 scouts and 15,117 scoutmasters. The Boy Scouts' rapid national acceptance reflected turn-of-the-century concern over the perpetuation and validation of American masculinity."[109] Hantover argues that "the Boy Scouts served the needs of adult men as well as adolescent boys" in shoring up a flagging national vim: "Scouting assuaged adult masculine anxiety not only by training boys in the masculine virtues. The movement provided adult men a sphere of masculine validation."[110] Though Hemingway was never a Boy Scout, his passion for taming the outdoors, be it the Michigan woods or the Kenyan savannah, surely shares an affinity with the organization's prime directive.

This *new* American male was not just heterosexual but *hyper*masculine in his social image—the cowboy turned soldier. Even by the time Freud's version of psychoanalysis had finally begun entering mainstream America through its pop culture of the Jazz Age—e.g., via its advertising, songs, art, and literature—what was privileged in America remained heterosexual in nature, serving only to dichotomize masculinity further and consolidating that image indeterminately.[111] Thus, if sexuality had begun dominating the national discourse after World War I, it was stylized around essentially heteromasculine constructs alone, with the *new* homosexual in America being driven to the margin of this emerging gender spectrum that not only isolated the social pariah but also defined, preserved, and protected the "proper" masculine American male that was his determined opposite.

In *The Sun Also Rises*, then, Hemingway is less interested in capturing the traditional gender role reversals of the 1920s in Paris (the masculine flapper or the effeminate bachelor/dandy) and more concerned with exposing the social mechanisms of gendered sexuality in general. As such, he arguably produces what Sedgwick describes, namely that many male writers—gay and heterosexual alike—at the turn of the century purposefully articulated the space of the closet since the then-current psychoanalytical trend was to explain and/or correct homosexuality, and literary modernism partly evolved from its partnership with Freudian psychoanalysis. As we have seen, though he will never achieve the kind of sexual identity that Hemingway himself enjoyed throughout most of the twentieth century, Jake can at least blend in for a while among the many heterosexual men who have found a haven between the sexual polarities of the gender spectrum. Yet unlike James or Proust, Hemingway more directly addresses male-male desire through the (apparent) binarized homophobia in both macho American mentalities and more liberal European ones, for if Jake represents emerging sexual mores in postwar Europe, Bill clearly encapsulates the polarized American ones, and together they exhibit the "gender trouble" inherent in culture-clashing sexual politics.

For example, Bill admires Jake a lot, and unashamedly tells him: "Listen. You're a hell of a good guy, and I'm fonder of you than anybody on earth" (*S* 116). Bill can express his admiration for Jake because he feels freer in Spain to do so than if they were in America: "I couldn't tell you that in New York. It'd mean I was a faggot" (*S* 116). Though Axel Nissen, like several recent critics, suggests that Bill here, via his edgy admission, is coming out of the closet, and even later tries to draw Jake with him, what is more plausible is that Bill, a sensitive writer as well, also recognizes that his social identity is as fragile as Jake's, for even without his additional anxieties of the hidden wound (the truth about which even Bill does not know), his unconventional life in New York risks exposing any sexual fissure in his image more readily than does Jake's in Paris.[112] As Debra Moddelmog writes of him, "Outside the geographic and psychological boundaries of New York and its taxonomy of deviance, Bill's feelings are platonic; inside those boundaries, they are homosexual. Bill's concern about the boundaries for same-sex relationships indicates that he cannot be sure about the 'purity' of his feelings for Jake or of Jake's for him."[113]

George Chauncey, Jr.'s *Gay New York* describes at length this fairy/queer binary that Bill fears, noting how the "effeminate 'fairy' put on stage at the Bowery resorts in the 1890s and at massive drag balls in the 1910s, '20s, and '30s, and highly visible on the streets of New York throughout this period, came to represent all homosexuals in the public mind:"[114]

> The determinative criterion in the identification of men as fairies was not the extent of their same-sex desire or activity (their "sexuality"), but rather the gender persona and status they assumed. It was only the men who assumed the sexual and other cultural roles ascribed to women who identified themselves—and were identified by others—as fairies. The fairies' sexual desire for men was not regarded as the singular characteristic that distinguished them from other men, as is generally the case for gay men today. That desire was seen as simply one aspect of a much more comprehensive gender role inversion (or reversal), which they were expected to manifest through the adoption of effeminate dress and mannerisms.... In the dominant turn-of-the-century cultural systems governing the interpretation of homosexual behavior, especially in working class milieus, one had a *gender* identity rather than a *sexual* identity or even a "sexuality"; one's sexual behavior was thought to be necessarily determined by one's gender identity.[115]

And yet, for those men at the time who were forging a gay identity but who could not or would not "adopt the fairies' highly visible style,"[116] they had to turn to more queer tactics, "restrict[ing] themselves to the role of 'trade'" or becoming the "'normal' partners of 'queers'";[117] these gay men were "unwilling to become virtual women" yet sought "to remain men who nonetheless loved other men."[118] As Chauncey contends, these "queer men constituted the majority of gay-identified men in New York in the early decades of the century."[119] The fairies had simply "diverted attention from other, more guarded men, and made it relatively easy for them to pass as straight."[120]

Hemingway demonstrates these problems of sexual identification and classification in an earlier draft of *The Sun Also Rises* where Bill and Jake discuss the latter's impotence, even to the point of showing Jake's growing awareness of how others pry into one's personal sexuality: "It is funny that a thing that ninety nine times out of a hundred you yourself never even think about, other people should mind so."[121] Curious about fashionable sexual politics in America, Jake then asks Bill how he was viewed by New York society, to which Bill responds:

> I'm crazy. Also I'm supposed to be crazy to get married. Would marry anybody at any time. Then I'm tight. And I get all my best stuff from Alice in Wonderland. Since Charley Gordon and I had an apartment together last winter, I suppose I'm a fairy. That probably explains everything. . . . My God it would make you sick. They don't talk about complexes anymore. It's bad form. But they all believe it. And every literary bastard in New York never goes to bed at night knowing but that he'll wake up in the morning and find himself a fairy. There are plenty of real ones too.[122]

In a very telling monologue, Bill is not so much admitting his homosexuality as he is pellucidly describing how American society "minds so"; because he shares an apartment with another man, New York "reads" him as gay. It is his disgust for gossip and supposition that Bill is expressing here through his trademark irony and not some closet-liberating declaration that he is gay. What is clear to Bill is that society will systematically declare it for him because it privileges homosexual signs over acts, and each morning that Bill wakes up in America without having countered those signs, he runs the risk of being identified as queer, whether or not he really is. For Bill and for Jake, this process of insinuation is the most deplorable of all social ills because, as Jake learned, gender signs are culturally constructed and prove nothing in the end sum of identity politics; for Hemingway, this would appear to be the most unforgivable of all American sins, despite the fact that he committed it more than most, because it unconditionally queers his own homoerotics at the same time.

With the episode at Burguete, then, Hemingway purposefully challenges the homosocial rules, as he had the sexual ones earlier in the novel, and recalibrates the sexual existentialism earlier in the novel toward a form of masculine existentialism here. In other words, while Jake's first time with Brett in the taxi served to exacerbate his existential feelings since he could not act upon a desired heterosexual identity, and he finally performs a *non*-heterosexual one in searching for all-male company—as with his male-bonding fishing trip with Bill Gorton—in order to alleviate this sexual angst, Jake simultaneously leaves himself vulnerable to social suspicion (at least to his American readers and critics). Only when he is by himself in San Sebastián, after all of his friends have left him, male and female alike, is Jake freed from the anxiety of socially positioning himself sexually between their two genders. But sociosexual liberation has its price, which the humanist Jake is unwilling or incapable of finally paying, despite the fact that he has been "paying" all along.

During his brief sabbatical in the queerly-coded city San Sebastián, for instance, Jake is given time to reflect upon and contemplate the fact that his injury has two meanings, one for him and another for society.[123] All he needs in order to temporarily abate his sexual existentialism is to learn how to balance these two perceptions. Jake's final lesson on existential identity, then, comes when he meets the team manager on the Tour de Pays Basque and has dinner with the racers. Here, Jake curiously watches the bicycle racers eat and drink to excess, despite the physical demands that will be placed on them in the next morning's grueling ride. But, as the manager reassuringly informs Jake, their unbecoming behavior matters very little in the end because "it did not make much difference who won" the day's stage as "the money could be arranged" (*S* 236). In sum, it was the outsider who spoiled the integrity of the race by imposing on it his external wants and desires, impressions and analyses, judgments and criticisms. The meaning of the race itself, however—that is, its essence—was essentially protected, for no matter how the fans and sponsors viewed it, the bicycle racers "did not take the race seriously *except among themselves*" (*S* 236, my emphasis). The racers had learned to project what the fans wanted, while remaining essentially true to themselves.

For Jake, this is the decisive lesson of his sexual education, and only someone truly at peace with himself and his physical injury could wear a revealing swimsuit in public without the slightest expression of anxiety. But just as the race only exists *because* of the fans, Jake realizes too that his sense of personal identification only exists because of his relationship to others: there is no such thing as a one-man *race*. So when Brett's two telegrams arrive and he accepts that San Sebastián was, like his penis, "all shot to hell" (*S* 239), there is no use in *not* answering them, or in turning his back entirely on Brett and remaining isolated, for she will always be there, present in any company with which he will surround himself daily. To be with her (or any female) will forever bring about his sexual angst; but to deny being with her, forever his queerness. Therefore, though his impotence seemingly grows less troubling for him by the end of the novel when he is alone, in returning to the world and its constructionist politics, Jake is accepting that his sexual identity will remain forever in flux, his sexual existentialism forever unresolved, which is why the second taxi ride and his ironic line are so essential to the novel and to our understanding of his growth by its end.

"A Matter of Measurement": Jake and the Signifying Lack

If Jake, like Hemingway, forged his sexual education in Europe, he certainly acquired his tastes for masculinity at home. As such, his injury accounts for many or all of the reasons why he decides to stay on in postwar Europe. For though he had all of the signs of American masculinity before the war (for instance, Jake tells us he had played football, the American equivalent of Spanish bullfighting culture), upon his return he lacked what was essentially needed to continue to underpin that identity: his intact penis. To have survived the war was one thing; to have been injured in it another; to have lost a limb in combat all together something completely different, something *manly*. If visible, his injury could have become a permanent war medal to a society that valorizes war, which America did up until the Vietnam War. That wound was the signifier of his masculinity, proof of his fearless sacrifice for the patria. As Rena Sanderson writes, which Dana Fore revisits years later with aplomb,

> The consequence of a physical wound incurred in battle, his impotence is paradoxically a badge of manly courage. By standards of earlier time, when respectable women were not supposed to enjoy sex anyway, Jake's handicap might have made no difference to a woman who did not want to bear children. But Brett will not accept sexual deprivation, will not suffer just because Jake suffers. His impotence, then, needs to be seen as more than just a physical wound or a personal dilemma: It reflects the sexual attitudes and gender conflicts of the time.[124]

But the "time" in postwar America was not the same as the "time" in postwar Paris, which complicates even further Jake's response to his sexual existentialism in the novel.

The Great War had an unexpected, and undesired, effect upon Victorian fathers and their sons. Initially, many men welcomed the coming of the War with its promise of a recovered, all-male Eden, uncomplicated by the presence of women who were, paradoxically speaking, both the purveyors of purity and the Victorian "guardians of morality" who policed male desires.[125] As Michael Kimmel writes, "Heroism had lost its currency in the postwar world. . . . Wartime victories had allowed a generation of men to rescue a threatened sense of manhood, and the expanding peacetime economy augured well for economic success. . . . But such reassurances soon gave way to a new restiveness."[126]

Yet the soldier's masculine identity was not so easily won, for while some had learned that individual acts of heroism were less demonstrable in the modernist War's mass destruction, others, victims of shellshock, had returned home a hysteric, whimpering, and crying shell of the man he formerly was. Joanna Bourke notes that only after the Great War did the "innocence" of male-male desire come "to be questioned by popular psychology," arguing that the War did more to destroy homosocial bonds between men than, as is traditional thought, engender them.[127]

In her study of male homosociality and the war wound in *Dismembering the Male: Men's Bodies, Britain and the Great War*, Bourke writes that the "male body was no more than the sum of its various parts and the dismembered man became Everyman."[128] During, and immediately after World War I, a "disabled soldier was 'not less but more of a man,'" Bourke writes. So great were the number of maimed men, however, that by the late 1920s in Europe, "the respect that had initially been given to the fragmented bodies of war-mutilated men had ended."[129] As Bourke posits, despite the "early sentimentalization of the war-wounded during the war and in the early 1920s" where "[p]ublic rhetoric judged soldiers' mutilations to be 'badges of their courage, the hallmark of their glorious service, their proof of patriotism,'" even "maimed ex-service men also rapidly lost their claim to special consideration."[130] "Limblessness," she concludes, "became normalized."[131]

The war wound, then, a one-time symbol of pride and sacrifice for the patria, had become nothing more than a collective signifier of the human tragedy that the War had visited upon an entire continent, and to ignore the wound was to help appease the psychic angst that had come with it. Given the fact that visible wounds, such as the loss of limbs, had been greater than in any previous war, to ignore them now constituted a denial so complete that it nearly erased all visible scars of the War. Arms, hands, feet, and legs could not be replaced, their dismemberment never undone, but prosthetics could at least provide visible substitutions for the lack that was all too real. And when amputees were not given plastic substitutions for their missing parts, Bourke adds, they were allotted symbolic ones: sub- or unconscious efforts on the part of society to fill that lack with imaginary limbs that would counter the realities of the wound itself. As long as people wanted to forget the horrors of the War, such denial, she concludes, was essential.

Non-visible wounds, however, such as shell-shock, posed a greater problem. They were not only impossible to erase through the use of prosthetics or some fantastic effort of symbolic substitution but also difficult to alter concerning the soldier's image of himself as a man. If anything, severed limbs could, at least for a while any way, signify bravery through their lack; male neurasthenia, on the other hand, was "a badge of shame," and "amounted to a flight from manhood."[132] Writing about the shell-shock debate and its relation to shifting gender paradigms, Angus McLaren concludes: "Even the manhood of the survivors appeared to be undermined. Thousands of men in regiments across the western front, after being subjected to weeks of terrifying bombardments, broke down and were wracked by the bouts of weeping, depression, nightmares, and nervous fits commonly associated with hysterical women."[133] The War had not created men, as many had thought it would; rather, it created lack, real, symbolic, and imaginary in the Lacanian sense.

"The Meaning of the Phallus" is Jacques Lacan's most direct explanation on the role of the phallus in the psychoanalytical acquisition of sexuality, where the phallus is not to be understood in the Freudian sense as instinctual codifier but rather in the symbolic sense as linguistic signifier. In the essay, Lacan introduces his concept of desire, which is characterized by lack—a desire for that which is missing. If all language for de Saussure is premised, like some dismembered limb, on the idea of metonymic absence defining difference, for Lacan the castrated phallus denotes the moment of individuation and the language acquisition which accompanies it: "For the phallus is a signifier, a signifier whose function in the intrasubjective economy of analysis might lift the veil from that which it served in the mysteries. For it is to this signified that it is given to designate as a whole the effect of there being a signified, inasmuch as it conditions any such effect by its presence as signifier."[134] Castration, then, is the cost of becoming the Self and of entering the symbolic order of language acquisition and the lack that it requires, and the phallus as transcendental signifier becomes forever unattainable.

Such contextual and theoretical backdrops to *The Sun Also Rises* help to frame the sexual existentialism Jake experiences in the novel. He is wounded during the War, but his injury cannot serve to signify his bravery, if even for only a few years, since it is not a wound he is willing to show people, as the Count willingly displays his arrow wounds from a "business trip" he was on "[i]n Absysinia" when he was "twenty-one years old" (*S* 60):

> "You see them?" . . .
> Above the small of the back were the same two scars, raised as thick as a finger. (*S* 60)

Nor could Jake simply drop his trousers and show his wound as the Count does his, for the wound itself would counter any masculine directive in displaying the wound in the first place. His lack, then, which normally could have served to petrify his masculinity in America after the war—just as it does the one-armed soldier in San Sebastián (*S* 237)—is now the one thing that will paradoxically undermine it by signifying his queerness.

In a chapter entitled "Ford Maddox Ford and the Devil's Disciple" in *A Moveable Feast,* Hemingway distinguishes at length between those veterans who paraded their war medals to signify a masculinity and those who overcame their handicaps, such as a lost limb or eye, without wearing their lack as a badge of honor (such as the bartender Jean later on in the chapter entitled "Evan Shipman at the Lilas"):

> Most of the clients were elderly bearded men in well worn clothes who came with their wives or their mistresses and wore or did not wear thin red Legion of Honor ribbons in their lapels. . . .
>
> There were other people too who lived in the quarter and came to the Lilas, and some of them wore Croix de Guerre ribbons in their lapels and others also had the yellow and green of the Médaille Militaire, and I watched how well they were overcoming the handicap of the loss of limbs, and saw the quality of their artificial eyes and the degree of skill with which their faces had been reconstructed. (*MF* 82)

The loss of a limb was not a sign of masculinity for Hemingway if one drew excessive attention to that lack: "In those days we did not trust anyone who had not been in the war, but we did not completely trust anyone, and there was a strong feeling that Cendrars might well be a little less flashy about his vanished arm" (*MF* 82).

Unlike Swiss-French poet Blaise Cendrars's war injury, Jake's loss is not something that could be worn proudly like a badge, and the fact that he received it on "a joke front" (*S* 31), too, does not help him much. At least, he thinks to himself, he is not like Mike, who borrowed war medals to dupe the English socialites into thinking him a war hero. And yet, no matter how we look at it in *The Sun Also Rises,* Jake's involvement in the war can no longer serve to underwrite his masculinity at home. If anything, his injury would ultimately call his masculinity later into question, for as a childless bachelor, Jake would begin raising public suspicion because American society demanded proof of sexual identity and, when there was little in the offering, was only happy to supply it for itself.

Doubly damned, Jake must find a means to resignify his masculinity, both for himself and for his society. Language, of course, is one such avenue, and as a writer Jake is able to recover or, at least, substitute a sense of a newly fashioned self. As noted earlier in this chapter, Jake at the beginning of the novel cannot look at his wound: "Undressing, I looked at myself in the mirror of the big armoire beside the bed. That was a typically French way of furnishing a room. Practical, too, I suppose. Of all the ways to be wounded. I suppose it was funny" (*S* 30). By the end of the novel, Jake has more or less come to terms with his wound, which his experience on the beach at San Sebastián suggests and his "pretty" rejoinder to Brett confirms. Therefore, if his lack of a phallus signifies his inability to perform heterosexually in the Freudian sense of the term, it does empower him with language, which, in narrating the story of this lost generation of expatriates to us, fills his lack, satisfies his desire (physical and linguistic), and sees him through his existential crisis.

What had disarmed the first readers of the novel, which has subsequently become its standard mark of excellence, is Hemingway's neutered style and Jake's linguistic suggestiveness. Even in the example just cited, where Jake looks at himself in the mirror of a French armoire, language is economized to such an extent that its essential lack of words carries the sentence's real meaning. In other words, Jake frequently keeps meaning from us by talking around the facts, by not supplying them, or by bridging those linguistic gaps with seemingly innocuous details that serve, through metonymy, to defer meaning. In other words, Jake's lack of a real phallus is reflected in his lack of a symbolic one, though both give him power over language games. But such a lack does not impoverish his desire, and as we have seen earlier in this chapter, the one thing that fuels Jake's existential angst is his desire—sexual and linguistic alike. For Jake to satisfy that desire, he needs access to his Other, both sexual and linguistic, and Brett serves as both in the novel.

Later in his essay, Lacan describes the relationship between the subject and his Other, in whom he finds the lost phallus, and in their mutual desire, the symbolic order is obtained: "If the phallus is a signifier then it is in the place of the Other that the subject gains access to it. But in that the signifier is only there veiled and as the ratio of the Other's desire, so it is this desire of the Other as such which the subject has to recognize, meaning, the Other as itself a subject divided by the signifying *Spaltung*."[135] The *Spaltung* is for Lacan the "splitting" of desire as appetite and demand for love, "the difference resulting from the subtraction of the first from the second. . . ."[136] Since the subject locates his lack of the phallus in the presence of the Other, the Other becomes that subject's phallus. He "has" what the Other one "is," namely that phallus. Lacan explains further what "appearing" to be the phallus (the subject) and "having" the phallus and the desire (the object of sexual fulfillment) encompasses: "Let us say that these relations will revolve around a being and a having which, because they refer to a signifier, the phallus, have the contradictory effect of on the one hand lending reality to the subject of that signifier, and on the other making unreal the relations to the signified. . . . These ideals gain new strength from the demand which it is in their power to satisfy, which is always the demand for love, with its complement of reducing desire to demand."[137] Therefore, in order to be the subject's phallus as his Other, "the woman will reject an essential part of her femininity, notably all its attributes through masquerade": "It is for what she is not that she expects to be desired as well as loved. But she finds the signifier of her own desire in the body of the one to whom she addresses her demand for love. Certainly we should not forget that *the organ actually invested with this signifying function takes on the value of a fetish.*"[138]

If we consider Jake to be the subject to Brett's Lacanian Other, what we understand about the novel is that Jake's continued pursuit of Brett, knowing fully well that he will never satisfy her sexually, is reflected in his desire to see his lack through her. What he literally is missing (the "fetish" organ of lovemaking), he symbolically projects upon her, and when he cannot satisfy her sexually, he pimps her off to other men, such as Cohn or Romero, to recover that lack. Similarly, Brett needs to be Jake's Other, his phallus, so as to assure herself that he will have one again. Since Jake lacks the penis and thus does not "have" the phallus, unfortunately Brett cannot be his Other (the woman) and "have" the phallus at the same time. As a result, she undergoes a gender-inversion of sorts, which many critics have discussed, where Jake's introduces her in the novel as a sexually-alluring boy: "Brett was damned good-looking. She wore a slipover jersey sweater and a tweed skirt, and her hair was brushed back like a boy's. She started all that. She was built with curves like the hull of a racing yacht, and you missed none of it with that wool jersey" (*S* 22). Similarly, Jake later describes how she wears a "man's felt hat" (*S* 28), how she frequently addresses him and the other men in the novel with the masculine term "chaps," and how Romero demanded that she grow out her short hair because "'[h]e said it would make [her] more womanly'" (*S* 280). Brett is, by definition, that liberated woman who rejects the conservative notions of Victorian women, and who smokes, drinks, and wears short hair. Yet her masculine signification makes Brett more than a flapper;[139] she is also Jake's Lacanian Other and essential to his entrance into the symbolic order, of which the substitution of language for his missing penis is a primary example.

With Brett as his Other, Jake must learn to move beyond genital signification, of the kind that we find in his and Brett's first taxi ride where she rebuffs his sexual advances because she does not want to "go through that hell again" (*S* 26), and onto symbolic signification, one that would demonstrate that his desire has transcended all physical needs. Lacan describes further in his essay how sexual intercourse for the man helps fulfill this symbolic transcendence:

> In men, on the other hand, the dialectic of demand and desire gives rise to effects, whose exact point of connection Freud situated with the sureness which we must once again admire, under the rubric of a specific depreciation (*Erniedrigung*) of love.
>
> If it is the case that the man manages to satisfy his demand for love in his relationship to the woman to the extent that the signifier of the phallus constitutes her precisely as giving in love what she does not have—conversely, his own desire for the phallus will throw up its signifier in the form of a persistent divergence towards "another woman" who can satisfy this phallus under various guises, whether as a virgin or *a prostitute*. The result is a centrifugal tendency of the genital drive in the sexual life of a man which *makes impotence much harder for him to bear*, at the same time as the *Verdrängung* inherent to desire is greater.[140]

Jake's encounter with the prostitute Georgette discussed earlier in this chapter is such an attempt to "satisfy this phallus under various guises," for the "sex" he cannot have with her would at least be devoid of the love he feels for Brett, and thus give him the phallus he seeks in Georgette without the emotional entanglements.

Jake's "infidelity" should not be considered one-sided, however, for Brett similarly sleeps with other men, like Cohn and Romero, to fulfill her need to be Jake's Other. As Lacan concludes, "We should not, however, think that the type of infidelity which then appears to be constitutive of the masculine function is exclusive to men. For if one looks more closely, the same redoubling is to be found in the woman, except that in her case, the Other of love as such, that is to say, the Other as deprived of that which he gives, is hard to perceive in the withdrawal whereby it is substituted for the being of the man whose attributes she cherishes."[141] To the extent that both seek the phallus—Jake finally to "have" it, because he does not; Brett finally to "be" it, because with Jake she is not—we can understand more clearly why Jake hates the gay men at the *bal musette* and Brett adores them. For them, and for all of her affairs with other men, Brett can "be" the phallic Other (because they "have" the phallus in terms of their sex organs, regardless of their sexual desire); whereas Jake, who does not "have" the phallus, literally "is" the phallus for them, their emasculated sexual Other.

For all of these reasons, Jake's impotence "is harder for him to bear" than perhaps for other men of his time who still had their penises intact, which returns us to the notion of sexual existentialism in the novel and how Jake manages to avoid *bad faith* and define his *soi* in terms appropriate to himself and not to society. One means to achieve this is through the concept of "mystery," or epistemological deferral. As Nina Schwartz writes about Jake in *The Sun Also Rises*, both existentialism and the Freudian/Lacanian castration complex "function as strategies of deferral" where

> both invent the possibility of a transcendent ego by defining the obstacle to autonomy as the signifier of what lies behind it. . . . And, like both the child and the existential hero that he has come to represent, Jake Barnes depends upon similar strategies of deferral to transcend his impotence. Incorporating several modes of self-representation—the writing itself, the "affair" with Brett, the ritual of the bull-fight—Jake's narrative simultaneously exploits and exposes the strategies of deferral that underlie these and all signifying systems.[142]

Though only Brett and Jake's Italian physician know the real extent of Jake's injury, many in Jake's circle of friends and acquaintances have already begun speculating about it. As Bill plainly asserts to Jake in Burguete: "One group claims women support you. Another group claims you're impotent" (*S* 115).[143] Though Jake says that he "just had an accident," Bill responds in words that prepare us for Williams's description later of Brick's sexual dysfunction in *Cat on a Hot Tin Roof*: "Never mention that. . . . That's the sort of thing that can't be spoken of. That's what you ought to work up into a mystery" (*S* 115).

The mystery here, and Bill's subsequent comment ("Like Henry's bicycle"), is in real life the story of Henry James and his suspected impotence brought about by a childhood biking accident.[144] Bill's implication that James invented the injury so as to preserve his sexual identity as a childless bachelor later in life is not entirely lost on Jake. Jake also recognizes that, like the real-life James, his critical years of performed heterosexuality are fast approaching. Why else would Hemingway make Jake, an ex-war hero at twenty-five or so in a war where the average age for a soldier was eighteen (as it was for Hemingway himself when he left for Paris, then Milan), a middle-aged man in this thirties, especially if we consider that in the summer of 1925 when the novel is set, Hemingway himself, upon whom Jake is modeled, was only twenty-six? These nine or ten years are clearly not superfluous.

Since America was refashioning its masculine iconography around an image permanently unattainable for Jake, he is forced now into finding a version that appealed more to his new sense of sexuality. He encounters this viable masculine gender in postwar Europe, where the image of the heterosexual male was not as bifurcated or as limiting as its American counterpart's, as we have already seen. In Europe, Jake discovers a social climate more tolerant and flexible, or at least less rigid, toward gender constructs outside of the sexual norm than in America, one that provides him with ample gender space in which to grow with his injury. Among the many differences in European notions of masculinity, for example, is the role that human touch played in male-male desire. Poisoned by the Freudian psychoanalysis that was at the same time sexually liberating it, America chose the safest route to consolidating its ideal masculine identity, and intimate male-male contact, an obvious attribute of homosexuality (outside of physical combat, that is to say, as in football or boxing), was too volatile a signifier of homosocial desire. Thus American social mores stigmatized all male touching outside of a handshake or a brief, fraternal hug, and Jake's homophobia at the *bal musette* early in the novel clearly displays this sexual epistemology. Later in the novel, however, Jake encounters similar signs of touching among straight men in Europe, which he finds comforting because they imply that masculine signifiers here are different from those he grew up with at home.

For instance, Jake finds Montoya's cultural touching, a shared emotional expression limited to the real men with *afición*, a little disconcerting from the start: "When they saw that I had aficion, and there was no password, no set questions that could bring it out, rather it was a sort of oral spiritual examination with the questions always a little on the defensive and never apparent, there was this same embarrassed putting the hand on the shoulder, or a 'Buen hombre.' But nearly always there was the real touching. It seemed as though they wanted to touch you to make it certain" (*S* 132). Half embarrassed, half honored, Jake soon recognizes that since the image of masculinity can change per culture, so too can the role of the gendered male. The aficionados were not only very expressive physically with each other, but they also had a privileged, if not protected, social identity as the real Spanish *hombre*.[145] Welcomed into this select circle, Jake discovers a new cultural performativity that is equally homoerotic and yet assuredly masculine. There is no need to prove his heterosexuality here because, as along as he is identified as having *afición*, his sexual identity (in Spain, at least) is assumed a priori.[146] And if the gender laws are more flexible here, so must be the sexual ones, and his injury in Spain will not mean the same thing as it would in America.

However, when Jake figuratively cashes in his membership into Montoya's masculine club by handing Romero over to Brett (though having once refused the same transaction for the American ambassador, much to Montoya's pleasure), he also severs these bonds that had preciously served to hold his sexual identity intact. From that moment onward, Jake plunges back into an existential mire from which he had achieved some temporary respite. He is now running out of gendered identities behind which he can hide, and each passing day signals for him the encroaching identity crisis that his sexual injury will inevitably bring about.

Therefore, when Jake chooses the feminine word "pretty" in his rejoinder, he is not just "choosing to sound like the homosexuals whose language he had earlier presented as effeminate"[147] and thus freeing himself from Brett's Circean spell but, more significantly, ironically inverting their earlier exchange where Brett had shown her repeated insensitivity to Jake's existential plight. He has, in short, acquired through Lacanian castration of the phallus the power of language, specifically a word he would never has used himself throughout the novel in describing his and Brett's unattainable dream.[148] Feminizing himself by choosing the non-neutered adjective does not make Jake gay, but it does allow him the opportunity to weigh his personal view of the sexual self against that of the body politic's and gives Hemingway the chance to thumb his nose at gender roles and sexual mores that were taking shape in America after the War.

Whether or not Jake is a closeted homosexual in the end matters very little, and even suggesting it would surely raise the hackles of many a Papa-loving audience, critical and popular alike. In fact, declaring Jake to be gay neuters the novel of its more powerful challenge to call "into question conventional understandings of sexual identity by deconstructing the categories, oppositions and equations that sustain them."[149] What lies beyond dispute, however, is the fact that Hemingway was among those modernist American writers who challenged convention, who did court the queer by inextricably yoking it to the macho. In so doing, and for whatever his original intent, Hemingway maintained the patriarchy's homophobic grip on sexual identification and simultaneously exposed its epistemological fissures. For this reason, bullfighting, Hemingway's signifier for all that is masculine in the novel, and Jake, the aficionado who is welcomed into its select minority that speaks in codes or in knowing looks, as the Davidsons have shown,[150] are susceptible to the queer: "He smiled again. He always smiled as though bull-fighting were a very special secret between the two of us; a rather shocking but really very deep secret that we knew about. He always smiled as though there was something lewd about the secret to outsiders, but that it was something we understood. It would not do to expose it to people who would not understand" (*S* 131).[151] Since Hemingway deconstructs the whole premise of heteromasculinity in the novel in the first place, cannot bullfighting here be equally read as a signifier for the closet?

"The sun also rises (like your cock if you have one)"

In the existentialist novel, there is a point where the hero must face a moment of crisis in order to preserve his individual identity. For Killinger, it was in Hemingway the moment when the bullfighter confronts the passing of the bull's horn; for Schwartz, the moment in that second taxi ride when Jake, the feminized matador, kills Brett's masculine bull, their dream of idealized love.[152] It is, in short, that moment when the hero emerges from the shadows of his existence to assert, despite all social repercussions, his individuality in face of those who would snuff it out: "I exist, and furthermore I exist among you."[153] That moment of personal existential declaration is certainly on par with a homosexual's emergence from the closet, which cannot be understood as a moment of psychosexual definition (since no doubt that was already defined by the retreat *into* the closet) but of sociopolitical definition.

Hemingway's *The Sun Also Rises*, then, which places impotence, castration, and male-genital obsession at the center of its traumatic *nada* feeling, whose title itself, like many of the sexual puns throughout the book, reinforces this preoccupation with sexual politics,[154] is clearer today in part due to contemporary queer theorists who have given us, like the existentialists before them, a rhetoric with which to articulate today what at a time most writers could, for reasons personal, social, or political, only conventionalize or broach by innuendo: the historization of modernist male-male relationships and identity politics. As Debra Moddelmog writes,

> Hemingway's novel puts gender and sexuality into constant motion. Although modern society attempts to stabilize conduct and appearance as masculine or feminine, and desire as homosexual, heterosexual, or bisexual, it is still not easy to contain and categorize desire and behavior. Actions, appearance, and desire in *The Sun Also Rises* spill over the "normal" boundaries of identity and identification so that categories become destabilized and merge with one another.
>
> This is not to say that Brett and Jake have discarded society's scripts for femininity and masculinity, or for heterosexuality and homosexuality, in favor of more contemporary concepts such as transgendered or queer. Their actions, particularly Brett's flirtations and Jake's homophobia, show that they know these scripts well. Nevertheless, . . . both Jake and Brett continually stray from the lines the scripts demands.[155]

Jake and Brett's first and second taxi rides are finally the events that define not only the nature of their relationship in the novel, where Jake is both Brett's desire and her comfort, both her heterosexual stud and her homosexual drinking buddy, but also the nature of their sexual identities at the beginning and end of the novel. His self-education comes through this relationship, and, by the end, he either accepts his dual role or at least mocks it with his comment "Isn't it pretty to think so?" For in using the masculine word "damned" to describe the good time that they could have had together, Brett challenges Jake to hold on to the dream, which has been the source of his existentialism from the start. At the end of the novel, it is now Jake who, like Mike earlier, is being "pretty" in light of Brett's treatment of him vis-à-vis Cohn first, then Romero (*S* 181). Already by the middle of book 2, Hemingway had foreshadowed his novel's final line—something Williams would do as well in his original version of *Cat on a Hot Tin Roof*, with Brick echoing Big Daddy's ironic rejoinder to Big Mama's declaration of love, just as Maggie challenges Brick to hold onto the dream of a good time together.

3

"A Dying Gaul": The Signifying Phallus and Williams's "Three Players of a Summer Game"

> "I liked your trenchant letter to the Times about the Goetz play. David Stewart wrote me about it, saying it was 'dull, unimaginative', so I'm not surprised at your reaction. But I'd like to see it for the performances, and I do hope I'll get back while Eliot's play [*The Confidential Clerk*] is still running. I have a feeling the critics must have missed the point of it. I am longing to see the book. Eliot and Dr. Kinsey are the two nicest men that I've ever met. They radiated a similar kind of honesty and warmth."
> —Tennessee Williams letter to Donald Windham, February 20, 1954

> "I take only an academic interest in homosexuality."
> —Ernest Hemingway, *Islands in the Stream*

> "Once the penis itself becomes merely a means of pleasure, pleasure among men, *the phallus* loses all of its power."
> —Luce Irigaray, *This Sex Which Is Not One*

IN APRIL 1952, TENNESSEE WILLIAMS COMPLETED AND THEN PUBlished in the *New Yorker* his short story "Three Players of a Summer Game," a nostalgic tale about a middle-aged alcoholic's crisis of masculinity. Begun the previous summer in Rome and Venice, when Williams was in the middle of reading Hemingway's "good" but "superficial" novel, *A Farewell to Arms* (*NB* 525),[1] "Three Players" would eventually find its larger treatment in *Cat on a Hot Tin Roof*, which, Brian Parker informs us, Williams began drafting the following year.[2]

Since "Three Players" contains the genesis of what would later become the celebrated play, most of its academic criticism has focused on what the story essentially brings to the play's historical dialogue concerning Brick's notorious "mystery."[3] What the early critics had overlooked, however, is that there is a first-person narrator here who, in

Al Hirschfeld cartoon of Hemingway with Truman Capote on the Left Bank in Paris, with Williams sitting on the left, August 13, 1950. © AL HIRSCHFELD. Reproduced by arrangement with Hirschfeld's exclusive representative, the MARGO FEIDEN GALLERIES LTD., NEW YORK. WWW.ALHIRSCHFELD.COM

relating Brick's story of emasculation, provides a queer dimension to "Three Players" that Williams could not sustain in transporting Brick's alcohol-cum-sexual dilemma from the story to the play.[4] Brenda Murphy has brilliantly corrected this oversight in a recent article by pointing out this narrator's role as spectator to the story's summer game that personifies the agon between Brick and Margaret. In arguing that the story recounts both Brick's crack-up and the narrator's "awakening to his homosexuality" through the voyeuristic predilections that make Brick at once his "role model and object of desire,"[5] Murphy not only rightly recalibrated the story's focus from Brick's summer onto that of the narrator's, but she also uncovered its potential homosexual link with *Cat*, locating it specifically in the narrator's reincarnation as Skipper.

While I find Murphy's reading cogent and stimulating and her argument insightful and ground-breaking, I equally feel that at crucial times she oversimplifies the story's sociohistorical context and the importance Williams places on transgenerational sex/gender roles within that timeframe. In claiming, for instance, that "it is not Mary Louise but Brick who is central to the narrator's memories of that summer,"[6] she dangerously neglects nearly *half* of the story's narrative content, which, once removed, alters considerably our understanding of the narrator's interests in Brick and his motives for retelling the events of this one summer to us. Brick's emasculation in the story, in fact, serves more as an analogous backdrop to the narrator's own emerging struggle like Hemingway's Jake to signify his masculinity and thus understand his sexuality than it does as a purely voyeuristic fantasy into which the narrator enters the homosexual world. Reading the narrator's passage into sexuality through his troubled relationship with Mary Louise demonstrates how both Brick and the narrator suffer identical crises of emasculation, one which leads the heteromasculine Brick to the bottle and the protosexual narrator into questioning the nature of gender and sexual identification. It is in this, the narrator's preoccupation with both Brick *and* Mary Louise, that the story reveals an insight not only into the awakening of the narrator's homosexual consciousness but also into the crises of masculine and sexual identification that filled a nation's agenda between the wars.

The Freudian Phallus in the Victorian "Cult of Masculinity"

"Three Players of a Summer Game" is most like *Cat on a Hot Tin Roof* in that it records the sexual politics of an aloof husband and a disgruntled wife and even begins by raising questions behind the reasons for that confrontation and the central role alcohol plays in it. As the story's narrator explains early on,

> Brick seemed to be throwing his life away as if it were something disgusting that he had suddenly found in his hands. This self-disgust came upon him with the abruptness and violence of a crash on a highway. But what had Brick crashed into? Nothing that anybody was able to surmise, for he seemed to have everything that young men like Brick might hope for or desire to have. What else is there? There must have been something else that

he wanted or lacked, or what reason was there for dropping his life and taking hold of a glass which he never let go of for more than one waking hour?[7]

Unlike the play, however, the story *seemingly* provides an answer, for though the Brick we encounter in the story is a much paler version of the antihero who suffers from any range of problems in *Cat,* he is certainly more vocal about the source of his troubles and explicitly identifies it for us as his conjugal castration. As Brick says to the men repainting his mistress Isabel Grey's house, "the meanest thing that one human can do to another human being is take his respect for himself away from him" (*CS* 328).

For Brick, that respect is tantamount to his masculinity, which, for a former athlete in a society that partly judges manhood by good looks and physical prowess, he locates, as had many men of his Freudian generation (Jake Barnes included), in the phallus: "I had it took away from me! I won't tell you how, but maybe, being men about my age, you're able to guess it. That was how. Some of them don't want it. They cut it off. They cut it right off of a man, and half the time he don't know when they cut it off him" (*CS* 328). Parroting the many case studies Freud published in the opening decades of the twentieth century concerning the psychosexual development of young boys, Brick here represents a clinical example of how the "phallus" is not meant to be understood simply as a signifier for the penis, but rather, as Freud had intended, as a signifier for power or control over one's external world whose necessary "castration" insures the development of heterosexual drives in children.[8] That Brick, recognizably beyond Freud's stages of infantile sexuality, should still express his lost male prerogatives through the watered-down language of Freudian psychoanalysis demonstrates less explicitly his inability to master psychoanalytical nomenclature and more implicitly his generation's need for and fascination with the scientific language of sexuality denied them for centuries. This phallic crisis plunges Brick into a bout with masculine existentialism, an angst derived from the inability of American men in the opening decades of the twentieth century to determine and construct a masculine gender in the face of enormous sexual and cultural changes taking place in the nation.

The cult of the phallus is surely nothing unique to Freud, nor to America. With a history dating back millennia to Hellenist *pæderastia* and Roman *stuprum,*[9] the phallus has invariably signified masculinity in the Western imago. And yet, what classical and modern historians have repeatedly informed us is that the phallus cyclically reenters cultural discourse at times when gender and sex are most in flux and men feel most threatened sexually speaking, that is, when clear distinctions between male and female, freed and enslaved, enfranchised and oppressed, *vir* and *cinædi* are required to negotiate the sociopolitical distinctions that maintain an ordered (i.e., patriarchal) polity.[10] Social historians like Anthony Rotundo and Michael Kimmel (among others) have convincingly argued that the signifying phallus only entered dominant American thought during the cultural watershed of the Victorian period when significant changes in the American ethos and body politic irreparably split old and new epistemologies of sexual and gender identification, transforming, in effect, American manhood into American masculinity.[11]

Under the onslaught of industrialization, the restructuring of a corporate economy, the rise of feminism, and the influx of immigrants who imported conflicting notions of masculinity discussed earlier in chapter 2, men's relationships with women, with other men, and with themselves altered considerably. They had not only to liberate space (real, social, and psychological) for the emancipated woman and the ubiquitous immigrant to accommodate their necessary mobilization, but also to reconstitute the masculine signification that work had once afforded them as breadwinners. Therefore, with their fathers increasingly becoming shadowy figures at home and their mothers inculcating them with a maternal ethos that often ran counter to the *paternus* of self-reliance once handed down through the generations, Victorian boys like Brick—and like Jake or later Big Daddy, for that matter—were becoming a species of young men whose ideologies about gender and sexual identification were, for the first time in American history, growing vastly different from those of their fathers.[12]

In addition to American manhood readily being challenged from the outside, an increased awareness of the sexual inversion debate—which had culminated in the wholesale declaration that the fin de siècle Aesthete was just another assault on masculinity[13]—further alarmed an already sensitive male public of the "specter of femininity" emerging from within.[14] Coupled with an existent sissified American culture were the findings of numerous European and American sexologists such as Edward Carpenter, Magnus Hirschfeld, and Havelock Ellis, whose research in same-sex eroticism declared homosexuality to be not only the result of psychic hermaphroditism, or the feminine soul in a male body, but also congenital and therefore present in a significant portion of society; such declarations had begun raising fears that unmanliness could imply sexual transgression as well.[15] Aided in part by the growing visibility of a gay subculture in large cities,[16] it took subsequently little effort to lump gay and effeminate men in the same category against manhood, as Rotundo notes: "The homosexual male and the man who was insufficiently manly were understood in the same figure of speech

.... The longer the association lasted between the homosexual and the unmanly man, the greater the power of the homosexual label to stigmatize any man."[17] With heterosexuality now being understood as the homogenizing agent to a culturally melting nation and homosexuality defined in terms of it congenital relation to effeminacy, the *un*masculine man in his many avatars became the national anathema, and American men quickly learned that perceived or performed masculinity was not only desirable but essential to one's heteronormative identity.

By the late nineteenth century in America, then, with the New Woman and the sexual invert challenging not only male hegemony but the definition of masculinity itself, heteronormative men began reasserting the phallus as a consolidating signifier of masculine authority, manifested in the many newly-founded all-male social and fraternal orders, in the religion of Muscular Christianity, and even in Teddy Roosevelt's Rough Riders discussed earlier.[18] At the dawn of the century, when G. Stanley Hall's influential recapitulation theory in his best-selling *Adolescence: Its Psychology and Its Relation to Physiology, Anthropology, Sociology, Sex, Crime, Religion, and Education* (1904) began informing American fathers that the sissy or the Miss Nancy were signs of coddled Victorian boys who would lack the necessary vim to see America through its own imperialist endeavors, the phallus was finally accorded clinical approval, one readily grafted onto various signifying activities which would detect, correct (or at least protect) the boys' emerging masculine image — such as the Boy Scouts or active participation in sports and bodybuilding.[19] That Hall was also one of America's foremost advocates of Freudian ideas had a lot to do with introducing psychoanalysis and its phallogocentrist theories to America, though its real impact would not be felt until the War and the debate on treating shell-shock.[20]

Freud, of course, did not produce the American cult of the phallus in the twentieth century, but his scientific discourse surely did provide men the opportunity to understand their modern anxieties and reaffirm their paternal authority. As David Greenberg suggests, Freud and his American supporters like Hall first helped men through their crisis of masculinity:

> Freud's influence, of course, extended far beyond the Austrian border; he became especially popular in early twentieth-century America. It has been suggested that this popularity stemmed in part from the sorts of problems psychoanalysis purported to cure: nervousness, lack of self-confidence, over-conscientiousness, feelings that life was meaningless — all problems one might expect to encounter in the professional classes in a society that encouraged hard work, had a high level of geographic and social mobility, and

was absorbing immigrants whose traditional cultures failed to provide interpretive meanings and behavioral guideposts in the New World.[21]

Then, once Freudian psychoanalysis finally entered American pop culture en masse after the War—through Jazz Age advertisements, songs, films, art, and literature, as well as a host of pop-psychoanalysis books that exploded on the market, sold even in Sears, Roebuck's catalogues[22]—men began exploiting it more fully. For phallogocentrism not only provided them with an authoritarian language, though "often in vulgarized form,"[23] in which to explain the recent shift in Victorian sex/gender roles and the medical legitimacy to justify it, but did so in strict heteronormative terms.[24] As the Plecks note, "Whereas once ministers and medical doctors had set the standard for male sexual purity, by the early twentieth century, Freudian-influenced psychiatrists held that men must develop 'sex-role identity' from suitable male role models and from reinforcement in learning masculine behaviors."[25] Freud was now as accessible to middle-class America as was the automobile, allowing women and men to discuss more frankly what their Victorian mothers and fathers would never have dreamed of doing. The residual effect further dichotomized American masculinity and consolidated its various images indeterminately.[26]

If in Freud could be found answers to the rise of the flapper or the pathology of the homosexual, both were now be understood only in relation to the phallic Law. As John D'Emilio confirms, "Although the diffusion of Freudian psychoanalysis in the 1920s helped a rapidly growing public discourse on sexuality that substantially replaced late nineteenth-century reserve, the decade's much heralded revolution in manners and morals was an exclusively heterosexual upheaval."[27] It is not coincidental, then, that of all the theories Freud postulated during the opening decades of the twentieth century, the one most popular in America was his castration complex,[28] whose phallogocentrism helped heterosexual men to simultaneously combat the rise of the flapper (through their misappropriation of the term "penis envy") and isolate their homosocial inklings from homosexual ones (with male bonding being understood as a social privilege in recovering one's masculinity, and homosexuality a psychological disorder). "Scientific studies of sexuality such as those produced by Sigmund Freud and the popular sex manuals like those of 'Dr. Jaf,'" Angus McLaren posits, demonstrate "how widespread were both the new, vulgarized notions of the sexologists and older sexual beliefs."[29]

Nor is it coincidental that American men would never warm up to Freud's bisexual theory outlined in *Three Essays on the Theory of Sexuality* where he postulates that homosexuality is a natural phenomenon, neither advantageous nor disadvantageous for an individual, and that everyone carries in him- and herself innate homosexual tendencies: "all human beings are capable of making a homosexual object-choice and have in fact made one in their unconscious."[30] According to Freud, humans possess "an originally bisexual physical disposition" which, over time, becomes "modified into a unisexual one, leaving behind only a few traces of the sex that has become atrophied."[31] As he would later explain in his famous 1935 letter to an American mother distraught by the fact that her son was homosexual: "Homosexuality is surely no advantage, but it is nothing to be ashamed of, no vice, no degradation, it cannot be classified as an illness, we consider it to be a variation of the sexual function produced by a certain arrest of sexual development."[32]

Unlike Carpenter, Ellis, or Hirschfeld, whose earlier third-sex theories on homosexuality were systematically banned in America as socially deviant or morally corrupt, Freud had confounded heterosexual American men because his theories spoke to their need to recovery their lost masculine identities but simultaneously threatened their heterosexuality. In other words, Freud's theory that sexuality was not only something to be attained, with heterosexuality as its goal, but that those failing to achieve it were somehow destined to a life of homosexuality pushed American men, particularly its burgeoning psychoanalysts themselves, to be selective in adopting certain Freudian ideologies on scientific means while rejecting others on purely moralistic grounds. As historian Henry Abelove writes, "It was in America, however, that Freud's viewpoint on homosexuality was least accepted or maybe most resisted," due mostly to its national obsession with sexual "overrepress[ion]."[33] Now more than ever, masculinity had become a means not only to recover lost gender privileges vis-à-vis the New Woman or the "effeminate" immigrant, but also to insure one's successful passage into the heterosexual world. As Abelove intimates, Freud's castration theory spoke more to what American men had wanted to hear about why they felt their masculinity was under assault, and how they might correct it, than anything else the Austrian psychoanalyst had written about the harmlessness of homosexuality.

Brick's signifying "phallus" in the story, then, is essentially Freudian, for in truth it could not have been anything else. Thus, when Williams develops a noticeable shift in gender roles in "Three Players of a Summer Game"—with Margaret losing her "feminine prettiness" for a "rough-textured sort of handsomeness" (*CS* 323) and, like Brett Ashley, cutting her hair short like a flapper's "so that she didn't have to 'mess with it'" (*CS* 323),[34] and Brick clinging desperately to any vestige of fin de siècle masculinity only to end up an outfitted doll in the back seat of his Pierce Arrow touring car—he is simply rendering a wider postwar cultural phenomenon in America more than he is queerly challenging it. With this in mind, reading Brick's cult of the phallus in "Three Players" defers from the attempt to isolate something that Margaret did or does to Brick that led to his alcoholism, which nothing in the story can finally proffer anyway,[35] and privileges instead a reading based on masculine existentialism: the need to understand why Brick unconditionally blames his alcoholism on Margaret's emasculating him. To be sure, if Brick's diminishing sense of masculinity ended with Margaret, it certainly did not begin with her.

"Bulls Have No Balls": Brick's Signifying Phallus

To understand Brick's Freudian sense of his emasculation, we need to view it through this contextual lens, one which no doubt would have had a strong hand in shaping his sexual epistemology. Only by recognizing what social influences had worked, for good or for bad, to construct Brick's personal and political self as it is revealed to us are we able to negotiate our way through Brick's mystery, one that has left its impression firmly etched on the history of American masculinity in crisis. Within this context, Brick's emasculation reveals itself to us not only when it becomes apparent that his alcoholism hides the loss of certain masculine signifiers afforded him by his society but also, and perhaps more significantly, when those *same* phallic signifiers are subsequently taken up by his once domesticated wife.

The first loss of the Freudian phallus comes when "Brick's driving license [is] revoked" (*CS* 323), and he is no longer able to project a masculine front from behind the wheel of his luxurious touring car, a ubiquitous badge of masculinity ever since Victorian America equated manhood with consumption and Ford made the mass-produced automobile one of its staple indicators in the 1920s.[36] Williams, in fact, repeatedly calls our attention to the gendered identity of cars, for not only is Brick's expensive (and patriarchal) "Pierce Arrow touring car" a marked contrast to Margaret's "little runabout" (*CS* 323) and Isabel's "ladylike electric" (*CS* 341),[37] it is also signified by a proper name that, given the story's obsession with the phallus, is more than merely suggestive.[38] But Brick's emasculation does not end with just the loss of his car or his license to drive it, for when Margaret usurps his Pierce Arrow, taking with it its masculine signification, she conspicuously begins performing, and even *phallicizing*, her newly acquired gender at Brick's expense: "She had a practice of releasing the clutch on a car and shooting off in high gear at the exact instant that her laughter boomed out, not calling good-bye but thrusting out one bare strong arm, straight

Pierce Arrow touring car, ca. 1925. Courtesy of the author.

out as a piston with fingers clenched into a fist, as the car whipped up and disappeared into a cloud of yellow dust" (*CS* 323).

Brick's touring car, then, along with the legal power to drive it, becomes an obvious signifier for all that is masculine in the story, whether lost or transgendered, something the younger narrator even acknowledges when he describes Brick's emasculation as an abrupt and violent "crash on the highway" (*CS* 322).

Brick's second loss of masculine signification comes when Margaret equally usurps his patriarchal privileges as landowner by wresting away his power of attorney, effectively making him a kept man in a Reconstruction South that resented the New Woman's challenge to gender roles. Completely denuded by his dependency upon alcohol, for example, Brick is unable to challenge Margaret's increased strength, which culminates in her taking "hold of Brick's ten-thousand-acre plantation as firmly and surely as if she had always existed for that and no other purpose" (*CS* 322). The more the effeminate Brick retreats into the bottle, the quicker the masculine Margaret steps into his financial shoes, ultimately managing "all of his business affairs with celebrated astuteness" (*CS* 322). Again, though not in itself a visibly emasculating act (even her society "admired her as a remarkably fine and brave little woman who had too much to put up with" [*CS* 322]), Margaret's machinations are portrayed as such when the narrator's nostalgic tone turns blatantly sardonic. Now, he begins pitting her Machiavellian ethics against Brick's drunken reverence for the lost Eden of his youth: "It was as though [Margaret] had her lips fastened to some invisible wound in his body through which drained out of him and flowed into her the assurance and vitality that he had owned before marriage" (*CS* 322), a vampiric image repeated in the story's summer mosquitoes whose bites Mary Louise tries to soothe with pieces of chipped ice. No irony is withheld either when that "invisible wound," that Brick specifies later as his castration, is rendered here through a cannibalistic image of the act of fellatio as a *vagina dentata*.

Left bereft of two traditional signifiers of post-Progressivist American masculinity, Brick gradually wastes away. It is only when Margaret leaves for Memphis to attend a funeral that spring and, appropriately enough, "collect her inheritance" (*CS* 323) that Brick manages, like Hemingway's Francis Macomber in "The Short Happy Life of Francis Macomber" (1936), to conquer his fears and restore some of his usurped masculinity.[39] First, Brick regains his right to drive, which is no insignificant feat for him since, as the narrator points out, "Brick's driving license had been restored to him, and it was an important step forward in his personal renovation—being able to drive his own car again" (*CS* 326). As Brick himself proudly announces to the painters, "That's my car out there and I drove it up here myself. It's no short drive, it's almost a hundred miles, and I drive it each morning and drive it back each night" (*CS* 329). Next, he wrests back his power of attorney, which he exercises immediately by purchasing the Greys' Victorian house, an act more out of vengeance against his wife than love for Isabel: "I got back my power of attorney which I'd give to that woman and I got back my driver's license and bought this piece of property in town and signed my own check for it . . ." (*CS* 329). Both signifiers are finally coupled to achieve a more fully realized attempt of performative masculinity—the taking of a lover—for the recently widowed Isabel Grey "was now his mistress" (*CS* 324). Having restored his driver's license and power of attorney, then, all that now remains for Brick to do to fully recover his phallus is to beat his drinking problem.

Though he in many ways has shown himself to be the archetypal Freudian analysand obsessed with masculine signification and the castration complex that defines it by negation, Brick most poignantly reveals his fixation with the phallus by couching it in a Freudian language of condensation (metaphor) and displacement (metonymy). For example, in describing analogously how he will conquer his alcoholism in the same manner as a player proceeds through the "summer game" of croquet "from wicket to wicket" (*CS* 330), Brick employs metaphor, that is, in resignifying the "sissy" sport as masculine because of its required precision (why precision should signify masculinity here, we are never told). When the wicket, croquet balls, and mallet/pole within that metaphor become obvious tropes for the vagina and the dismembered male sex organ that Brick nostalgically bemoans, he seamlessly moves toward metonymy: "I'm just going to prove I'm a man with his balls back on him! I'm going to do it step by little step, the way that people play the game of croquet. You know how you play that game. You hit the ball through the wicket and then you drive it through the next one. You hit it through that wicket and then you drive on to another one . . . until you arrive at that big final pole, and then, bang, you've hit it, the game is finished, you're there!" (*CS* 330).

While the innuendo of sexual climax as restituted manhood seems fairly sophomoric here by post-Freudian tastes,[40] the metonymy becomes more complex when we recognize its attachment to the sexual potency of the act of driving itself, which Williams had established earlier in the story with Brick's Pierce Arrow. When emasculated, Brick loses his driver's license; now that he is "masculine" again, Brick can drive both physically his car and sexually the widow Grey, proving to himself that he is no longer the impotent or castrated man that Margaret had earlier made him.

On a surface level, Brick's problem mirrors Jake's: both men, whose sexual identities have been challenged, confront their loss of manhood first by hiding behind the bottle, and second by defying the most immediate source of their emasculation—their women. For the impotent Jake, it was eluding Brett's impossible dream of their "damned good time together" (*S* 193), a battle Hemingway metaphorically equates with a bullfighter's need to kill that which would kill him. For the psychologically impotent Brick, it is proving his masculinity in the affair with Isabel and simultaneously battling his alcoholism, which he similarly personifies as a *torero* or *matador* in the bull ring: "The thing to do, the way to handle the problem, is like a bullfighter handles a bull in a bull ring. Wear it down little by little, get control of it gradually. That's how I'm handling this thing!" (*CS* 327). Because Brick's alcoholism is directly linked to his emasculating wife, the battle with one is ostensibly a battle with the other. Later, Brick even describes the triumphant manner in which he will, like the bullfighter, prevail in the end: "Then slowly, slowly, the way a bull trots back from its first wild, challenging plunge into the ring, he would fasten one hand over his belt and raise the other one hesitantly to his head, feeling the scalp and the hard round bowl of the skull underneath it . . ." (*CS* 331). Given Jake's earlier admiration of how Romero "smoothly worn down" (*S* 193) his bull before killing it, Brick's allusion here to how he will defeat his alcoholism/wife is not coincidental.

3: "A DYING GAUL"

In fact, by no small coincidence, many of the governing themes and symbols of Hemingway's *The Sun Also Rises* are in some way present in Williams's "Three Players of a Summer Game"—the rise of the flapper in sexual politics and its metaphoric transference onto the "game," the loss of masculinity via castration, the loss and forced recovery of marital fidelity, the abuse of alcohol to counter all three realities, and the ironic first-person narrator who views it all. Even the reference to bullfighting was present in the 1952 version of the story published in the *New Yorker*, which suggests that, in drafting the story in 1951 Hemingway's novel may have already been on Williams's mind. To be sure, Williams was passionate about bullfighting and did not need to posture to Hemingway about it when they met in Havana in 1959.

In his letters and notebook entries of the late 1940s and throughout the 1950s, for example, Williams frequently talks about attending the bullfights whenever he and his traveling companions visited Spain. On June 6, 1945, Williams wrote to Donald Windham,

> And yesterday went to the bull-fights, which were sickening and fascinating *as ever*. One matador wore white silk with silver sequins and bougainvillea pink stockings. He had to stab his bull nine times before he killed him, and the crowd was disgusted with him, but my attitude was indulgent. After each fight the matador marches around the ring, bowing at each section to receive his plaudits. This poor youth was hissed and booed until he came to my section. I stood up and yelled "Bravo!" so fervently that he made a bow directly to me. (*TWLDW* 171–72, my emphasis)[41]

Then in a letter to Cheryl Crawford dated August 1954, he wrote that he and Maria Britneva met up with his poet friend Oliver Evans "and took a trip by car along the Costa Brava, two weeks in Barcelona in which we saw seven bull-fights" (*SL II* 540). Almost a year later, on July 22, 1955, he wrote to Robert MacGregor that he was "flying to Valencia tomorrow to attend a week of bull-fights with the English critic, Kenneth Tynan, who's doing a piece about me for Harper's Bazaar and is getting altogether too much confidential material here in Spain, though I am also getting a lot on him!" (*SL II* 585; cf. 586). Williams also demonstrated (though no where near the extent of Hemingway's) his earnest knowledge of the bullfights and of several celebrated matadors. In a "Drama Mailbag" letter to the *New York Times* about Tallulah Bankhead's 1956 performance of Blanche, he notes, "To me she brought to mind the return of some great matador to the bull ring in Madrid, for the first time after having been almost fatally gored, and facing his most dangerous bull with his finest valor, a bullfighter such as Belmonte or Manolete, conquering himself and his spectators and his bull, all at once and together; with brilliant cape-work and no standing back from the 'terrain of the bull'" (*SL II* 602–3).

While none of this proves that Williams's reference to bullfighting in "Three Players" was a conscious reference either to Hemingway or to *The Sun Also Rises*, each reference does offer circumstantial evidence that, when weighed against comments Williams would make later about Hemingway—and not just in his public interviews but also in these private letters and notebook entries—combines to show that Hemingway was never far from Williams's thoughts during the 1950s, conscious or otherwise. Arguably, then, Brick Pollitt in "Three Players" reincarnates Jake Barnes to a great extent as a man whose alcohol abuse is identified as a symptom of his greater male anxiety, namely impotence; but unlike Jake, Brick can *attempt* to prove his masculinity to others. Therefore, all masculine symbols in the story, just as they do in the novel for Jake, ironically remind Brick (and us) of the permanence of his impotence.

Moreover, like Brett's control over the equally impotent though queerly masculine Jake, Margaret's sexual politics and gender reversal finally serve to destroy any advances Brick might have made in his recovery. By once again wresting away his power of attorney over their estate at the end of the story (in the *New Yorker* version of the story, we are informed that she immediately puts the Grey house up for sale again), Margaret humiliates him socially; by recommandeering his fancy Pierce Arrow after "Brick's driver's license [was] revoked again for some misadventure on the highway due to insufficient control of the wheel" (*CS* 342), and now driving it through town with "a wonderful male assurance"—"her bare arms brown and muscular like a Negro field hand's" which she repeatedly "thrust[s] out" (*CS* 342) as she passes people on the street—she succeeds in humiliating him sexually. The story's tableau, then, which portrays a masculine Margaret behind the wheel *driving* a feminized and "sheepishly grinning and nodding" Brick around town with "the car's canvas top . . . lowered the better to expose [him]" (*CS* 342), completes the transference of gender signification. Brick, "clothed and barbered . . . like the president of a good social fraternity in a gentleman's college of the South" (*CS* 342), has become signified, a mannequin whose plastic masculinity serves finally to legitimate Margaret's usurped social image. We are left, as is the narrator, with the impression that Brick will never again gain control of his life. Nothing directly links the story to the novel more than this final image of the emasculated male in the phallicized car with his emasculating lover/wife controlling him. Yet, whereas Jake arguably detaches himself from Brett in their second taxi ride, Brick, equally being taxied around town, is incapable of Jake's irony and has clearly fallen back under Margaret's Circean spell.

Unlike with Brick's mystery in *Cat on a Hot Tin Roof*, then, Williams does provide some answers as to why the story's Brick is estranged from Margaret, and we are left with the conclusion that Brick's alcohol abuse in both works is a symptom of his greater male anxiety, namely his emasculation, which his liquor temporarily alleviates by either clouding his ability to reason why he feels the way he does or at least providing a physiological equivalent to the impotence he is attempting to mask with drinking. Either way, though, Margaret will always be present in his Collins glass. For these reasons, searching for answers as to *why* Brick drinks is perhaps less problematic in the story than in the play, for though both Bricks experience a crisis of masculinity on par with the men of their respective generations, only the play's hero suffers one of sexual identification as well. It would appear, then, that Brick in the story has very little in common with Brick in the play.

In truth, there is little reason to doubt Brick's own explanation for his alcoholism. With neither the latent homosexuality that haunts the play as a potential objective correlative for his "crack-up" here (since Brick publicly and privately engenders a heterosexual bent in the story) nor the existential angst that daunts his dramatic namesake (since Brick in the story is drawn much more like a clown than a nihilist), we are hard pressed to link the two texts thematically. Lacking both critical distance to understand from whence his emasculation derives and the intelligence to theorize himself out of it, Brick has little else to arm himself against his sexual marasmus than the childlike finger pointing he resorts to in the story, an accusation which, by the story's end, even proves entirely justified given that Margaret's actions are presented as those of an emasculating wife. Brick simply identifies his wife as the source behind his loss of masculinity because she is his most immediate and tangible force behind a national crisis of masculinity of which Brick can only intuit.

The Narrator and Lacan's Phallus

If the phallogocentrism of Freud's castration complex in many ways could be understood as a discrete byproduct of a Western crisis of masculinity, it could be equally recognized as one of its continued instigators. With Brick's implied knowledge of the loss of the phallus as both an assault by those forces working to undermine the masculine privileges his father's generation attempted to instill in him *and* the fear of that father's castrating him to help preserve those masculine privileges vis-à-vis his wife/mother for himself, how could a man like Brick ever hope to develop normally? Or, for that matter, how could that young man's own impressionable son? In other words, if we consider Brick to be the sexual role model for the young narrator (as Brenda Murphy has suggested)[42] who, as his "father," is already "castrated," how might that "son," involved in his own castration complex (and now old enough to contemplate it), actually develop once he recognizes that his "father" poses no real masculine threat to his own phallus?

Though we are to understand that the narrator is now much older, perhaps even middle-aged as Brick is when he pens this story, we figure him in the story's narrative to be a young boy around Mary Louise's age of twelve (the *New Yorker* version says explicitly that he is fourteen).[43] Like her, he is currently discovering sexuality and its inescapable politics. As the older narrator confesses, the events of this story took place during one "long ago summer" (*CS* 320), a summer that he admits was "the last one of my childhood" (*CS* 321).[44] What in this surrogate father-son relationship was significant enough for the boy to have passed from childhood into early adulthood? In the Bildungsroman tradition, that passage invariably recounts a recognition of the hero's mortality, immorality, or Narcissistic self as being different from the image afforded by his or her parents or immediate environment. Though there is a death in this story, it is not one that contributes to the narrator's education as it apparently does Brick's. And though there is a level of social and religious impropriety in Brick's drunkenness and adultery, neither is given enough narrative weight to suggest that the narrator judges them improper and redirects his life toward something more morally or socially acceptable as a consequence. Rather, the narrator first identifies with Brick as the Freudian father of the castration complex who, himself castrated, fails to properly initiate the young narrator into a traditional sex role. Then, confronted with a similar struggle to signify his own masculinity in the face of a hostile world demanding that he measure up, the narrator, in post-Freudian hindsight, identifies Brick as his Lacanian Other, the anchor of the chain of masculine signifiers, which subsequently reveals to us and to the confused young narrator his future sexual identity. Brick's story of castration, like Jake's, serves as a catalyst behind the story's subversive theme of sexual initiation; and in recounting that story to us, the narrator exorcises his own "hidden truth" of a latent homosexual desire in the same way Jake puts to rest his "damned good time" with Brett.

With Brick being the only father-figure present in the story for the young narrator on whom to fashion his own emerging sense of masculine identity, it becomes understandable why the boy is at first obsessed with telling us Brick's story and how Brick's emasculation not only realizes the boy's anxiety of the castration complex but also informs him of the familial and social orders inscribed on his phallus. Though he frequently appears to be in the background of Brick's story—for example, a mere bystander reporting for us, as would some tabloid journalist in a gossip column for his intoxicated readers, the salacious rise and fall of a local hero—the narrator also surfaces at significant moments in the story. These occasions of self-reproduction, in fact, situate the narrator centrally within Brick's story, intimating that the history of Brick's loss of masculinity is equally the narrator's. Since he can now talk about these events with a candor and a lucidity that Brick, given his alcoholism, never could, what we recognize is that beyond their shared experience of the castration complex, the narrator has the added anxiety of self-referentiality, that is, he is looking for his masculinized self in the world around him, not finding it, then determining for himself what that absence implies. This anxiety, then, makes him less Freudian in the traditional sense that Brick represents, where the latter only fears the loss of his masculine phallus through castration, and more Lacanian in recognizing that his loss is more the *phallus comme significant* (phallus-as-signifier)—in other words, the phallogocentrism which defines and represents the self. This explains why the older narrator returns to the scene of the castration so as to piece together his own understanding of its effects upon him later in life.[45]

The first striking detail of how the narrator's story of his own emasculation shadows that of Brick is encountered in his relationship with Mary Louise. The narrator admits being "her only close friend," for example, just as "she was mine" (*CS* 321), forging to some extent an adolescent version of marriage where Mary Louise, in searching for her passage into feminine adulthood, begins reflecting Margaret more than she does her own mother, Isabel. For instance, despite all of her attempts to be like her mother, who is a "thin woman with long bones and skin of a silky luster" and whose voice "has a pleasantly resonant quality that carries it farther than most voices go" (*CS* 320), Mary Louise's "plump bare legs and arms" (*CS* 325)[46] and her affected attempts to imitate "the elegant manners and cultivated eastern voice of her mother" (*CS* 321) intimate that she will never carry off her mother's grace. Her mother admits as much herself when she calls Mary Louise a "fat little monster!" and repeatedly tells her that her "cushions of flesh were going to dissolve in two or three years and then she would be just as thin and pretty as her mother" (*CS* 333). Because the narrator frequently isolates these faults in her, such as "her plump little buttocks and her beginning breasts" (*CS* 333)[47] and her "endless . . . copying [of] her mother" (*CS* 331), we are left with the impression that being a twelve year old girl whose feminine precociousness is hampered by her boyish body is making it difficult for her to mature into that woman she is rushing headlong into becoming.

Having informed us that Mary Louise will fail to recapitulate Isabel's femininity, the narrator begins portraying her as he did Margaret, though without the bitterness in her characterization since he realizes now the girl's innocence in that duplicity. Like Margaret, for instance, she too takes pleasure in the masculine act of driving. Sitting in "the electric automobile sometimes all afternoon by herself as if she were on display in a glass box," Mary Louise adopts the posture of her flapper double, "uttering treble peals of ladylike laughter" and "using grown-up expressions such as, 'Oh, how delightful' and 'Isn't that just lovely'" (*CS* 321). Even in her obsession with "sucking" her mosquito bites (*CS* 338), despite the fact that her mother tells her to numb them with chips of ice, she is aligned with Margaret, whose sucking Brick's invisible wound like the "metamorphoses that occur in insect life" (*CS* 322) established the narrator's misogynistic stance toward her. By intimating how Mary Louise, when older, will be more like Margaret than Isabel, an emancipated woman who will demand her equal place in society, the narrator equally informs us of her potential to castrate men in order to secure that place, which is something she will innocently do to the narrator. This is what finally meshes the narrator's story with Brick's.

The narrator's masculine castration arrives that summer when he describes how he and Mary Louise "took a drive" in the electric car to "a little art museum that had recently been established in the town" (*CS* 325). Once there, Mary Louise, bypassing all the other reproductions of classical works, leads the narrator directly to a "reclining male nude" entitled *The Dying Gaul*, whose penis is covered up by "a fig leaf, which was of a different colored metal from the bronze of the prostrate figure" (*CS* 325), a detail Williams takes pleasure in adding.[48] Unlike Margaret, or even Brett in *The Sun Also Rises* and Maggie in *Cat on a Hot Tin Roof*, Mary Louise innocently emasculates the narrator when, after raising the conquered Gaul's fig leaf, she demands, "Is yours like that?" (*CS* 325). Displaying a look of "astonished horror" (*CS* 325) that not only discomforts him but directly challenges his sexual identity, the boy laconically responds, "My answer was idiotic; I said, 'I don't know!' and I think I was blushing long after we left the museum . . ." (*CS* 326, Williams's ellipses).

None of this, of course, suggests that the narrator is prehomosexual, only that he, at an impressionable age, suffered a psychological blow to his emerging and delicate masculine ego (though many modernist thinkers had frequently linked the two). In fact, it would appear that the narrator was anything but homosexual, since, like most teenage boys, he is intrigued with the "plumpy" girl as a sex object and even drifts into recalling this episode of his youth after having just recollected Mary Louise's "ravishingly smooth and tender" skin: "The association is not at all a proper one, but how can you recall a summer in childhood without some touches of impropriety?" (*CS* 325). The narrator's recalling this event immediately after a heterosexual reverie prepares us, however, for the emasculation that follows; that he should also lose his power of speech following the emasculation announces the impact the loss of the phallus has on the boy, particularly when the narrative from this moment onward begins focusing on the events surrounding Brick's castration.

In Lacanian terms, anxiety over language articulates "the crisis of male self-definition that throws into question the very category of male heterosexuality."[49] In his *Écrits*, Lacan argues that since language is rooted in unconscious desire, where the id and not the ego contains "the whole structure of language,"[50] any moment of verbal prohibition in a sexually developing child signals that child's preconscious confrontation with the Name-of-the-Father, the paternal law of the Phallus that controls the gateway between the Other and the self, between the imaginary and the symbolic realms through which the child must pass in order to become a functioning—that is, a signifying—adult. Differing from Freud, who saw the phallus simply as the desire for power (whether in men or in women, like with Brick or Margaret) and thus castration the fear of its usurpation or unattainability, Lacan sees the Phallus as the center of all language, and thus the imaginary *signified* that anchors the entire signifying chain. A prelinguistic child need not desire the Phallus because he is not yet conscious of its existence, or its absence for that matter, and only comes to desire it when he is aware of its lack. Therefore, the Phallus, whose castration denotes the moment of language acquisition—which for de Saussure is premised on the idea of metonymic absence defining difference (that is, words are only necessary when the object you desire is gone and you need to identify what that desire was in order to recover it)—becomes the signifier of that absence: "the phallus is a signifier, a signifier whose functions, in the intrasubjective economy of the analysis, lifts the veil perhaps from the function it performed in the mysteries. For it is the signifier intended to designate as a whole the effects of the signified, in that the signifier conditions them by its presence as a signifier."[51]

In pursuit of this nonexistent but eternally desired signified in which to stabilize the meaning around which the self/other dichotomy is constructed, the "I"dentity passes from (mis)identifying its self as other (the *méconnaissance* of accepting its mirrored reflection to be the real, fixed and unified self when it is only an external image) to understanding its self as Other (the concept that others are not the self). Yet once the child has established this idea of Otherness in relation to his self as other, he achieves the self/Other split, recognizes the self as "I" and the language that signifies it, and thus enters the symbolic order, the structure of language itself. Now encultured, the child is forever castrated of the Phallus, whose lack will produce a desire in him for the Other to fill it.

For these reasons, the narrator at the museum cannot respond to Mary Louise's inquiry into the size of his penis reflected in the mirror image of the Roman statue because he has not yet formulated the phallus-as-signifier, that is, he has not yet passed into the symbolic order of masculine signification. Since the statue both has a penis (when Mary Louise unveils it) and lacks one (suggested by the fig leaf,), the narrator is incapable of (mis)identifying with it and thus psychosexually remains in Lacan's realm of the prelinguistic Real. His language only comes to him after he identifies his Other as Brick, whose castration of the Freudian phallus leads the narrator into recognizing that his own castration at the art museum provided him with the power to signify. Thus, while Brick loses his Freudian phallus, the narrator loses his Lacanian Phallus, for if he were laconic as a boy at the sight of the fraudulent penis, he is certainly more Lacanic now in his semantic effusiveness in recounting his emasculation, and that of Brick's, for us.

That the narrator has entered the symbolic order via his *méconnaissance* of Brick as the Other (just as Jake had with Brett and the gay men at the *bal musette*) is established immediately from the story's opening words, where he uses the game of croquet—which, as we have seen, was a means for Brick to signify the recovery of his lost masculinity—to recapture the poetic truth behind Brick's story. As the narrator says, "Croquet is a summer game that seems, in a curious way, to be composed of images . . ." (*CS* 319), fragments of truth that, when recollected and *re*collected, form a mosaic "that may be closer than a literal history could be to the hidden truth of it" (*CS* 321).[52] The narrator even employs the same metonymic references of the "delicate wire wickets," "the strong rigid shape of the mallets that drive the balls through" them, and finally its "wooden poles gaudily painted" (*CS* 319) that Brick will later use in the story to signify the game as heterosexual potency. But because the narrator's use of the images here *presignify* those of Brick's in the story, they can only serve to foreshadow the alcoholic's half-poetic, half-scatological analogy of how he plans on recovering his Freudian phallus and thus counters any attempt to see them as forming a metonymic continuum with Brick's. We need to remember, however, that potentially twenty years separates the event from its recollection, time enough for the now mature narrator to have appropriated Brick's signifier of the phallus and manipulate it to serve his own needs in the writing of that story, even providing, through his own references to penetrating an orifice, a homoerotic gloss on the erstwhile heterosexual image. Given that the narrator again enters the narrative later in order to recount a significant experience he had with this summer game, one that equally calls into question his degree of performed masculinity, his use of the game of croquet here appears to be anything but artistically innocent.

For example, the young Mary Louise (like the real Hazel Kramer, Williams's adolescent love) is sexually advanced for her age and likes the sexual signifying of the game of croquet; though, as a girl on the cusp of femininity, she perhaps only intuits that signification in her desire to play with the older Brick. When Mary Louise repeatedly asks, "Do you think he will get here in time to play?" to which her mother can only respond, "I hope so, precious. It does him so much good to play croquet" (*CS* 332; cf. 337), we are led into reading the game on two levels: as sexual intercourse and as sexual innuendo. If Brick does come to play croquet, then his presence for Isabel implies another *game* of sorts, for while Mary Louise is out preparing the lawn for the match, Brick and Isabel fill that time in her upstairs bedroom (*CS* 333). Therefore, when Mary Louise responds "in a voice that trembled just at the vision of it," "'Oh, I think it does all of us good to play croquet'" (*CS* 332), we can only assume that she now too understands the subtleties of innuendo even if her own pleasure derived from the game remains liminal. By substituting herself in this game of sexual signification for her mother, whose "summer game" with Brick has a much more literal meaning, Mary Louise is vicariously initiated into the (hetero)sexual world of adults.

Therefore, when Mary Louise asks the narrator at times to substitute for the absent Brick, we are also meant to recognize that the game carries some level of significant sexual import for the narrator as well (with the advantage of maturity and hindsight in his narrative recollection). Though, like Mary Louise, he reads the game at the time only liminally, the older narrator can now extemporize with ironic distance what he had then only intuited with dissatisfaction: "she was not at all satisfied with my game" (*CS* 333). Because he is still an undeveloped and unmasculine boy, the narrator is incapable of satisfying her unconscious heterosexual needs through the game of signification. As he admits, "I had had so little practice and she so much, and besides, more importantly, it was the company of the grown-up people she wanted" (*CS* 333). Taken by itself and out of the context of sexual initiation, this experience, like the one in the art museum, could resemble one that most boys of the narrator's age might have encountered at some point during their childhood — namely, sociosexual inadequacy. However, given the narrator's sensitivity to have felt something in her response to his own incapacities, as well as his self-established link not only with

Brick but also with his signifying the game of croquet as the recovered phallus, the event seems too important to be glossed over as merely anecdotal.

With this "sissy" sport being transformed from a metonymy for masculinity into a poetic means of rendering the fragmented truth of the past—that is, from Freudian power to Lacanian wholeness and self-referentiality—we discover that croquet had ultimately failed not only Brick in his struggle to signify his masculinity but the narrator as well.[53] By importing a sexual reading to the game of croquet from the start of the story, the narrator in fact *back*shadows its signification. In other words, the older narrator appropriates Brick's masculine signifier in order to recount the history of that signifier's designification, all the while using that signifier subversively to prepare us for his own parallel story of emasculation as a young boy. As such, when the narrator describes how it "would be absurd to pretend that this is altogether the way it was, and yet it may be closer than a literal history could be to the hidden truth of it" (*CS* 321), the phallus he is now attempting to recover through the game of croquet is not the Freudian one of masculine signification lost in the castration complex but the Lacanian phallus-as-signifier, the fixed center of the symbolic order of language itself that fills the lack he encountered through the silence of the years he had endured before authoring his sexual self through Brick's struggle. Therefore, in retelling for us these "moments that stand out in a season that was a struggle for something of unspeakable importance to someone passing through it . . ." (*CS* 319), the narrator is, in addition to speaking about Brick here, speaking about himself, about his castrated introduction into the symbolic order.

Masculine Signification: "Three Players" as Ur-*Cat*

Though the appropriation of Brick's croquet metaphor establishes him as the narrator's other (seeing the castrated self as being reflected in the mirrored narrative), it does not yet show that the narrator is conscious of Brick *as* Other (recognizing that sexual self as being different from that mirror image and desiring to be the Other). That moment comes when the narrator gazes upon Brick as he had *The Dying Gaul* in the art museum, again providing a mirror for the narrator in which to measure his phallus. Since the narrator at the time had not yet entered the symbolic order of masculine signification and could only see the statue's penis as a representation of the perfect (and thus nonexistent) phallus, he did not "possess" the language necessary to react to Mary Louise's innocent emasculating question; in other words, the mirror image of the penis on the statue merely reinforced the boy's notion of what masculinity is, will be, or at least should be for him when he grows up, just as its lack on Brick had informed him of what masculinity was not. Now that he is older and speaks freely about these events of that one summer, of his and of Brick's castration, the narrator demonstrates that his masculine signification is complete, though the transference of his gaze from the statue's penis onto that of Brick's later in the story intimates for the narrator that his fascination with the castrated Other was anything but boyishly innocent.

In the narrative, for example, the narrator is of course a boy who is neither straight nor gay because he is too young to comprehend sexuality beyond its relationship to gender types. As such, he finds Isabel Grey "pretty," especially when he sees her bare breasts for the first time: "That was the time when I saw, between the dividing gauze of the bedroom curtains, her naked breasts, small and beautiful, shaken like two angry fists by her violent motion" (*CS* 333). Yet, pages later, we find the boy equally intrigued with Brick, watching, as he adds years later in his recollection, "with unabated interest" (*CS* 336):

> That evening was a fearfully hot one, and Brick decided to cool and refresh himself with the sprinkler hose while he enjoyed his drink. He turned it on and pulled it out to the center of the lawn. There he rolled about the grass under its leisurely revolving arch of water, and as he rolled about, he began to wriggle out of his clothes. He kicked off his white shoes and one of his pale green socks, tore off his drenched white shirt and grass-stained linen pants, but he never succeeded in getting off his necktie. Finally, he was sprawled, like some grotesque fountain figure, in underwear and necktie and the one remaining pale green sock, while the revolving arch of water moved with cool whispers about him. (*CS* 335)

Certainly, the boy's descriptions in both scenes are innocent enough, as we would expect the impressions of a young boy's to be at the sight of two semi-naked bodies. But, if we again remember that the narrator is now much older, we recognize that there lie deeper implications behind his descriptions here, as Brenda Murphy has already noted,[54] ones that distinctly reveal the development of a homoerotic gaze in him.

Within "normal" sexual development, Lacan continues in *Écrits*, heterosexuality is determined by "reference to the function of the phallus."[55] To the traditional model of heterosexual development as put forward in Freud's Oedipal complex, where the young boy, in recognizing that his mother lacks a penis and figures that she had had one but that at some point had it cut off, desires to have sex with her so as to make her complete again, Lacan adds desire to the act of castration: "What analytic experience shows is that . . . it is castration that governs desire.... Castration turns fantasy into that supple yet inexhaustible chain by which the arrest of the object-investment, which can hardly go beyond certain natural limits, takes on the transcendental function of ensuring the *jouissance* of the Other, which passes this chain onto me in the Law."[56]

If in the Freudian model, the castration complex evolves from the anxiety that the father will make the boy experience the lack that his mother has, in Lacan the father *is* the Phallus, making castration essential for the boy to become a signifying (and heterosexual) adult. In Lacanian terms, this "having" the Phallus (the father/masculine subject) is defined only by its lack in the Other (the mother/feminine object), who is the object of that subject's desire and who becomes that subject's signifier. In "being" the Phallus, this Other becomes the object of male heterosexual desire and reflects the power (and subsequently controls it) of the Phallus to establish the subject's reality. As Lacan writes in "The Meaning of the Phallus" cited earlier in chapter 2, "Let us say that these relations will revolve around a being and a having which, because they refer to a signifier, the phallus, have the contradictory effect of on the one hand lending reality to the subject of that signifier, and on the other making unreal the relations to the signified."[57] Women, then, must "be" what men "have," and "in being" define men through this lack.

Since language is the direct result of desire (the need to express what we feel is lacking in our lives after we realize that it is gone, such as oneness with the mother) and lack signifies the moment of language acquisition (the desired return to that center of oneness we left when we entered the symbolic order, when we became "I"), castration of the phallus paradoxically produces desire for the Phallus, for the Other. In terms of heterosexual identification, then, a man desires a woman because her lack is the mirror image of the phallus he wishes to recover: "Such is the woman concealed behind her veil: It is the absence of the penis that turns her into the phallus, the object of desire...."[58] Since what straight men desire most in women is that mirror image of their own phallus, gay men, in identifying with the mirrored Other's lack of a penis (which is the mother), desire to "be" the phallus that straight men want.[59]

If, however, that mirrored Other is already a man who, like the woman, lacks the phallus, then the self, which always desires to fill the lack in its Other, becomes the object of the Other's desire—in short, he will no longer "have" the phallus and instead "*be*" the phallus to compensate for the castration that created lack in the Other. For the narrator as a young boy, who encounters lack not only in the penisless Margaret but also in the equally penisless Brick, his *méconnaissance* of the Other as the *castrato* produces in him the desire to "be" that phallus for the male Other and not for the female Other. Therefore, in his desire to ensure Brick's *jouissance* by filling his lack created by Margaret's castration (the *real* Name-of-the-Father here in the narrator's gender-inverted world), the narrator summons all his signifying power to reinscribe Brick's phallus into the narrative, not only in the masculine signifiers of the sprinkling garden hose and the conspicuously hanging necktie, both symbols of the absent referent as is the sign of the signified, but in the retelling of Brick's story itself *through* the interplay of his and Brick's voice.[60] Because he acquired the phallus-as-signifier through his desire to fill the lack in Brick, when he normally should have desired to do so in his mother, the narrator interprets his developing voice later in life as having been the defining moment of his homosexual awakening.[61]

The innocence of his embarrassed response to Mary Louise's inquiry into the nature of his penis becomes homoerotic (though still very much latent for the boy) when the older narrator substitutes Brick for the Roman statue, since both are portraits of a "reclining male nude."[62] It is surely not coincidental either that the statue's title, *The Dying Gaul*, should be echoed in the narrator's final tableau of Brick, a dying Gaul himself figuratively being led in chains through Rome by a conquering Caesar Margaretus: "It was exactly the way that some ancient conqueror, such as Caesar or Alexander the Great or Hannibal, might have led in chains through a capital city the prince of a state newly conquered" (*CS* 343).[63] Therefore, the projection of his brief and uncomfortable public glimpse of the statue's nakedness onto the protracted private gaze years later of Brick's half-naked final battle before succumbing to his chains—first to those of the arresting police chief's handcuffs used for his drunken disorderly conduct (*CS* 335), then to Margaret's "two bands of gold, one small one about a finger, a large one about the wrist" (*CS* 342), complementary signifiers of acquiescence/dominance—demarcates the narrator's unconscious development from sexual curiosity to retrospective desire. In looking upon the one as a young boy, be it in fascination, in obsession, or even in curiosity, the older narrator is now figuratively looking upon the other, whom he describes as the "handsomest [man] you were likely to remember" (*CS* 342). With Margaret chauffeuring Brick around in the masculine Pierce Arrow, just as the narrator had been led by Mary Louise in the "ladylike electric" (*CS* 341) after they left the art museum, the transgendered signification is made complete.

This final detail points to "Three Players of a Summer Game" as being a story not only about Brick's crisis of masculinity but also about the narrator's transgenerational sexual identification, particularly given how Margaret and Mary Louise, though for clearly different reasons, psychologically castrate the two males in the story—one at a time when sexual identity *was* a social identity, and the other when it was just emerging. Like *Cat on a Hot Tin Roof*, then, "Three Players of a Summer Game" *is* about masculine signification and sexual awakening, but not in Brick alone, which is why the story has repeatedly troubled critics who wish to read it primarily as Ur-*Cat*. What *Cat on a Hot Tin Roof* appears to have evolved from, as Brenda Murphy has suggested, is the grafting of this nostalgic study of psychosexual development onto the turbulent history of Brick's marital problems vis-à-vis the absent Margaret, with the story's narrator emerging as the specter of homosexuality that haunts the margins of the play. Simply put, if *Cat*'s Brick does not entirely resemble the story's Brick, it is because he is as much a reincarnation of this sexually confused narrator as he is the story's drunken hero. Therefore, though neither wholly Jake nor the Brick of *Cat*, Brick in "Three Players" has certain elements of both and provides us with a clearer literary transition between the two characters, especially when we consider this Brick and the story's narrator to be an amalgamation not only of Williams's sexually existential hero but Hemingway's as well.

"A Dying *Gaule*": Impotence and (Homo)Sexual Identification

In their 1936 study *Sex and Personality*, Lewis Terman and Catherine Cox Miles introduced their famous "M-F" scale to help measure, through an inventory of 456 items, the degree of masculinity and femininity of its subjects, a test Michael Kimmel describes as "perhaps the single most widely used inventory to determine the successful acquisition of gender identification in history and was still being used in some school districts into the 1960s."[64] Engineered to identify physical, emotional, and psychological impotence in American boys and tomboyishness in American girls, the Terman-Miles "M-F test" equally weeded out its potential gender (and, by association, sexual) deviants, effectively banishing them to the sociosexual borders of heteronormative society lest they be taught how to perform their genders properly. Such a test, we have come to understand today, is more a byproduct of half a century's struggle to save the American male than it is an isolated example of post-flapper gender warfare.[65] It is surely not coincidental that Williams would note in his private journal of August 1936 that he believed he was "acquiring a little masculinity as I go along. I feel a good deal tougher and firmer in some ways than before . . ." (*NB* 46–47).

Twelve years later, America would encounter one of its first *queer* practitioners, predating by half a century those academics whose theoretical work has served the very real struggle to depoliticize gender and sexual identification, for in arguing against the polarizing of sexual identities that emerged from gender-biased institutions such as the national administering of the "M-F test," Alfred Kinsey had politicized not just the boundaries between sociosexual communities but also the epistemologies used to construct and police them. In his chapter "Early Sexual Growth and Activity," for instance, Kinsey describes how the homosexual play of preadolescent boys of ages ten to eleven frequently carries signs of later adult heterosexuality, thus rendering sexual profiling ineffective:

> On the whole, the homosexual child play is found in more histories, occurs more frequently, and becomes more specific than the pre-adolescent heterosexual play. This depends, as so much of the adult homosexual activity depends, on the greater accessibility of the boy's own sex. . . . In the younger boy, it is also fostered by his socially encouraged disdain for the girls' ways, by his admiration for masculine prowess, and by his desire to emulate older boys. The anatomy and functional capacities of male genitalia interest the younger boy to a degree that is not appreciated by older males who have become heterosexually conditioned and who are continuously on the defensive against reactions which might be interpreted as homosexual.[66]

Such behavior, Kinsey continues, does not lead to homosexuality; on the contrary, "In many cases, the later homosexuality stops with the adolescent years. . . ."[67] Yet, he concludes, "many of the adults who are actively and more or less exclusively homosexual date their activities from pre-adolescence."[68]

When Kinsey and his research team published *Sexual Behavior in the Human Male* in 1948, Tennessee Williams was already thirty-seven years old (he was forty when he began writing "Three Players" three years later, which could put him and the narrator at roughly the same age). While the extent to which Williams was familiar with the report remains conjecture, there is little doubt that he had at least dipped into its pages, perhaps even beyond the book's controversial twenty-first chapter on homosexuality. In a letter to Kinsey, dated January 18, 1950, Williams expressed his heartfelt gratitude for the zoologist's work, which even included an extensive study of the sexual histories of many of the cast members of *A Streetcar Named Desire:* "I am gratified by the attention you have given 'Streetcar' since I feel that your work, your research and its revelations to the ignorant and/or biased public, is of enormous social value. I hope that you will continue it and even extend its scope, for not the least desirable thing in this world is understanding, and sexual problems are especially in need of it" (*SL II* 286).

Later, in 1954, just four months after writing to Donald Windham about Kinsey (cited in the epigraph to this chapter) and during his stay in Rome where he was drafting what would become his intended third act for *Cat on a Hot Tin Roof*, Williams wrote to Cheryl Crawford: "Dr. Kinsey, after a four and a half hour talk in 1949 or 50, told me that I needed analysis and that he would recommend a good man for me. He seemed to realize that I was facing an eventual impasse, at which I am now arriving (*SL II* 535).[69] Again, though this does not reveal in any irrefutable way how closely Williams had read the report, it does show that Kinsey's study was on his mind when he was turning the story into the play.[70]

Given that the events of "Three Players of a Summer Game" take place in a town called Meridian, and one of its principle characters is named Grey, what else might Williams be implying if not precisely the Kinseyan notion that gender and sexual boundaries are social constructs and therefore susceptible to reconfiguration? Simply put, with Brick's alcoholism (and Jake's as well for Hemingway), Williams realistically limned the self-destructive existentialism that gender ideals have repeatedly bequeathed to American men cognizant of those ideals but incapable of attaining or sustaining them; with the narrator's sensitive reading of Brick's emasculation as reflecting his own as an influential boy, Williams sympathetically captured the quiet struggle certain American boys had in negotiating their sexuality with their masculinity—or lack of it. For this reason, Williams and the narrator draw the young boy in "Three Players"—not entirely unlike the fallen macho-hero Brick—as a counter-example to the protomasculine model forced upon them from birth since he lived on the border of something psychological and implicitly sexual, who is finally neither homoeffeminate nor heteromasculine simply because he existed between them, between society's *grey meridian* rules of gender and sexual identification.

In describing the problems reconstituted autobiography has with respect to developing sexuality, Judith Butler writes:

> The constitutive identifications of an autobiographical narrative are always partially fabricated in the telling. Lacan claims that we can never tell the story of our origins, precisely because language bars the speaking subject from the repressed libidinal origins of its speech; however, the foundational moment in which the paternal law institutes the subject seems to function as a metahistory which we not only can but ought to tell, even though the founding moment of the subject, the institution of the law, is equally prior to the speaking subject as the unconscious self. (*GT* 85)

While I do not wish to suggest here that Williams was consciously resorting to Kinseyan taxonomy (let alone Lacanian psycholinguistics) in portraying the narrator's struggle to signify what masculinity and heterosexuality ultimately meant for him as an adolescent boy, I do want to suggest that what the narrator recalls in his youthful experiences reflect both what Williams no doubt intuited while growing up and what Kinsey scientifically posited two decades later. Though Williams certainly did not need any scientific research to prove to him that he was homosexual, the study no doubt supported Williams's sense of his sexual identity at a time when social and political homophobia were reaching fever pitch levels.[71] That *The Dying Gaul* episode at the art museum should have a historical precedent in Williams's own life at a time when he too was discovering his sexuality perhaps only reinforces this supposition, for in his *Memoirs*, Williams admits that Mary Louise is based in part on Hazel Kramer,[72] who made him blush "like a maiden" when she asked him the same question Mary Louise asks the narrator (*M* 29).[73] Similar to Hemingway's linguistic fun with French, Williams's poignant inversion of the slang expression *"faire la gaule"* in the statue's title (that is, "having an erect penis," an expression Williams would have frequently heard during his stays in North Africa in the late 1940s) further intimates his own impotence vis-à-vis the heterosexual impulse that the question attempts to raise.

What Alfred Kinsey was to the science of sexology, then, Tennessee Williams (and Ernest Hemingway, evident in his posthumous works) was to its art, for both had struggled to denature a postwar-American heteronormality that had been fixed a generation earlier; but unlike Kinsey, Williams never affronted his society directly with stark figures and clinical charts showing precisely where its national "open secret"[74] was to be uncovered, which is why Williams's *New Yorker* readers could have understood the story's gender war and would have intuited Brick's crisis of masculinity presented therein, whereas only his gay readers would have recognized the narrator's sexual crisis. No doubt this double reading accounts for the fact that while "Three Players of a Summer Game" could have appeared in *New Yorker* and later included in the collection *Best American Stories of 1953*, more openly gay stories of the era, like "Two on a Party," which was written around the same time as "Three Players," could have only appeared in Williams's queer collection *Hard Candy*. Williams simply chose instead to sublimate Kinsey's numbers by portraying heteronormality as hetero*abnormality*.

4

"sneakin' an' spyin'" from Broadway to the Beltway: Cold War Masculinity, Brick, and Homosexual Existentialism

"*Macho:* male, masculine, abundantly endowed with male reproductive organs; *torero macho:* bullfighter whose work is on a basis of courage rather than perfected technique and style, although the style may come later. . . .

Maricón: a sodomite, nance, queen, fairy, fag, etc. They have these in Spain too, but I only know of two of them among the forty-some matadors de toros. This is no guaranty that those interested parties who are continually proving that Leonardo da Vinci, Shakespeare, etc., were fags would not be able to find more. Of the two, one is almost pathologically miserly, is lacking in valor but is very skillful and delicate with the cape, a sort of exterior decorator of bullfighting, and the other has a reputation for great valor and awkwardness and has been unable to save a peseta. In bullfighting circles the word is used as a term of opprobrium or ridicule or as an insult. There are many very, very funny Spanish fairy stories."
—Ernest Hemingway, *Death in the Afternoon*

"Read 'Death In the Afternoon' [*sic*] by Hemingway with ever increasing respect for it as a great piece of prose, and honest acknowledgment of a lust which is nearly always concealed. H's great quality, aside from his prose style, which is matchless, is this fearless expression of brute nature, his naively candid braggadocio [*sic*]. If he drew pictures of pricks, he could not more totally confess his innate sexual inversion, despite the probability that his relations have been exclusively (almost?) with women. He has no real interest in women and shows no true heterosexual eroticism in any of his work.
  (I don't think this is just the usual desire to implicate others in one's own 'vice'.)
  Hemingway calls El Greco, whom he greatly admires, 'El Rey de Maricones'—perhaps in literature H. deserves the same crown."
—Tennessee Williams, *Notebooks*

"The key to the recovery of masculinity lies . . . in the problem of identity. When a person begins to find out who he is, he is likely to find out rather soon what sex he is."
—Arthur Schlesinger, Jr., "The Crisis of American Masculinity"

4: "SNEAKIN' AN' SPYIN'" FROM BROADWAY TO THE BELTWAY

O<small>N</small> NOVEMBER 31, 1954, WHILE STRUGGLING TO SATISFY ELIA KAZAN'S demands for revisions to act 3 of *Cat on a Hot Tin Roof*, Williams sent his director the following letter wherein he declares not only his perception of Brick's homosexual latency but also his rationale for not revealing it to the audience at the play's end:

> Here's the conclusion I've come to. Brick *did* love Skipper, "the one great good thing in his life which was true". He identified Skipper with sports, the romantic world of adolescence which he couldn't go past. Further: to reverse my original (somewhat tentative) premise, I now believe that, in the deeper sense, not the literal sense, Brick *is* homosexual with a heterosexual adjustment: a thing I've suspected of several others, such as Brando, for instance. (He hasn't cracked up but I think he bears watching. He strikes me as being a compulsive eccentric). I think these people are often undersexed, prefer pet raccoons or sports or something to sex with either gender. They have deep attachments, idealistic, romantic: sublimated loves. . . . Their innocence, their blindness, makes them very, very touching, very beautiful and sad. . . . But if a mask is ripped off, suddenly, roughly, that's quite enough to blast the whole Mechanism, the whole adjustment, knock the world out from under their feet, and leave them no alternative but—owning up to the truth or retreat into something like liquor. . . .
>
> . . . In a way, this is progress for Brick. He's faced the truth, I think, under Big Daddy's pressure, and maybe the block is broken. I just said maybe. I don't really think so. I think that Brick is doomed by the falsities and cruel prejudices of the world he comes out of, belongs to, the world of Big Daddy and Big Mama. Sucking a dick or two or fucking a reasonable facsimile of Skipper some day won't solve it for him, if he ever does such "dirty things"! He's the living sacrifice, the victim, of the play, and I don't want to part with that "Tragic elegance" about him. You know, paralysis in a character can be just as significant and just as dramatic as progress, and is also less shop-worn. (*SL II* 555–58)[1]

Confessional letters are certainly more forthcoming than public declarations, so when Walter Kerr criticized Williams in his famous 1955 review of the Broadway debut of *Cat* for being "either less than clear or less than candid" in addressing Brick's homosexuality,[2] Williams defended himself and his choices in characterizing Brick immediately in an article for the *New York Herald Tribune:* "I know full well the defenses and rationalizations of beleaguered writers, a defensive species, but I still feel that I deal unsparingly with what I feel is the truth of character. I would never evade it for the sake of evasion, because I was in any way reluctant to reveal what I know of the truth" (*WIL* 76). Near the end of this rejoinder, Williams passionately defends his artistic stance, reasserting the need for Brick to remain *heterosexual* in the play: "Was Brick homosexual? He probably—no, I would even say quite certainly—went no further in physical expression than clasping Skipper's hand across the space between their twin beds in hotel rooms—and yet his sexual nature was not innately 'normal.' . . . But Brick's overt sexual adjustment was, and must always remain, a heterosexual one" (*WIL* 77–78).

Kerr, like Kazan before him, had undeniably touched a nerve, yet Williams remained steadfast to both in his decision not to "out" Brick. A few months later, in an interview for *Theatre Arts*, Williams would reiterate his theory to Arthur Waters:

> Brick is definitely not a homosexual. . . . Brick's self-pity and recourse to the bottle are not the result of a guilty conscience in that regard. When he speaks of "self-disgust," he is talking in the same vein as that which finds him complaining bitterly about having had to live so long with "mendacity." He feels that the collapse and premature death of his great friend Skipper, who never appears in the play, have been caused by unjust attacks against his moral character made by outsiders, including Margaret (Maggie), the wife. It is his bitterness at Skipper's tragedy that has caused Brick to turn against his wife and find solace in drink, rather than any personal involvement, although I do suggest that, at least at some time in his life, there have been unrealized abnormal tendencies.[3]

Worried perhaps that his message of artistic integrity would not reach posterity in such ephemeral sources, Williams added to the published version of *Cat* the now-notorious extended "bird" stage direction, which appears immediately after Big Daddy's initial intimation of Brick's latent homosexuality: *"The bird that I hope to catch in the net of this play is not the solution of one man's psychological problem. I'm trying to catch the true quality of experience in a group of people, that cloudy, flickering, evanescent—fiercely charged!—interplay of live human beings in the thundercloud of a common crisis. Some mystery should be left in the revelation of character in a play, just as a great deal of mystery is always left in the revelation of character in life, even in one's own character to himself"* (*C* 3:114–15).

Given the seemingly contradictory nature between Williams's letter to Kazan and his published declarations, is it valid to say that the post-*Cat* Williams is simply refuting in public what the pre-*Cat* Williams had expressed in private? If that is the case, can we find Williams guilty of dodging the crucial bullet that could have denied him critical and popular success with *Cat*, as Kerr and others have suggested?[4] Perhaps. Certainly, it was dangerous for Williams to write openly about homosexuality at a time when Congressional witch hunts of artists were daily fare, as David Savran and Steven Bruhm have competently informed us,[5] and honest treatments of homosexuality onstage were not the stuff of Pulitzer's,[6] an award Williams openly coveted. Perhaps what is equally plausible is that Williams found it more dramaturgically significant (if not also more politically subversive) to intentionally articulate the uncertainty of Brick's Cold War masculinity, the vagueness with which he, given the various contradictory rules and mores of his society, does or does not understand the limits of his male desire.

For instance, Brick developed from the story "Three Players of a Summer Game" and through the many drafts of the play, including *A Place of Stone*, as a psychologically-castrated alcoholic whose sexual identity itself, and no longer his masculinity alone, is now being challenged.[7] Perhaps he is now questioning his own sexual identity based on what others have informed him homosexuality meant in his day. That definition, largely challenged by the two Kinsey reports on male and female sexual tastes and habits (1948 and 1953) that documented a paradigm shift governing sexual identification in American since World War I, discerned a homosexual identity based on same-sex genital acts or, more problematically, perceivable gender sensibilities. Brick may drink to hide his doubts from everyone or to avoid contemplating their sexual taxonomies himself, either out of disgust for the world that has underwritten them, guilt in his role in choosing to sustain them with regards to Skipper, or fear that what his society and his family are intimating may in fact be true.

To be sure, any—or, more precisely, *all*—of these suppositions are valid and, as I will argue in this chapter, collectively essential to understanding the angst-ridden truth behind Brick's existence and the strength of Williams's play. For at the heart of Brick's reticence to *name* his relationship with Skipper is his inability to understand *what* homosexuality is or how it is precisely defined or even vaguely *knowable*, an epistemological mire for which Williams holds his Cold War society ultimately responsible. My point here is not to determine whether or not Williams knew if Brick was gay (I do not think he did, since his vision of the play, and of Brick, kept developing over the years that separated the story's drafting in 1951 to the play's final revisions in 1974),[8] but to argue that the question itself has more significance than its answer, given our own needs throughout the years to finally *know* Brick's "truth."

Choice—Angst-ridden existence—Epistemology—the Cold War—Responsibility

Any faithful discussion of *Cat* within its contextualized 1950s must reckon with some combination of these words and with the two sources upon which they collectively converge: existentialism and Jean-Paul Sartre. While Kierkegaard's doctrine of the individual's existence with respect to his or her a priori essence had emerged more fully in the dialectical theories of Heidegger, Marcel, and Jaspers in the inter-war years, it was through Sartre that the American intelligentsia would mostly acquire its postwar knowledge of and taste for existential thought. At first only an admirer of Sartre (he had wanted to meet Sartre while visiting Paris in August 1948,[9] and eventually did meet him in October 1960 at the Hotel Nacional in Havana with Marion Vaccaro)[10] and of Sartrean existentialism, Williams would later count himself briefly among its many American practitioners.

For in his 1950 introduction to Carson McCullers's *Reflections in a Golden Eye,* Williams wrote of the undeniable link between Sartre's existentialism and his Southern Gothic's "sense" or "intuition" of the "underlying dreadfulness in modern experience" (*WIL* 49), noting that while "the motor impulse of the French school is intellectual and philosophic," that of his American school "is more of an emotional and romantic nature" (*WIL* 49).[11] Intellectual or emotional, Williams's existentialism in *Cat* has undeniable Sartrean roots,[12] inevitably refracted through the American prism of Cold War identity politics.[13]

Williams and Marion Vaccaro with Jean-Paul Sartre and Simone de Beauvoir at the Hotel Nacional in Havana, October, 1960. Courtesy of the Richard Leavitt Collection, Special Collections Library, University of Tennessee.

As noted in chapter 2, Sartre's *Being and Nothingness* theorizes how we are born devoid of any known or knowable essence to our lives, be it a preordained or objective signification, and must supply ourselves with that essence or meaning to our existence in order to define our individuality and thus abate those fears that would consume us. A pre-discursive power exists within us to help determine the self, but this is not in itself an innate essence; rather, it is more like an instinctive physical drive (one could say even sexual) that pushes us daily to chose to act upon our conscious thoughts and thereby give meaning to our daily existence. For Sartre, to choose not to act, or to remain passive to others' actions working upon us, is to give in to nothingness, to live an inauthentic life, to commit what he calls "bad faith." As Sartre writes, "I am passive when I undergo a modification of which I am not the origin; that is, neither the source nor the creator. Thus my being supports a mode of being of which it is not the source. Yet in order for me to support, it is still necessary that I exist, and due to this fact my existence is always situated on the other side of passivity" (*BN* 19). Only through action (if even in a determined passive opposition) is the self defined.

Existentialism, then, implies the concerted efforts of conscious man to assert himself in spite of all the external social forces working to identify him (be it Kierkegaard's corporate Christianity, Jaspers's *masse-Mensche* of technological conformity, de Beauvoir's collected ethics, or Sartre's *en-soi*). While the existent's essence (literally his past experiences as he lives them, which constitute the sum of his existence) is heavily formulated by the nothingness imposed upon it by the Other, it is ultimately the individual's responsibility to preserve his integrity by making honest choices with respect to those external forces. Already, in spite of the metaphysical complexities, it is relatively easy to understand the particular anxiety that permeates *Cat* and renders Brick impotent—physically, spiritually, and morally—in Sartrean terms.[14] Freely choosing abstinence, silence, and alcohol as active means to counter the gross attempts of his anxious wife, his prying father, and his pragmatic brother to package him materially as the wayward stud, the prodigal son, or the effete drunkard—all indirect epithets of his homosexuality—Brick becomes the archetypal existentialist hero.[15] Once he recognizes his own participation in Skipper's death in like manner, Brick becomes the modern nihilist. The basic question that remains is whether Brick's actions and *in*actions vis-à-vis his family, his best friend, and himself constitute bad faith or not.[16]

Brick, it must first be acknowledged, is honest, even priding himself on having never lied to his father (*C* 3:111) nor to Maggie, which nothing in the play can contradict. It is, for instance, Brick who does not "want to fool" (*C* 3:35) Big Daddy into thinking that it was he, and not Maggie, who bought him his birthday present, just as it is only Brick who finally reveals to Big Daddy that he is dying (*C* 3:128–29) or responds to Skipper's confession of love for him with blatant disgust. Though unquestionably hard and selfish, each act is honest and contrasts sharply with the sugar-coated lies (white or otherwise) that the rest of the family exchange as currency, and that Big Daddy, Brick, and undoubtedly Williams so detest. Similarly, Brick never lies to or for Maggie, supported by his ironic curtain-line in the original ending of act 3 and by his refusal to uphold her declaration of pregnancy to the Pollitt family (which also proves how Brick could not, in any real truth of the play, go back to her in the end, which he does in both the Broadway and film versions). His integrity toward the truth (for the moment, the Others' truths), then, helps Williams to establish Brick's authentic existence.

So, when questions of authentic existence (internal and external to the play) readily give rise to veiled accusations of a homosexual identity, both Brick and Williams are pressured to fess up. That both should respond to these charges in existential terms is equally telling of their *situation* with respect to the truth, not only in their all-too-real need to protect their respective privileged social stations from exclusionary homophobia but also, and more fundamentally, in their epistemological plight to negotiate what they know of the truth with what society informs them it is. Admittedly, Brick shies away from addressing the latency of his relationship with Skipper, which for many in (and outside of) the play is proof of it by omission (in Sartrean terms, committing bad faith):

> *Big Daddy.* Who's been lying to you, and what about?
> *Brick.* No one single person and no one lie. . . .
> *Big Daddy.* Then what, what then, for Christ's sake?
> *Brick.* —The whole, the whole—thing. . . . (*C* 3:107)

Yet, beyond the generality of his words and the suppositions they may entertain, we are given no single piece of conclusive evidence in the play that can isolate why Brick drinks or why he never names his disgust outside the term "mendacity." Given Brick's honesty in the play and his inability to articulate (let alone comprehend) complex problems, need we unconditionally read his reticence toward the provocative evidence leveled against him by Maggie, Big Daddy, and Gooper as a wholesale lie? Could it not also be that perhaps it is precisely this "evidence"— socially manufactured as it is through innuendo, hearsay, and imagination—that might be lying or at least promoting confusion in Brick since it counters his empirical knowledge of homosexuality? For in the play's final tally, it is surely only Brick who is incapable of lying, whereas all those responsible for the manufacturing of his gay identity repeatedly demonstrate through their manipulation of Brick's truth that they have much to gain or lose in the balance.

Similarly, Williams's language in the "bird" stage direction explaining Brick's "mystery" also seems more to be hiding behind Sartrean existentialism than it does evoking it. Like his hero, Williams too appears to be guilty of bad faith in his intentionally obfuscated reply to questions concerning Brick's homosexuality. And yet, Williams had indirectly provided an "earlier version" of this stage direction in his McCullers's introduction, long before the controversy surrounding Brick's "mystery" ever began raising doubts about Williams's artistic integrity, as it had done Henry James's and Jake Barnes's sexual dysfunction for Hemingway. The explanation to his Southern Gothic school's fascination with the "Sense of Dreadfulness" (one which Williams later echoes in his *Memoirs* to capture the "mystery" of his own life)[17] resembles more closely the existential angst just explored in Brick and thus makes Williams's "bird" comment sound more authentic:

> All of these things that you list as dreadful are parts of the visible, sensible phenomena of every man's experience or knowledge, but the true sense of dread is not a reaction to anything sensible or visible or even, strictly, materially, *knowable*. But rather it's a kind of spiritual intuition of something almost too incredible and shocking to talk about, which underlies the whole so-called thing. It is the uncommunicable [*sic*] something that we shall have to call *mystery* which is so inspiring of dread among these modern artists that we have been talking about. . . . (*WIL* 50–51, Williams's emphasis and ellipses)

In Sartrean terms, this anxiety of the incommunicable sublime, the nothingness that feeds the *pour-soi*'s epistemological encounters with the Other, results from repeated attempts to discern the self's truth from the Others' convincing lies, a necessary distinction if one is to stave off bad faith and live life authentically.

Surely, if Brick were more philosophic than dogmatic, he would have reasoned something like this in response to Maggie's and Big Daddy's inquiries into the source of his alcoholism. But his inability either to articulate to others why he feels so disgusted with everyone and everything, or to assimilate for himself this "experience or knowledge," results more from his lack of critical self-distancing from the truth than it does from his affected staging of it. Williams is simply resorting to the basic tenets and vocabulary of existentialism to explain Brick's dilemma. However, if Brick (and Williams, by extension) has little else to specify the nature of his angst and is not shrouding it in "mystery," the burning question still remains: *What did Brick know?* Pure existentialist readings of the play are hampered, then, not just because they are stymied by the lack of certain knowledge but more because it is impossible for readers/audiences to penetrate Brick's mind and to know for certain what lies behind the spoken and unspoken. As such, it is difficult for them to imagine how Brick could *not know* if he were gay or not (thus inherently lying behind his "mendacity") or how Williams could contend truthfully that such basic knowledge of sexual identity in Brick ever posed an epistemological dilemma in the first place (thus disingenuously posturing behind his "mystery"). Their doubts, to be sure, are just.[18]

We should remember, however, that even *Being and Nothingness*, like *A Sun Also Rises*, was not written in a political vacuum. Influenced to a great extent by the spread of Nazi collaborators in France and shaped by Sartre's eventual incarceration in 1941 for his role in the Resistance, the essay's self-as-activist credo flirts openly with nationalist sedition against the Occupation. The extent to which Williams fully understood this fact, or French existentialism as a theory in general, is contentious, but there is no doubt that he admired its general tenets as well as Sartre's ardent political commitment. In a 1953 letter to *New York Times* theater critic J. Brooks Atkinson, Williams writes,

> But I catch flashes of a "tortured sensibility" in the best of Sartre. I don't mind a work being dark if it is rooted in compassion. In a notebook I once copied the following bit from Sartre's "Age of Reason":—"Various wellbred moralities had already discreetly offered him their services: disillusioned epicureanism, smiling intolerance, resignation, common sense, stoicism—all the aids whereby a man may savor, minute by minute, like a connoisseur, the failure of a life."—The sadness in this reflection is a genuine thing, truthful and therefore moving. Of course there must be more comfort in his existence than in his "existentialism" or he couldn't endure it, I agree with you about that. I'm sure he is comforted by the esteem of his followers, for instance, and by the excellent French wines and restaurants and the civilized freedom of thought that still prevails and is the great tradition in his country. (*SL II* 487)

If nothing more, Williams at least understood the Sartrean tenet of existence before essence as well as the human difficulties in respecting it throughout one's life.

From all of this, we should also recognize that *Cat*'s existentialism can—and should—be studied as a product of its own incendiary times. If we read the play precisely as an epistemological inquiry into the politics that governed Cold War identities, then what we discover is an existentially honest Brick, whose *situation* fails to sustain in him the nothingness he needs to determine the truth, and a dramatically honest Williams, whose locating of those external forces at work on Brick may begin with Maggie, Big Daddy, and Gooper but, and perhaps more importantly, ends with implicating *everyone* who makes up Brick's society, including Williams's 1955 audience and reader. As real questions of identity pass from the metaphysical to the political, as they certainly did for many a gay man in the hyperhomophobic 1950s, purely theoretical concepts like bad faith seem arbitrary and even dangerous. In Cold War terms, Williams expresses existentialism in *Cat* not in phenomenological but rather in sociopolitical terms, where Brick's "moral paralysis" (*C* 3:168) results not from his failure to act but rather from his failure to know *how* to act in sexual and masculine terms befitting his evolving sense of self. Despite the "open secret" of his own homosexuality during the 1950s with Frank Merlo, Williams clearly understood Sartre's Other in America as the powerful entities of government, commerce, and Hollywood, whose job it was precisely to manufacture "normality."

Robert J. Corber and Suzanne Clark, for example, explore the problems of sexual identity responsible not only for the resultant hypermasculinity that infused Cold War discourse, but also a nation's sexual self-destruction, captured to some extent by Arthur M. Schlesinger, Jr.'s 1958 essay "The Crisis of American Masculinity" and *Look* magazine's 1958 series on "The Decline of the American Male."[19] To counter the effects of this post-World War II challenge to American masculinity, political men consciously resorted to poignant heterosexist language or affected masculine sensibilities, both of which helped to project a strong national image abroad as much as it did stave off sexual suspicion at home. As Corber and Clark separately argue, the American male was effectively on trial to prove that he had the muster to earn the respect of a nation built on the myth of the cowboy warrior, and *Cat* in particular was an "examination of the closet" as being part of a "larger critique of postwar structures of oppression."[20] At a time when identity was essentially what *others* considered it to be, regardless of the truth about where one's political or sexual sympathies lay, American men had to perform their masculinity or effectuate it by ridiculing the effeminacy in others.

When Roosevelt's New Deal and later Truman's "Fair Deal" agendas were simply brandished Democratic versions of the bull-moose Progressivism that ushered in socialist ideologies and left-leaning proactivism, it was not difficult for the conservative pundits of the 1950s to carve out their needed masculine niche after the war. The quickest strike American men could launch was against the left, the visible agent of an anti-masculinity that had held sway during the era of the New Deal preceding World War II.[21] American men found the only way to protect and preserve their masculinity still left them was to push effeminate men further and further to the borders of a gendered identity. The collective "left" became that man. Or, in Geoffrey Smith's wry words, "On the colour spectrum, it is but a short jump from pink to red to lavender, and in the early 1950s the distance became even shorter."[22] With the specter of communism now firmly entrenched in postwar discourse, Cold War demagogues had little else to do than simply reawake the sleeping bugbear that had haunted a nation earlier in the century, which had then also carried with it an effeminate challenge to masculinity. Homosexuality, then, was simply grafted onto this leftist/communist specter since it too was in many ways considered its equal—morally corrupt, suspiciously invisible, politically dispersed, and femininely corrosive to the male fiber of the patriarchal society.

To effectuate this communist-cum-queer erosion of postwar American masculinity, politically "right" men consciously resorted to heterosexist language or affected masculine sensibilities, both of which helped to project a strong national image abroad as much as it did to stave off any sexual suspicion at home. Just as some men named names or draped themselves in the American flag in order to project this image and thus avert communist suspicion that inextricably accompanied the effete male, others resorted to more proactive sexual politics: privileging the "inflated manly bravado, the hard/soft dualisms, the excessive scorn for the feminine, and the language of perversion and penetration in so much political discourse of the early Cold War era" in order to separate and ostracize unAmerican (i.e., unmanly) men from the "healthy," heteromasculine stock.[23] By having assigned alleged communist sympathizers and their fellow travelers effeminate characteristics in contrast with their more "masculine" ones, these voices of national identity—from Washington (such as George F. Kennan and J. Edgar Hoover, to say nothing of Nixon and McCarthy) to Hollywood (including, though certainly not limited to, those men like John Wayne speaking through such popular films as *The Red Menace* [1949] and *Big Jim McLain* [1952])—effectively controlled identity politics for more than a decade. Their message was loud and clear: the only *true* American male was, in Clark's terms, the "hyper-male," the Cold Warrior: "reasonable, penetrating, vigorous, and healthy."[24]

Every political action generates a critical reaction, and Cold War America was not without its doves, though they were arguably more vocal in American bookstores and theaters than in the Capitol's rotunda. John Proctor, Tom Lee, Bo Decker and Virgil Blessing, Kilroy and Val Xavier onstage, and Matthew Garth (Montgomery Clift),

Terry Malloy (Marlon Brando), and Jim Stark (James Dean) onscreen reflected the liberal's vision of the masculine male whose softness deliberately countered Washington's hard-line gender propaganda (with these last three film stars successfully sporting the cowboy-warrior image while playing characters nonetheless thoughtful and sensitive). They were not entirely like the heterosexually troubled protagonists Bob Ford and David in Gore Vidal's and James Baldwin's openly homosexual novels, *The City and the Pillar* (1948) and *Giovanni's Room* (1956). But, then again, plays and films are plastic arts motivated by money, and Williams clearly recognized that these two fictional characters were not feasible models for Brick on the Broadway stage.[25]

Choked daily with images of these two diametrically opposed realities of proper manly thought and conduct, repeatedly underscored in the popular and literary fiction of the day,[26] what was the average white American male to think or do? The question, Clark posits, "plunged American men into a confusion about identities that literature as well as mass culture struggled to address."[27] Fears of homosexuality, then, just like those of communism fueled by HUAC, did not emerge in a vacuum and thus cannot be claimed as having sole claim to what has repeatedly been labeled "the crisis of American masculinity" in the twentieth century. Recent critical studies have competently informed us how both, in fact, appeared simultaneously as inevitable products of a fin de siècle post-industrial push to usher in colonialization, which had loosened the Monroe Doctrine's grip on demarcated American borders and consequently toyed with once-uniformly masculine national mores, including those governing commercial, political, and gender roles.[28]

With a political discourse delineating hard from soft, penetrating from penetrated, and a national conscience reflecting its uneasy mélange, many American men like Brick who did not know with which to identify often found themselves trapped in what Richard Vowles pertinently calls "that shadowy no-man's land between hetero- and homosexuality."[29] Publicly, Brick is the archetype of heteromasculine America with his good looks, his strong athletic build, and his fawning wife cheering him on from the sidelines as he scores the winning touchdown in the championship bowl game. Privately, he is its anathema with his suspiciously intense relationship with his best friend Skipper, his refusal to sleep with the seductive Maggie, and his emasculating alcoholism that has resulted from one or the other, or both. Even in the early drafts of the play, as Jeffrey Loomis notes, Brick is "a demoralized, existentially dread-ridden gloomster not very prepared to make quick alterations in his behavior, whatever the quickening motivation might be."[30] Caught in this archetypal Sartrean struggle between authentic self-actualization and inauthentic bad faith, Brick freely chooses the bottle, an act which simultaneously diverts thoughts of social responsibility in Skipper's death as well as sexual responsibility toward his agitated wife. Like other existentialist heroes in the 1950s, then, Brick struggles to *authenticate* his existence by denying all external efforts to assert its essence; however, unlike those other heroes, the origins of Brick's epistemological disgust are fused with questions surrounding his sexual orientation, making his form of existentialism sexual in nature and inevitably entwined with the externalized forces at work on him internally as well.

BECOMING A WOMAN: MAGGIE, MAE AND THE SEXUAL OTHER

In *The Second Sex* (*Le Deuxième sexe*, 1949), Simone de Beauvoir, Sartre's significant/intellectual other, applies Sartrean existentialism to define the existence/essence dualism of modernist woman, whose own a priori lack of female selfhood is further compounded by the fact that feminine essence is singularly imposed upon a woman from forces outside her body. This is the essential meaning behind her now famous phrase, "One is not born, but rather becomes, a woman."[31] In the introduction, for example, she notes that her "perspective is that of existentialist ethics," almost singularly Sartre's:

> Every subject plays his part as such specifically through exploits or projects that serve as a mode of transcendence; he achieves liberty only through a continual reaching out towards other liberties. . . . Every time transcendence falls back into immanence, stagnation, there is a degradation of existence into the *"en-soi"* . . . and of liberty into constraint and contingence. This downfall represents a moral fault if the subject consents to it; if it is inflicted upon him, it spells frustration and oppression. In both cases it is an absolute evil. (*SS* 28)

Yet, because she implicates human nature in sexual terms (a woman and not a man), whereas Sartre had argued strictly in asexual terms of "being" (again, though, understood by many to be masculine), she cannot avoid the "passive" existence that Sartre had argued is "truly unthinkable" (*BN* 16). By asserting that "the sexual role of woman is largely passive" (*SS* 419) and still arguing for woman's independently formed essence, de Beauvoir paradoxically challenges Sartre's existentialism *and* remains loyal to it.

To be sure, since precisely "men compel her to assume the status of the Other," woman is forever doomed to transitiveness and thus prohibited from ever transcending to "another ego (consciousness) which is essential and sovereign" (*SS* 29) — in effect, being only the sexual equivalent of Sartre's *pour-autrui*. For this reason, de Beauvoir writes, "Woman is not a completed reality, but rather a becoming, and it is in her becoming that she should be compared with man; that is to say, her *possibilities* should be defined" (*SS* 66). Therefore, the "drama of women lies in this conflict between the fundamental aspirations of subject (ego)—who always regards the self as essential—and the compulsions of a *situation* in which she is inessential" (*SS* 29, my emphasis). As it is "civilization as a whole that produces this creature" (*SS* 295), de Beauvoir can no longer adhere strictly to pure existential thought; woman's social position vis-à-vis man simply lacks the freedom that Sartre maintains is essentially coextensive with human existence. Though she retains faith in the individual's free choice to act responsibly in establishing her essence, de Beauvoir cannot entirely exclude—as Sartre had effectively done in his metaphysics—the practical exchange of identity-forming values consistent with social constructionism. If Sartre's *pour-soi* sees the Other only as a means towards self-actualization, de Beauvoir's second sex sees the Other *as self* and thus cannot pretend that self-actualization is an inherent privilege of humanity. The existent is a sexual being, and sexuality inevitably plays a role in establishing that essence.

As Sartre had already acknowledged, "the proposition 'Sexuality is co-extensive with existence' can be understood in two very different ways; it can mean that every experience of the existent has a sexual significance, or that every sexual phenomenon has an existential import" (*SS* 70). Yet sexuality for Sartre remains ancillary to the existent's transcendence. De Beauvoir, however, cannot but privilege this sexuality since woman-as-Other's transcendence depends upon her interaction with her own Other: "The existent is sexual, a sexual body, and in his relations with other existents who are also sexual bodies, sexuality is in consequence always involved. But if body and sexuality are concrete expressions of existence, it is with reference to this that their significance can be discovered" (*SS* 77). Be it another woman or a man, her Other is inescapably sexually signified, and for that reason the "body" becomes "not a *thing*" but "a situation" (*SS* 66), again in the Sartrean sense of the word. By emphasizing sexuality in the construction of an existential identity, de Beauvoir fills the gap of modernist theory that held Sartre and his purely suprarational definition of human ontology at polarities with those of Freud or Alfred Adler (who had articulated that development in social terms passed strictly through biological ones). Though more self-defined than self-defining, de Beauvoir's woman still "has the power to choose between the assertion of her transcendence and her alienation as object" (*SS* 82), and this is how de Beauvoir finally returns to Sartre's existentialism. Even if "in sexuality and maternity woman as subject can claim autonomy," to be "a 'true woman' she must accept herself as the Other" (*SS* 291), placing her at direct odds with her own sexuality.

Already we have moved out of the pure notion of human definition in Sartrean existentialism and into the role sexuality and society play in a woman's sense of autonomous self in passive relation to a man. De Beauvoir takes the next logical step by looking at how sexuality specifically contributes to that defining matrix, studying homosexuality (in women exclusively here) as a natural/cultural phenomenon that further complicates the ordering of an individual's existential *situation*.[32] "Sexologists and psychiatrists," she writes, "confirm the common observation that the majority of female 'homos' are in constitution quite like other women. Their sexuality is in no way determined by any anatomical 'fate'" (*SS* 424). Loyal again both to Sartrean tenets of an individual's complete freedom to choose and to her own claim that woman is essentially an agent of an existent's transcendence, de Beauvoir explains homosexuality as a choice but one motivated by external forces: "Woman's homosexuality is one attempt among others to reconcile her autonomy with the passivity of her flesh. And if nature is to be involved, one can say that all women are naturally homosexual" (*SS* 426–27). Consequently, sexuality both objectifies and *subjectifies* an existent, acting simultaneously as the *pour-soi* and the *pour-autrui*. As such, she concludes, we need to be wary of "the many ambiguities the psychoanalysts create by accepting the masculine-feminine categories as society currently defines them": "The truth is that man today represents the positive and the neutral—that is to say, the male and the human being—whereas woman is only the negative, the female" (*SS* 428).

If Brick in many ways incarnates the Sartrean existential hero, Maggie certainly appears to be de Beauvoir's second sex, a being whose signifying femininity is constructed through her negative relation with her two defining Others: Brick and Mae. As Brick's wife, she is Margaret Pollitt, the sexual Other who defines him as heteromasculine patriarch but whose "passivity of [the] flesh" equally depends upon him for self-definition. In the play, for example, Maggie would cease to exist (socially and sexually speaking) were it not for Brick: he is her meal ticket (and she knows it) and her defining sexuality since she is existentially bound to him only through her desire. As Mae's sister-in-law, she is Maggie the Cat, the Other's Other equally seeking to justify her existence through opposition with Mae despite the fact that she and Mae are pursuing like identities—mistress of the plantation. To secure her place in this world, Maggie must maintain both transitive identities. To fail as Brick's wife would mean losing not only the plantation but her need for reciprocated desire as well, something she attempts without success to relocate in other men (such as Big Daddy's "lech" [*C* 3:23] for her). To fail as Mae's rival for Big Daddy's estate would mean losing not only her title as Big Mama's heir-apparent but also her feminine essence since her sexuality would not have served her in her defining *situation*. To be sure, Brick and Mae are everything Maggie detests but have everything Maggie wants; and Maggie recognizes that, in the heteromasculine economy of the Pollitt family, a child is what will ultimately secure that identity on both fronts.

Fertility is, to be sure, *the* leitmotif of the play, running "neck and neck" with sterility as Reverend Tooker's Stork does with the Reaper (*C* 3:72). If, with her five "no-neck monsters" (and number six on the way), Mae is a "monster of fertility" (*C* 3:22), to whom Big Daddy says he will have her "bones pulverized for fertilizer!" (*C* 3:72), then Maggie, "jealous [she] can't have babies" (*C* 3:61), is the childless Diana/Artemis who mythically killed the boastful Niobe's six daughters, just as Maggie says she would like to do to Mae's children. So too does Williams instill fertility in men to contrast the play's theme of sterility. The macho Big Daddy *seeded* the plantation left fallow by Straw and Ochello so that it "got bigger and bigger and bigger and bigger and bigger!" (*C* 3:77) until it became, like Mae herself, the most fertile in the Delta. Later, the effete Gooper carries a "pregnant-lookin' envelope" (*C* 3:204), which contains papers that he hopes will secure the fertile plantation for himself. Both expressions of male fertility prove ineffectual, however, since Big Daddy's plantation will not flourish under Brick's reign and the contents of Gooper's envelope remain unexamined.[33]

Thus, when Maggie returns from Memphis where her gynecologist informed her that "there is no reason why" she and Brick "can't have a child whenever they want one" (*C* 3:62), she seizes the opportunity to assert her Othered identity by using sexuality to realize a maternal essence. Literally ovulating at the moment and informing Brick that "this is my time by the calendar to conceive" (*C* 3:164), Maggie only needs now to coax Brick back into bed to impregnate her, which he unconditionally rejects. And therein lies her sexual existentialism: as passive existent to Brick's nihilist inaction, Maggie is forever denied the means to fulfill her own essence.

In an early draft of the ending to *Cat*—one which directly follows the draft Williams had entitled "*Cat* number one"[34] in which he established Brick's ironic rejoinder, "Wouldn't it be funny if that was true?," as the play's desired curtain-line—Williams even toyed with the idea of explaining Brick's sexual dysfunction as the result of his impotence (though the reasons behind that impotence still remain obscure).[35] After Maggie asks Brick where he wants his pillow for the night, on the sofa or on the bed, Brick responds: "Turn out the light, Maggie. . . . I might be impotent."[36] Jeffrey Loomis points out that, as late as December 9, 1954, Williams was still making changes in the play to "help signify that Brick retained some heterosexual tendencies."[37] That impotence, along with the ironic ending established prior to it, alert Maggie to the truth that her desired essence will require more than a little seduction. It also demonstrates that Hemingway's Jake Barnes may well have been on Williams's mind while drafting the play's ending.

All problems are seemingly rendered moot, however, when Maggie announces to Big Mama in front of the family the she and Brick "are going to—*have a child*" (*C* 3:158). Though her pregnancy seemingly confirms that essence, Maggie's declaration could eventually impede her long-term efforts toward self-actualization. For while Maggie's ingenious lie successfully assuages the anxiety produced by her sexual existentialism in that it confirms her maternal femininity (defining her as Earth Mother and besting Mae's Sister Woman), assures the family of Brick's heterosexual potency, and potentially secures her the family fortune, it also draws Brick out of his insular world and forces him into asserting an identity that potentially could undermine the one Maggie has conveniently established for him. In other words, because her declaration is a truth that will soon be borne out (or not, as the case might very well be), it reignites an existential crisis in Brick, but one that moves beyond earlier questions of heteronormality and now towards those of homosexuality.

Acting a "Man": Brick and the Kinsey Report

While de Beauvoir had effectively spoken for and to the women of her generation and of those which followed, her theories of sexual existentialism generated one obvious drawback. In working out her positive/negative binary of male and female identities, she made men existentially and sexually inclusive. Around the same time that de Beauvoir was penning her feminist manifesto, Alfred Kinsey was proving that American men did not in fact constitute such a binary (even in purely theoretical terms), and as such any universalizing sense of maleness was effectively self-defeating. In its attempt to provide a scientific taxonomy of American male sexuality, Kinsey's popular 1948 study, *Sexual Behavior in the Human Male* (which, despite its own delusions of inclusiveness, was only about the sexual behaviors of white, American males, from young boys to old men), inadvertently supplied clinical evidence that demonstrated what de Beauvoir's book had established about women could also be applied to men, namely that man-as-Other not only existed but was omnipresent and fluid.[38]

Kinsey's study may have done more to damage the psyche of Cold War heteromasculinity than it did to transfigure it. For, among the surprisingly eclectic sexual habits Kinsey documents that effectively reaffirmed the hegemonic control heteromasculinity had in America, one equally served to deconstruct it: the homosexual outlet. In the study's controversial twenty-first chapter, Kinsey records how almost forty percent of the total male population he and his colleagues had interviewed admitted to having had "at least some overt homosexual experience to the point of orgasm," though only four percent identified themselves as exclusively homosexual.[39] Accounting for "nearly 2 males out of every 5 that one may meet,"[40] the frequency of homosexual activity in America led Kinsey to conclude that "a considerable portion of the population, perhaps the *major portion* of the male population, has at least some homosexual experience between adolescence and old age" without ever considering itself as being homosexual.[41] By the chapter's end, Kinsey had not only portrayed *heterosexual* America as the problematic source of identity politics, but he had also singularly dismantled the hetero/homosexual continuum fashioned in Victorian America that had controlled those politics for more than a half-century.[42]

The question Kinsey's report quickly generated, then, was not *who* was homosexual but *what* constituted homosexuality and, by extension, heterosexuality. By arguing against polarized sexual identities, Kinsey had effectively blurred not just the boundaries established between sociosexual communities but also the political, economic, and legal precepts that had underwritten them: "It would encourage clearer thinking on these matters if persons were not characterized as heterosexual or homosexual, but as individuals who have had certain amounts of heterosexual experience and certain amounts of homosexual experience. Instead of using these terms as substantives which stand for persons, or even as adjectives to describe persons, they may be better used to describe the nature of the overt sexual relations, or of the stimuli to which an individual erotically responds."[43] Cold War heteromasculinity had been dealt a significant blow, and even more than before the War, American men and boys grew "confused about what they should and should not do to fulfill their masculine roles."[44] Left bewildered, defensive, and paranoid over the uncertainties governing traditional definitions of sexual identification, heteromasculine American men began demanding proof of heterosexuality, as much for themselves as for those who were (given these politically-charged times) inevitably to judge them.

What any astute gay man like Williams in the hyper-homophobic 1950s would have learned from Kinsey's study was that his sexual habits had confirmed a psychological abnormality no more than it had constituted a social anomaly.⁴⁵ What the average heterosexual man would have learned was in many ways what Brick reveals in *Cat on a Hot Tin Roof*: that straight America had disingenuously been reared into privileging certain signs of a homosexual identity, all the while destabilizing those signs through its own acts of male-male desire writ large.⁴⁶ To be sure, Kinsey publicly assured the gay community that they were not perverted or isolated, privately persuaded some closeted homosexuals to emerge and join the body politic, openly alarmed a bigoted and conservative community of the prevalent "feminizing" of the American male, and thoroughly confused heterosexual society, male and female alike, as to what caused, shaped, or even defined homosexuality. Thus, if Sartre's existentialism informed certain American men like Brick that their identities were solely of their own making (with the implication being that socially-formed identities were to be combated), and de Beauvoir's sexual existentialism insisted upon the fact that certain social imperatives could not be excluded from their identity, then Kinsey's homosexual existentialism popularized the de facto ruling that one's social and sexual identities were inextricably bound, both for the existent's sense of essence as well as for his Other's sense of that essence.

In expressing mutual appetites for male exclusivity and masculinist iconology but lacking the performative heterosexuality to anchor them, Brick is a Kinseyan male through and through—a sociosexual conundrum, a Cold War signifier without a signified.⁴⁷ On the surface, he represents what a significant portion of (white) American men of his era had aspired to be; underneath, he is perhaps more like them than either would have ever wanted to acknowledge or admit. A "prisoner of conventions and of the *image* of virility American society has imposed upon him," as Georges-Michel Sarotte writes,⁴⁸ Brick was simply for Williams—always the consummate Broadway playwright who knew well the politics setting commercialism against artistic integrity and who repeatedly portrayed this Cold War identity crisis throughout the 1950s—his best literary expression of this emerging *queer* heteromasculine male in America.⁴⁹

Though he is no longer of an age of sexual awakening, Brick is certainly of an age of social definitioning based on sexual conditioning. As such, Brick is now sensitive to the social implications of his and Skipper's relationship, but he was not always aware of them, and that is where his troubles first began. When Skipper was alive, for example, Brick treated their friendship as he had when they were younger, which significantly removes from it any stigma of harbored or conscious desire, regardless of how it was externally perceived at the time. While in college, he and Skipper belonged to a fraternity and played football together; given their youth and participation in a socially-sanctioned, all-male milieu, society did not challenge them. No one—Brick and Skipper especially—would have suspected that there was an ulterior motive to their friendship other than its youthful male-bonding or camaraderie. Life was presumably simpler then for Brick because he understood homosexuality solely as gay sex, evidenced in Brick's story about the suspected homosexuality of a fraternity brother: "Don't you know how people feel about things like that? How, how disgusted they are by things like that? Why, at Ole Miss when it was discovered a pledge to our fraternity, Skipper's and mine, did a, attempted to do a, unnatural thing with—We not only dropped him like a hot rock!—We told him to git off the campus, and he did, he got!" (*C* 3:119). In Brick's eyes, one was homosexual simply by *what* one did, not by *who* one was, with that act threatening the benchmark of homosocial American society (here, the college fraternity, but in reality any all-male institution, such as the Elks, Masons, and Rotary clubs which Big Daddy significantly despises [*C* 3:108]) that both Brick and his patriarchal society felt the need here to protect.[50]

Yet, when the primacy of his and Skipper's communion endured long after their college days and up to the point where they began sharing hotel rooms during away matches and refused to be apart, society began having its doubts. Maggie acknowledges this, perhaps in convenient hindsight, when she tells Brick that, even while on a double-date during their college days, she and Skipper's girlfriend Gladys felt that they "were just sort of tagging along . . . to make a good public impression" (*C* 3:57). Brick, though, failed or refused to see how any innocent, male-male bond beyond a certain age or off the football field alone could be perceived as queer: "Normal? No!—It was too rare to be normal, any true thing between two people is too rare to be normal. Oh, once in a while he put his hand on my shoulder or I'd put mine on his, oh, maybe even, when we were touring the country in pro-football an' shared hotel-rooms we'd reach across the space between two beds and shake hands to say goodnight, yeah, one or two times we—"(*C* 3:121).[51]

As an icon of Cold War heteromasculinity and (presumably) free from the stigma of having actually committed a homosexual act, Brick rejects Maggie's and Big Daddy's external readings of his and Skipper's relationship: "Why can't exceptional friendship, *real, real, deep deep friendship!* between men be respected as something clean and decent without being thought of as—. . . .—*Fairies.* . . ." (*C* 3:120). By not acknowledging or even recognizing how society's rules of normalized sociosexual behavior had changed for him or, more importantly, why, Brick is guilty here only of having failed to discern that modern social mores of intimate male companionship come with an expiration date, an idea Williams clearly expounds in the stage note that follows Brick's outburst: "*In his utterance of this word, we gauge the wide and profound reach of the conventional mores he got from the world that crowned him with early laurel*" (*C* 3:120, [*sic*]).⁵² As Michael Paller puts it, "Is this—the fear of being *thought* a homosexual—finally more important than whether or not Brick actually is gay? . . . What is clear is that he fears being *perceived* as gay, and while this fear of what others think may be a projection of his own fears, the most important point would be not his shame at being gay, *but his shame at denying* it."⁵³

In *Epistemology of the Closet*, Eve Sedgwick historicizes the changes in these sociosexual conventions that, in many ways, recapitulate Kinsey's startling numbers at the time. In arguing that the modern homosexual was not a fixed, sexual identity but rather a fluid, socially-heterogeneous type that grew out of a bourgeois society's developing need to police its gender borders, Sedgwick sides with the many social constructionists who, like de Beauvoir, began isolating the increasingly powerful role of the Other in determining an individual's sexual identity. Contending that homosexuality as a social identity sprung "precisely from the inexplicitness or denial of the gaps *between* long-coexisting minoritizing and universalizing, or gender-transitive and gender-intransitive, understandings of same-sex relations,"⁵⁴ Sedgwick intimates that the homosexual was not born, per se, but evolved gradually through the increasingly bipartisan agendas of modern scientific, judiciary, and political discourses that were attempting to qualify and proscribe the limits of male-male desire. In other words, she writes, "constructions of modern Western gay male identity tend to be, not in the first place 'essentially gay,' but instead (or at least also) in a very intimately responsive and expressive, though always oblique, relation to incoherences implicit in modern male *hetero*sexuality."⁵⁵

The implication behind Kinsey's figures and Sedgwick's theory is not that certain men just shied away from admitting (either to themselves or to another) that they were gay but that a good many men categorically separated a homosexual *identity* from a homosexual *act* so as to avoid having to do so in the first place—a phenomenon that significantly altered modern epistemologies of sexuality in America. Constructed homosexual identity based uniquely on gender and sexual inversion allowed for masculinist male-male desire, whether homosocial or not, to persist free from suspicion. Even communities of gay men themselves formulated such a distinction. As George Chauncey, Jr. describes in *Gay New York*, the gay world divided itself between the fairies (a gay identity) and the queers (a gay act), with gender inversion effectuating that distinction. While the queer male—the homosexual male who maintained the gender constructs of heteromasculinity—despised the fairy for conjoining homosexuality to effeminacy, he also privately lauded him/her for giving him the closet space in which to practice his homosexual tastes among heteromasculine, middle-class culture.[56] Thus if Cold War heteromasculinity had responded to its crisis by extracting homosexuality from sexual performativity and relocating it in an effeminate identity, Cold War *homo*masculinity had effectively done the same. But with the fairy safely catalogued as the (homo)sexual Other, what then distinguished the two forms of masculinity from each other?

It is precisely this question that troubles Brick now in the play and that has triggered his homosexual existentialism, for though he recognizes the obvious heteromasculinity in himself and Skipper, he cannot unilaterally deny their homomasculine traits and remain completely honest with himself. Caught in this metaphysical struggle to separate homosexual identity from a homosexual act, a dialectic upon which his very sexual identity hinges, Brick relies on what many heteromasculine and queer men before him did in order to protect their sexual identities: enact homophobia, that performative tool par excellence to justify homosocial bonds and marginalize homosexual ones, as Gayle Rubin and Sedgwick have convincingly argued.[57] By systematically defaming all the gay men in the play, Brick enacts homophobia as unimpeachable proof of his heterosexuality, just as Jake does at the *bal musette* episode of *The Sun Also Rises*. In addition to recounting his fraternity story, for instance, Brick denigrates the "dirty old men" Straw and Ochello by labeling them "ducking sissies" and "Queers" (*C* 3:118). For Brick, what separates him and Skipper from the old couple is that he and Skipper had never slept together, with Brick still insisting on the primacy of the homosexual act over the identity because it is tangentially more viable as proof and also consistent with his existential nature.

For these reasons, when Big Daddy suggests that Brick and Skipper might have been in love, Brick immediately accuses Big Daddy of believing that he and Skipper "did, did, did!—sodomy!—together" (*C* 3:117), which was not Big Daddy's implication at all.[58] Unlike most men of his time, precisely because he exudes heteromasculinity and unashamedly "knocked around" (*C* 3:115) in his time (he did not get to be heir to Peter Ochello and Jack Straw's plantation for nothing), Big Daddy offers Brick an alternative route to sociosexual identification, one that seamlessly integrates a homosexual act with a heteromasculine identity.[59] To claim this route, however, Brick would first have to admit that he was gay (certainly in identity more than in act) and then accept the responsibility of having rejected Skipper's confession of love for him—arguably his most flagrant act of homophobia. Instead, Brick rejects his father's attempt to define him (even if it represents the most enlightened definition in the play) and chooses to maintain his homophobia, which for the moment secures his heteromasculine identity and relieves him of any culpability he might be feeling concerning his friend's resultant suicide.

In retrospect, then, Brick's defining moment of heterosexual identification came when he refused to respond to Skipper's "drunken confession[al]" phone call of homosexuality (*C* 3:124)—an act that precisely parallels his ironic curtain-line to Maggie, as we will see later. In Sartrean terms, Brick simply chose to reject the Other's efforts to define him, for Skipper's admission of his own (apparent) homosexuality would implicate Brick's by default. In hanging up the telephone on Skipper and thus precipitating his suicide, Brick re-enacts his determining essence of heteronormality. Yet Brick's guilt over Skipper's death and drinking to hide his "mendacity" with himself for "passing the buck" (*C* 3:124), as Big Daddy says, conjures up once again that Sartrean specter of bad faith. If Skipper were everything that Brick was and turned out to be queer (perhaps), what would suggest that Brick would not as well? Though Brick insists that Skipper's homosexuality was "*His* truth, not *mine!*" (*C* 3:125), there is no way for us to know if Brick is being honest or not—nor is there any need to either, and that is my point here. For Williams, such a question is ultimately irrelevant, in spite of the fact that he has insisted all along that Brick never lies. Given Brick's existential nature to know the truth of his and Skipper's relationship in light of modernist sexual epistemologies and to control his identity accordingly, it is easier for Brick just to reject Skipper's efforts, as he would later Big Daddy's, than to question contradictory notions of "truth." As both figures emerge from the nothingness of Brick's *pour-soi*, he sees them collectively as being predatory in nature. In their mutual rejection, then, lies Brick's "truth" to preserve his identity by himself.

Endemic homophobia was (and still is) undoubtedly a powerful performative tool with which to enact a hetero/homosexual distinction, but one exploited equally by gay and straight men alike to simultaneously excoriate the homosexual and secure one's heteromasculine alignment.[60] As such, it serves little in the way of truthfully informing the public sphere what Kinsey and Sedgwick said simply did not exist in the private one—the legitimacy of that binary. Brick's homophobia, then, in no way serves to prove Brick's attitude towards homosexuality, despite the fact that it has been the locus of critical readings of the play, homophobic and homophiliac alike, since 1955. While it does admittedly reflect his inner struggle to find a safe haven between homosocial and homosexual desire—not so much as to retroactively clear Skipper's name but rather to reassure himself that *his* desire would not have eventually extended beyond the football player's sanctioned embrace *on* the field but its *required* handshake *off*—Brick's homophobia is more a way for him to thwart any external effort to define him, since any social identity afforded him would be contained within his sexual desire. But if being the model of American masculinity and voicing public declarations of virulent homophobia were not singular proof of one's heterosexuality, what did Brick have to do to prove to his father, his wife, his society, and, ultimately, himself that he was not gay? Perhaps a more appropriate question should be, what did *Williams* have to do to prove it to his audience? The answer, Chauncey informs us, lies in proof of the performative *hetero*sexual act.[61]

Sexual Performativity: HUAC and Homosexual Existentialism

While the uncertainties and inconsistencies surrounding the "conventional mores" of heterosexuality are undeniably at the heart of *Cat*, it is Williams's distaste for a society that first determines someone's private identity and then systematically marginalizes those who do not fit its model of normalized sociosexual behavior that mostly drives the play's sociocritical engines. Arguably, Brick had never desired Skipper sexually—at least not consciously—but his desire for Skipper socially over all other things now makes him equally susceptible to being labeled a homosexual since he can no longer balance his homosocial desire (Sedgwick) with a heterosexually performative one (Butler), which could at least legitimate that friendship.[62]

Hemingway had understood this dilemma as well, perhaps more clearly in the McCarthy 1950s than he had in the Parisian 1920s. In the Africa of *True at First Light/Under Kilimanjaro*, and again with the distance of an ocean between him and his native country, Hemingway was able to explore the limits of homosocial desire more safely. In his "African book," which he was writing around the same time that Williams's *Cat on a Hot Tin Roof* was running on Broadway,[63] Hemingway writes a passage strikingly similar in sentiment to Skipper's relationship with Brick and Maggie, where the Hemingway persona must rebuff another man's homosexual advances at the risk of losing the male bond on which they, like Brick and Skipper, thrive:

> Arap Meina worshiped very few things as his religion had become hopelessly confused but he had moved into a worshiping of Miss Mary that, occasionally, reached peaks of ecstasy that were little short of violence. He loved G.C. ["Gin Crazed," a character in the book] but this was a sort of schoolboy fascination combined with devotion. He came to care greatly for me carrying this affection to the point where I had to explain to him that it

was women that I cared for rather than men though I was capable of deep and lasting friendship. (*UK* 289–90)

In the passage, Hemingway describes how sexed identities, particularly during the Cold War, were an American obsession, one entirely lost on certain African tribes since Arap Meina could equally desire "men, women, children, boys and girls" (*UK* 290) and not think twice about it.

Desire, as Hemingway would repeatedly demonstrate throughout this fictional memoir, takes all shapes and forms, but only in America does it need to be so strictly codified: "The Wakamba are not homosexual. I do not know about the Lumbwa because Arap Meina was the only Lumbwa I had ever known intimately but I would say that Arap Meina was strongly attracted to both sexes and that the fact that Miss Mary with the shortest of African haircuts provided the pure Hamitic face of a boy with a body that was as womanly as a good Masai young wife was one of the factors that channeled Arap Meina's devotion until it became worship" (*UK* 290).

Unable to let the issue rest, Hemingway returns several chapters later to the idea that "[t]here is no homosexuality among the Wakamba people" (*UK* 336), but now he explains why: there is no homosexuality because little distinction is made between same- and other-sex desire. That had not always been the case in sub-Saharan Africa, however, as in "the old days homosexuals . . . were condemned" and then "tied in the river or any water hole for a few days to make them more tender, and then killed and eaten" (*UK* 336). To this explanation, Hemingway wryly adds: "This would be a sad fate for many playwrights, I thought" (*UK* 336).[64] Because "homosexuals tasted worse than a waterbuck" (*UK* 336), he jibes, it was easier simply to do away with sexual labels altogether and accept a more holistic outlook on desire, one that Hemingway finds in Arap Meina and other tribal members.

Simply put, for Hemingway and for Williams, performing one's heteromasculinity required much more than "being manly" and "hating queers," which Brick was successful at doing. American society demands evidence of a sexual identity that homosexuality (which could equally achieve both signs of heteromasculine homophobia) could not faithfully reproduce. At a time when evidence of an alternative family was perhaps what America most needed, Cold War society (Brick's and Williams's, as well as Hemingway's) privileged the recapitulation of the nuclear family, the backbone of consumerist American society.[65] What else but his five "no-neck monsters" could have (albeit artificially) insulated the effete Gooper from similar suspicion?[66] For that reason, we have to return to Maggie's declaration, for in its attempt to secure her identity in light of her own sexual existentialism, it subsequently enforces an external identity upon Brick. And since Brick had systematically rejected Skipper's homosexual proposal, and Big Daddy's homosocial one, it is only natural that he should now reject Maggie's heterosexual one as well.

Because Maggie, like Big Daddy, has the consumerist need to sanction Brick and Skipper's relationship—for the finance-obsessed Maggie, to produce an heir to secure Big Daddy's estate; for the dying Big Daddy, to learn before his death that an heir will come from the only son he deems worthy of his legacy—she takes it upon herself to finally *assert* its heterosexual nature.[67] The keenest of all the Machiavels in the play, Maggie manipulates society's unwritten handbook of male-male conduct by first psychoanalytically pouring into Skipper's mind "the dirty, false idea" that what he and Brick were "was a frustrated case of that ole pair of sisters that lived in this room" (*C* 3:123).[68] Of course, Maggie has no proof of Skipper's homosexuality except for the fact that he could not perform, for any number of reasons, a heterosexual act of love-making for her upon demand (he was, after all, drunk at the time, as Brick is now). Consequently, she labels him queer and furthermore makes him believe that he is too—whether or not Skipper really is gay. Maggie wanted only to break up the friendship in question by forcing Skipper to sleep with her, believing, perhaps naively so, that once she "proved" Skipper's suspected disloyalty or homosexuality, Brick would come running back to her, disgusted by the thought that his best friend turned out to be a cheat or a queer.

What Maggie did not expect in the bargain was the resultant challenge to Brick's sexual identity as well. For now, in adopting Maggie's method of supposition and dubious tactics in eliciting the truth (albeit *her* truth), Mae and Gooper can equate Brick's refusal to sleep with Maggie with his incapacity for heterosexual performance. This psychological impotence with regards to his seductive wife, coupled already with his exclusively homosocial preference for Skipper, allow these eavesdropping (and vindictively greedy) brother and sister-in-law the opportunity to deduce Brick's homosexuality accordingly and thereby secure the plantation for themselves. Given HUAC's "guilt by association" politics toward American artists, who were communists simply because they were not publicly flag-waving patriots, Williams appears to be precisely critiquing Cold War society's role in determining someone's private identity, be it political or sexual, based solely on the *lack* of some positivist performative act. In his 1945 essay, "Something Wild . . . ," published in the *New York Star* a decade before *Cat* appeared on Broadway, we already find proof of Williams's conscious efforts to denounce McCarthyism and HUAC (something Hemingway would do in *True at First Light/Under Kilimanjaro*):[69]

> Today we are living in a world which is threatened by totalitarianism. The Fascist and the Communist states have thrown us into a panic of reaction. Reactionary opinion descends like a ton of *bricks* on the head of any artist who speaks out against the current of prescribed ideas. We are all under wraps of one kind or another, trembling before the specter of investigating committees and even with Buchenwald in the back of our minds when we consider whether or not we dare to say we were for Henry Wallace. *Yes, it is as bad as that.* (*WIL* 46, first emphasis added)

When Big Daddy finally bellows his response to Mae's persistent intrusiveness into his and Brick's private conversation, Williams certainly intended it to be heard all the way from Broadway to the Beltway: "... I hate eavesdroppers, I don't like any kind of sneakin' an' spyin'.... You listen at night like a couple of rutten peekhole spies and go and give a report on what you hear to Big Mama an' she comes to me and says they say such and such and so and so about what they heard goin' on between Brick an' Maggie, and Jesus, it makes me sick.... I can't stand sneakin' an' spyin', it makes me sick...." (*C* 3:82).

Such collectivist power is not only dangerous (it killed Skipper after all) but socially immoral and, ironically, entirely unAmerican.[70] When Big Daddy next warns Brick to keep his voice down because the "walls have ears in this place" (*C* 3:84), Williams cleverly turns his attack directly upon the viewing audience as well, where we too become government spies and eavesdroppers during this private scene between father and son; and when we leave the theater asking ourselves, as Walter Kerr did in 1955, "Was Brick gay?" or "Why didn't Williams just come out and say that Brick was gay instead of hiding behind all this 'mystery' business?," we are aligning ourselves more with the rumor-mongering Maggies and Maes of the world than we are with the victimized Bricks and Skippers. In other words, we too are guilty of determining a man's sexual nature based solely on our *reading* of his social identity, and forever marginalizing him socially, sexually, and politically in the process.[71]

Williams only complicates matters further when he makes Brick, à la HUAC, refuse to confirm or deny the charges of homosexuality (as with Maggie and Big Daddy) or name names (as in the case of Skipper's alleged homosexuality) if he were not gay. Consequently, Brick is being forced existentially into either redefining his heterosexual role along personal epistemological lines of desire or accepting his society's vague definition of homosexuality with all of its transparent and plastic components. Like many existentialists, Brick chooses a third option: escape. Since Brick's recourse is through the bottle and not, as it was with Skipper, through suicide, alcoholism becomes the perfect cover—socially and physiologically—to justify his impotence and refusal to confront or exclaim the truth of his sexual identity. Throughout the play, Brick only needs to wait long enough for his "click," for that moment of artificial detachment when he can free himself from his accusers or from any personal reflection he imposes on himself as a result of his homosexual existentialism.

But because any private answer Brick might be seeking about his desire is also contingent upon his accepting society's already grey rules of sexual definitioning, he cannot secure Charles May's "possible palliative" to his homosexual existentialism without first satisfying (or not) his wife's sexual demands, and therein lies the locus of his, and of *Cat's*, problematic. While her demands that he return to their bed are successfully avoided throughout the play, parried either by his referencing the conditions of their earlier agreement to stay together or by his dependence upon the bottle, Maggie finally challenges Brick into heterosexual performativity with her public declaration that she is already carrying Brick's child. For everyone, especially Brick, this is Judith Butler's "defining moment of performativity" where Maggie's declaration "not only perform[s] an action, but confer[s] a binding power on the action performed."[72] Maggie backs Brick into a corner where he can no longer hide (or plead the Fifth) and has given him as much time to confront the truth of his sexuality as Big Daddy has in accepting his own impending death. So, when he rejects Maggie's love with his ironic "Wouldn't it be funny if that was true?" in the original ending of act 3, it is not just out of the need to preserve his sense of self or to confirm or deny his homosexuality but also to reject all socially-based definitions of heterosexuality that Maggie upholds with her declaration, making his tragedy a more caustic indictment of society's omnipotence over the individual.[73] Either way, Maggie wins, and Brick is forced into accepting one identity or the other on society's terms alone, just as Jake is at the end of *The Sun Also Rises*.[74] His and Brick's irony may export poignant literary commentaries, but neither man carries the power or the force in his rejoinder to counter his lack of heterosexual performativity per their respective societies.

"*NO HAY REMEDIO*": JAKE AND BRICK AS *HOMO AMERICANUS*

If existentialism describes the angst an individual suffers when faced with the choice of either accepting his place among the conforming masses or detaching himself from the artificial constraints of that external reality in order to assert or confirm his individual presence, then homosexual existentialism describes that same individual, now locked in the vacuum of gender identification and confronted with the choice of either proving his society wrong or right in its sexual labeling of him or detaching himself altogether from the socially-artificial constraints that impede his process toward self-actualization. Though it in no way provides a final assessment of the individual's definitive sexual identity, homosexual existentialism does portray that individual's crisis of homosexual identity by exhibiting his struggle to negotiate his society's collective epistemologies of what heterosexuality is, or at least ought to be, with what he knows or thinks he knows it entails. As de Beauvoir writes, "Like all human behaviour, homosexuality leads to make-believe, disequilibrium, frustration, lies, or, on the contrary, it becomes the source of rewarding experience, in accordance with its manner of expression in actual living—whether in bad faith, laziness, and falsity, or in lucidity, generosity, and freedom" (*SS* 444). For Brick, as well as for Jake, certainly the former applies; for Williams himself, arguably the latter.

The original ending of *Cat*, then, is undeniably more powerful than its Broadway rewrite, for its strength comes in part from its wry, ironic detachment of a man whose sexual identity can be nothing less than a social identity no matter how much he tries to preserve its private nature. Brick clearly understands the stakes behind Maggie's public declaration, as did Williams when he restored his ending for *Cat*'s 1974 revival and republication the following year.[75] As such, when Williams added the extended "bird" stage direction to the play that addresses *"the inadmissible thing that Skipper died to disavow between them"* (*C* 3:114),[76] which John Clum sees as Williams "proceed[ing] with a scene about homosexuality while denying that that is what he is doing,"[77] he was not attempting to mire Brick's sexuality in half-truths or evasive rhetoric but rather to underscore the consequences—social, political, familial, and personal—of Brick's homosexual existentialism, demarcating more clearly the *Homo americanus* in him, that species of queer heteromasculine men who have haunted the pages of the American canon since Charles Brockden Brown at least.[78]

Williams understood the importance of invoking suggestiveness in dealing with Brick's problem in the play and worked throughout the manuscripts to move away from homosexuality as the end-all reason for his "moral paralysis" (*C* 3:168) and toward something more enigmatic and endemic in nature. In an entry in his personal notebooks, dated April 3, 1954, Williams describes his attempt to avoid making *Cat* singularly about homosexuality: "I wrote sort of messy today on 'Place of

Stone' [a working title for *Cat*]. The intrusion of the homosexual theme may be fucking it up *again*" (*NB* 631, my emphasis; cf. *SL II* 524, 525). When he changed genres by adapting "Three Players of a Summer Game" into *Cat,* Williams simply lost the necessary narrative thread found in the story to explain Brick's alcohol-cum-sexual dilemma in the play that his rather curious "bird" insertion now attempted to provide. Williams was simply following Bill's advice to Jake in *The Sun Also Rises* about downplaying the rumors surrounding Brick's impotency: "Never mention that. . . . That's the sort of thing that can't be spoken of. That's what you ought to work up into a mystery" (*S* 115). What is most important for Brick, then, is that he, like Jake, remain heterosexual, for it better explains both of their struggles to negotiate personal reflections on what homosexuality is, underpinned no doubt by the stereotypes their societies have supplied for them, as well as by their faith in the purity of homosocial relations.

Questions surrounding Jake's and Brick's sexual identities are not, and perhaps should never be, conclusively affirmed or denied, for such certitude would surely depoliticize the novel's and play's intent of turning that suspicion back upon the reader's/audience's desire to know, implicating their own sexual epistemology as being at the core of the two texts' final tragic ambiguities.[79] As the narrator in "Three Players of a Summer Game" says in defense of Brick's private life, a judgmental voice that carries the weight of Williams's message in the story, and of Hemingway's in the novel: "It is only the outside of one person's world that is visible to others, and all opinions are false ones, especially public opinions of individual cases" (*CS* 324). In this respect, *Cat* is extremely adroit and sincere in its representation of Brick's response to homosexuality. The ambiguities are not in the play itself, Williams seems finally to be saying, but are imported by the prying audience, who, because of its own ambivalent attitudes toward male-male desire, is truthfully reflected in Brick, and in Jake for that matter.

5

The Impotence of Being Ernest: Scott and Hemingway's "Gender Trouble" in Williams's *Clothes for a Summer Hotel*

> *Playboy:* Do you believe that, in the final analysis, a man follows his phallus?
> *Williams:* I hope not, baby. I hope he follows his heart, his frightened heart.
>
> —Tennessee Williams,
> *Playboy* Interview

> *Max.* And you are still straight?
> *Philip.* I hope so. Does it show when you're not?
> *Max.* Oh, yes.
> *Philip.* How do I look then? . . .
> *Max.* You look pretty straight to me.
>
> —Ernest Hemingway,
> *The Fifth Column*

> "The constitutive identifications of an autobiographical narrative are always partially fabricated in the telling."
>
> —Judith Butler,
> *Gender Trouble*

BETWEEN *CAT ON A HOT TIN ROOF* AND STONEWALL, THE GAY PLAY AND gay theater in America had made considerable strides on Broadway, though repeatedly the dominant image, as that delivered in Mart Crowley's *The Boys in the Band* (1968), underscored traditional heterosexual views of homosexuality as either pathetically self-destructive or comically urbane.[1] The queer play, on the other hand, that which had often couched gay allusions, argot, camp, and/or sensibilities within typical bourgeois theatrical productions, worked to undermine those stereotypes heteronormative America relied upon to police its identity borders, on and off the stage, with the gay playwright either mocking his unwitting audiences or at least profiting from their ignorance or inexperience with gay aesthetics.² It was the fear of this *"disguised* homosexual influence" that prompted theater critic Stanley Kauffmann in 1966, continuing in the tradition of *New York Times* theater critic Howard Taubman before him, to write his now-notorious article, "Homosexual Drama and Its Disguises."³

Disingenuously writing from behind a liberal mask, Kauffmann helped to fan the flaming homophobia of a destabilized America in the mid-1960s by "decoding" the gay language of the queer play, which had come to occupy "the main traffic of our stage."⁴ By "convert[ing] their exclusion into a philosophy of art that glorifies their exclusion," Kauffmann contends, and by favoring "manner and style" over "character and idea" because they are "legal tender in their transactions in their world," the homosexual playwright threatened the heterosexual viewer by masquerading the psychological neuroses of a minority population as authentic social drama.⁵ In other words, if openly gay plays were fine in the 1960s because they allowed the heteronormative public to safely identify the sexual Other, and thereby police it, the queer play was not because, just like the unidentifiable communist who had upended identity politics during the Cold War, the queer play was seen as counterfeit, subversively attacking the hegemonic ethos from within. Gay plays, like those performed in Off Off-Broadway venues such as Caffe Cino, La Mama, or the Judson Poets' Theatre, were a matter of public choice; queer plays were not.⁶ As a result, the queer play proved, though in hindsight alone, a more effective tool in serving the needs of gay liberation than the combative armada of gay pride plays that paraded across the Broadway stage during the 1970s because it surreptitiously conditioned heteronormative America in to quietly absorbing gay aesthetics into mainstream epistemologies rather than inadvertently buttressing the more prevalent *us and them* politics.⁷

One of Kauffmann's unidentified triumvirate homosexual playwrights was Tennessee Williams, who, curiously enough, did not write a "gay" play in the 1960s at a time when it was perhaps most ripe to do so, especially for a playwright who, though not yet clearly out of the closet, had never denied the "open secret" of his sexuality and who had brazenly flirted with homosexuality onstage, whereas William Inge and Edward Albee—the two other gay playwrights in Kauffmann's notorious trio—had not. Instead, Williams continued writing queer plays in the 1960s, those like *The Milk Train Doesn't Stop Here Anymore* (1963), *Slapstick Tragedy* (1966), *Kingdom of Earth* (1966–1967), *I Can't Imagine Tomorrow* (1966), *The Two-Character Play* (1967), and *In the Bar of a Tokyo Hotel* (1969), which were not *about* homosexuality per se, but whose quirkiness, easily filed under the rubric "absurd" at that time, also belied the traditional heterosexual material that each play contains within its matrix: a dying prima donna and her handsome gigolo/angel of death; two "mutilated" whores—"the strange, the crazed, the queer" (7:81)—searching for human compassion on Christmas Eve; the seduction of a half brother's wife; a Pinteresque sketch of a lonely man and woman's search for meaning to their lives; the incestuous desires of a brother and sister; and the suffering of a marriage neglected for art's sake. Because they were not categorical gay plays but resembled none of the traditional bourgeois parlor play that had held sway in American theater since the Provincetown Players (the formula Williams had successfully queered in the 1940s and 1950s), each became a target of Kauffmann's and other openly homophobic theater critics' attacks,[8] with their explicit or implicit critical impetus taking the form of the Albertine strategy of labeling his heroines as simply queens in drag.[9] Williams, of course, would adamantly deny this assessment of his work as myopic at best, damaging at worst.[10]

If Williams had predictably been the repeated target of homophobic critics in the pre-Stonewall years for subversively concealing homosexual style within heterosexual content, after Stonewall he surprisingly came under attack from the homophiliac critics *for precisely the same reason:* that is, for not having dramatized homosexuality more openly in his plays during the liberating 1960s and for having come out himself only when it was safe to do so.[11] This was something gay playwright "Lee Barton" in his article "Why Do Homosexual Playwrights Hide Their Homosexuality?" charged Williams with having done throughout his career: "One work of art dealing truthfully with homosexual life is worth a hundred breast-beating personal confessions. Who really gives a damn that Tennessee Williams has finally admitted his sexual preferences in print? He has yet to contribute any work of understanding to gay theater, and with his enormous talent one of his works would indeed be worth any amount of personal data."[12]

Though Williams *had* no doubt advanced the honest treatment of homosexuality on Broadway with *Cat on a Hot Tin Roof* and more fully with *Suddenly Last Summer,* such treatments were still deemed offensive to some of the gay public because the homosexual in them was once again portrayed as an antisocial degenerate meriting his unfortunate and untimely end, whereas in his short fiction and poetry—mediums less exploitive and, they are quick to add, less lucrative—Williams frequently treated him with more tea and sympathy. "The homosexual as a person," "Barton" concludes, "will never know freedom until his artists stand up for him," which Williams apparently had not done.[13] Williams, it had no doubt seemed to "Barton" at the time, could simply placate neither camp, for if before he had had to mobilize against marginalization for being homosexual in the 1950s, now he had to do so for not being gay enough. As Michael Paller summarizes, "Changes in the social and political climate, as well as in coverage of gay playwrights in the New York press, and, most importantly, changes in the attitudes of gay men and women themselves, would turn Williams into a figure of ridicule, when not ignored altogether, for many in the emerging gay community of the early 1970s."[14]

A strange case of *déjà lu* arises here, for just as he had to defend himself back in 1955 against Walter Kerr concerning Brick's "mystery" in *Cat on a Hot Tin Roof*, Williams was now finding himself twenty years later in an identical position. This time, though, the charges against him for not having outed Brick, or any other of his principal characters prior to Quentin in *Small Craft Warnings*, were emerging from the gay community itself.[15] And just as he had responded to Kerr back then, Williams was to dismiss his gay critics by arguing that his plays were never about homosexuality from the outset since their themes were much larger than the sexual identification of one character: "Frankly, and at the risk of alienating some of my friends in Gay Lib, I have never found the subject of homosexuality a satisfactory theme for a full length play, despite the fact that is appears as frequently as it does in my short fiction. Yet never even in my short fiction does the sexual activity of a person provide the story with its true inner substance" (*WIL* 172).[16] Significantly, Williams would repeat this sentiment often, even directly to the gay community itself, where, in his 1976 interview with George Whitmore for *Gay Sunshine*, Williams reiterated that he did not want to "write a gay play" simply because he did not "find it necessary."[17] Williams knew that such a comment would "bring down on my cracked head the wrath of all the Gay Libs to whom my heart is committed, categorically, in a bruised-ass way," as his self-identified narrator said a year earlier in *Moise and the World of Reason*.[18] Yet he also knew that his Broadway audience and theater critics were not yet warm to the idea of an honest "gay" play, despite the financial and critical success that plays like *The Boys in the Band* had enjoyed a few years earlier.

One wonders, then, just as we had back in 1955, whether Williams was in earnest or not in his proclaiming that he had never written, nor would ever write, a gay play because if was not "necessary." Was Williams again consciously trying not to limit his audience and, with it, any potential rewards, lucrative or otherwise? One recurrent theme in all of Williams's unpublished nonfiction writings of the 1970s was, indeed, his need for another critical and commercial success (as well as his bitterness toward the critics whom he felt repeatedly denied him this); and while it is true that he never "sold out" his artistic sensibilities by returning to the nostalgic plays that had earlier established his career (save, perhaps, *Vieux Carré*), he also knew that a "gay" play like *Small*

Craft Warning, which he felt at the time was one of his best later plays, would not garner the erstwhile accolades. To be sure, after Williams "officially" came out in 1970 on the David Frost Show, his art did increasingly turn rhetorical, even confessional, as if to satisfy both of his opposing critics' needs for him to write *that* didactic gay play. And surely, it is not entirely coincidental either that Williams should have written his only gay plays for Broadway—*Small Craft Warnings* (1972) and *Vieux Carré* (1977)—*after* Stonewall, while most of his plays written prior to Stonewall, culminating with *Cat on a Hot Tin Roof* and *Suddenly Last Summer,* contain various degrees of queerness.[19]

To a certain extent, one great limitation of Williams's art in the better part of the 1970s—in his plays (*Small Craft Warning, Vieux Carré*), in his fiction (*Moise and the World of Reason, Eight Mortal Ladies Possessed*), and in his nonfiction (*Memoirs*)—stems from the fact that he exchanged the queer, on which he established himself not only as America's preeminent playwright but also one of its leading gay polemicists, for the gay. To many of his critics, gay and straight alike, if it seemed that Williams had before only broached the subject of the love that dare not speak its name in his one-act and full-length plays, now in the 1970s he simply could not shut up about it. To them, Williams had done so apparently less out of the need to finally assert ideas he felt he never had the opportunity before to express (which he certainly had done with Brick and company) and more to deflect mounting criticism from the gay libbers who were, or so it seemed, doing very well without him. Williams's love/hate relationship with gay liberation during the 1970s led him to confess to C. Robert Jennings in their *Playboy* interview that "I am bored with movements. . . . The gay libs' public displays are so vulgar they defeat their purpose. . . . Fantastic transvestites in open convertibles making absolute asses of themselves are only hurting their cause—ridiculing homosexuality" (*CTW* 249). Williams would echo these words later in his *Memoirs:* "Of course, 'swish' and 'camp' are products of self-mockery, imposed upon homosexuals by our society. The obnoxious forms of it will rapidly disappear as Gay Lib begins to succeed in its serious crusades to assert, for its genuinely misunderstood and persecuted minority, a free position in society which will permit them to respect themselves, at least to the extent that, individually, they deserve respect—and I think that degree is likely to be much higher than commonly supposed" (*M* 50).

Even by 1979, following the shooting deaths of San Francisco Mayor George Moscone and Harvey Milk that previous November, Williams would even speak entirely detached from the gay lib movement: "'I think the gay population was quite rightly outraged. Of course, I don't believe they expressed it properly in burning police cars, creating a riot

... I'm afraid that militant movements of any kind often use the wrong tactics'" (*CTW* 322–23).

Paradoxically, Williams was putting many of these gay transvestites onstage all the while denouncing them in print. As Paller contends, "... when Williams returned to writing gay characters, increasingly putting them in the center of his plays, what he was doing would strike many gay theater-makers and activists not only as old-hat but also not nearly gay enough. For them, Tennessee Williams would be offering too much too little far too late."[20] Given this discrepancy in truth between word and deed, then, it would appear that, if Brick's silence was indeed at the heart of his own mendacity in *Cat on a Hot Tin Roof* then, so too was Williams's now, with Kerr finally appearing vindicated in the end. For this reason, perhaps one of the most polemical questions in Williams studies today is less what did Williams do to advance American drama but rather what, within the evolution of his dramaturgy, what did Williams do to advance the gay cause?[21]

And yet, in Williams's defense, I think we would do better to recognize again how, just as he had proclaimed back in 1955 in his rejoinder to Kerr, his dramatic subjects were not essentially about homosexuality at all, not even those of the outwardly gay plays *Small Craft Warnings* and *Vieux Carré*? Rather, his plays were more about the identity politics that underwrite them, about society's need to know if you are, or if you are not, *one of them*. Twenty years had passed, for example, and Williams was still proselytizing that "the major thrust of my work is not sexual orientation, it's social": "the theme of the play, if it's important, should not be impeded by fending people right off by a tangential thing like the precise sexual orientation of a character; in fact I don't think there is such a thing as a precise sexual orientation. I think we're all ambiguous sexually."[22] It could be argued that these words show how little America had changed since *Cat on a Hot Tin Roof* and the Cold War as far as sexual differentiation was concerned, or how far Williams was willing to play the game for fear of retribution, real or professional, with his vogue phrase "ambiguous sexually" only slightly camouflaging the former word "mystery." I believe this not to be the case. To be sure, after 1975, his gay *annus mirabilis* with the publication of *Moise and the World of Reason* and his confessional *Memoirs*, there would have been little reason for him to continue posturing.

While it is true that Williams could not really have admitted to Brick's homosexuality back in 1955, given his free currency of the word *gay* throughout his post-Stonewall canon by 1976 (the year of Whitmore's interview), he certainly could have finally outed Brick, or any of his queer characters, if he had so desired. Few critics, gay or otherwise, would have chided Williams for long, since most would have considered that confession a fait accompli. Instead, Williams chose the more subversive route again, one consistent with his earlier stance that prejudiced epistemologies, and not the human condition itself, were at the heart of sociosexual identification. True "revolution is implicit," he said, "not explicit, but woven into the fabric."[23] If Williams were only *saying* now that he believed sexual ambivalence, and not sexual orientation, to be congenital, with social pressures ultimately being responsible for (often inaccurate) sexual labeling—that is, nature artificially influenced by constructionist ideologies based on policed sociosexual identities—he had certainly been intimating it throughout his dramatic work for decades.[24]

A transitional year for Williams, 1975–1976 saw not only the publication of his openly gay works but also the gestation period of what would later become a return to his queer thesis, evidenced not only in his remarks to Whitmore but also in his theatrical productions written that year: the subversively bourgeois *Crève Cœur* and the surrealistically paranoid *Red Devil Battery Sign*. It was also in 1975 that Williams began drafting *Clothes for a Summer Hotel* (1980) and returned to *Cat on a Hot Tin Roof* for the last time, publishing yet another version of the play that he had reworked the year before for the American Shakespeare Theatre. This definitive version significantly reasserts Brick's sexual ambiguity and restores to him his ironic curtain-line that Williams describes in his 1973 essay, "Let Me Hang It All Out," was cut to make room for a "sentimentally ingenuous solution of the marital problem between Maggie and Brick" (*WIL* 171).[25] For all of these reasons, then, it is perhaps not coincidental that in his final run at Broadway, Williams would attempt to recapture the recipe that had made him so successful and so subversive with *Cat on a Hot Tin Roof*, for *Clothes for a Summer Hotel* is a "ghost play" of lost youth and predatory marriage *and* an encomium to sexual ambivalence. Only superficially a gay play, where Zelda's accusations of Scott Fitzgerald's latent homosexuality dominate the more suggestive language of innuendo and incompletion between Fitzgerald and Hemingway, just as Maggie's had been with Brick, and Brick's had been with Skipper and Big Daddy, *Clothes for a Summer Hotel* is more a queer play polemically aimed (as *Cat on a Hot Tin Roof* was) at exposing the identification politics of society and its role in marginalizing homosexuality. As such, it serves as a final chapter in the history linking Jake and Brick, where once fictional characters trapped within their homosexual existentialism have now been replaced by the real authors responsible for having put them there in the first place.[26] Such a reading reflects how Stonewall both changed the manner in which the avowed homosexual Williams saw his role as a postmodern playwright emerging and helped him to negotiate his alterity to the homophobic *and* homophiliac discourse he had experienced for nearly two decades.

Unlike in *Cat on a Hot Tin Roof*, Williams's characters here are real people, with documented histories, so if anyone seems guilty of the gossip-mongering slander behind the identity politics that he had repeatedly criticized in his work, it would certainly appear to be Williams himself. And therein poses our greatest problem: did Williams practice what he bitched?[27] Perhaps he was only attempting to write himself back into the gay community, from which he had personally feared being ostracized, by promoting renewed accusations of both writers' latent homosexuality. Or perhaps he was only gratuitously wagering to increase the play's sensational appeal to draw more box-office receipts, which is what *New York* drama critic John Simon felt.[28] Williams certainly realized that few audiences in the polemical 1970s would care whether a fictional character like Brick was gay or not, whereas baiting the sexual identities of historical figures, particularly that of a notoriously heteromasculine and/or outspokenly homophobic celebrity like Hemingway, piqued public prurience. Though both views are valid, I feel that Williams exploited the innuendoes to redirect his attack away from the heteronormative society of *Cat on a Hot Tin Roof* and onto that of the closeted gay community exposed in *Clothes for a Summer Hotel*. For Williams by the late 1970s, closeted homosexuals did more to harm gay liberation, either by speaking and acting directly against it as demagogues of heteronormativity (i.e., Hemingway), than those who, like himself, were out before Stonewall but simply did not feel the need to boast about it. Williams's subversiveness now was no longer aimed at the homophobic community but at the gay community itself, whose internalized strife within gay liberation caused as much damage to gays and their acceptance within a heteronormative society as had done those demagogues of heteromasculinity before. The argument is familiar enough; only the target had changed, and with it came Williams's double-edged response to both communities.

"Truth of Character," Language Games, and Paralogy

Like most of Williams's late plays, *Clothes for a Summer Hotel* was frequently considered as another embarrassing blemish on a rather illustrious career. It is not coincidental, then, that such a work of then-minor standing should have met with so little critical attention from the theater public whose ennui could not keep the play's Broadway production alive for even a month nor sustain its 1995 York Theatre revival, or from the academic community whose tolerance with the play was surpassed only by the dearth of pages dedicated to its interpretation, something Jackson Bryer reported in his millennial retrospect of the play's critical reception nearly a decade ago.[29] Those critics who did venture intrepidly into analyzing the play have studied it as either a psychodramatization of Williams's guilt-ridden relationship with his sister Rose,[30] a mimetic representation of his auto-da-fé at the hands of belligerent critics,[31] or a personal exegesis on the tortured psyche's struggle to produce art with impunity.[32] In a telling piece of commentary Clive Barnes wrote for the *New York Post,* he concludes, "Time and time again, Williams is like a matador who canaassess [*sic*] the bull but is less certain in handling his cloak and has almost forgotten his sword."[33] To be sure, such readings are insightful in light of Williams's biography and dramaturgy and do reveal consistent truths about the play; that the majority of this criticism should have come from the play's initial theater critics nearly a quarter of a century ago, however, is perhaps most telling.[34] With only five serious treatments prior to Bryer's to have appeared since the play's publication in 1983, we would do better, it would seem, to let sleeping "ghost plays" lie.[35]

A spate of criticism on the play, however, appeared the same year as Bryer's essay. These essays proposed a reexamination of the play's postmodern characteristics and subsequently renewed scholarly interests in Williams's anti-mimetic literary efforts, here and elsewhere in his late canon.[36] Working from various drafts of *Clothes for a Summer Hotel* and with Williams's unfaltering echoes of Strindberg and Lawrence, for example, Linda Dorff shows how the play "rejects the earlier plays' redemptive paradigms" of modernist resurrection mythologies (from which he frequently drew in the 1940s and 1950s) by using fire and ash metaphors within a postmodern discourse of doubt and distrust to foreground "the artificiality/artifice of the denaturalized ghost form as an ultimate simulacrum . . . a reproduction of a reproduction—what Jean Baudrillard has defined as 'that which is already produced. The hyperreal, . . . which is [already] entirely a simulation.'"[37] Similarly, George Crandell looks at the postmodern representation of time in the play which "substitutes for historical time an *aesthetic space,* a representation of time that permits the exploration of an alternative temporality and a virtual reality that bears no mimetic relationship to the world outside of the play's dramatic boundaries and yet, paradoxically, illuminates that *real* world."[38] Finally, Norma Jenckes examines the play's postmodern flippancy toward serious modern issues, here love, to demonstrate how "an historically constructed emotion and state of being . . . can be and is affected by the material conditions of society in which it rises and falls"—in other words, how love has become a commodity, a postmodern spin on romanticism.[39]

5: THE IMPOTENCE OF BEING ERNEST

While each of these three essays is excellent in its own right, together they provide a mere postmodern gloss on the play's problematic with simulacra, historicity, and the era of late capitalism, as if all challenges to modernity could fall under one banner postmodern heading. To be sure, there *is* something postmodern about the play, but it is not one or the other of the things these critics discuss above. It is rather *all* of them, inextricably bound and gagged together in a maddening mishmash of reproduction and representation. One cannot properly talk of postmodern simulacrum, for example, outside of a late-capitalist context, no more than one can imagine anti-mimetic space without its contemporaneous historicity. Postmodernism is simply a gestalt, a process and not a product, a discourse and an aesthetic that is evolving as I write these words. To give a postmodern reading of the text is to accept a priori that such a reading cannot stand on its own but must draw from the past and speak to the future through the limited words and tools of today. Perhaps *Clothes for a Summer Hotel* is only successful today because we are that future Williams was speaking to back then, which his contemporary audience was either ill-prepared or openly hostile to deem intelligible, let alone responsible, writing.[40] If Williams were a postmodernist, and there is much in his later career to suggest that he was,[41] it was not just through any effort he did then but what we today recognize that he had done and will confirm tomorrow. And if *Clothes for a Summer Hotel* is a postmodern play, it is so largely because of its message that we (both the characters in the play and the audiences who observe them) retract a future and project a past, and wretch out our "truth" from the wreckage of our todays.

In this regard, *Clothes for a Summer Hotel* could be understood as a response to the time's larger conflict with what Williams's contemporary Jean-François Lyotard calls in *The Postmodern Condition* (*La Condition postmoderne*, 1979) metanarratives (*grands récits*), those universalizing truths that adjudicate disputes between opposing discourses of knowledge once embraced by modernism but which postmodern culture frequently harbored "incredulity toward" (*PC* xxiv). I do not wish to suggest that Williams had ever read Lyotard's book when it was first published in French in 1979 (Williams's level of French was not high enough to meet the demands that Lyotard's book commands, and he was already dead by the time the first English translation appeared in 1984);[42] nor do I wish to use Lyotard's theory, which has had its many detractors anyway, as a critical metanarrative with which to legitimate Williams's postmodernist tendencies. Rather, I wish only to assert plainly that what Lyotard had theorized about Western culture in the late 1970s (a theory frequently taken up, both directly or indirectly, by contemporary theorists after him, such as Jürgen Habermas, Fredric

Jameson, Jean Baudrillard, and Linda Hutcheon, to name but a few) Williams had put onstage, and in understanding the observations and ramifications of one, we might be able to interpret the motives of the other.

Around the time that Williams was revising *Clothes for a Summer Hotel* for its Broadway debut, Lyotard was preoccupied with defining a culture's crisis in accepting its inherited modernist truths that had worked their way into daily practices of legitimating knowledge. His central argument that postmodernism is a rejection of these metanarratives used since the Enlightenment to prescribe universal meaning to human experiences has, in fact, provided a useful rhetoric to our understanding of the increased play with modernist ideas that postmodernist culture has resorted to as it began growing tired of the diametrically opposed "isms" that sustained the Cold War. In the hope that a reevaluation of the individual's perception in the production of knowledge would legitimate truth more faithfully than any universalizing one had ever claimed to do before—be it capitalism or Marxism—a postmodernist began privileging the combination of several smaller, often competing and contradictory truths (*petits récits*) that the metanarratives had overridden. These little narratives, the anomalies or paradoxes inherent to the metanarratives, are thus woven together to reconstruct truth via "paralogy," Lyotard's term for the interplay of individualistic ideas that, through localization (the temporal assigning of meaning to particular terms or ideas that refuse fixed definitions), attempt to apply new rules to the old language games of denotative truth—those "various categories of utterances [that] can be defined in the terms of rules specifying their properties and the uses to which they can be put . . ." (*PC* 10). By opening up the possibility of hearing the once marginalized voices of these little narratives, a postmodernist seeks to reincorporate the individual back into the production of knowledge from which he had been displaced once scientific discourse became the gatekeeper of truth's legitimatizing.

In post-Enlightenment modernism, for example, Lyotard argues that scientific discourse (based on reason and rationality and logic) emerged as a competing legitimizer of truth with pre-modern narrative knowledge (fables, legends, myths, folklore, religion, history). It soon grew more dominant because its refusal to allow for language games (connotative utterances as the basis of truth, which narrative discourse privileges) forced narrative knowledge into accepting that it could not validate truth outside of itself. In other words, one narrative truth, say religion, is based on another, say history, with no center upholding the whole system of knowledge. In accepting this critique because it "does not give priority to the question of its own legitimation," narrative knowledge was not acquiescing to the fact that science maintained categorical control over truth. Instead, it saw scientific discourse precisely "as a variant in the family of narrative cultures" (*PC* 27). Though science refused to share this understanding and faulted narrative knowledge for its inability to answer to argumentation or proof, narrative knowledge internally "certifies itself in the pragmatics of its own transmission" (*PC* 27). Narrative knowledge was truth simply because modernism accepted it as such, whereas scientific knowledge was truth because it could be proven.

Despite their unavoidable agon in modernity, narrative knowledge and scientific knowledge found a useful partner in one another. Just as narrative knowledge began looking to scientific knowledge for the legitimation that it felt it was nonetheless losing out to scientific discovery—in short, for the justification of its truth value—scientific knowledge soon recognized that it too could not "make known that it is the true knowledge without resorting to the other, narrative, kind of knowledge, which from its point of view is no knowledge at all"—"[w]ithout such recourse it would be in the position of presupposing its own validity and would be stooping to what it condemns: begging the question, proceeding on prejudice" (*PC* 29). Since science could not legitimize itself either, it had to create a discourse that would offer it that sense of legitimacy, and thus looked to narrative discourse with its grand narratives as a potential means to provide that validation. As a result, Lyotard posits, knowledge was no longer the subject but "in the service of the subject" (*PC* 36), with the fact remaining that "knowledge has no final legitimacy outside of serving the goals envisioned by the practical subject, the autonomous collectivity" (*PC* 36).

Modernist scientific knowledge, then, had itself become a metanarrative, having established a narrator on which to underpin its own empirical phenomena, and thereby opened itself up to equal incredulity. This is precisely what took place during postmodernism, those years following World War II where the "decline of the unifying and legitimating power of the grand narratives of speculation and emancipation" (*PC* 38) at the end of the nineteenth century splintered the grand narratives. Legitimation through "the principle of consensus as a criterion of validation seems to be inadequate" (*PC* 60) to the postmodernist. As Lyotard contends, "What saves them [postmodernists] from it [barbarity, in having rejected the grand narratives] is their knowledge that legitimation can only spring from their own linguistic practice and communicational interaction" (*PC* 41).

For Lyotard, this was the "striking feature of postmodern scientific knowledge," that is, "the discourse on the rules that validate it is (explicitly) immanent to it" (*PC* 54). And while this observation led to the "loss of legitimacy and a fall into philosophical 'pragmatism'" at the end of the nineteenth century, in postmodern scientific discourse the paradox was found to be the legitimation of knowledge which it tended to exploit for performative purposes. Consequently, scientific discourse shifted from the prescriptive toward the pragmatic mode of validation, moving away from essentialists questions like "Is it true?" and onto to those like "Is it efficient?" (*PC* 51).

Though this valorization of performativity as legitimation brought about the internal erosion of the metanarratives, it meant an equal threat to notions of justness implicit in truth because it neglected humanist interests; that is, in dismantling the metanarratives, it removed any external value to its drive for validation. This led to a resurgence of narrative knowledge, but one which was no longer based on the grand narratives. Instead, it followed the effectively skeptical means of postmodern scientific discourse in optimizing performativity of a given system (e.g., a car's engine or a political state)—in other words, searching for "new" rules to govern the old language games—though it ultimately abandoned that discourse's end for progress's sake alone. Postmodern narrative knowledge thus emerged when the little narratives of knowledge—those instabilities or anomalies, the "quintessential form of imaginative inventiveness" (*PC* 60) that inevitably haunt modern scientific discourse (which could never "prove the proof" [*PC* 29] anyway) and postmodern scientific discourse (which dehumanizes its truth through performativity)—were combined through the practice of paralogy to form a newer knowledge whose legitimation was local and contextual and thus non-totalizing. Postmodern narrative knowledge, then, which recognized the inherent flaw within modernist conceptions of truth value and turned to the non-teleos of knowledge—not what end is produced in an action but what means are used to arrive at that end (a significant distinction in the politics of gender identities, as we will see later)—is "changing the meaning of the word *knowledge,* while expressing how such a change can take place" (*PC* 60). It is, in other words, producing "not the known, but the unknown"; not the plausible, but the possible (*PC* 60).

If we understand biography as a concrete example of Lyotard's concept of narrative knowledge, we could recognize how an emerging level of distrust against modernist ideas of fact have colored postmodernists' views of history, especially biographical history with its claims of truth. Since postmodernism is precisely skeptical of such totalizing knowledge, postmodern biography, or even autobiography, should necessarily challenge traditional notions of historical facts relating to one's life.[43] Williams, on a fundamental level, precisely resorts to this distrust in a veracious biography in *Clothes for a Summer Hotel* since the truth of the story of the Fitzgeralds that he tells is derived from several competing biographical sources from which Williams readily and freely draws and interprets for various ends. These "facts" are unabashedly filtered through him, where Williams's own life is transparently grafted onto that of Scott Fitzgerald, where *Clothes*'s Scott loosely hovers between the historical Fitzgerald and the real Tom/Tennessee Williams.[44] Williams openly invites this cross-identification in the play, either to exorcize personal demons deftly projected through Fitzgerald, as Thomas Adler and Elliott Martin argue, or to endear himself to a canonized writer and thus assure himself a place in America's literary pantheon at a time when he felt his inclusion in jeopardy, as Peter Hays contends.[45] For whatever the reason behind his motives, Williams's "truth" about Scott's and Zelda's lives (together or apart) is historically confounded, loosely interpreted, or expressionistically fabricated, though at no point does Williams acknowledge this as being somehow *untruthful* or disrespectful to the Fitzgeralds or to our memory of them.[46]

In the Broadway production's playbill, for instance, which he reproduced in the New Directions edition, we find the play's foreword explaining the reasons behind his poetic license with time and history surrounding the lives of his real characters:

AUTHOR'S NOTE: This is a ghost play.
   Of course in a sense all plays are ghost plays, since players are not actually whom they play.
   Our reason for taking extraordinary license with time and place is that in an asylum and on its grounds liberties of this kind are quite prevalent: and also these liberties allow us to explore in more depth what we believe is truth of character.[47]

Williams is, of course, recounting his truthful experiences with mental hospitals and its patients from first-hand knowledge—be they from his visiting his sister Rose in Ossining or from his own short stint at the Renard Psychiatric Division of Barnes Hospital in St. Louis in 1969—and artistically reproducing through a distorted mimesis notions of time and space as they might appear to a schizophrenic mind. We bring our sane and rational truths and realities into the theater to suspend our disbelief and accept that truth does not always come in tidy, boxed-up facts but rather in incidents, hyperbolic or realistic, fantastic or expressionistic, which show us a form a truth that we either carry with us upon leaving the theater or dutifully exchange at the coat check in return for our umbrella and overcoat.

When we go and see a play that deals with real *historical* people, however—and not just any tom-dick-or-harry, but beloved figures who have contributed a great deal to our nation's collective consciousness—that disbelief is frequently met with hostility, as was the case with *Clothes for a Summer Hotel*. And when those truthful and biographical "facts" are not only stretched to their "suspended" limits but even threaten the delicately constructed security of that national consciousness (as they were with Williams's implication that Fitzgerald not only admired but desired his friend Ernest Hemingway and, moreover, that Hemingway secretly felt the same toward Fitzgerald), we can understand a bit of the hostility the Williams encountered in the play's notices. The year was 1980, and though we seemed revolutions away from the Cold War anxieties of *Cat on a Hot Tin Roof* and Brick and Skipper, gender-benders and homosexuals were still a national bugbear and would become more so under the Christian demagoguery of President Reagan.

If we recall, however, that Williams at no point said that his play dealt with the "truth of historical fact" but rather with the "truth of character," then we recognize how Williams, like his contemporary Lyotard, understood historical truth as yet another incredulous metanarrative, no more valid as fact than the many fragmented narratives which, through paralogy, underscore or counter it. For postmodern biography is as concerned with the unknown as it is with the known. And although Williams is certainly not voicing anything particularly new about the histories of his characters, his compilation of these competing narratives and his moving them off the page and onto the Broadway stage, was certainly inventive, if not entirely inviting of hostility.

This notion of "truth of character," in fact, has had a long epistemological history in Williams, one that is key to understanding his repeated treatment of ambiguities in his characters, which have frequently been termed deceptive or manipulative by critics who viewed Williams as having frequently avoided dealing directly with difficult issues for fear of critical reprisal or public retribution. For example, as a response to Walter Kerr's attack on Brick's mysterious angst in 1955, Williams added the now-notorious stage note that attempts to explain Brick's reticence during the scene where Big Daddy tries to draw Brick out of the closet, one which we find later echoed in *Clothes for a Summer Hotel*'s "Author's Note": "*The bird that I hope to catch in the net of this play is not the solution of one man's psychological problem. . . . Some mystery should be left in the revelation of character in a play, just as a great deal of mystery is always left in the revelation of character in life, even in one's own character to himself*" (C 3:114–15).

That Williams would repeat these words, almost verbatim, in his own *Memoirs* twenty years later is a testament not only to his attempt to preempt any false truth, intentional or not, that he may have committed in rendering his life on paper, but also to challenge the sacrosanct belief that biography (auto-, ghost-scripted, or otherwise) can lay claim to a definitive, historical truth: "Truth is the bird we hope to catch in 'this thing,' and it can be better approached through my life story than an account of my career. Jesus, career, it's never been that to me, it has just been 'doing my thing' with a fury to do it the best that I am able" (*M* 173).

While the plays "speak for themselves" (*M* 154; cf. *M* 144), Williams continues, he still feels that he must explain himself to his *Memoirs'* readers, choosing here again "truth of character" (and all of its historical inaccuracies) over "truth of fact" (and its inability to tap into the nature of the inexplicable human condition) because he sees truth, as does Lyotard (and Hemingway, for that matter),[48] as being bound not by teleological fact derived from universal experience but rather by multidimensional truths wrapped up in new meanings to the old language games. In other words, if truth is finally rendered in the end product, as Williams has repeatedly intimated that it has, need we be so concerned about the facts that got us there? Could we not, he implores, simply accept his means to that end, despite their inconsistencies and perhaps even inaccuracies, if what is concluded remains consistent with our prior knowledge of it from the start? To do so would be accept that those ends, though they may satisfy a teleos-hungry audience, are less significant than what lies behind them, a notion that has surely fueled identity politics for over a century.

If Williams's own autobiography can be historically inaccurate but characteristically truthful, could not also those histories of other people, of other epochs? As he says in his "Author's Note" to *Clothes for a Summer Hotel*, "This must be regarded as a ghost play because of the chronological licenses which are taken, . . . the purpose being to penetrate into character more deeply and to encompass dreamlike passages of time in a scene" (*CSH* 8:n.p.). This is Williams's equivalence to Lyotard's paralogy. His "ghost play" as truth is a language game, and its foreword an attempt to define Williams's intentions locally and contextually so as to legitimate, not totalize, his view of the truth of Fitzgerald and Hemingway. Lyotard concludes his report by suggesting that we should no longer try to seek "a universal consensus" because consensus can never be an end in itself, only a process toward an end, one that moreover has become "outmoded and suspect" (*PC* 66). Instead, we would do better to recognize, first, "the heteromorphous nature of language games" and, second, "the principle that any consensus on the rules defining a game and the 'moves' playable within it *must* be local, in other words, agreed upon by its present players and subject to eventual cancellation. The orientation then favors a multiplicity of finite meta-arguments, by which I mean argumentation that concerns metaprescriptives and is limited in space and time" (*PC* 66). In attempting to establish a temporary "consensus" among his players and viewers by defining the rules of his "ghost play" with its "extraordinary license with time and place," all the while admitting that such a consensus cannot be sustained given the competing truths of the biographies from which he drew, Williams fulfills this earnest "quest for paralogy" (*PC* 66).

For whatever his intended aim in fictionalizing fact (either directed through his own lens or refracted through the lenses of those before him), immutable truth remains for Williams noncategorical, placing him clearly in the company of such postmodern giants as Don DeLillo, E. L. Doctorow, J. G. Ballard, and John Updike. As such, *Clothes for a Summer Hotel* reveals Williams's affinities with his era's postmodernist tastes in relativizing historicity and thus refutes any claim that his later work was just rehashed success from the 1940s and 1950s.

From Freud to Foucault: Sexuality as Metanarrative

Among the many metanarratives that Lyotard describes and that Williams challenges, we could readily add sexuality and its legitimizing judicio-scientific infrastructure established at the end of the nineteenth century and reinforced in the twentieth through psychoanalysis. Independently of Lyotard, Michel Foucault argued in *History of Sexuality* that the scientific discourse established in late Victorian Europe worked to legitimate its narrative truth of the sex-gender binary in order to meet the exponentially expanding desires of a burgeoning capitalist society, with the homosexual emerging as a tool within that construction to control and police heterosexuality for "economically useful and politically conservative" ends.[49] The metanarrative of psychoanalysis entered the sexology debate in America through Freud via Ulrichs, von Krafft-Ebing, Hirschfeld, and Ellis. Though it was first dubbed "maternal attachment" or "sexual inversion"—a residual of Claude Levi-Strauss's incest taboo—sexuality soon took on its own status as a metanarrative in Freud's Oedipal complex (and its two corollaries, castration theory and the phallus). Modern society was content to have been granted certain scientific legitimacy to its questions surrounding sexual and gender identities. Freud's primary bisexuality theory outlined in *Three Essays on the Theory of Sexuality*, in fact, served to reinforce that sexuality metanarrative, confirmed later by Alfred Kinsey with his findings in *Sexual Behavior in the Human Male*. Despite the attempts of these modernists to counter existing judicial prejudices against homosexuality by deeming it congenital or widespread, both Freud and Kinsey inadvertently relegitimized the nineteenth century's narrative of sexual inversion and fueled a half-century of hostility toward homosexuality.

Postmodern attempts to upend the sexuality metanarrative, like those of Mattachine in the early 1950s or Jonathan Katz with his monumental *Gay American History* in 1976 for instance, met with similar results.[50] While their political and sociohistorical agendas to promote multiple sexualities and genders in the face of a modernist binary varied, each unavoidably reinforced the metanarrative by challenging it with a series of mini-narratives that either never reached the masses who helped shape or police the sex/gender binary or were categorically dismissed as reflecting esoteric moments in U.S. history that, though indisputably true, were the exception more than the rule of American sexual life. For this reason, modern and postmodern affronts to heteromasculinist domination proved to be little more than what Lyotard would later deem as "noise." If Foucault's study added anything radically new to the assault against the sexuality metanarrative, it was in his inverted polemic that sexuality was not a true metanarrative at all—not in the sense that it naturally emerged from the "sex" narrative—but instead had appeared prior to "sex" through the concerted efforts of those in power to repress or conceal certain moral issues that challenged heteromasculinist hegemony. In other words, it was akin to a myth or a fable that earned truth-value after its dissemination and not a legitimate narrative in proper terms from the beginning.

None of these previous works, then, had considerably altered public opinion enough to constitute the type of challenge that Lyotard would describe as necessary for paralogy, at least not outside American academic circles. True paralogy for the sexuality metanarrative would have to wait a few more years for Judith Butler's *Gender Trouble*, a self-described "genealogy of gender ontology" that examines the competing roles feminism paradoxically played in confirming sexed identities in what could be identified as a postmodern *"bricolage"* (*PC* 44) of structuralist and poststructuralist psychoanalytical theories. By challenging the fixed "truth" of the gender/sex binary first expounded in the metanarrative of Victorian sexuality through a paralogic analysis of the many psychosexual mininarratives of the twentieth century (e.g., Freud, Lacan, de Beauvoir, Irigaray, Wittig, Kristeva, Rubin, and Foucault),[51] Butler hoped to "... understand the discursive production of the plausibility of that binary relation and to suggest that certain cultural configurations of gender take place of 'the real' and consolidate and augment their hegemony through that felicitous self-naturalization" (*GT* 43).

An erudite study whose influence has inexplicably spilled over the university borders and into popular culture, *Gender Trouble* would take as its central argument that, like Foucault's "sex," gender too is not a stable signifier but a socially-enacted phenomenon that carries little to no truth value about the perceived notions of identity. If "sex" had emerged from the sexuality metanarrative to serve the heteromasculinist powers that be, so too did "gender," with science no longer being able to account for what made a man different from a woman since even basic biological assumptions were inaccurate determiners of sex or gender. That emergence as a fixed, biological phenomenon was not through social construction alone but also through the individual's performance acting upon that construction, where the human body does not contain "a signifiable existence prior to the mark of gender" (*GT* 13) but rather reflects the individual's sexed or gendered action that through time carries "a performatively enacted signification" (*GT* 43–44). We have already seen how this theory applied to Jake Barnes in Hemingway's *The Sun Also Rises*. Here, I'd like to turn to how it works in Williams's *Clothes for a Summer Hotel* and in Williams's own struggle to negotiate his way through the troubled gay waters of the 1970s.

For Butler, gender is never the noun we have perceived it to be, and thus not a metaphysical substance consistent with the various competing feminist theories that insist first on there being a "doer" behind the action; instead, gender is a verb, a performance through which the individual adheres to (or not) the prescribed role afforded to him or her by the Symbolic law of phallogocentrism: "Gender ought not to be construed as a stable identity or locus of agency from which various acts follow; rather, gender is an identity tenuously constituted in time, instituted in an exterior space through a *stylized repetition of acts*. The effect of gender is produced through the stylization of the body and, hence, must be understood as the mundane way in which bodily gestures, movements, and styles of various kinds constitute the illusion of an abiding gendered self" (*GT* 179). As a result, gender cannot verify the "identity behind the expression of gender" since "that identity is performatively constituted by the very 'expressions' that are said to be the results" (*GT* 33)—once again, the non-teleological approach to the study of alterity. In other words, a man's heteromasculinist exterior is in no way proof of his resultant heterosexual identity since it is really just an act anyway; rather, his heterosexuality is a social assumption resulting from his performing the necessary gender signs to assure such a reading.

Such gender performance is not an isolated act, Butler adds, but precisely demands "the repeated stylization of the body, a set of repeated acts within a highly rigid regulatory frame that congeal over time to produce the appearance of substance, of a natural sort of being" (*GT* 44). Consequently, both sex and gender produce "regulatory fictions that consolidate and naturalize the convergent power regimes of masculine and heterosexist oppression" (*GT* 44) and thus lack inherent scientific truth-values on even the biological level. Working through paralogy to legitimate each other's existence, which, in turn, reinforces the social identity for which they ultimately serve, sex and gender open themselves up to postmodern scrutiny bent on exposing the political motives luring behind the mask of their everyday use. To be sure, this notion of "performativity" is where Lyotard and Butler meet, where for Lyotard what is legitimized in the narrative (i.e., its optimized functionality) is for Butler just another example of a language game with one's performed gender not always being a truthful representation of one's real sexual identity, let alone the most productive one. Any failure—unintentional or otherwise, isolated or repeated—for a male to perform a gender consistent with the "regulatory fiction" of what a *he-man* is, or should be, opens that male up to signification via society's gendered reading; in other words, as Butler notes, "Not to have social recognition as an effective heterosexual is to lose one possible social identity and perhaps to gain one that is radically less sanctioned. The 'unthinkable' is thus fully within culture, but fully excluded from *dominant* culture" (*GT* 99).

Butler's polemic in *Gender Trouble* lies in its "subverting and displacing those naturalized and reified notions of gender that support masculine hegemony and heterosexist power" in order "to make gender trouble": "not through the strategies that figure a utopian beyond, but through the mobilization, subversive confusion, and proliferation of precisely those constitutive categories that seek to keep gender in its place by posturing as the foundational illusions of identity" (*GT* 44).[52] Though not stated in precisely the same manner, Williams's "Author's Note" implies a similar agenda, for the "truth of character" behind his gay Scott and his queer Hemingway in *Clothes for a Summer Hotel* contains his own efforts to subvert those "constitutive categories" that have contributed to their "illusions of identity" in an adoring America. By portraying an effeminate F. Scott Fitzgerald and a macho Ernest Hemingway as potentially closeted homosexuals, Williams demonstrates how he too had envisaged gender as a performance through which an individual projects an identity to the world inconsistent with his real sexual desires. If "gender proves to be performative—that is, constituting the identity it is purported to be," as Butler posits, any sexual identity that is determined *propter hoc* must be proscribed and necessarily inaccurate (*GT* 33).

To be sure, the stories behind Williams's Fitzgerald and Hemingway were not revelatory in their historical sense, given that Williams was not the first to make such claims about either men. In fact, the play's initial criticism wavered between condemning Williams either for outing obscure theories from their biased academic sources (Nancy Milford's *Zelda*) or gossipy, self-aggrandizing memoirs (Hemingway's *A Moveable Feast*) and placing them indiscriminately on the democratic stage for all to see; or for not advancing our knowledge of those theories beyond what we had already known of them. For these reasons, it is not surprising that his re-appropriation of the past was viewed in the play's theater notices as being merely a repetition of the past, with John Simon criticizing Williams's "typical gossip-mongering approach" and Douglas Watt intimating he wished Williams would have gossiped more.[53] And yet, since Williams's sole intent was not merely to dramatize what the numerous biographies had already established about the two men's sexual incongruities but rather to revisit those stories in order to expose how society had forced the two men into performing their genders and questioning each other afterward as to what those identities behind them actually were, any alteration of the biographies would (scientifically speaking) have contaminated Williams's study. Williams thus remains loyal to the apocrypha (for that is all that postmodernism would be ready to call it anyway) so as to precisely call its "truth" into question.

In terms of Fitzgerald's troubling gender, for example, Williams has Zelda allude to the notorious photo of a "stunning" Fitzgerald in drag for the Princeton Triangle Club (which Williams enlarges and has projected onstage in his play) to call our attention not only to the Fitzgerald during the drag performance of the Triangle Club but also to the one now standing before us onstage whose gender performance in marrying the Jazz Age darling made him a male impersonator. Williams then has Zelda push Scott into acknowledging that he married her so as to preempt any social reading of his feminine gender, which she suggests signifies his latent or closeted homosexuality:

> *Zelda.* Just crept in against orders, to admire you at work. . . .
> *Scott.* I don't work to be admired at it.
> *Zelda.* I know, for the work to be admired. But, Goofo, you look so pretty working, at least till — [*She points at the bottle.*]
> *Scott.* [*still facing front*] *Pretty* did you say?
> *Zelda.* Admirable, and pretty. At first, you know, I had reservations about marriage to a young man prettier than me. . . . I'm not pretty, only mistaken for it. . . . But, Goofo, you really *are*. (*CSH* 8:234, emphasis added)

In reading Scott's homosexuality from the outside in, that is, from his visible body language and effeminate appearance toward his unknowable desire, Zelda is perhaps only guilty of remaining consistent with her day's social praxis of determining psychosexual identity from external gender signs. But, as Butler would argue, determining Scott's sexual identity based upon our or Zelda's reading of his gender performance in no way legitimizes the truth of that identity. If Fitzgerald had already performed his effeminacy once during his drag role at Princeton, why should his "real" life's effeminacy be considered as anything more than just another performance, and therefore not telling of his "real" sexual identity?

Without a doubt, Williams is exploiting here not only the performativity of marriage as a truth-laden act of heterosexuality but also the given assumption that gender faithfully mirrors the sexual identity involved in this act. Though he may *look* gay in appearance, Williams's Scott is not in appetite, or so it seems at this point of the play:

> *Scott.* [*with an edge*] Don't keep on with that, Zelda, that's insulting.
> *Zelda.* . . . I don't understand why you should find it so objectionable.
> *Scott.* The adjective "pretty" is for girls, or pretty boys of—ambiguous gender. . . . (*CSH* 8:234)

Zelda fully understands what being "pretty" implies for a man, and that it challenges his masculinity and has so since at least the end of the nineteenth century when it was a metonymy for sexual inversion, and Scott is quick to point this out: "Being called pretty implies—. . . . A disparagement of—. . . . You know as well as I know that what it disparages is—the virility of—[*He takes another drink.*]" (*CSH* 8:235). By substituting alcohol for a public declaration of the word itself, let alone the sexual identity that potentially accompanies it, Scott successfully parries the insinuation for the moment, temporarily eluding the need to admit any possible truth to Zelda (and perhaps to himself), for as long as the drink holds out, that his femininity hides a homosexual bent.[54]

That Williams should substantiate Zelda's inquiry here with the reference to the word "pretty" hardly seems coincidental, given the fact that Hemingway, who was just mentioned a few lines earlier, appears later in the play and Scott boasts to him that he saved Hemingway's first novel "from starting with the entire past history of Lady Brett Ashley . . ." (*CSH* 8:269). The intertextuality recalls both Hemingway's description of Fitzgerald in *A Moveable Feast* as "a boy with a face between handsome and pretty" (*MF* 149) and Jake Barnes's ironic "pretty" (*S* 247) at the end of *The Sun Also Rises*. It also problematizes a socially-perceived sexual identity since Jake is not gay in the novel and consistently performs a masculine gender, but, because of his impotence, he cannot perform his heterosexuality and possibly abuses alcohol like Scott, and Brick Pollitt, to hide that fact from others or to placate its effects on him, thus opening himself up to queer suspicion. No irony is lost either when Scott, just like Jake in the Hemingway novel and Brick in *Cat on a Hot Tin Roof*, predictably resorts to homophobic panic as a secondary means to counter society's reading of his sexuality and protect his private self.

For example, in an attempt to undermine, first, Zelda's description of his gay sensibilities, which she felt helped him as a writer and, second, Hemingway's disparaging affronts to his masculinity, Scott initially responds with the same pejorative language to which both Jake and Brick retreat when trapped in a similar confrontational situation:

> *Zelda.* I think that to write well about women, there's got to be that, a part of that, in the writer, oh, not too much, not so much that he flits about like a —
> *Scott.* Fairy?
> *Zelda.* You're too hard on them, Scott. I don't know why. Do they keep chasing you because you're so pretty they think you must be a secret one of them? (*CSH* 8:235)

When language fails to convince her (or the Williams's character "Hem" later), Scott takes to launching racial epithets and gender slurs at an exotic black male Moulin Rouge dancer, whom Sara and Gerald Murphy had flown in from Paris for their May 1926 party in Antibes: "HEY! MILK-CHOC'LATE, WANTA ASK YOU SOMETHING! Which gender do you prefer?" (*CSH* 8:266). However, in response to the drunken Scott's maligned act of bravado, the equally effeminate dancer easily *"flattens him with one blow"* (*CSH* 8:266), which does nothing to help Scott's masculine image or our contemporary distinction between gender and sexual alignment.

While the black singer is not actually in drag here, his feminine traits coupled with his performing the song "Sophisticated Lady" lead Scott nonetheless to pronounce him a "fairy" (*CSH* 8:266). Unluckily for Scott, the singer's effeminate exterior hides a masculine interior (if we consider the boxer, as Hemingway did, as an archetype of masculinity), and Scott reaps the fruits of the androgynous man's wrath. That the effeminate singer should perform two genders simultaneously — Scott's in his queer nature and Hemingway's in his pugilist one — only demonstrates how inappropriate gender readings are as determiners of identity, sexual or otherwise, in the play.[55] If, as Butler writes, we consider gender to be *"a corporeal style,* an 'act,' as it were, which is both intentional and performative, where *'performative'* suggests a dramatic and contingent construction of meaning" (*GT* 177), then Scott's performance is as indeterminate as the exotic black performer's, with Williams again suggesting that gender signification is finally impossible; ambiguity and androgyny win the day.

Furthermore, even when gender is intentionally performed as a public spectacle, as in the case of female or male impersonation—the kind of which we see in the black singer's performance and in Scott's bellicose attitude—it not only inverts normative identity types but equally refuses all attempts at codification. As Butler notes,

> The performance of drag plays upon the distinction between the anatomy of the performer and the gender that is being performed. But we are actually in the presence of three contingent dimensions of significant corporeality: anatomical sex, gender identity, and gender performance. If the anatomy of the performer is already distinct from the gender of the performer, and both of those are distinct from the gender of the performance, then the performance suggests a dissonance not only between sex and performance, but sex and gender, and gender and performance. As much as drag creates a unified picture of "woman" (what its critics often oppose), it also reveals a distinctness of those aspects of gendered experience which are falsely naturalized as a unity through the regulatory fiction of heterosexual coherence. *In imitating gender, drag implicitly reveals the imitative structure of gender itself—as well as its contingency.* (*GT* 175)[56]

All gender is drag for Butler, meaning that we are all performing a particular role that we wish to be read as consistent (or not) with compulsive heterosexuality's "regulatory fiction." One cannot *not* perform gender, and therefore performativity makes all sexual assumptions behind it moot. In attempting here to perform a masculine gender through the fight, then, Scott is no more signifying his heterosexuality than the black singer is performing his homosexuality through his effeminate act.

To be sure, Williams was not being overly inventive in this scene, since others with whom Fitzgerald was intimate, particularly his wife Zelda and friend Hemingway, had long intimated that homosexuality lurked behind Scott's feminine mystique (though the black dancer episode was an original contribution, which exhibits Williams's intention to toy with gender and racial notions). Williams's own dialogue was, in fact, heavily influenced by Nancy Milford's in her biography *Zelda*, where she notes repeatedly Zelda's efforts to drive a wedge between her husband and Hemingway by implying that Fitzgerald's attraction for him went beyond "hero worship" and even bordered on sexual desire: "On the boat to Europe . . . she accused Scott of a homosexual liaison with Ernest Hemingway. Scott, who had gone without Zelda to have a drink one evening with Hemingway and his wife, had returned home intoxicated and had fallen into a deep sleep. In his sleep he had murmured, 'no more baby', which was taken by Zelda as absolute proof of her suspicions."[57]

Hemingway (and others) believed that Zelda used the gay insinuation, as Maggie had with Skipper, to belittle Fitzgerald in their ongoing marital disputes,[58] an effort, Milford adds, which proved effective:

> Several months later Robert McAlmon told Hemingway that Scott was a homosexual. Hemingway must have relayed the accusation to Fitzgerald, for Scott mentioned in a letter to Maxwell Perkins: "Part of his [McAlmon's] quarrel with Ernest some years ago was because he assured Ernest that I was a fairy—God knows he shows more creative imagination in his malice than in his work. Next he told Callahan that Ernest was a fairy. He's a pretty good person to avoid." . . . By the spring of 1929, the Fitzgeralds' own physical estrangement all but complete, Zelda turned the charge against Scott. It took surprising effect. For a while at least Scott had begun to believe her. (*Z* 154; cf. *Z* 211)

Fitzgerald became for Williams the poster child of accusative sexual politics, where gender readings not only tainted an individual's social identity but worked to breakdown his own certainty of who he was, or thought he was.

Significantly, each reading of the real Fitzgerald's apparent homosexuality relied solely upon his feminized beauty, irrespective of any proof of his acting upon a homosexual desire. For this reason, we have arguably entered Skipper and Brick's world in *Cat on a Hot Tin Roof*, where the fictional Scott is equally forced into either accepting (as Skipper had done) or denying (as Brick does) how others perceive his sexual identity.[59] Though he never does emerge from his closet, Scott begins admitting to harboring a homoerotic desire, or is at least persuaded by Zelda as possessing one. By perceiving Scott as a homosexual because of his effete sensibilities first and his overt homophobia second, where he admits not liking to be "touched by men!" (*CSH* 8:258), Zelda is simply reflecting the twentieth-century trend of sociosexual identification, perhaps more recognizable by 1980 than it had been by 1955, or even by 1926. But that trend in no way captures the truth behind the suspected homosexual's real sexual identity, as we have seen, and the individual is left with no choice but to accept his society's definition or to challenge it, and Scott does both.

If Williams first dramatizes Scott's refusal of his wife's definition of homosexuality, Williams next dramatizes his evolving self-awareness of it, countering all that he (and Williams, for that matter) had asserted up to that point in the play about the dangers of sexed readings of gender. In fact, Scott soon begins camping up his own queer sensibilities for, if not sexual attraction to, Hemingway himself at the Murphys' party:

> *Hemingway.* Scott, I've always had a feeling that it's a mistake for writers to know each other. The competitive element in the normal male nature is especially prominent in the nature of writers.
> *Scott.* With so much in common? As you and I?
> *Hemingway.* A profession—only.
> *Scott.* Not sensibilities?
> *Hemingway.* Yours and mine are totally different, Scott.
> *Scott.* And yet—it's said of us both that we always write of the same woman, you of Lady Brett Ashley in various guises and me of—
> *Hemingway.* Zelda and Zelda and more Zelda. As if you'd like to appropriate her identity and her—. . . . Sorry, Scott, but I almost said gender. (*CSH* 8:267–68)[60]

To be sure, in exploiting the suspected homosexuality of Fitzgerald and promulgating it with that of Hemingway within his postmodern biography, Williams is challenging modernist sexual epistemology itself, revealing in practice what contemporary queer theorists would later provide a rhetoric for. Yet, despite Williams's public protestations to society's reading of his gender as homosexuality, which would suggest that Williams was trying to show how gay signification of this sort often proves damaging, Scott privately begins validating it, parroting what others have been telling him throughout the play: a man who is homosexual, who knows it, and who has been hiding that truth from everyone despite the fact that they had already suspected it from the start.

In now reading Fitzgerald's feminine features, fragile sensibilities, and heterosexual dysfunction as signifiers of a homosexual identity, is Williams revealing his own prejudices against masculine signification and demonstrating how inescapable the Phallic law can be in establishing sexual identity from gender performance alone? And, if this is the case, is he not precisely doing what he has just warned us all against doing, that is reading a sexed identity through a gendered one? I do not think so. Instead, I think that there is something more political at stake here. As Linda Hutcheon has said of all postmodern production, a text likes *Clothes for a Summer Hotel* "exploits and yet simultaneously calls into question notions of closure, totalization, and universality that are parts of those challenged grand narratives" that the play recalls.[61] Certainly, Williams could be demonstrating how damaging social pressure can be for an individual whose insecurities lead him to doubt his personal epistemologies in favor of those of the masses, just as he had shown with Brick in *Cat on a Hot Tin Roof*. But I believe Williams had moved beyond that polemic by 1980, for if he had found himself in the years prior to Stonewall paring attacks from homophobic critics for making homosexuality the stuff of Broadway, by the 1970s he was to find himself the target of the gay community itself for not having done it enough; and when he did do it, it was only after gay activists had already paved the way with the Stonewall riots that resulted in gay liberation. In this way, then, Scott moves further away from being a postmodern incarnation of Brick Pollitt and begins merging with a post-Stonewall Williams, where Scott now flirts with outing himself and grows hostile toward those, namely Hemingway, who do not have the *cojones* to do so as well.

Postmodern Pastiche and the "Queer" Hemingway

In his "intimate" memoir of Williams, *Tennessee: Cry of the Heart*, Dotson Rader supplies a conversation Williams was said to have had with Margaux Hemingway about her father and Williams's characterization of him, as well as the work involved in writing a biographical play: "I think *Clothes* was the most difficult play, of all my plays, to write. Because of the documentation that I had to do. I had to spend four or five months reading everything there is about Fitzgerald and Zelda. There's a huge amount of material!"[62]

Though apocryphal in nature, Williams's comment is at least legitimated by the indisputable fact that Williams's research for *Clothes for a Summer Hotel* was vast, evidenced by the glaring similarities between the play's text and those sources Williams's used in its composition. While we will probably never know exactly how much "everything there is" included, what we do know is that the two most significant sources for the play were Milford's biography *Zelda* and Hemingway's *A Moveable Feast* as ideas and even language found in each are readily traceable in the play.[63] To be sure, Williams's choice of sources for the documentation he uses to fill his play is not at all innocent. If reading Milford's feminist *Zelda* purposely gave him the thesis that "the entire fabric of their life was [Scott's] material, none of it was Zelda's" (*Z* 273)[64]—through which Williams expiates feelings of guilt he might have had for turning his sister's life into his artistic material—then reading Hemingway's *A Moveable Feast* and posthumously published novel *Islands in the Stream* fueled Williams's bias into reading Scott's emasculation as linked directly to charges of sexual impotence and latent homosexuality by those nearest to him, to say nothing of Hemingway's as well.[65]

Opposing Milford's pro-Zelda thesis with Hemingway's vituperative bitch-Zelda one provided Williams the opportunity to explore theories of emasculation in relation to sexual orientation and identification consistent with the times. The most flagrant difference between these two biographers and Williams, however, is that while all provide historically-slanted views of Scott, only Williams's version has Hemingway appear as a character to deliver them. In other words, though Williams passes Milford's thesis through the mouth of his play's Zelda, Hemingway's appraisal of Scott is given by his fictionalized self. If Milford's book provides the play's essential thesis, then, Hemingway's memoir provides the play's pastiche, and Williams's reading of Hemingway through Hemingway's reading of Scott further establishes *Clothes for a Summer Hotel* as a critique of biography (and autobiography, like his *Memoirs*) being nothing more than postmodern fiction.

In *Postmodernism, or, The Cultural Logic of Late Capitalism* (1991), Fredric Jameson describes how modernity "characterizes the attempt to make something coherent" out of the relationship between the changes to a society and "the form the superstructure takes in reaction to that ambivalent development" (*P* 310). As there is no longer enough critical distance between modernism and postmodernism, postmodernism has proved incapable of breaking with tradition and criticizing modernism through parody; instead it has become a pastiche of high modernist style, where the "disappearance of the individual subject" imitates the idea of the original without actually mocking it directly: "Pastiche is, like parody, the imitation of a peculiar or unique, idiosyncratic style, the wearing of a linguistic mask, speech in a dead language. But it is a neutral practice of such mimicry, without any of parody's ulterior motives, amputated of the satiric impulse, devoid of laughter and of any conviction that alongside the abnormal tongue you have momentarily borrowed, some healthy linguistic normality still exists. Pastiche is thus blank parody, a statue with blind eyeballs . . ." (*P* 16, 17).[66]

In combining old and new aesthetics, pastiche plays with images not so much as to challenge or debunk history but, precisely, to recover it, or at least some semblance of what history was ever since its postmodern degradation.[67] As Jameson notes, "The new spatial logic of the simulacrum can now be expected to have a momentous effect on what used to be historical time" (*P* 18). Pastiche, then, is the result of this transformation from a society with a historical sensibility to one that can now only play with a degraded historicism, reshaping notions of subjectivity and objectivity along the way. In other words, what was history then is to a postmodernist pastiche, "a vast collection of images, a multitudinous photographic simulacrum" (*P* 18) in search of its transcendental signified.[68]

Any postmodern attempt at recovering historicity, such as biography, can only hope to do so through pastiche, since history's fragmentation is all that we have to establish our continuity with the past that is being studied. To lay claims to producing biographical authority today is complicated by the subject's "cannibalized" (Jameson's term) image, making it nearly impossible to attempt a truly historicized reading without having already been contaminated by being in contact with its simulacrum first. Therefore, as Jameson writes,

> The historical novel [or biographical play] can no longer set out to represent the historical past; it can only "represent" our ideas and stereotypes about that past (which thereby at once becomes "pop history"). Cultural production is thereby driven back inside a mental space which is no longer that of the old monadic subject but rather that of some degraded collective "objective spirit".... If there is any realism left here, it is a "realism" that is meant to derive from the shock of grasping that confinement and of slowly becoming aware of a new and original historical situation in which we are condemned to seek History by way of our own pop images and simulacra of that history, which itself remains forever out of reach. (P 25)

This "objective spirit" that Jameson describes once again returns us to Williams's "truth of character" credo in *Clothes for a Summer Hotel*, for any prior understanding that he had of Fitzgerald or of Hemingway first passed through his contact with them as Goofo or Papa—the icons, literary and cultural, and not the men/writers themselves. While there is a certain amount of pastiching of Fitzgerald's character going on in the play to represent the truth behind his constructed sexual history, as we have just seen, Williams's use of Hemingway material to portray the reasons behind that writer's eventual suicide are also very telling, not just about the "real" Hemingway's view of the "real" Fitzgerald but also about Williams's view of that "real" Hemingway within pre- and post-Stonewall contexts, about which Williams himself felt more and less divided.

To be sure, Ernest Hemingway's unabated homophobia and celebrated macho image throughout his life belied his sexual dysfunction, inner femininity, and fascination with gender bending, repeatedly documented in his biographies and evidenced most strikingly in his posthumously published novels *Islands in the Stream*, *The Garden of Eden*, and *True at First Light/Under Kilimanjaro*. Thus when Zelda suggests in *Clothes for a Summer Hotel* that "Scott is magnetized, infatuated with Ernest's somewhat too carefully cultivated aura of the prizefight and the bullring and the man-to-man attitude acquired from Gertrude Stein" (*CSH* 8:261), Williams is once again simply recycling the well-worn homosexual gossip involving Zelda's use of her husband's friendship with Hemingway as fodder against him in their marriage disputes, as well as against Hemingway himself for his obsession with masculinity and its many representations.[69] Hemingway would parody these accusations, of course, writing in a December 1927 letter to Fitzgerald: "You are right about the Spanish wine skin and I find it very comfortable but it has nothing so unhemanish as a zipper. I have to watch myself that way and deny myself of many of the little comforts like toilet paper, semi-colons, and soles to my shoes. Any time I use any of those people begin to shout that old Hem is just a fairy after all and no He man ha ha" (*SL* 268). Still, critics and biographers alike have repeatedly wondered "what if?" Williams crosses this historical line of wondering and has Hem publicly respond to Zelda's charge with a queerly encoded comment, "I'm acquainted with the other side of the coin" (*CSH* 8:261),[70] and privately admit to Scott his gay sensibilities and reciprocated attraction for the writer.

Curiously enough, Hemingway's *The Garden of Eden*, published six years after *Clothes for a Summer Hotel*, would support many of Williams's intimations here about Hemingway's fascination with homosexuality and obsession with androgyny. In the opening scene of a novel that explores lesbianism more fully than in Hemingway's short stories "Mr. and Mrs. Elliot" and "The Sea Change," we discover Catherine Bourne, a woman who crops her hair so short that she looks like a boy and even says to David, "I'm a girl. But now I'm a boy too and I can do anything and anything and anything."[71] During her lovemaking with David, they switch sex roles, and David is sodomized by Catherine with a wine bottle after she asks him, "Will you change and be my girl and let me take you?": "He had shut his eyes and he could feel the long light weight of her on him and her breasts pressing against him and her lips on his. He lay there and felt something and then her hand holding him and searching lower and he helped with his hands and then lay back in the dark and did not think at all and only felt the weight and the strangeness inside and she said, 'Now you can't tell who is who can you?'" (*GE* 17). Had Williams lived long enough to read this novel, he would surely have been as moved by it as he was by *Islands in the Stream*.

Hemingway's posthumous works simply provided Williams with the material to question further those initial reports of Hemingway's queer side that had been dismissed for half a century or more. Williams uses Hemingway's *A Moveable Feast*, then, not to characterize Scott in the end as effeminate but precisely to interpret Hemingway's memoir as an unspoken confession of admiration-cum-fascination in the very homoerotic sense, similar to Willie's repeated declaration of love (like Big Mama's and Maggie's in *Cat on a Hot Tin Roof*) to the dying Thomas Hudson at the end of *Islands in the Stream*:

> "Tommy," Willie said. "I love you, you son of a bitch, and don't die."
> Thomas Hudson looked at him without moving his head.

"Try and understand if it isn't too hard." . . .
"I think I understand, Willie," he said.
"Oh shit," Willie said. "You never understand anybody that loves you." (*IS* 446; cf. 263)

If Williams only pastiches the Hemingway sources at first to buttress his dramatized interpretation of a sexually-confused Fitzgerald, he then turns Hemingway on himself in the play to consider what those obsessions with gender inversion and homosexuality might actually entail.

For example, in the opening words of Hemingway's "Scott Fitzgerald" in *A Moveable Feast*, Williams encountered this description of Fitzgerald, which he subsequently worked into *Clothes for a Summer Hotel* with Zelda's "pretty" comment and Hemingway's admission of Scott's tender and vulnerable beauty:

> Scott was a man then who looked like a boy with a face between handsome and *pretty*. He had very fair wavy hair, a high forehead, excited and friendly eyes and a delicate long-lipped Irish mouth that, on a girl, would have been the mouth of beauty. His chin was well built and he had good ears and a *handsome*, almost beautiful, unmarked nose. This should not have added up to a *pretty face*, but that came from the coloring, the very fair hair and the mouth. The mouth worried you until you knew him and then it worried you more. (*MF* 149, my emphasis)

No doubt incensed by his own times's reading sexual identity through gender (specifically Zelda's), Hemingway describes Scott's prettiness over his handsomeness not so much to fuel the existing theories of his homosexuality but rather to inveigh against them. In other words, Hemingway repeatedly casts Scott's effeminacy in a heterosexual light, just as he had Jake's heterosexuality in an effeminate light. If anything was to suggest that Fitzgerald was gay, Hemingway polemicizes here, it was only to be found in the emasculating machinations of the "hawk" Zelda.

And yet, for Williams, this chapter complicates Hemingway's reasons behind his portrayal of Fitzgerald in *A Moveable Feast*. Though Hemingway's relationship to irony poses all sorts of problems and repeatedly denies us access to a definitive interpretation, it equally supposes the alternative; that is, what is being said is completely truthful, partially truthful, or not at all truthful, each becoming plausible since that we cannot isolate one from among the many layers of irony. As such, in turning descriptive prose into dramatic declaration, Williams forces a queer reading upon his Hemingway, just as Hemingway had forced one upon Jake in the closing line of *The Sun Also Rises*: "—Scott, you had the skin of a girl, mouth of a girl, the soft eyes of a girl, you—you solicited attention. I gave it, yes, I found you touchingly vulnerable" (*CSH* 8:270).[72] In other words, regardless of whether or not Hemingway was using the word "pretty" ironically (or even homophobically), both he and Jake (the paradigmatic male pimp/healer in the Hemingway canon if ever there was one) are conscious of their self-stylizing and relationship to the word "pretty" and frequently perform a macho, rugged handsomeness in order to distance themselves from it.[73] Williams thus questions: what if the memoir's bitingly nostalgic portrayal of a roughly maternal Hemingway nursing the febrile Fitzgerald back to health is another example of his many sincere nurse portraits, from Catherine Barkley in *A Farewell to Arms* to Bugs in the short story "The Battler"? Moreover, when that nurse is male, as with Bugs, what happens to that bond between patient and healer?[74]

In *Clothes for a Summer Hotel*, Williams provides his answer to these questions by "outing" Fitzgerald explicitly and "queering" Hemingway implicitly. When everyone at the Murphys' Antibes party leaves to attend dinner, for example, Hemingway lags behind to talk to Scott "*mano-mano?*" (*CSH* 8:267), with the Spanish bullfighting term for a duel between two matadors now taking on a queer English metonymy. While it first appears that Hemingway might soon emerge during this private moment from his well-guarded closet, however, he remains coy and laconic: "[*He approaches Scott. For a moment we see their true depth of pure feeling for each other. Hemingway is frightened of it, however*]" (*CSH* 8:268). Even when Scott, sensing Hemingway's struggle to want to open up to him emotionally, begins coaxing him into accepting that his homosocial desire harbored more sentiment than Hemingway is willing to admit, as Zelda had said of Scott earlier, Hemingway maintains his resolve:

> *Scott.* We do have multiple selves as well as what you call dual genders.—
> Hem? Let's admit we're—
> *Hemingway.* What?
> *Scott.* Friends, Hem—true and very deep friends. (*CSH* 8:269)[75]

Yet, just as Scott had done after his homophobic outburst with the black singer, Hemingway begins letting down his macho guard and delivers those words that Williams lifted directly from *A Moveable Feast* concerning Fitzgerald's voluptuous mouth and doe-like eyes. Williams's Hemingway never moves beyond the ambiguous or the ironic or the encoded, however, for even when Scott asks him if these traits repelled him, Hemingway replies, "They were disturbing to me" (*CSH* 8:270). Though Scott prods him "[i]n privacy, under such special circumstances" (*CSH* 8:271) to analyze that response and explore their mutual attraction, Hemingway responds that he would "rather not examine the reason too closely" (*CSH* 8:270). All that is finally agreed upon is that Scott had "a sleepless night when the rain stopped [them] on the way back" (*CSH* 8:267), and Hemingway cared for him "with the tenderness of [the night/knight]—" (*CSH* 8:270).[76]

At this point of their conversation, Scott continues his overtures about Hemingway's queerness and cites many of the closeted characters in Hemingway's work.[77] In the first, Scott recalls Hemingway's story "A Simple Enquiry" where a potentially gay (or at least heterosexually unsatisfied) Italian officer inquires about the marital status of young orderly, Pinin, whose "androgynous appeal" is similar to the one that Hemingway said Scott had "had in wherever after Lyon" (*CSH* 8:271). In the story, the major wonders at the end if the "little devil . . . lied to me" (*CSS* 252) about his being straight, just as Scott questions Hemingway here about his telling him the truth. Hemingway counters Scott's accusations by saying that he has written other works where homosexuality or homoeroticism plays a significant role, including the story "Sea Change" [*sic*] that has a "protesting" young man on "a ship sailing to Europe" who eventually "reconciled to his patron's attentions" (*CSH* 8:271).[78] But Hemingway defends himself by saying that a writer's profession is "to observe and interpret all kinds of human relations": "That's what serious writers hire out to do. Maybe it's rough, this commitment, but we honor it with truth as we observe and interpret it" (*CSH* 8:271). Whether or not Hemingway would have actually said something like this matters little since he frequently demonstrated it in his work, which for Williams was proof enough that Hemingway was at least capable of saying it.[79]

Conflating a writer with his work, as Williams repeatedly does here, is dangerous territory to be sure; when questions of a writer's sexual identity are at stake, such an inquiry even replicates in kind the sociosexual stereotyping of which Zelda was certainly guilty. And yet, in observing and interpreting "human relations" and offering "truth of character" in the form of a pastiche that captures biographical historicity without ever claiming to be historically true, Williams becomes this writer that Hemingway describes. As his gendered body is to his sexual desire, a writer's words are merely isolated performative acts that reveal little inner truth about their source's identity. The Butlerian corollary, however, is equally true: those performed words, like the body in drag, not only influence the reader's impression of the writer's identity, but also the writer's of himself—and Hemingway was the perfect case in point.

With all of his paeans to heteromasculinity, which helped to shape his public image, Hemingway could not entirely escape honest queer treatments of male-male and male-female relations, for *Islands in the Stream* and *The Garden of Eden*, penned around the same time as *A Moveable Feast*, reveal a Hemingway that the public had never before known and would have to wait another thirty years or more to meet: one obsessed as much with homoeroticism and gender-bending later in his career as he apparently was with heteronormative sex and gender in his early works. Thus, if Scott's conclusion in *Clothes for a Summer Hotel* is that Hemingway's unacknowledged homosexuality was at the source not only of his frequent marital strife and alcoholic depression but also of his suicide, it is a reading of a man's *corpus* as one reads his *corps*, and making damning generalizations in the process about the identity behind the performance.[80] This conclusion is, of course, Williams's as well, and despite the fact that he earnestly defends Hemingway's right to denial based only on the proof that he treated homosexuality fairly in his canon, Williams again proves seemingly incapable of transcending the identity politics that his play critiques. For though he proffers no indisputable answers concerning the real Hemingway's sexual identity, Williams's pastiche ends with a foreshadowing of Hemingway's queer portrayal of Fitzgerald in *A Moveable Feast*, as well as with the reproduction of the ending to Hemingway's *Islands in the Stream* where Scott's trying to coax Hemingway out from his closet replicates the ambiguity the latter chose to conclude his novel.[81]

While the conclusion to their dramatic inquiry in *Clothes for a Summer Hotel* is drawn directly from *Islands in the Stream*, the fact that Hemingway's novel was left incomplete in 1950–1951 and published posthumously by Scribner's in 1970 in no way provides convincing evidence as to what Hemingway had really intended with the ambiguous ending, or even if he had meant to conclude it in this manner. Again, my point here is not to implicate Hemingway one way or another but rather to apprehend what Williams had implicated from reading the novel. In other words, while Scott and Hemingway's conversation was historically unfounded, the "fictive incident might be argued to be historically accurate as a metaphor of the two men's relationship."[82] And for Williams, a Hemingway who had treated homosexuality and homoerotics more directly in this novel than in his other works, particularly where he says the hero makes a "beautiful declaration of his love for a man at the end," was proof alone of his queer side: "They say he was 'often inebriated' when he wrote it, but if you like Hemingway the man, here you get the man more truly than in any other work. I admired above all his poet's feelings for words. And here, finally, whether or not he intended to, he told the complete truth. For that reason, it is his greatest work. I like all of it" (*CTW* 222). Williams was simply as interested in Hemingway's portrayal of Fitzgerald and of his fear that Zelda's emasculation was evidence of his homosexuality as he was intrigued by the fetishist role Hemingway took in recounting that emasculation in his memoir. For Williams, Hemingway's positioning himself as "the objective spirit" (to borrow Jameson's term again) within this historicist economy belied his innocence, leaving him with a troubled subjectivist role open to interpretation.

While Williams chose to include Hemingway's theory about being "pretty" in his pastiche of him, and make explicit references to his homosexual canon, Williams did not allude to the more illuminating stories in *A Moveable Feast* which recast that "queer" argument in more telling light. For example, later in his chapter "Scott Fitzgerald," Hemingway recalls their trip to Lyon in the topless Renault where Hemingway cared for the sick Fitzgerald, who imagines that he is dying, despite Hemingway's efforts to comfort him by telling him that he does not have a fever. Wanting proof by having his temperature taken, Fitzgerald pushes Hemingway to find a thermometer, but with all of the pharmacies closed, the only one he can find is one that is not taken orally but held under the arm. Though Fitzgerald complains that he cannot put it into his mouth (and therefore have a more accurate reading), Hemingway, who administers the thermometric reading, jokes that Fitzgerald should be glad it is not a "rectal thermometer" (*MF* 170).

Similarly, Williams curiously leaves out one of the most significant chapters from *A Moveable Feast* whose understated homoeroticism would have played directly into Williams's gay Scott/queer Hemingway interpretation. This entire chapter, which deals with Zelda's belittling Fitzgerald's sexual prowess, is unsatisfactorily summed up in one curt sentence in the play and, even then, put into Scott's mouth despite the fact that Williams encountered it in Hemingway's memoir: "I'm not satisfactory to you?" (*CSH* 8:236). In fact, Hemingway describes at length in "A Matter of Measurements" how Fitzgerald came to him one day distraught by the fact that Zelda had told Fitzgerald that he was not "built" to ever "make any woman happy":

> "She said it was a matter of measurements. I have never felt the same since she said that and I have to know truly."
> "Come out to the office," I said.
> "Where is the office?"
> "*Le water*," I said.
> We came back into the room and sat down at the table.
> "You're perfectly fine," I said. (*MF* 190)

Hemingway's ellipsis between the request and the response is pregnant with homoerotic tension (to say nothing of his equating the toilet with the workplace), more so than if he had described sophomorically the action of examining the size of Fitzgerald's penis. While that in itself might not have made an impression on Williams's reading into Fitzgerald's homosexuality or even Hemingway's, what Hemingway describes next in the chapter certainly would have:

> "You are O.K. There is nothing wrong with you. You look at yourself from above and you look foreshortened. Go over to the Louvre and look at the people in the statues and then go home and look at yourself in the mirror in profile."
> "Those statues may not be accurate."
> "They are pretty good. Most people would settle for them." (*MF* 190)

Hemingway then describes taking Fitzgerald over to the Louvre where they "looked at the statues," though Fitzgerald was still "doubtful about himself" (*MF* 191). When Fitzgerald asks Hemingway why Zelda had said it to him in the first place, Hemingway responds, "To put you out of business. That's the oldest way in the world of putting people out of business. . . . Zelda just wants to destroy you" (*MF* 190–91). While emasculation in itself does not stand up to the litmus test of homosexuality, this passage, written after 1957 when Hemingway began writing *A Moveable Feast,* curiously replicates the scene in the earlier Williams's story "Three Players of a Summer Game," where the proto-homosexual narrator's measuring of his penis against that of the classical Greek statue *The Dying Gaul* is used to problematize questions of gender and sexual construction/identification. While there is no knowing if Hemingway had read "Three Players of a Summer Game" before writing this passage, or if the similarities between them were purely incidental, no doubt reading it while researching for *Clothes for a Summer Hotel* struck Williams as being highly suspicious—and queer.

Williams encountered enough material in both Fitzgerald's and Hemingway's primary works to suggest that what was being spoken of in the secondary sources merited serious attention. Yet, to return to the early question, why did Williams chose not to include these obvious homoerotic passages from *A Moveable Feast* in his pastiche of Hemingway, since they are already fraught with the kind of unspoken homoeroticism that he had tried to work into *Clothes for a Summer Hotel* in the first place? In other words, were his intentions merely to "out" Hemingway here, Williams certainly passed up some prime opportunities. I believe that Williams's intention was never to out Hemingway but rather, as was the case with his treatment of Fitzgerald's sexual identity, to politicize our wanting him to. This inquisitive thrust of our desire to *know*, tempered by the liberalist recognition that it is none of our business, to which I will now turn, is precisely was haunts *Clothes for a Summer Hotel*. As Fredric Jameson writes, the "political content of postmodernist art" (*P* 158) lies in its representation of cultural schizophrenia.[83]

The Postmodern Phallus, or the Body without "Organ"?

Since any contemporary moment within a material production of pastiched images essentially erases history by encouraging a "breakdown of the temporality" necessary to focus on the subject and "make it a space of praxis," the present (what Jameson calls a "signifier in isolation") will always remain disconnected from the past (e.g., its transcendental signified). Postmodernism suffers, then, from a state of cultural schizophrenia, where the individual, lacking the continuity with the past to establish an ego, redirects the burden of that individuation process through the interpretation of those "isolated, disconnected, discontinuous material signifiers which fail to link up into a coherent sequence."[84] For Jameson, this postmodern aesthetic recalls Lacan's theory of schizophrenia where "a breakdown in the signifying chain, that is, the interlocking syntagmatic series of signifiers which constitutes an utterance or a meaning" (*P* 26), destroys the schizophrenic's ability to locate reality. Lost forever in the realm of the Symbolic self and thus at one with the signifying Phallus that anchors the signifying chain, the schizophrenic never experiences the necessary castration of the Phallus that initiates the self's entrance into the symbolic order of language. Any attempt to join these ego-forming signifiers only reproduce "a series of pure and unrelated presents in time" (*P* 27–28), an effacing of the epistemic past altogether.[85]

In terms of cultural identity, these ego-building signifiers are the various pastiched images that we are confronted with daily (be they T.V. commercials, magazine ads, or even McDonald's restaurant chains reproduced in suburbia's McMansions), which, in lacking continuity and contiguity, force us into reconstructing a past based on "pure material signifiers" (*P* 27) that do not form coherent knowledge—our historicity. We are all condemned, as it were, to the repetitive writings and rewritings of our own "ghost plays," where the re-encountered simulacra of our pasts prove no more or less fictive than our presents given their unavoidable dependence upon the cultural images we consume daily that helped give them shape. Our loss of history most resembles this sense of cultural schizophrenia, where the "rubble of linguistic and unrelated signifiers" (*P* 26) awaits permanently in vain for its eventual castration of the Phallus.

Like Lyotard's explanation of postmodernism's rejection of metanarratives, Jameson's cultural schizophrenia theory insists upon the "death of the subject" but from a cultural rather than an epistemological point of view. Postmodern societies within late capitalism, such as that which frames the modernist aesthetic of *Clothes for a Summer Hotel,* have become necessarily schizophrenic, culturally speaking, because the various fragments of modernism from which it has evolved, detached as they are from the original truths once immanent to them, serve to form the egoless society capitalism needs if it is to continue. Unlike modernism's assault on bourgeois culture, postmodernism simply replicates, reproduces, and reinforces "the logic of consumer capitalism."[86] Lacking the ability to link its signifiers together and therefore comprehend that logic, postmodern culture remains culturally schizophrenic and incapable of challenging capitalism's control over it.

Notions of schizophrenia have, of course, preoccupied Williams throughout his life and career, and *Clothes for a Summer Hotel* is, if nothing else, a play about schizophrenia on many levels. But in moving the discussion/representation of mental illness out of its psychological state and into its historical one, as he does in *Clothes for a Summer Hotel* where the real Zelda's schizophrenia (like the real Rose Williams's) is portrayed as being perhaps less pathological with respect to society's definition of sanity, Williams saves the play from having an overtly sentimental nostalgic feel (such as we find in *Vieux Carré* or *A Lovely Sunday for Crève Coeur*). In fact, if we look into Williams's entire canon, what we find consistently is this presence of cultural schizophrenia, be it those characters from his journeyman plays out of step with Roosevelt's New Deal, those from his Cold War plays who combat sociosexual classification, and those from his post-Stonewall plays who denounce gay oppression *and* liberation simultaneously. In short, cultural schizophrenia in nearly all of Williams's plays stands up against this logic of late capitalism and its economic reliance upon heterosexual norms. *Clothes for a Summer Hotel* simply balances that cultural schizophrenia, which cannibalizes the Fitzgeralds and the Hemingways to serve its desires for glitz and masculine icons, against the mental schizophrenia of Zelda and Scott's crack-up—*which* is finally the metaphor of *which* in Williams's play, however, remains conjecture.

In this sense, Williams exposes the various elements of cultural schizophrenia, and perhaps Hemingway was for him the perfect example given his complex relationship to sexual identity and gender performance, in and out of his work, especially after the publication of *Islands in the Stream* (confirmed sixteen years later with *The Garden of Eden*). Williams simply resorts, as many male writers do—gay, queer, or heterosexual alike—to examining that relationship through the phallic economy, which Hemingway himself had repeatedly done given his response to Fitzgerald's emasculation in *A Moveable Feast*: it is not what you have but what you do with it. But what happens when one does not *have* it, such as is the case with the castrated Jake Barnes or the psychosexually castrated Brick or Scott? In Lacanian terms, they become the female Other who "has the phallus" and thus define the masculine state of "being the phallus" though they cease "being" it themselves. Surely, they could perform a masculine gender and thereby assure themselves of an externally-supplied heterosexual identity (which is something Jake does but which Brick refuses to continue doing). Yet, once even that option of performativity is lost to them, as it is for Scott, what avenues are left available to confirm one's desire, both for oneself and for the all-too-eager-to-know outsider in the audience?

Heterosexual non-performativity does not have to be limited to castration, of course, but can also suggest impotence, if even in the metaphorical sense. Therefore, Hemingway's "A Matter of Measurement" parodies itself, for if size does not matter, neither "in repose" nor in what "it becomes" (*MF* 191) as Hemingway had assured Fitzgerald, when it simply does not become at all, which was a not-too-infrequent case with Hemingway himself, castration and impotence become potent signifiers of the same phallusless reality.[87] Therefore, when Scott suggests in *Clothes for a Summer Hotel* that Hemingway was lonelier than he was and even as lonely as Zelda, his insinuation is that Hemingway could not actualize in private the sexual identity he performed in public. Annoyed with the accusation, Hemingway's rejoinder proves as polysemic as it does queer: *"Fuck it! Hadley, Hadley, call me, the game's gone soft, can't play it any longer!"* (*CSH* 8:272). The "game" is, of course, his marriage to Hadley, here reconstituted as a poker hand a player must convince or "bluff" his opponents into believing is superior to theirs. Since Hemingway replaced Hadley with Mary immediately after their 1926 visit to Antibes, Scott suggestion is used as proof that Hemingway's eventual solitariness resulted from his inability to function heterosexually in any relationship (which Scott then suggests led Hemingway to kill himself, since he could not keep substituting wives and putting the blame on them). The "gone soft" is Williams's interpolation that Hemingway's phallogocentric impotence later in his life signified his repressed homosexual desire—to say nothing about his own sexual prowess. In other words, having lost the phallus, Hemingway lost the Phallus, and with it came an impotence immeasurable either "in repose" or in what "it becomes."

What can be deduced from these comments and from *Clothes for a Summer Hotel* in general is that Williams's insistence on flirting with the historical unknown while refusing to confirm or deny its veracity is consistent with postmodernism's "doubly coded" agenda, which "both legitimizes and subverts that which it parodies."[88] Where the modernist phallus as signifier of male prerogatives was replaced by a poststructuralist Phallus as transcendental signifier, the castrated or impotent phallus of postmodernism represents the cultural schizophrenia that has challenged the phallogocentric economy all the while faithfully reproducing it. While this phallic lack might define the deplorable state of (heteromasculinist) affairs, as Jameson insists upon, Gilles Deleuze and Félix Guattari find it more performatively beneficial.

In *Anti-Oedipus: Capitalism and Schizophrenia* (*L'anti-Œdipe: Capitalisme et schizophrénie*, 1972), Deleuze and Guattari attempt to expose the limited nature of the Freudian castration theory and its metonymic lack as a form-giving and unifying concept to psychoanalysis and replace it with a theory of the unconscious as producing positive "multiplicities" and "flows," potentially not just "two sexes, but *n* sexes":

> It is simply that castration, instead of being the principle of sex conceived as the masculine sex (the great castrated soaring Phallus), becomes the result of sex conceived as the feminine sex (the little hidden absorbed penis). We maintain therefore that *castration is the basis for the anthropomorphic and molar representation of sexuality.* Castration is the universal belief that brings together and disperses both men and women under the yoke of one and the same illusion of consciousness, and makes them adore this yoke. . . . Long live castration, so that desire may be strong? Only fantasies are truly desired? What a perverse, human, all-too-human idea![89]

To be concerned with the proper construction of one's identity in Freudian terms is to be resigned "to Oedipus, to castration: for girls, renunciation of their desire for the penis; for boys, renunciation of male protest—in short, 'assumption of one's sex.'"[90] In other words, the subject locks himself into standardized sex/gender molds in Freud, whereby any deviation from the norm generates in him a certain amount of anxiety not found in the schizophrenic, who has avoided those norms altogether by denying the need to be *sub*jectified in the first place. Like the schizophrenic, the homosexual has also "resisted oedipalization" and has "invented for himself other territorialities" within to define his or her self.[91] In breaking the Oedipal cycle of ego individuation and the castration law it upholds, the schizophrenic is not damaging the unconscious as an ideal of static being but rather embellishing it as the locus of active production (again, Lyotard's and Butler's "performativity") since only the schizophrenic is capable of interpreting or decoding the incomprehensible hodge-podge of postmodernist pastiche culture. In short, to challenge the Oedipal complex and its phallic lack—for them, a theory "more powerful . . . than psychoanalysis, than the family, than ideology, even joined together"[92]—is to disrupt the whole of Western culture's hegemonic (hence heteromasculine) and phallogocentric regime.

Given the role that the phallus plays in Freud's Oedipal theory, its lack in schizoanalysis is therefore not considered as a late stage toward developing consciousness but rather, to the postmodern schizophrenic like Williams (and Williams's Hemingway, for that matter), one of the many potential Body without Organs, a term coined by Antonin Artaud in his "Theatre of Cruelty," which Deleuze and Guattari use to describe, among countless other things, the limit that attracts and repels the "flows" (e.g., ideas, culture, money, capital, information, etc.), and, in interrupting them, gives them meaning and coherence.[93] Deleuze and Guattari envision a "post-Oedipal" world, itself castrated of the organizational Phallus characteristic of Western culture. The loss of this traditional genital economy would produce this radically liberated Body without Organs, "the unproductive, the sterile, the unengendered, the unconsumable. . . . surface for the recording of the entire process of production of desire."[94] In other words, a body without the phallus as its signifying or, at least, organizing "organ" would be one that identifies the more ideal state of men and of women, one no longer hindered by genital politics—in essence the state of pure androgyny.

Like schizophrenia, androgyny was one of Williams's literary obsessions (and Hemingway's)[95] which, after Stonewall, also became one of his political ones as well. Williams frequently voiced in his interviews during the 1970s that what he had been experimenting with in his drama (*Out Cry*), his fiction ("Miss Coynte of Green" or *Moise and the World of Reason*), and his poetry (*Androgyne, Mon Amour*) was a poetics of androgyny, or a "a duality not reconciled" (*CTW* 209).[96] As Kari Weil notes in *Androgyny and the Denial of Difference*, the androgynous differs from the hermaphrodite in a political sense in that while the latter describes more a physiological phenomenon, the former recalls the transcendental signified that "asserts original difference (the male and the female 'halves' it unites), and claims to transcend that 'most virulent' of binary oppositions by defining our origin as one."[97] This "oneness of the origin posited by the androgyne" and the "differences it engenders through opposition" are best defined "by the exclusion of an origin that is not determined by the phallus, in other words, by the exclusion of a 'differ*ant*' sexual and textual body."[98] Williams was not only attracted to the androgynous physically, as it is often said Hemingway was, but ideologically as well; it was for Williams "the truest human being" (*CTW* 212). Since Williams struggled throughout his career to upend the authority of any one-to-one signification between gender and sexuality—from *The Glass Menagerie* and *Summer and Smoke* to *Cat on a Hot Tin Roof* and *Camino Real*, androgyny became the logical conclusion to that dialectic.

Like the BwO, the androgyne lacks the signifying phallus as organ of oppressed Western ideology. This androgynous BwO, then, is

> not a joining of two plenitudes, but a confluence of masculine and feminine that blurs the distinction between them. The irony of irony is that one loses all ability to designate the difference between the ironic and the non-ironic, between rhetoric and truth, (sexual) performance and (sexual) identity. This loss of control results, in fact, in a breakdown of difference, bringing questions of language in touch with questions of the body by feminizing the (male/ironic) subject through the association of his state with the female reproductive process, regarded as a form of productivity over which one is powerless.[99]

If anything brings Williams and Hemingway together into the same theoretical bed, it is certainly this conceptual understanding of androgyny as the only potential panacea to counter (homo)sexual existentialism. Williams clearly understood this, too, which is why he has his Hemingway repeat the words to Scott that Williams himself had said during those many interviews: "It's often been observed that duality of gender can serve some writers well" (*CSH* 8:268). Perhaps what irritated Williams the most was Hemingway's unwillingness to acknowledge it for himself in public, not only as a literary aesthetic to his work but also a political avowal about his life.

Whether or not Hemingway's implied impotence in *Clothes for a Summer Hotel* can be read as a signifier of heterosexual dysfunction brought on by his homosexuality does not matter in the end, for both still suggest that he lost the phallus and the Phallus, the power to perform and the power to signify his heteromasculine performance. Androgyny is not castration, to be sure, as Roland Barthes notes in *S/Z*, distinguishing between those who have the phallus but are not the phallus, and the castrated characters who neither have it nor are it.[100] And yet the result is essentially the same, leaving Williams's Hemingway, like Brick, a cultural schizophrenic unable to define or even know where his signified body leaves off and his body politic begins. In other words, for Williams, Hemingway the man and Hemingway the writer were opposing egos locked in competitive battle within the same body, both struggling to overcome the homosexual existentialism that had warped the internal truth with persistent external lies. But whereas Brick was fictional, Hemingway was real, and that raises all sorts of epistemological problems, the least of which implicates Williams's as one of those gossip mongers whose sources he chose to pastiche. As Barthes informs us, the power of "The Proper Name" is "to emphasize the structural function of the Name, to state its arbitrary nature, to depersonalize it, to accept the currency of the Name as pure convention"; but it is also "to maintain that the patronymic substitute is *filled* with a person (civic, national, social), it is to insist that appellative currency be in gold (and not left to be decided arbitrarily). All subversion, or all novelistic submission, thus begins with the Proper Name. . . ."[101] For Williams's making Hemingway queer in 1980, that subversion was all but guaranteed.

Again the question rises, though, if Williams were not, under the guises of defining Hemingway's cultural schizophrenia, simply resorting to the same type of name-calling he was accused of having done with Fitzgerald discussed earlier in this chapter. And once again, I would argue that, as with the questions surrounding Fitzgerald's sexual identity, Williams was not out to *out* Hemingway, nor to keep him in the closet, but rather to use Hemingway as he had used Scott and Brick before: to show the psychosexual effects upon the individual who cannot internalize the truth of sexual epistemology or who is afraid to examine it altogether out of fear of what he might reveal to others or to discover for himself. For this reason, Williams does not expose the liminal homoeroticism present in Hemingway's chapter "A Matter of Measurement." To draw upon the more homoerotic passages from Hemingway's *A Moveable Feast* to declare Papa a pansy would have undercut the more troubling queer Hemingway, in language and in subject material, which in the end would have undermined his overall intent in exposing the workings of cultural and psychosexual schizophrenia. Simply put, Williams was more interested in making the phallus absent by calling attention not to its role in homoerotic literature but rather precisely to its lack. As Barthes writes, this type of symbolic transposition of turning history into narrative ". . . hinges on a structural artifice: identifying the symbolic and the hermeneutic, making the search for truth (hermeneutic structure) into the search for castration (symbolic structure), making the truth be *anecdotally* (and no longer symbolically) the absent phallus."[102]

Drawing Hemingway as the world felt it knew him (before *The Garden of Eden*) and how Hemingway repeatedly (that is, schizophrenically) reproduced *and* refuted that image in his work as in his life—the macho, big game hunting homophobic womanizer who frequently and sympathetically wrote about queers and gender-benders—Williams was turning historical truth into anecdotal truth, though nonetheless inaccurate given a postmodernist's relationship to historical facts. Resounding Deleuze and Guattari's anti-Oedipal critique of genital economy and portending Jameson's notion of the postmodern pastiche, *Clothes for a*

Summer Hotel, then, can be read as a critique not only of Hemingway's phallogocentrism but also of the agenda behind sexual identification which has constructed, and no doubt will continue to construct, Western social hierarchies.

"Love in 'Ernest'": Williams, Hemingway, and the Politics of Sexual Identification

If Fredric Jameson's definition of postmodernism as a "random play of signifiers" that "ceaselessly reshuffles the fragments of preexistent texts" to produce "metabooks which cannibalize other books" (*P* 96) is valid, and there is a resounding consensus that suggests that it is, then *Clothes for a Summer Hotel*'s distrust of modernist metanarratives, its play with sex and gender as free-floating signifiers, and its pastiche of historicity on micro- and macro-levels readily confirms the play's postmodern status. This fact alone, were there no *Out Cry* before *Clothes* or *Something Cloudy, Something Clear* after it, serves to establish Tennessee Williams as one of the few American dramatists to have bridged the century's two major aesthetic periods. Reproducing on stage what readers had repeatedly encountered in the historical novels of the 1960s and 1970s, *Clothes for a Summer Hotel* dramatizes changes that postmodernism has imposed upon American culture by challenging history and its ownership of facts. As Linda Hutcheon rightly asks, "Which 'facts' make it into history? And *whose* facts?"[103] To provide definitive answers in *Clothes for a Summer Hotel*, say, to Scott's gay identity or Hemingway's queer one, is to lay claim to a totalizing theory that accepts the authority of those troubling metanarratives, to reproduce biographical narrative without subverting it at the same time, which Williams finally never does here. It is better to queer those facts, Williams seems to say here, than to replicate let alone legitimate them.

But if a postmodern text needs be politically motivated as well, what in *Clothes for a Summer Hotel*'s critique of identity politics differentiates it from Williams's Cold War productions, notably the modernist *Cat on a Hot Tin Roof*? If Fitzgerald and Hemingway are essentially flesh and blood embodiments of Skipper and Brick, then what had Williams done differently in finally giving a voice to their unspoken homoeroticism? And doesn't such a declaration finally undercut the power of irony and ambiguity and feed into our voyeuristic need to know what lies behind the gender mask, an inquiry that *Cat on a Hot Tin Roof* had so successfully critiqued back in 1955? What was Williams finally accomplishing in *Clothes for a Summer Hotel* beyond its appearance as a postmodern pastiche of the identity politics *Cat on a Hot Tin Roof* had already exposed? To answer these questions is to attempt to understand what motivated Williams to write a historical play in the first place, something he had never attempted before outside of autobiography, and why he specifically chose Fitzgerald and Hemingway and his subject. Was it that Williams simply became intrigued with Fitzgerald because of the 1970 publications of Milford's *Zelda* and Hemingway' *Islands in the Stream?* Certainly, an argument could be made that both books' stellar popularity piqued an interest in Williams, who felt perhaps literarily exhausted at the time and in need of material. Anyone familiar with the vast unpublished Williams archives and their trunks full of drafts of plays, complete or otherwise, to which Williams could have turned his attention would quickly recognize this theory as being dubious. Rather, Williams wrote the play partly because he saw the potential in it not only to expiate certain personal ghosts he may have had concerning his relationship with his sister, but also to silence the critics, theater and sexual alike, who had haunted him since Stonewall about his homosexuality.

In Scott Fitzgerald, for instance, Williams had encountered a soul mate, an artist whose public support waned later in his career; whose chemical dependency may have been the cause of that decline, or the result; whose artistic endeavors were fed with the lifeblood of a loved one; whose guilt for having turning the life of another into his work haunted him until his remaining days; and whose sexual exploits began eclipsing his literary achievements. To be sure, finding or defending one's sexual identity had always been a staple theme in Williams's work, but, more so than ever, it seemingly rose to personal heights in the 1970s, with Williams turning away from writing about sexual identity in general to writing about *his* sexual identity in particular. In this sense, Scott and Brick become two versions of Williams at two very distinct homophobic moments in American history, fighting not for privacy but for the power of self-determinacy outside of a rule-bound binary that controls sexual identity politics. As Judith Butler writes in *Gender Trouble*, "If sexuality is culturally constructed within existing power relations, then the postulation of a normative sexuality that is 'before,' 'outside,' or 'beyond' power is a cultural impossibility and a politically impracticable dream, one that postpones the concrete and contemporary task of rethinking subversive possibilities for sexuality and identity within the terms of power itself" (*GT* 40).

Were these words written a decade earlier, perhaps Williams would have chosen them to shore up his play's thesis that sexuality is not something to be commoditized within the genital economy, that identity cannot be reduced to the polarities of a binary system, and that notions of originality in the postmodern world are only misappropriated myths used to legitimate those binaries which maintain that economy. If "gay is to straight *not* as copy is to original but, rather, as copy is to copy," Butler adds, and the "parodic repetition of 'the original' . . . reveals the original to be nothing other than a parody of the *idea* of the natural and the original" (*GT* 41), then Williams is no more or less a parody of Fitzgerald than Scott is of Brick. Instead, each is a parody of that transcendental homosexual whom heteromasculinist America helped construct in order to protect its homosociality, secure its traffic in women, and sustain its genital economy, whose hegemony was "threatened" by so many pink Bolsheviks.

Concerning Williams's relationship to Hemingway in the play, the stakes are entirely different. If Williams could be paralleled with the "real" Fitzgerald in *Clothes for a Summer Hotel*, his Hemingway *is* the "real" Hemingway, and therein lies the play's postmodern political agenda. Repeatedly in his interviews, Williams remained deferent to Hemingway the artist; it was Hemingway the man with whom he had had issues. If homophobia was an unavoidable reality among gay American men in the 1970s, it was certainly abetted by Hemingway, who, like Brick, only became a harmless alcoholic after the damage had already been inflicted. What did not sit well with Williams, which is perhaps why he characterizes Hemingway in the play as being queer, was that Hemingway used his public imago to deflect attention away from the gay aesthetics that preoccupy his fiction. For Williams, this made Hemingway a much more dangerous obstacle to gay liberation than he was—not because Hemingway did not come out as Williams had done but because he abused his position within heteromasculinity as a bully pulpit to incite and coalesce homophobic discourse and reaction.[104] In giving his Hemingway gay sensibilities without making him gay, Williams is simply castigating both society for its inscience in determining sexual identities *and* the individual for his role in the resultant cultural schizophrenia "that makes all of us somewhat neurotic" (*CTW* 322).[105]

The difference here, though, between Williams's view of Scott and of the fictional Hemingway is reflected in Williams's view of the difference between himself and the real Hemingway: though perceived as effeminate, he had the courage to admit to his homosexuality, whereas Hemingway, ardently masculine in a cultivated image that even helped fuel homophobia throughout the 1970s to fever-pitch levels in the decade that followed, might have been masking a homosexual identity, which, for Williams, belied the image's projection of strength. Consequently, *Clothes for a Summer Hotel*, though arguably inferior drama in its substitution of thesis for poetics, of masked knowledge for confused epistemology, is superior to *Cat on a Hot Tin Roof* as a polemic against sexual oppression—there is no "mystery" here as to who is responsible for the construction of the closet, who is forced into it, and who had mustered the strength on June 27, 1969, to break out. As such, Williams is as unforgiving of Hemingway and his cult as the homosexual community was of Williams after Stonewall for not, according to Michael Paller, having addressed their concerns: "Of what use, what relevance to their lives was a gay playwright who wrote by indirection, was even-handed in his treatment of heterosexual and homosexual characters, who did not use his fame to speak out and be 'proud' in an era that would increasingly insist on pride and political correctness as artistic criteria?"[106] The answer to that question is located in Williams's cultural schizophrenia: the *gay* playwright who is not a "gay playwright" at all because he never felt it necessary to "write a gay play" but who nonetheless celebrates his gayness here and demands others like Hemingway (though long since dead) to do so as well.[107]

Though never wanting to make homosexuality an issue in his work, Williams could not avoid doing just that, for all the while he deconstructs the hetero-homosexual binary that had marginalized him socially over the years, he reconfirms that binary within the gay community itself by privileging his queer homosexuality over the more visible fairy one after Stonewall, which had kept him out of the Gay Lib ranks.[108] As he would reveal in his 1976 interview for *Gay Sunshine*, such exclusionism did not entirely trouble him, however: "I think the great preponderance of them [transvestites or transsexuals] damages the gay liberation movement by travesty, by making a travesty of homosexuality, one that doesn't fit homosexuality at all and gives it a very bad public image. We are *not* trying to imitate women. We are simply trying to be conformably assimilated by our society."[109]

In denying the "us/them" duality of the heteromasculinist world and reproducing it in the gay one, Williams finally proved incapable of escaping the genital economy that he had long since combated.[110] Therefore, his intended goal in *Clothes for a Summer Hotel* was not to declare definitively whether the "real" Fitzgerald or the "real" Hemingway were gay or not, nor even to mock the chauvinist Hemingway for his unabashed slurs against fellow homosexual artists, but rather to demonstrate once again how society has grown culturally schizophrenic from its sexual politics. Williams unavoidably reproduced that which he set out to critique. For that reason alone, Williams himself, perhaps more than any play he ever wrote or could have ever hoped to write, is the best argument against the identity politics practiced in America: no matter how hard he tried to defend the forgotten, the disenfranchised, and the persecuted in his work, he could not truthfully position himself outside of the powers that had put them there.

Clothes for a Summer Hotel, then, documents not just the reemergence of an era's intolerance toward sexual diversity but also Williams's own problematic relationship to that intolerance and to the strides gay liberation had made in the intervening years to neutralize it, with or without his help. In the final line of his "Author's Note" preceding *Clothes for a Summer Hotel,* Williams provides what is perhaps his definitive response to a political agenda whose cause he had taken up years before—the unconditional protection of the individual's right to an identity not bound by the rules and mores of any establishment, but rather by the inner truths of that individual's search for self-knowledge—and also his truce with an offended gay public. For in justifying his playing with the facts concerning the history behind this play, Williams remains loyal to the existential credo he had established with Brick's "bird" mystery, namely, that truth is an essence more than an existence: "Our reason for taking extraordinary license with time and place is that an asylum and on its grounds liberties of this kind are quite prevalent: and also these liberties allow us to explore in more depth what we believe is the truth of character. And so we ask you to indulge us with the licenses we take for a purpose which we consider quite earnest" (*CSH* 8:n.p.).

The final pun on "earnest" also winks playfully to his gay audience. That is, it fits nicely within a play that places a good deal of value on being "earnest" in the truthful sense of being open and liberated from one's confinement—be it an asylum, a closet, or even the self—*and* on being "Ernest" in the ironic sense (that is, while nearly every American male had wished to be Hemingway, or at least the image he had cultivated, only Hemingway did not wish to be *him* any longer). That both uses should be tied up with the queer allusion to Oscar Wilde's play and to John Gambril Francis Nicholson's collection, *Love in Earnest: Sonnets, Ballads, and Lyrics* (1892), seems the most appropriate way for Williams to introduce his final queer play for Broadway and show deference to the gay Broadway community to whom it is quietly dedicated.[111]

Conclusion

"[Amado 'Pancho' Rodriguez y Gonzalez] reminds me rather pathetically of a bull in the arena with his black hide full of fancy darts from the picadors, charging madly this way and that, whenever the red silk flashes until finally sometime the sword behind the red silk will put a stop to him. A brave and wonderful black bull—but I am not a bull-fighter! My veronicas were not as quick as the horns."
—Tennessee Williams letter to Carson McCullers,
July 5, 1948

"... *the great North American playwright, Tennessee Williams.*"
—Ernest Hemingway note to Fidel Castro,
April 1959

"We have now been to five bullfights, and reading Hemingway's book gives one a wonderful added concern and understanding of everything. It makes the theatre pallid.... Tenn thinks Hemingway is really queer as he has an unnatural concern about queens—and, Tenn says, writes uninterestingly about women."
—Maria St. Just,
Five O'Clock Angel: Letters of Tennessee Williams to Maria St. Just, 1948–1982

HEMINGWAY AND WILLIAMS SURELY MAKE FOR STRANGE BEDfellows in a literary monograph, but they do share quite an interesting literary history, and I have attempted here to show exactly where, how, and why their literary productions crossed paths. Though that relationship was often unidirectional, the polemical subtext of this study suggests that Hemingway was aware of Williams's work in sexual identity politics (because it reflected to some extent his own, though it would be a couple decades before we would see that in print) and was perhaps as influenced by it in the writing of his later fiction as Williams was by Hemingway's earlier work.[1] Though the latter theory is more difficult to prove beyond speculation and circumstantial evidence, the former is not, and it is here that I have tried to focus my critical attention in this study. For, despite Margaret Thornton's recent revelation in the *Notebooks* that "perhaps most surprisingly" (*NB* xi) Hemingway's name figures among the many who influenced Williams's work, Williams was simply no Hemingway novice.[2]

In 1970 to Don Lee Keith, for instance, Williams described their personal relationship, which included that one, brief encounter in Castro's Cuba: "Hemingway and I never established a rapport either. One night Frank Merlo and I were at a dinner party with him. Kenneth Tynan had arranged it. Hemingway seemed shy to me; we didn't have much to talk about. In a way, it was embarrassing. Tynan later wrote something rather unkind, something about the gay company, but I don't think Frank and I came off very gay in the situation" (*CTW* 155).[3] Of his respect for Hemingway the artist, Williams told Jim Gaines in 1972, "I think Hemingway was unquestionably the greatest. I think *Islands in the Stream* is his most important work, epic in scope" (*CTW* 222).[4] And of his admiration for Hemingway the intellect, Williams admitted to John Gruen in their 1965 interview, "Hemingway had the great feeling for man's ability to choose. He was an existentialist—he understood it long before Sartre did, you know. Perhaps we all understood existentialism before Sartre did" (*CTW* 121).[5]

Despite their apocryphal nature, each comment reveals a Williams appreciative of Hemingway and of his work on various levels.[6] That appreciation is perhaps best expressed in two of Williams's statements on Hemingway, the first from a college essay he wrote dating back to 1936–1937, and the second from his eulogy of Hemingway the day following his suicide.

By the time Williams was an undergraduate student at Washington University in St. Louis in 1936, he had read most of Hemingway's works published to date. In an English course essay entitled "A Report On Four Writers Of The Modern Psychological School" written that fall, Williams expounds at length about what he perceived as the best and the worst in Hemingway and in his writing (I am quoting the passage on Hemingway in its entirety):

> According to Gertrude Stein's "Autobiography" it was [Sherwood] Anderson who introduced Hemingway to the literary world and chiefly influenced his development as a writer. It is true that there is a good deal of similarity in the work of these two writers. Hemingway probably learned a good deal from the older writer: but what he learned was just a starting point. He went on and developed a very distinctive method and style of his own.
> With the exception of one book, "The Torrents Of Spring", I have read all of Hemingway's published works. The book which I selected for this report is his latest "The Green Hills Of Africa." This is not a novel, but like "Death In The Afternoon" a detailed study of a sport. The sport is game-hunting, apparently Hemingway's favorite preoccupation at the present time. It's object, as the author put it, is to see if a perfectly true account of a month's action and description of a country can successfully compete with a work of fiction. The main character is Hemingway himself. Or what is

supposed to be Hemingway. Hemingway defines himself as a braggart and probably isn't far wrong. The book leaves you with a distinct impression that Hemingway is a pretty good guy. That was very likely the impression which the author wished to create, though it must be admitted that he went about it with considerable subtlety. Other characters are Hemingway's wife (known as P.O.M. or Poor Old Mom) Karl, a lucky hunter, Pop, a professional guide and various native hunters and guides of the African game country.

The most dramatic action of the book is the pursuit of the elusive kudu. I had never heard of a kudu before but apparently it is a very important animal. It certainly gave Hemingway plenty of excitement. It seems that Karl, the rival hunter, bagged a magnificent kudu, so Hemingway felt obliged to duplicate this feat or die in the effort. In the end he succeeds. But there are many kudu-less nights when poor Ernest has to drown his mortification in drink. There is a good deal of drinking all through the book. A characteristic of Hemingway's works. There is also a lot of literary talk. A good many bad words and frank language. Hemingway speaks right out about Gertrude Stein. Says that Thomas Wolfe ought to exile himself in Siberia. Admires Thomas Mann and Tolstoi, Stephen Crane and Henry James. Thinks most other modern writers aren't worth their salt. Hemingway's opinions are always interesting and his flair for dialogue is nowhere better exhibited than in this book.

The style of the book is nearly perfect. Hemingway's crisp phrases present the country and the action with marvelous clarity. But the revelation of Hemingway's own self is the most impressive thing. He tells more about himself that [*sic*] he probably wishes to. He is trying to present himself as a very happy, perfectly satisfied out-doors man. But reading between the lines you can see a good deal of bewilderment and frustration. This complete absorption in hunting and killing is not a healthy symptom. Hemingway is very likely the pursued as well as the pursuer. Pursued by what? Possibly an increasing sense of his own limitations as a writer. He takes his writing very seriously. And lately he has just been marking time. He hasn't produced a novel since "A Farewell To Arms". I think in his game-hunting, fishing, drinking, Etc., he is very likely trying to escape from the uncomfortable awareness that his greatest achievements are already behind him. However you can't tell about that. He is still a relatively young [*sic*], he has developed a fine technique. Perhaps he may surprise his critics by coming out pretty soon with another first rate piece of fiction.[7]

Perhaps echoing what many of Hemingway's critics themselves were saying in the press, Williams's comments are nonetheless astute and eerily prophetic. Himself a young writer of twenty-five at this time and with some professional acclaim—as was Hemingway when he wrote *The Sun Also Rises*—Williams clearly identifies that what attracted him most about Hemingway was not only his style and its truth-driven clarity but also his persona as "the pursued" and "the pursuer." Williams's fascination with these two sides of Hemingway's nature was to follow him for another half-century until he finally confronted them directly in *Clothes for a Summer Hotel.*

Williams would repeat these sentiments throughout his private notebooks for the next twenty years, as we have seen, at no point recanting on anything that he had said about Hemingway the artist in this college essay. He would later go public with his admiration, writing glowingly of Hemingway in an obituary the *New York Times* ran on July 3, 1961:

> Tennessee Williams, playwright—To begin with a somewhat obvious statement, twentieth-century literature began with Proust's "The Remembrance of Things Past" and with Hemingway's "The Sun Also Rises," since literary history has already established the fact that Joyce was not and never was meant to be an artist with a comparably wide audience. Hemingway never retired from his life into his workshop. He knew that an artist's work, the heart of it, is finally himself and his life, and he accomplished as few artists that have lived in our time, or any, the almost impossibly difficult achievement of becoming, as a man, in the sight of the world and time he lived in, the embodiment of what his work meant, on its highest and most honest level, and it would seem that he continued this achievement until his moment of death, which he would undoubtedly call his "moment of truth," in all truth.[8]

In situating the birth of modern American literature with the publication of *The Sun Also Rises* (Hemingway himself had opted for Mark Twain's *Huckleberry Finn*), Williams is at once elevating Hemingway to the rank of deity in the nation's literary pantheon and reconfirming the novel's central position within his own literary epistemology. By 1961, Williams had also come to empathize with Hemingway in ways he could never have imagined in 1936: a highly successful artist who, many critics believed, had already produced his best work, and yet who was on the cusp of another critical success and, perhaps, even winning the Nobel Prize for Literature. It would not be long before *The Night of the Iguana* would win the New York Drama Critics' Circle Award for best play and *Time* magazine would place Williams on its March 1962 cover, proclaiming him to be "the greatest living playwright in the English-speaking world." The Nobel, alas, was not to be for Williams.

Among all the writers mentioned in the criticism as having influenced Williams throughout his career, surprisingly Hemingway has received noticeably little recognition.[9] One reason for this oversight might owe to the fact that among the several writers Williams often cited as his early literary mentors, Hemingway's name never appears; another reason, no doubt, is connected with the fact that when Hemingway's name does appear, it occurs relatively late in Williams's career at a time when critics stopped looking for the established playwright's literary influences. Perhaps it was because he found himself battling different demons later in his career that Williams precisely looked to Hemingway—himself an embattled writer, man, and icon—to help him quell them; but, as Williams's notebooks reveal, those demons were there from the start, and so was Hemingway:

> Dec. 19 [1946]
> Later—I managed, remarkably, to go down town and mail "chart" [*Summer and Smoke*] to Audrey. Had an oyster stew on the way home. No appetite but no nausea. Now back home in bed with newspaper and Crane and Hemingway. Two of the best bed-partners a sick old bitch can have. (*NB* 453)[10]

Williams drew from Hart Crane his inspiration to romanticize the tortured artist's struggle against a philistine and myopic public; from D. H. Lawrence, his passion for dialectizing the flesh and spirit; and from Anton Chekhov, his obsession to poeticize the pariahs of dying social orders—all of which served Williams well in forming his early dramatic voice. But it was only from Hemingway's dual role within the American canon *and* the American myth as heteromasculinity incarnate that he could draw the power to politicize sociosexual identification, something Williams certainly felt conscious of, being a semi-outed homosexual during the Cold War. That Williams would eventually dramatize Hemingway the writer in his final play on Broadway serves to confirm this respect; that he would also question Hemingway's integrity about his iconic role in American culture suggests what Williams also thought about Hemingway the man—or at least the image behind it—and the whole political agenda in ascribing a sexual identity to the body politic.

To be sure, Hemingway's relationship to homosexuality both in his life and in his art interested and confounded Williams. Both were fighting the same cause, Williams must have felt, but from opposite ends of the sociosexual continuum. In reading Hemingway's *The Sun Also Rises*, Williams's learned how irony was the only way to treat those sociosexual identity problems, especially in a country whose discourse on homosexuality at the time was limited to banned sexology books like Havelock Ellis's, turgid legal torts taken up against various writers and playwrights, and weighty psychoanalytical studies from Freud to G. Stanley Hall. In Jake Barnes, Williams discovered an alternative American hero, one whose sexed and gendered identities are completely transformed with the loss of his penis, and who waits until the novel's close to address the inevitable questions awaiting him about his sexual identity. By terming this phenomenon "sexual existentialism," where an individual is provided an identity by society based not only on what he does but also on what he *does not do* sexually, I have attempted in this study to show how the novel supports the idea that sexual identity politics in America had no place to go other than in the direction of the gay and communist witch hunts of the Cold War. Hemingway simply predicted this political providence in the novel's closing lines where the final exchange between Brett and Jake—where he delivers his uncharacteristic "pretty" rejoinder in their taxi ride through Madrid—reflects more Jake's inability to understand the rules of sexual identification that govern his concept of heterosexuality than it does his acceptance of the sterility of their relationship confined by those rules.

So appropriate was Jake's "Isn't it pretty to think so?" comment to the emasculating Brett in its anti-establishmentarian irony that Williams saw it as a potential statement for the plight of sexual politics in the twentieth century in general. It is not by accident, then, that his Brick Pollitt should recapitulate in action, if not also in words, Jake's sexual existentialism and ironic response to his emasculation to the equally voluptuous and sexually insatiable Maggie: "Wouldn't it be funny if that was true?" The only way to respond to compulsive heterosexuality—for which Maggie fights in *Cat on a Hot Tin Roof* and championsin its original ending, first by announcing her pregnancy, and second by pleading to Brick to make the lie come true—was not to ignore it but to expose its manipulating mechanics, that is, to demonstrate how economics lies behind all notions of sexed identities because society, and not the individual, is at their root. Like Hemingway with Jake, Williams relied on a bitter cocktail of irony and the unspoken to help deliver his message. Perhaps the sexual implications behind Jake's use of irony in *The Sun Also Rises* have only recently turned toward issues of homosexuality and gender trouble because Hemingway's own heterosexuality did not solicit queer readings in the same way that Williams's homosexuality did for Brick's irony. Were Williams heteromasculine like Hemingway in 1955, one wonders if Walter Kerr would have ever written his attack against Williams's evasiveness in dealing truthfully with the reasons why Brick drinks in the first place?

Williams, in fact, spent the better part of his career defending Brick's heterosexuality, and yet critics and scholars alike are still debating the fallout from Kerr's 1955 polemic concerning Brick's homosexual "mystery." I reopen that debate here, not with the intent of siding for or against Williams in his response to Kerr and others but rather in the interest of understanding what Williams meant by refusing to label Brick's "mystery" homosexuality. In reading Brick and the play against their Cold War and existential contexts, I argue that Williams was finally less interested in outing a gay character than he was in demonstrating how that character's sexual uncertainty could belie his model heteromasculinity, both for himself and for his society. Such a message, one upheld by the play's original ending, is for Williams more socially significant (and politically subversive) because it debunks society's myth of polarized sexual identities. Though undoubtedly queer, Brick in the play is not gay, and for Williams that fact is more troubling for audiences who need to see that Brick is finally not one of them. Were Brick determinately gay, the play itself would be emasculated, denuded of its political weapons against Cold War "gendermandering."[11]

Williams's critics have always made homosexuality an issue in his work, and Williams's own treatment of gay themes throughout his dramatic canon had brought about as many attacks against him later in his life for addressing homosexuality candidly as it had earlier in his career when he avoided dramatizing gay subjects altogether. Though Williams quietly addresses homosexuality in *A Streetcar Named Desire* and, to an even lesser extent, in *The Glass Menagerie, Summer and Smoke,* and *Camino Real,* nowhere in Williams's early Broadway plays does he explore the social implications of homosexuality in a homophobic society more forcefully than in *Cat on a Hot Tin Roof.* For this reason, it has become the locus of all dramatic homosexual representations in Williams studies. Despite the obvious politicizing of this fact, which has given many a critic fodder for siding with or taking aim against Williams, nearly all have agreed that Williams, for whatever reason, intentionally obfuscates the theme of homosexuality in the play, pointing to the various ambiguities vis-à-vis Brick's sexuality as evidence. Certainly, the necessary changes Williams made to his third act—from where Brick remains aloof from Maggie in the original to where he nearly reconciles their marriage in the rewrite—are partly responsible for the play's apparent ambiguity. Yet, critical complaints aimed specifically at Williams's coy treatment of homosexuality in either ending of *Cat on a Hot Tin Roof* are, I feel, unwarranted, since he did not make the play as ambiguous in its final assessment of homosexuality as many theater critics and drama scholars have charged him with having done. I feel that Williams was much more forthcoming with his characterization of Brick in *Cat on a Hot Tin Roof,* not in defining Brick's homosexuality but rather in exploring the uncertainty of Brick's own knowledge of what homosexuality meant in the xenophobic 1950s.

Williams did not arrive directly at Brick's ironic rejoinder of the heterosexual imperative through Jake Barnes, but instead through the seemingly detached observations of a boy on the cusp of sexual identification who bears witness (as do the readers of Hemingway's *The Sun Also Rises*) to the emasculation of an older man for sociopolitical gains. In "Three Players of a Summer Game," the story that serves as the link between Hemingway's novel and Williams's *Cat on a Hot Tin Roof*, Williams provides a window through which to examine the long-troubling "mystery" concerning Brick Pollitt's alcoholism and troubled relationship with his wife Margaret: masculine existentialism. Reading the story against its contextualized setting (the transgendered 1920s), I explain how the first-person narrator (then only a boy) recalls his initiation into gender identification in order to explain (if not justify) his later sexual identification. Experiencing an act of emasculation similar to the one Brick confronts in *Cat*, the narrator demonstrates how linguistic fluency and its ability to negotiate the symbolic is bound as much by a sexual epistemology as it is by a psychological one. He only gains the voice necessary to narrate the two stories of castration when he acknowledges the object of his gaze as also being the one of his desires. Though not entirely autobiographical, the story does recall certain truths of Williams's own sexual development from the flapper 1920s to the homophobic 1950s, representing one among many of his reactionary statements against American heteronormativity that paradoxically celebrated him as a playwright and marginalized him as a homosexual.

*Homo*sexual existentialism is what connects all three works, where their two principal characters—Jake and Brick (in both of Williams's works)—are in a state of personal and cultural anxiety that emerges when their individualistic struggles to secure an identity based not on what they do or do not do, but rather on what they think and feel is countered when their respective societies care more for performativity than epistemology. What they *do* makes them what they *are;* or, in the case of Jake and Brick, what they *do not do* makes them what they are— that is, as non-performative heterosexual males they become queer by social default. Hemingway and Williams both, one in a post-World War I environment and the other in a post-World War II one, denounced this reality and created literary heroes who are masculine and heterosexual but whose lack of performance cannot sustain their social identities indefinitely. Both Jake and Brick, then, are queer heterosexual men whose desires and whose performed genders in no way reveal the truth about who they are—to others and, at times, to themselves. However, society values one's existence over one's essence, and the individual is forced to choose social definitions of personal epistemology or be ready to fight or assert an identity that might run counter to the one society has pre-supplied. Both *The Sun Also Rises* and *Cat on a Hot Tin Roof* end, unfortunately, before the hero takes up that challenge. That Brick in "Three Players of a Summer Game" does act before the story's end, and his final act is of one of quiet acquiescence, gives us some insight into what Williams at least thought would be the consequence of an individual's homosexual existentialism.

If irony was a potent tool to subversively attack heteronormality during the high modernist period, it proved ineffective during postmodernism, where everything deemed normal was systematically upended, with Jean-François Lyotard and Fredric Jameson positioning terms like *bricolage* and pastiche in the once privileged place that irony had held in literary production. Irony could no longer effectively challenge what society had already lost faith in—totalizing narratives of truth. If sexuality were itself one of these metanarratives that modernism fully embraced, a post-Stonewall society would certainly have had to contend with its systematic deconstruction, whether or not that gradual ideological (and eventual political) dismantling was deemed acceptable to heteronormativity. Surely, Hemingway had quarreled with sexuality, and its twin "gender," in novels that proved way ahead of their day as far as sexual politics were concerned. It seems only fitting that Hemingway would being pushing the sexual envelope in drafting *The Garden of Eden* at the same time that Williams was enjoying success with his sexually conventional (though unquestionably "queer") play, *The Glass Menagerie*, and was headily involved in drafting *A Streetcar Named Desire*, where the gay poet Allan Grey was to announce on Broadway that homosexuality was not so easily typecasted. As Blanche says to Mitch, "There was something different about the boy, a nervousness, a softness and tenderness which wasn't like a man's, although he *wasn't the least bit effeminate looking*—still—that thing was there. . . . (1:354, my emphasis). Given that several of Williams's late plays, like *Out Cry* and *Something Cloudy, Something Clear*, challenge this sexual metanarrative as well, we could examine *Clothes for a Summer Hotel* as a conscious attempt to rewrite America's *grand récit* of sexual identity, with Williams emerging not only as its principal postmodern detractor but also its modernist challenger.

If anything, what brought Hemingway and Williams into the same camp was their vocal distain for "camp" or the effeminate parody of homosexuality. Hemingway had attacked the effeminate gay men at the *bal musette* in *The Sun Also Rises*, just as he did repeatedly throughout his canon: Robert Prentiss in *The Sun Also Rises*; the young writer in "Che Ti Dice La Patria"; the cook in "The Light of the World"; Paco in "The Mother of a Queen"; "Sliding Bill" Turner in "The Pursuit Race"; the older man and his younger lover at the "Café des Deux Magots" episode in *Death in the Afternoon;* Hal in "Birth of a New School" in *A Moveable Feast;* and the Consulate's "plucked eyebrows" desk clerk and Thomas Hudson's second houseboy in *Islands in the Stream*. In fact, Hemingway's "prejudices against homosexuality," as his narrator describes to Gertrude Stein in *A Moveable Feast*, was based on decadent and predatory homosexuals, of the type that pursued him, just as they had young Tom in *Islands in the Stream:*

> "Tommy is the only one of us who plays backgammon," David told the girl. "It was taught to him by a worthless man who turned out to be a fairy."
> . . .
> "I think fairies are all awfully sad," she said. "Poor fairies."
> "This was sort of funny, though," David said. "Because this worthless man that taught Tommy backgammon was explaining to Tommy what it meant to be a fairy and all about the Greeks and Damon and Pythias and David and Jonathan. You know, sort of like when they tell you about the fish and the roe and the milt and the bees fertilizing the pollen and all that at school and Tommy asked him if he'd ever read a book by [André] Gide. What was it called, Mr. Davis? Not *Corydon.* That other one? With Oscar Wilde in it."
> . . . Well, this man who'd taught Tommy backgammon and turned out to be a fairy was awfully surprised when Tommy spoke about this book but he was sort of pleased because now he didn't have to go through all the part about the bees and flowers and that business and he said, 'I'm glad you know,' or something like that and then Tommy said this to him exactly; I memorized it: 'Mr. Edwards, I take only an academic interest in homosexuality. I thank you very much for teaching me backgammon and I must bid you a good day.'" (*IS* 178–79)

Fairies, within Hemingway's epistemological system, were social flotsam. Masculine homosexuals, on the other hand—the kind that were neither decadent nor predatory but who had a keener, and a more aesthetic, insight into the psychology of human passions, desires, and sexual motivations than a heterosexual man was capable of—were what troubled, or perhaps intrigued, Hemingway the most.

Williams, too, repeatedly scorned homosexuals who drew excessive attention to themselves, thus making homosexuality synonymous with emasculation. Early in his active gay life, for instance, Williams never spoke out much against the fairy culture and no doubt paraded among them from time to time despite his attraction for masculine queer men, as Lyle Leverich notes: "Although in gay circles Tennessee Williams enjoyed the often hilarious ritual of antic camping—while seldom joining in himself—he was never able to reconcile himself to flagrant public displays, which he saw a mockery not simply of women but of his own sense of manhood."[12] Leverich drew his conclusion from reading the various references Williams makes in his extant letters from the 1940s, such as those addressed to Donald Windham, Paul Bigelow, or even Joe Hazen, where Williams candidly narrates stories of his cruising but also of his general amusement with or aversion toward the fairies he inevitably encountered.

In a letter to Bigelow, for example, dated September 25, 1941, Williams writes,

> I got reckless and invested half of my current checque [*sic*] in a membership at this rather exclusive Club [New Orleans Athletic Club], but it is worth it as there is a marvelous salt water pool, Turkish bath, Etc., and the prettiest Creole belles in town. I am already well-established in their circles and my particular intimate is a Bordelon [Eloi Bordelon], one of the oldest families in the city. Such delicate belles you have never seen, utterly different from the northern species. Everybody is "Cher!"—I actually pass for "butch" in comparison and am regarded as an innovation—"The Out-door Type"!—and am consequently enjoying a considerable succés [*sic*].[13]

Though attracted at times to the *belles*, Williams could not sustain any relation with them, as he writes again to Bigelow on November 2, 1941: "I had a violent and rather bloody matrimonial break-up with the Bordelon, and as she is the queen bee of the bitch society there, it would be unpleasant for me to remain during her displeasure which I must admit was somewhat unjustly provoked—Marriage is not for me! . . . I am quite fed up with piss-elegant bitches (don't you love that phrase?) of the New Orleans variety, and wish to get back to nature" (*SL I* 353).

Even in his own autobiography, Williams exhorts his complete disdain toward the "'obvious' types" of "'swish' and 'camp'" (*M* 50) that had again become synonymous with homosexuality in the public eye after gay liberation. In a revealing interview for *Gay Sunshine* the year following the publication of *Memoirs*, Williams would even openly attack the effeminate queens:

> I picked up a copy of *Gay Sunshine* (GS 29/30) saying that plays such as *Streetcar*, and virtually all of my plays, were lies because they were about homosexuals disguised as women, which is a preposterous allegation and a very dangerous one. . . . I don't understand transvestites or transsexuals. They are *really* outside my understanding. . . . I think the great preponderance of them damages the gay liberation movement by travesty, by making a travesty of homosexuality, one that doesn't fit homosexuality at all and gives it a very bad public image. We are *not* trying to imitate women. We are simply trying to be conformably assimilated by our society.[14]

In *Clothes for a Summer Hotel*, then, Williams challenges this notion of the masculine/feminine divide in sexual classification by replacing irony with pastiche as his postmodern tool to challenge sexuality. Using the documented events of the lives of F. Scott Fitzgerald and Ernest Hemingway in order to reconstruct a possible past—one that is not true to historical fact because nothing postmodern can claim authority anyway, but rather true to historical character—Williams explores not what necessarily happened between them, but what could have, perhaps what *should* have happened. As he reportedly told Dotson Rader in their 1981 interview for *The Paris Review*, "I think [Hemingway] may have been in love with Fitzgerald, or at least sexually desired him. That was why he treated him so abominably in *A Moveable Feast*, ridiculing his sexual prowess and his innocence, quite cruelly, too."[15] Williams would later expand upon his comment to Rader:

> Hemingway had a remarkable interest in and understanding of homosexuality, for a man who wasn't a homosexual. I think both Hemingway and Fitzgerald had elements of homosexuality in them. I make quite a bit of that in my rewrite of *Clothes for a Summer Hotel*.
> ... The final line in Hemingway's *Islands in the Stream* is one man saying I love you to another. It didn't mean they'd had homosexual relations, although Gertrude Stein intimated that Hemingway had. But does it matter? I don't think it matters. (*CTW* 347)[16]

Of course it mattered to Williams, despite the constant attempts in his work *not* to make it matter. By dragging out familiar gossip concerning both Fitzgerald's and Hemingway's sexual desires and having them intimate it to each other in private, Williams revisits the homosexual existential theme of *Cat on a Hot Tin Roof* and its voyeuristic corollary.

Now, though, in positioning himself in Scott as one whose sexual identity is socially constructed and individually confirmed, and the "real" Hemingway in his Hem as one whose sexual identity was fueled by his gendered performances that potentially belied his private desires (ones that at least provided him with sensibilities to write so accurately about gay issues), Williams enters the sexuality narrative and in effect provides explicit answers where irony and ambiguity once reigned. In short, with Scott's coming out of the closet and Hemingway's in/out status remaining undetermined, Williams supplies a more definitive conclusion to Brick and Skipper's ambiguous relationship that had once eschewed the truth of *Cat on a Hot Tin Roof*'s "mystery." We will never know what Brick decides to do with respect to Maggie's declaration of pregnancy and plea to him to make it come true, but we do get to know what Hemingway does, and that is certainly less reassuring for queer men, homo- and hetero- alike.

What makes *Clothes for a Summer Hotel* potentially more subversive than its predecessor *Cat on a Hot Tin Roof* is that, while Williams had then only written about the potential homosexuality of a fictive ex-football hero-cum-emasculated alcoholic, he now brazenly treads on the reputation of a factual ex-football hero-cum-emasculated alcoholic. In claiming moral integrity, Williams was also pandering to the gossipmongers, for Hemingway *was* a historical figure, unlike Brick, one whose actions dramatized in the play could not be simply brushed away with a "bird" commentary as Williams had done in explaining Brick's problems in *Cat on a Hot Tin Roof*. Just after affirming Hemingway's heterosexuality in the play, Williams then calls it into question, which is only partly dismissed by his "it's nobody's business" comment at the end. Williams was interested in Hemingway's sexual identity, plain and simple, if for the only reason that Hemingway perhaps seemed to him the living embodiment of Brick: heteronormative to excess, his homophobia helped hide a softer, call it "gay" sensibility, which belied that hardened façade. As such, where *Cat on a Hot Tin Roof* is only a challenge to the sex/gender binary and not finally its repudiation, *Clothes for a Summer Hotel* is the binary's wholesale refusal, a fact which makes *Cat on a Hot Tin Roof* and its reproduction of totalizing sexual theories the structuralist forerunner of the referentially-dependent, post-structuralist *Clothes for a Summer Hotel*.

What I have been arguing throughout this book has been precisely to show that Williams was never concerned with *confrontational* homosexual politics in his art (at least not before Stonewall in any case; afterward, he would only become concerned as it affected his standing within the homosexual community). He never felt the need to convince a prejudiced society that he was just like it, which he no doubt internally intuited. His argument has always been rather to show how that society influences personal reflections on sexual identity, how it works to counter intuition and create within the individual thoughts of doubt or guilt over sexual desire. What would, for Williams, separate a homosocial act from a homosexual act remains unclear, then and now. Certainly, male sodomy was considered in Williams's time, as it was in Hemingway's and still in ours today, the unconditional homosexual *act*. But does that act, which is repeatedly performed in male prisons, constitute a homosexual identity? Or, for that matter, do David and Catherine's inverted gender and sex roles in *The Garden of Eden*? What about a homoerotic *thought*? Or the homosocial act found repeatedly in the sports worlds of both Jake and Brick, where men can not only embrace in the ring but also pat each other's asses on the field without anyone batting an eye? Or the simple pleasures of male company over female company, as is evident with Jake's fishing trip with Bill or Brick's football games with Skipper, which are both deemed nonhomosexual simply because they are enacted within an accepted social milieu? Do any or all of these acts constitute the construction of a stable sexed identity? Those men who are sensitive enough to understand the inaccuracies of their society's rules defining sexuality, and yet who derive pleasure from their male companionships, are daily confronted with the problems of a homosexual identity—either for themselves, for their social image, or for both.

Williams's *Cat on a Hot Tin Roof*, then, shares much more with Hemingway's *The Sun Also Rises* than just a similar ending. What we find in both works, which passes through "Three Players of a Summer Game" and which culminates in *Clothes for a Summer Hotel*, is a complex queer relationship where the parameters of masculinity and sexuality are as unstable and irresolute as the frontier during a war or the line of scrimmage during a football game. In each of these four works, the line of demarcation between hetero- and homosexuality is not only blurred but necessarily in permanent flux—one moves the line when one conquers or loses space doing battle. Jake Barnes, physically impotent but heterosexual; Brick Pollitt, psychologically impotent and potentially homosexual (with strong emphasis on "potentially" here); Scott, physically, psychologically, and spiritually impotent—each of these queer men lives an existential relationship with his female "lover" and suffers equally from a meaningless sexual existence wherein he is socially defined (and even self-defined) by his heterosexual *inaction*. As such, each represents men of their respective modernist and postmodernist times who cannot possibly articulate, nor fully comprehend, their sexual natures because the social mores which govern sexual identities have not as of yet been codified beyond stereotyping and ill-formed prejudices. As a result, their resultant "male homosexual panic" documents not only their affiliation with but also their fears of those rules. Yet, while it seems that Jake has by the end of the novel learned to accept his situation, Brick by the end of Williams's original third act to *Cat on a Hot Tin Roof* has only begun contemplating his, which is a much more powerful social commentary insofar it implies that there are for Brick—or for any of us—epistemological problems with modern assessments of sexual identity that no "'pat' conclusions" (*C* 3:115) can sustain, as Williams had warned.

The Sun Also Rises was almost turned into a Broadway play in 1927, Leonard Leff notes, and perhaps it would have been had it a dramatizable plot.[17] Such was the destiny of many celebrated novels in the 1920s. Had it reached the stage, Jake's ironic rejoinder to Brett in the novel would also have been his ironic curtain-line for the play. And had it reached the stage, Williams might have had the opportunity to see it performed, for a year later, in July 1928, before embarking on a two-month European tour with his grandfather, Williams attended his first Broadway performance, *Show Boat*.[18] Two weeks later, as he would describe in a short piece on Paris for his high school newspaper, *U. City*

Pep, Williams described how he "descended" from a cab and, like Jake in the novel, strolled into "the Café de la Paix, the most celebrated of the Parisian cafés, intending to get some refreshments (*WIL* 233)."[19] While it is exciting to imagine the young, seventeen-year-old Williams unwittingly crossing paths with Hemingway at one of his favorite Parisian haunts, Hemingway had already left Paris that March with his newly wedded second wife Pauline Pfeiffer, headed, prophetically, to Key West via Havana. Williams would just "miss" Hemingway again in Key West when he fled there following the disastrous Boston premiere of *Battle of Angels* in February 1941; Hemingway had just divorced Pfeiffer that previous November and left Key West for Havana.

To push this imaginative scenario even further, were audience members or theater critics in attendance of the play version of *The Sun Also Rises* in 1927 *also* on Broadway to witness Williams's *Cat on a Hot Tin Roof* years later, they surely would have heard echoes of Jake's voice in Brick's ironic curtain-line to Maggie. That is, they "surely would have" had Williams's original ending been performed that night. Since Brick's original curtain-line was not to be heard by Broadway audiences for another fifty years or so, when *Cat on a Hot Tin Roof* was revived in 1974 for the American Shakespeare Theatre with the original ending restored, no echoes were to be heard, no comparisons were to be made. Only readers familiar with Hemingway and Williams, as well as with the endings of both of their works, have been able to explore any literary lineage between them, and this book is but a small attempt to bring these two literary giants closer together.

In August 1959, four months after he had met Hemingway in Havana, Williams typed the following unpublished essay, "~~12~~ 13 Golden (?) Rules for New Playwrights." In rule number 10 (appropriate enough), Williams writes, almost as if to himself:

> 10. Do not be intimidated or beguiled into writing sweet and gentle works for the stage merely because you have been warned that the violence and sensationalism of ~~yours truly~~ this writer has provoked a moral reaction against plays with strong themes strongly written, staged, and performed. If you can channel your creative urge, which to be true must be violent, into such beautifully serene works as "A Raisin in the Sun" [which premiered on Broadway March 11, 1959, one day after *Sweet Bird of Youth*], then you have done something that ~~yours truly~~ this writer has not been able to do in the last ten years, much as he would love to. But don't count on your ability to preserve *tranquillity* [*sic*] *under fierce pressure.* Prepare yourself for the time when you must imitate the fighting bull in the ring when he has taken the picadors and the banderillos and is now facing the matador and the "moment of truth" and don't forget to smile forgivingly at the note of bewildered challenge, like the doomed bull's snort, in this counsel just above. Here is

longest of my golden (?) rules, and the most self-favoring, the most shameless [. . .].[20]

Williams was rarely one to enact Hemingway's famed code, "grace under pressure," in the face of repeatedly hostile critics. If anything, what this essay (and perhaps even this book) reveals is that Hemingway was bound to the playwright (at least in Williams's cataract eyes) as the matador is to his bull.

Notes

Introduction

1. Kenneth Tynan, *Right and Left* (London: Longmans, 1967), 331.

2. In separate letters to Donald Windham and Edwina Williams from Havana (both dated April 6, 1959), Williams does not mention having met Hemingway or Castro, which he most certainly would have done. The April 8 edition of the underground newspaper *Revolución* carries the story of Williams's introduction to Castro. All of this suggests that they met on April 7. See Donald Windham, ed., *Tennessee Williams' Letters to Donald Windham, 1940–1965* (New York: Holt, Rinehart, and Winston, 172), 295–96, and Edwina Williams and Lucy Freeman, *Remember Me to Tom* (St. Louis: Sunrise, 1963), 246. All references to *Tennessee Williams' Letters to Donald Windham* noted in this study come from this edition and are hereafter cited parenthetically in the text and abbreviated *TWLDW*.

3. Kenneth Tynan, review of *Sweet Bird of Youth*, *The New Yorker*, Mar. 21, 1959: 98. In *Right and Left*, Tynan adds that was he nervous when seeing Williams at the Hotel Nacional in Havana: "I flinched; because a few days earlier I had given his latest play, *Sweet Bird of Youth*, an extremely damaging review that included references to dust bowls and sterility" (332).

4. Michael S. Reynolds, *Hemingway: The Final Years* (New York: Norton, 1999), 320.

5. Carlos Baker, *Ernest Hemingway: A Life Story* (1969; London: Penguin, 1972), 830.

6. Tennessee Williams, *Memoirs* (Garden City: Doubleday, 1975), 67; see also pp. 65, 111, and 112. All further references to *Memoirs* noted in this study come from this edition and are hereafter cited parenthetically in the text and abbreviated *M*.

7. See Kenneth Tynan, "A Visit to Havana," *Holiday* 27 (Feb. 1960): 50–58; and "Papa and the Playwright," *Playboy* XI (May 1964): 138–41. The title of the essay for *Playboy* carries with it all the prejudices that Tynan had in favor of Hemingway, who is referred to by his nickname, and against Williams, who remains a generic figure.

8. Qtd. in Tynan, *Right and Left*, 332.

9. Tynan, *Right and Left*, 332.

10. Qtd. in Tynan, *Right and Left*, 333.

11. In his glossary to *Death in the Afternoon*, Hemingway defines *cogida* (Spanish for "caught," or gore marks left by a bull's horn) thus: "the tossing of a man by the bull, means literally the catching; if the bull catches, he tosses" (396). See Ernest Hemingway, *Death in the Afternoon* (1932; New York: Simon and Schuster, 1996). All references to *Death in the Afternoon* noted in this study come from this edition and are hereafter cited parenthetically in the text and abbreviated *DA*.

12. Qtd. in Tynan, *Right and Left*, 334.

13. Ibid., 335. Williams met Pauline Pfeiffer in the winter of 1941 after having fled Boston for warmer climes in south Florida to meet up with his friend Jim Parrot and

to rewrite the failed *Battle of Angels* for the Theatre Guild. The Hemingways had divorced that previous November in 1940.

14. Qtd. in Tynan, *Right and Left*, 335.

15. Kenneth Tynan's version recalls that "Castro strode over to meet us," and in "clumsy but clearhearted English" he had told "Tennessee how much he had admired his plays, above all the one about the cat that was upon a burning roof" (*Right and Left*, 336).

16. John Hicks, "Bard of Duncan Street: Scene Four," in *Conversations with Tennessee Williams*, ed. Albert Devlin (Jackson: University Press of Mississippi, 1986), 321. All further references to *Conversations with Tennessee Williams* noted in this study come from this edition and are hereafter cited parenthetically in the text and abbreviated *CTW*.

17. We could even say there is a fourth version, since George Plimpton wrote about the encounter as well. Because it strays so far from the other three versions, it is likely to have been the product not of serious reporting but of grandstanding, which is what Hemingway felt of Plimpton when he came to interview him in Havana.

18. Elaine Dundy, *Life Itself!*, new ed. (London: Virgo, 2002), 213.

19. Ibid.

20. Ibid., 222.

21. Ibid.

22. Qtd. in Dundy, *Life*, 216.

23. Ibid.

24. Ibid., 223.

25. Ibid.

26. Ibid.

27. Ibid.

28. Ibid., 223–24.

29. Tynan, *Right and Left*, 333.

30. Dundy, *Life*, 224.

31. Qtd. in Turk Pipkin, *The Old Man and the Tee: How I Took Ten Strokes Off My Game and Learned to Love Golf All Over Again* (New York: St. Martin's, 2004), 122.

32. Qtd. in Tynan, *Right and Left*, 334.

33. Tennessee Williams, *Notebooks*, ed. Margaret Bradham Thornton (New Haven: Yale University Press, 2006), 684–85. All references to Williams's *Notebooks* noted in this study come from this edition and are hereafter cited parenthetically in the text and abbreviated *NB*.

34. In folder 46.4, Tennessee Williams Papers, Rare Book and Manuscript Library, Columbia University.

35. Dundy, *Life*, 224.

36. Ibid., 225.

37. Qtd. in Dundy, *Life*, 225.

38. Carlos Baker writes that Hemingway's "view of the play in November 1951 was that it [was] probably the most unsatisfactory thing he ever wrote": "After much bad luck and several false starts, the play was adapted by Benjamin Glaser and produced by the Theatre Guild in New York in the winter of 1940" (234). See his *Hemingway: The Writer as Artist*, 4th ed. (Princeton: Princeton University Press, 1972).

39. Baker, *A Life Story*, 830.

40. See Kenneth Lynn, *Hemingway* (New York: Simon & Schuster, 1987); James Mellow, *A Life without Consequence: Hemingway* (Boston: Houghton Mifflin, 1992); and Michael S. Reynolds, *Hemingway: The Final Years*.

41. Jeffrey Meyers, *Hemingway: A Biography* (New York: Harper & Row, 1985),

518. Meyers does recount more of the meeting earlier in his biography when he discusses charges that Hemingway was a closeted homosexual. He writes of Hemingway, "His notorious antagonism to homosexuals made Tennessee Williams quite nervous when Kenneth Tynan offered to introduce the playwright to Hemingway in 1959.... But his fears were ill-founded and their meeting was quite amiable" (202).

42. Donald Spoto, *The Kindness of Strangers: The Life of Tennessee Williams* (New York: Ballantine, 1986), 223.

43. Virginia Spenser Carr, *The Lonely Hunter: A Biography of Carson McCullers* (Garden City: Doubleday, 1975), 433–34.

44. Spoto, *Kindness of Strangers*, 258–59. Spoto does note that this was their second trip to Havana. Williams and Vaccaro went there on January 17, to celebrate her fifty-third birthday (259).

45. Philip C. Kolin, "Tennessee Williams, Ernest Hemingway, and Fidel Castro," *Notes on Contemporary Literature* 26.1 (Jan. 1996): 7.

46. Qtd. in Spoto, *Kindness of Strangers*, 258.

47. Kolin, "Castro," 7, *sic*. See also Ronald Hayman, *Tennessee Williams: Everyone Else Is an Audience* (New Haven: Yale University Press, 1993), 180–81, though his version of the story is essentially the same as Tynan's.

48. Hemingway's name appears repeatedly in Williams's personal notebooks from as early as 1936 to as late as 1954, when he was drafting his third act to *Cat on a Hot Tin Roof*. He would remain a key figure in Williams's literary life well up to and beyond the writing of *Clothes for a Summer Hotel* (1980). Martin Williams has apparently written a play entitled *Past Meridian*, which dramatizes (à la Tynan's "Imaginary Conversations") a fictional conversation Williams has with Hemingway about homosexuality, where both men in the end reveal their inner demons and emotional struggles never publicly revealed, which includes Hemingway's secret love for a bullfighter named Karl. See http://www.studyworld.com/newsite/ReportEssay/Literature/Play%5CPast_Meridian-38744.htm

49. Miriam Mandel informs us that "Hemingway's posthumous texts constitute a veritable library: *A Moveable Feast* (1964), *Islands in the Stream* (1970), "African Journal" (*Sports Illustrated*, 1971–1972), *The Nick Adams Stories* (1972), *Complete Poems* (1979), *Selected Letters* (1981), *The Garden of Eden* (1986), *The Complete Short Stories of Ernest Hemingway: The Finca Vigía Edition* (1987), *The Dangerous Summer* (1985), and *True at First Light* (1999).... But these texts, having been cut, emended, reorganized, and otherwise distorted by editorial intervention, could only yield tentative and uncertain analyses and interpretations" (95). See her article "Truer than the Truth," *The Hemingway Review* 25.2 (2006): 95–100.

50. Tynan, *Right and Left*, 336.

Chapter 1. *Cat* and *Sun*

1. Tennessee Williams, *The Theatre of Tennessee Williams*, 8 vols. (New York: New Directions, 1971–1992), 3:214–15. All references to *Cat on a Hot Tin Roof* noted in this study come from this edition and are hereafter cited parenthetically in the text and abbreviated *C*. For reasons of comparative analysis, I will also be citing from the Dramatists Play Service's edition of *Cat on a Hot Tin Roof* (1955; New York: Samuel French, 1986; hereafter abbreviated DPS), which is closest to Kazan's Broadway production, as well as from Williams's revised version of *Cat* in 1974 (New York: New Directions, 1975; hereafter abbreviated ND), published separately by New Directions the following year "with the third act completely rewritten" (inside jacket).

2. Brian Parker complicates matters further when he suggests that even this original ending was not Williams's first choice but rather "a revised composite of several early drafts, prepared especially for publication, *not* properly an 'original version' at all" (477). See his "A Preliminary Stemma for the Drafts and Revisions of Tennessee Williams's *Cat on a Hot Tin Roof* (1955)," *Papers of the Bibliographical Society of America* 90.4 (Dec. 1996): 475–96. It is perhaps worth noting here that Williams's thematic continuity was further compromised in the Elia Kazan rewrite when Maggie's foreshadowing of her final declaration of love earlier in act one—"Later tonight I'm going to tell you I love you an' maybe by that time you'll be drunk enough to believe me" (*C* 3:31)—is defused of its irony since she no longer keeps her promise by the end, as she does here in the original ending.

3. See Williams's "Note of Explanation" (*C* 3:167–68), and Kazan's *A Life* (New York: Knopf, 1988), 540–44, where Kazan claims that existing laws prevented him from ever demanding Williams to change the ending, maintaining instead that it was "Williams who wanted the commercial success" (544). For a more bibliographical approach to understanding the confusion behind the third act, which supports in part the theory that Williams desired the overall structure to the play that his third act supplies, see Parker, "A Preliminary Stemma," 482–84. For early treatments of the debate, see William Sacksteder, "The Three Cats: A Study in Dramatic Structure," *Drama Survey* 5.3 (Winter 1967): 252–66; William Peterson, "Williams, Kazan, and the Two Cats," *New Theatre Magazine* 7.3 (Summer 1967): 14–19; and R. M. Mansur, "The Two 'Cats' on the Tin Roof: A Study of Tennessee Williams's *Cat on a Hot Tin Roof*," *Journal of the Karnatak University: Humanities* 14 (1970): 150–58. For two recent treatments, see Brenda Murphy, "Brick Pollitt Agonistes: The Game in 'Three Players of a Summer Game' and *Cat on a Hot Tin Roof*," *Southern Quarterly* 38.1 (Fall 1999): 36–44, and Jeffrey B. Loomis, "Four Characters in Search of a Company: Williams, Pirandello, and the *Cat on a Hot Tin Roof* Manuscripts," *Magical Muse: Millennial Essays on Tennessee Williams*, ed. Ralph F. Voss (Tuscaloosa: University of Alabama Press, 2002), 91–110.

4. Brenda Murphy, "Seeking direction," *The Cambridge Companion to Tennessee Williams*, ed. Matthew C. Roudané (Cambridge: Cambridge University Press, 1997), 189. See also her *Tennessee Williams and Elia Kazan: A Collaboration in the Theatre* (Cambridge: Cambridge University Press, 1992), 98–108, 126–30.

5. Marian Price, "*Cat on a Hot Tin Roof:* The Uneasy Marriage of Success and Idealism," *Modern Drama* 38 (1995): 324–35. As Price writes, "Brick's stasis, then, can be understood as grief over the loss of an artistic integrity which Williams, in the very process of revising the play, was setting aside in favor of realistic material and artistic concerns. *Cat on a Hot Tin Roof* plays out the author's choice between suffering paralysis in the face of the unacceptability of his truth and allowing his desire for fame and fortune to become a reason for going on" (234).

6. Tennessee Williams, *The Selected Letters of Tennessee Williams*, Vol. II: *1945–1957*, eds. Albert J. Devlin and Nancy M. Tischler (New York: New Directions, 2004), 569. All letters noted in this study taken from this volume are hereafter cited parenthetically in the text and abbreviated *SL II*.

7. For an in-depth analysis of the realization of this 1974 version (published in 1975), see Brian Parker's "Bringing Back Big Daddy," *The Tennessee Williams Annual Review* 3 (2000): 91–99. Parker finally argues in favor of Williams's first version where Big Daddy does not return to the stage in act 3.

8. Jeffrey Loomis draws on "more than twenty draft versions" (91) of *Cat on a Hot Tin Roof* to show how "the entire manuscript progress[ed] toward the 1975 *Cat*" (92).

9. Mark Royden Winchell, "Come Back to the Locker Room Ag'in, Brick

Honey!," *Mississippi Quarterly* 48.4 (Fall 1995): 711–12. He adds: "What remains uncertain is the view [of Brick] of Williams himself. In the alternate third acts that he wrote for the play and the various contradictory comments he made about his intentions, Williams reflected an ambivalence that finally makes *Cat* a problematic, if undeniably powerful, work of art" (702). For the most recent summary of the debate surrounding this issue, see George W. Crandell's bibliographic essay on *Cat on a Hot Tin Roof* in *Tennessee Williams: A Guide to Research and Performance*, ed. Philip C. Kolin (Westport, CT: Greenwood, 1998), 109–25.

10. Charles E. May, "Brick Pollitt as Homo Ludens: 'Three Players of a Summer Game' and *Cat on a Hot Tin Roof*," *Tennessee Williams: A Tribute*, ed. Jac Tharpe (Jackson: University Press of Mississippi, 1977), 278. Representing a good many of the critics who share May's assessment of the play, S. Alan Chesler notes in the same collection that "neither ending of *Cat* satisfactorily concludes the play" (863). Even in his Mar. 22, 1990 review of Howard Davies's *Cat* revival Frank Rich, drama critic for the *New York Times*, complained of Williams's "curiously constructed" original third act: "Since Brick doesn't pull his weight in any of the playwright's third acts for 'Cat,' it hardly matters which one is used" (sec. 3: 22).

11. James Gilbert, *Men in the Middle: Searching for Masculinity in the 1950s* (Chicago: University of Chicago Press, 2005), 187, 188. Gilbert seemingly contradicts himself in the very next sentence, however, when he says that the "larger significance of the play is disclosed in Williams's commentary on the meaning of masculinity itself and its fragile dependence upon how we choose to perform it" (188). One wonders how the questioning of Brick's suspected homosexuality does not affect his worrying about his masculinity as well.

12. See Walter Kerr, "A Secret Is Half-Told in Fountains of Words," *New York Herald Tribune*, Apr. 3, 1955, sec. 4: 1. For a theatre critic's view opposite to Kerr's, see Henry Hewes, "A Streetcar Named Mendacity," *Saturday Review*, 9 Apr. 1955: 32–33. See also Williams's April 9, 1955 letter to Kerr, to whom he sent his rejoinder and asked that it be published (*SL II* 570).

13. Douglas Arrell has recently taken up this issue again, in particular how Brick denies sexuality altogether when he confronts his homosexual panic. See his essay "Homosexual Panic in *Cat on a Hot Tin Roof*," *Modern Drama* 51.1 (2008): 60–72.

14. Gilbert, *Men in the Middle*, 172.

15. As Michael Paller writes in *Gentlemen Callers: Tennessee Williams, Homosexuality, and Mid-Twentieth-Century Drama* (New York: Palgrave Macmillan, 2005): "Unlike critics, artists are rarely interested in putting their work in neatly labeled boxes. This may explain Williams's constant hedging over Brick's supposed homosexuality" (104). See also Michael P. Bibler, "'A Tenderness which was Uncommon': Homosexuality, Narrative, and the Southern Plantation in Tennessee Williams's *Cat on a Hot Tin Roof*," *Mississippi Quarterly* 55.3 (Summer 2002): 381–400, where he argues that the play's "textual indeterminacy" is based less on questions of whether Brick is gay or straight and more on how "the *way* in which homosexuality creates this narrative disruption . . . derives specifically from the play's setting on the Southern plantation," that is, "white male homoeroticism and homosexuality are actually consistent with the structure of the plantation as long as the patriarchal hyper-valuation of white masculinity remains intact" (381–82).

16. As Winchell wryly puts it, "If Williams's treatment of homoeroticism seemed scandalous in 1955, more recent theorists have chided Williams for his reticence and evasiveness" (711). Some critics, siding with Williams's original response to Kerr's attack, do not even feel that his ambiguity is the result of his being evasive. Nancy Tischler, for example, argues in *Tennessee Williams: Rebellious Puritan* (New York: Cita-

del, 1961) that there "is no evasion of Williams's part" because "Brick simply can't acknowledge the homosexual tendency within himself because he accepts the world's judgment upon it" (214). Though I agree with Tischler that Williams is not being evasive, I do not think we can lay blame on Brick either for not acknowledging what he perhaps cannot fully negotiate for himself.

17. See John M. Clum, "'Something Cloudy, Something Clear': Homophobic Discourse in Tennessee Williams," *Displacing Homophobia: Gay Male Perspectives in Literature and Culture*, eds. Ronald R. Butters, John. M. Clum, and Michael Moon (Durham, NC: Duke University Press, 1989), 149–67; George W. Crandell, "'Echo Spring': Reflecting the Gaze of Narcissus in Tennessee Williams's *Cat on a Hot Tin Roof*," *Modern Drama* 42.3 (Fall 1999): 427–41; and Collette Gerbaud, "Famille et homosexualité dans *Cat on a Hot Tin Roof* de Tennessee Williams," *Coup de Théâtre* 5 (Dec. 1985): 55–70.

18. See David Savran, "'By coming into a room that I thought was empty': Mapping the Closet with Tennessee Williams," *Studies in the Literary Imagination* 24.2 (Fall 1991): 57–74, and also his *Cowboys, Communists, and Queers: The Politics of Masculinity in the Works of Arthur Miller and Tennessee Williams* (Minneapolis: University of Minnesota Press, 1992), 99–110. See also Robert J. Corber, *Homosexuality in Cold War America: Resistance and the Crisis of Masculinity* (Durham, NC: Duke University Press, 1997).

19. Benjamin Nelson argues in *Tennessee Williams: The Man and His Work* (New York: Ivan Obolensky, 1961) that "A true quality of experience cannot be grasped when the situation and characters involved are left unexplained" (211). Signi Lenea Falk, in *Tennessee Williams* (New York: Twayne, 1961), adds that "Williams writes as if he himself did not know the physical and moral condition of his hero and the reason for his collapse" (107). See also Charles E. May, "Homo Ludens," 51.

20. Foster Hirsch, *A Portrait of the Artist: The Plays of Tennessee Williams* (Port Washington, NY: Associated Faculty, 1979), 48. Finding *Cat* to be Williams's "most dishonest play" (52), Hirsch complains that Williams "is obscuring the real subject of his drama with fevered language, and this plea for 'mystery' is a shabby ploy" (50).

21. Dean Shackelford, "The Truth That Must Be Told: Gay Subjectivity, Homophobia, and the Social History in *Cat on a Hot Tin Roof*," *The Tennessee Williams Annual Review* Premiere Issue (1998): 105.

22. Dennis W. Allen, "Homosexuality and Artifice in *Cat on a Hot Tin Roof*," *Coup de Théâtre* 5 (Dec. 1985): 72. Allen argues that the play is not even about homosexuality at all but that homosexuality appears on the surface to hide a deeper structure of "the sacralization of virility and the cultural worship of the male" (72), where homosexuality merely acts as a covert "artifice which conceals this latent ideal" (72). For more on this paradox, which I see as accurate though negligent of the larger context of a masculinity in crisis that the play invokes, see C. W. E. Bigsby, *A Critical Introduction to Twentieth-Century American Drama*. Vol. II: *Williams, Miller, Albee* (Cambridge: Cambridge University Press, 1984), 85–87.

23. See, for example, Williams's interview with Arthur B. Waters in "Tennessee Williams: ten years later," *Theatre Arts*, July 1955: 72–73, 96, and his November 31, 1954 letter to Elia Kazan, both examined further in chapter 4.

24. Fertility is, to be sure, *the* locus of the play, which I argue more at length in chapter 4.

25. David Savran, "'By coming into a room that I thought was empty,'" 57.

26. See Williams's 1955 essay, "Critic Says 'Evasion,' Writer Says 'Mystery,'" *New Selected Essays: Where I Live*, ed. John S. Bak (New York: New Directions, 2009), 76–78. Unless otherwise stated, all of Williams's essays noted in this study come from this edition and are hereafter cited parenthetically in the text and abbreviated *WIL*.

27. David K. Johnson, *The Lavender Scare: The Cold War Persecution of Gays and Lesbi-

ans in the Federal Government (Chicago: University of Chicago Press, 2003), 2. Johnson's book describes at length the methods the federal government used to persecute its gay employees in the 1940s and 1950s.

28. The "correct" date is actually 1869 when Westphal's "Die Konträre Sexlempfindung" was published, though we cannot even properly call this date correct. The year 1869 also saw the first appearance of the word *Homosexualität* in two anonymous pamphlets (later attributed to the German-Hungarian Károly Mária Kertbeny) published in Leipzig. Even then, both of these studies were greatly influenced by Karl Heinrich Ulrichs's *Der mannmännlichen Liebe*, which was published half a decade earlier. In fact, Urlichs's psychic hermaphrodite theory had already been outlined in *Vindex* and *Inclusa* in 1864, two studies that later influenced yet another eminent psychiatrist, Richard von Krafft-Ebing, whose *Psychopathia Sexualis* (1866) eventually turned Ulrichs's theory into a psychological pathology. In short, Foucault oversimplified the historical influencing here to arrive at his "species" theory. Rictor Norton thus concludes in *The Myth of the Modern Homosexual: Queer History and the Search for Cultural Unity* (London: Cassell, 1997) that Foucault's watershed year seems arbitrary at best, though Urlichs's earlier studies certainly did demarcate a paradigm shift (71).

29. Michel Foucault, *History of Sexuality*, Vol. I: *An Introduction*, trans. Robert Hurley (New York: Pantheon, 1978), 37. John D'Emilio and David Greenberg have both advanced this reading that the transition away from the household family-based economy to a fully-developed free labor one is in part responsible for the coalescing of various homosexualities. See John D'Emilio, *Sexual Politics, Sexual Communities: The Making of a Homosexual Minority in the United States, 1940–1970*, 2nd ed. (Chicago: University of Chicago Press, 1998), and David Greenberg, *The Construction of Homosexuality* (Chicago: University of Chicago Press, 1998), where he adds that "Capitalism reorganized the family, sharpened gender stereotypes, created and disseminated new ideologies of love and sex, and established new methods of socializing children. All these developments had an impact on social responses to homosexuality" (369–70).

30. John D'Emilio, for instance, argues in *Sexual Politics, Sexual Communities* that "Homosexuality and lesbianism have become less of a sexual category and more of a human identity" (248). Jeffrey Weeks posits in *Sexuality and its Discontents: Meanings, Myths & Modern Sexualities* (London: Routledge, 1985) that anyone who affirms his sexual identity must recognize that that identity "is provisional, ever precarious, dependent upon, and constantly challenged by, an unstable relation of unconscious forces, changing social and personal meanings, and historical contingencies . . . (187). See also David Halperin, *One Hundred Years of Homosexuality* (New York: Routledge, 1990), and David Greenberg, *The Construction of Homosexuality*, for more on this line of thought.

31. For studies of the fin de siècle crisis of masculinity in Western culture in general, see Angus McLaren, *Trials of Masculinity: Policing Sexual Boundaries, 1870–1930* (Chicago: University of Chicago Press, 1997), where he argues that doctors, sexologists, magistrates, and sex reformers during this period "exploited the stereotype of a virile, heterosexual, and aggressive masculinity," having selected and "declared preeminent one particular model of masculinity from an existing range of male gender roles" (2). See also Jeffrey Weeks, "Inverts, Perverts, and Mary-Annes: Male Prostitution and the Regulation of Homosexuality in England in the Nineteenth and Early Twentieth Centuries," and James D. Steakley, "Iconography of a Scandal: Political Cartoons and the Eulenburg Affair in Wilhelmin Germany," in *Hidden from History: Reclaiming the Gay & Lesbian Past*, eds. Martin Bauml Duberman, Martha Vicinus, and George Chauncey, Jr. (New York: New American Library, 1989), 195–211 and 233–63, respectively. See also Steakley, *The Homosexual Emancipation Movement in Germany* (1975; Salem, NH: Ayer, 1982).

32. See Jonathan Katz, *The Invention of Heterosexuality* (New York: Plume, 1995).

33. E. Anthony Rotundo, *American Manhood: Transformations in Masculinity from the Revolution to the Modern Era* (New York: Basic Books, 1993); Michael Kimmel, *Manhood in America: A Cultural History* (New York: Free Press, 1996); and Michael Kimmel, *Changing Men: New Directions in Research on Men and Masculinity* (Newbury Park, CA: Sage, 1987).

34. Elizabeth Pleck and Joseph Pleck, eds., *The American Man* (Englewood Cliffs: Prentice-Hall, 1980), 1.

35. Myron Brenton, *The American Male* (New York: Coward-McCann, 1966); Marc Fasteau, *The Male Machine* (New York: McGraw-Hill, 1974); Peter Filene, *Him/Her/Self: Sex Roles in Modern America*, 3rd ed. (Baltimore: Johns Hopkins University Press, 1998); and Joe L. Dubbert, *A Man's Place: Masculinity in Transition* (Englewood Cliffs: Prentice-Hall, 1979). As early as 1966, and in response to Betty Friedan's 1963 *Feminine Mystique*, Brenton had called for a "masculine mystique," one that would describe American masculinity in crisis long before the onslaught of masculine studies at the end of the 1980s and into the 1990s. He adds that the American male "nurses a fairly potent patriarchal hangover" that forces him into "juggling the forms of the present against the substance of the past" (40). In short, this patriarchal system, Brenton argues, which was evoked to underpin male masculinity, has "proved to be fairly costly to men, a cost that is considerably higher in today's shifting, complex society" (41).

36. Jonathan Katz, *Gay American History: Lesbians and Gay Men in the U.S.A.* (New York: Crowell, 1976).

37. Brenton, *American Male*, 32.

38. Bryce Traister, "Academic Viagra: The Rise of American Masculinity Studies," *American Quarterly* 52.2 (2000): 298–99.

39. Many critics and scholars have challenged this notion of "crisis" in explaining changes in masculine identity at the turn of the century. In addition to Rictor Norton, see Clyde Griffen, "Reconstructing Masculinity from the Evangelical Revival to the Waning of Progressivism: A Speculative Synthesis," *Meanings for Manhood: Constructions of Masculinity in Victorian America*, eds. Mark C. Carnes and Clyde Griffen (Chicago: University of Chicago Press, 1990), 183–204. As Griffen argues, "While the word 'crisis' presupposes a turning point, it remains unclear when this crisis began, how long it lasted, and when it was resolved, if at all" (184).

40. In other words, Traister satirically writes, ". . . the crisis theory of heteromasculinity circulates in North American popular culture with about same [*sic*] ubiquity that it proliferates in our academic worlds" (285).

41. Traister, "Academic Viagra," 278.

42. Les Wright, who edited this collection of essays for *Men and Masculinities*, announces his plan in the issue's introduction. See his "Introduction to 'Queer' Masculinities," *Men and Masculinities* 7 (Jan. 2005): 243–47.

43. George Chauncey, Jr., *Gay New York: Gender, Urban Culture, and the Making of the Gay Male World, 1890–1949* (New York: Basic Books, 1994).

44. See Robert Heasley, "Queer Masculinities of Straight Men: A Typology," *Men and Masculinities* 7 (Jan. 2005): 310–20, where he describes several effeminate heterosexual male types such has (1) straight sissy boys, (2) social justice straight-queers, (3) elective straight-queers, (4) committed straight-queers, and (5) males living in the shadow of masculinity.

45. For a recent examination of Hemingway's works via masculine studies that challenges the critics' views of the "stability of Hemingway's concept of manhood" (74), see Thomas Strychacz, *Hemingway's Theaters of Masculinity* (Baton Rouge: Louisiana State University Press, 2003). See also Nancy R. Comley and Robert Scholes, *Heming-*

way's Genders: Rereading the Hemingway Text (New Haven: Yale University Press, 1994); and Carl P. Eby, *Hemingway's Fetishism: Psychoanalysis and the Mirror of Manhood* (New York: State University of New York Press, 1999).

46. Debra A. Moddelmog, *Reading Desire: In Pursuit of Ernest Hemingway* (Ithaca: Cornell University Press, 1999), 92.

47. Elaine Dundy, *Life Itself!*, new ed. (London: Virgo, 2002), 223. See my introduction for more about this quote.

48. Michael S. Reynolds, *Hemingway: The Final Years* (New York: Norton, 1999), 319.

49. Hemingway scholars Robert W. Lewis and Robert E. Fleming have recently re-edited *True at First Light* (New York: Simon and Schuster, 1999) under the title *Under Kilimanjaro*, restoring nearly two hundred pages that Patrick Hemingway had originally edited out for publication. It is worth noting that *The Garden of Eden*, already scintillating in its depiction of un-Hemingway-like sexual transgression, was heavily edited as well.

50. Ernest Hemingway, *Under Kilimanjaro*, eds. Robert W. Lewis and Robert E. Fleming (Canton, OH: Kent State University Press, 2005), 178–79. Since *Under Kilimanjaro* is more faithful to the original manuscript of Hemingway's "African book" than *True at First Light*, I will cite only from it. However, any passages under consideration in *Under Kilimanjaro* that were expurgated from *True at First Light* will be noted. All further references to *True at First Light* and *Under Kilimanjaro* noted in this study come from these editions and are hereafter cited parenthetically in the text and abbreviated *TFL* and *UK*, respectively. Incidentally, the Albertine reference is perhaps a nod to critic Stanley Edgar Hyman's Albertine Strategy, which he applied to Tennessee Williams's writings in the 1950s. See his essays "Some Notes on the Albertine Strategy," *Hudson Review* 6 (Autumn 1953): 417–22, and "Some Trends in the Novel," *College English* 20.1 (Oct. 1958): 1–9.

51. During Miss Mary's short trip to Nairobi to buy Christmas presents and have her hair cut, Hemingway attempts finally to sleep with Debba, though his night is thwarted by the tribal elders who wish to uphold Kamba law: "Keiti killed it in the name of his loyalty to the bwanas, to the tribe, and to the Moslem religion. . . . This was the beginning of the end of the day in my life which offered the most chances of happiness" (*UK* 355). Hemingway manages to smooth things over with Keiti later, telling him that if Debba had gotten pregnant that night and gave birth to a son or a daughter, Hemingway would have raised the child as his own. Hemingway's earlier comment that he "proved mathematically" to himself that he "could not be" Ngui's father (*UK* 336) also suggests that he had slept with M'Cola's wife during his 1933–1934 safari with his wife Pauline (documented in *Green Hills of Africa*). The Hemingway persona, if not Hemingway himself, was frequently obsessed with interracial sex.

52. See chapter 4 of George Chauncey, Jr., *Gay New York*, and John D'Emilio, *Sexual Politics, Sexual Communities*.

53. For three in-depth studies of how the Wales-Padlock Law and Hays Code censored plays and movies that dealt with homosexuality, if even subversively, see Nicholas de Jongh, *Not in Front of the Audience: Homosexuality on Stage* (London: Routledge, 1992), Kaier Curtin, *"We Can Always Call Them Bulgarians": The Emergence of Lesbians and Gay Men on the American Stage* (Boston: Alyson, 1987), and Vito Russo, *The Celluloid Closet: Homosexuality in the Movies*, rev. ed. (New York: Harper & Row, 1985).

54. Foucault, *History*, 43.

55. Dundy, *Life*, 221.

56. James Weldon Johnson, *The Autobiography of an Ex-Colored Man* (1912; Ontario: Dover, 1995), 80.

57. See Robert Lynd and Helen Lynd, *Middletown: A Study in American Culture*

(1929; New York: Free Press, 1955), and Robert Lynd and Helen Lynd, *Middletown in Transition: A Study in Cultural Conflicts* (1937; New York: Free Press, 1966).

58. Alfred C. Kinsey, Wardell B. Pomeroy, and Clyde E. Martin, *Sexual Behavior in the Human Male* (Philadelphia: W. B. Saunders, 1948).

59. Ernest Hemingway, *The Sun Also Rises* (1926; New York: Scribner's Sons, 1954), 247. All references to *The Sun Also Rises* noted in this study come from this edition and are hereafter cited parenthetically in the text and abbreviated *S*.

60. May, "Homo Luden," 291.

61. Murphy, "Brick Pollitt Agonistes," 44.

62. Robert F. Gross, "The Pleasures of Brick: Eros and the Gay Spectator in *Cat on a Hot Tin Roof*," *Journal of American Drama and Theatre* 9.1 (Winter 1997): 24–25.

63. Winchell, "Come Back," 712.

64. Williams records in his notebooks having read "a pretty good book about a doomed matador" (*NB* 591) in September 1953. Though Margaret Bradham Thornton suggests that it was "[v]ery likely Hemingway's *Death in the Afternoon*" (*NB* 590n877), I would argue that Williams was referring to the "doomed" Romero in *The Sun Also Rises* and not *Death in the Afternoon*, which describes the fates of *several* "doomed" matadors. In all probability, Williams had first encountered *The Sun Also Rises* back in college in the mid-1930s, and reread it again in the 1940s and/or 1950s. As Williams attests later in a notebook entry for December 6, 1953: "I felt listless and heavy so I left Mike in a bar and came home to comfort myself with this journal and Mr. Hemingway's 'Green Hills of Africa' which I'm reading *again, as I do all of his works*" (*NB* 603, my emphasis). In an entry for the following day, Williams calls *Green Hills of Africa* "Hemingway's good book" and even attempts to reproduce Hemingway's prose style: "A hotel is no good when you have to put the glass on the floor because there's no table by the bed. (a Hemingway type sentence)" (*NB* 605, *sic*).

65. Tennessee Williams, "A Report On Four Writers Of The Modern Psychological School," box 10, folder 12, College papers, 1930–1938, n.d., Papers of Tennessee Williams, Harry Ransom Humanities Research Center, The University of Texas at Austin, 7.

66. In her journal entries for August 9, 1954, in *Five O'Clock Angel: Letters of Tennessee Williams to Maria St. Just, 1948–1982*, ed. Maria St. Just (New York: Knopf, 1990), Maria St. Just writes that she and Williams "have now been to five bullfights, and reading Hemingway's book [cf. "A copy of Hemingway," *NB* 647] gives one a wonderful added concern and understanding of everything" (96). Later she adds, "Tenn thinks Hemingway is really queer as he has an unnatural concern about queens . . ." (96). Williams, who was "[r]ead[ing] 'Death in the Afternoon' by Hemingway with ever increasing respect for it as a great piece of prose, and honest acknowledgment of a lust which is nearly always concealed" (*NB* 649), admits in the August 5 entry of his own notebook to "enjoying the brutal poetry of the Toros . . . 3 times in 1 week" (*NB* 651). Although they were reading *Death in the Afternoon* that summer, it is likely that she and Williams had also talked about or read *The Sun Also Rises*, since it is Hemingway's more famous bullfighting work.

67. See Brian Parker's "A Preliminary Stemma" where he argues that Williams was drafting his original third act during the summer of 1954 and not "*already* trying to revise his original third act to meet the Kazan objections to it that are specified in Williams's 'Note of Explanation' prefixed to the 'Broadway version' of Act 3 in the New Directions edition" (484n11). His reasons for this argument as based on the facts that Kazan did not join the project until the following fall. Williams's letters to Audrey Wood in September 1954 show that Kazan had still not signed on to the project (*SL II* 547–48), and those to Kazan in November illustrate the working out between their

disagreement over the changes (*SL II* 549–53, 555–59; see also another letter to Kazan reprinted in the *Notebooks* apropos their differing views on *Cat*'s ending, *NB* 658). By the end of November 1954, Williams would acknowledge in his notebooks having received Kazan's acceptance of his third act rewrite: "A wire from Gadg this A.M. expresses pleasure with the rewrite" (*NB* 659).

Chapter 2. *The Sun Also* Sets

1. Kenneth Lynn, *Hemingway* (New York: Simon & Schuster, 1987), 223–25, 242–44, 284–88, and 319–23.

2. James Mellow, *A Life without Consequence: Hemingway* (Boston: Houghton Mifflin, 1992), 313.

3. Jeffrey Meyers, *Hemingway: A Biography* (New York: Harper & Row, 1985), 202. Though Michael S. Reynolds, too, neither shies away from nor repudiates the charge of Hemingway's closeted homosexuality throughout his multivolume biography, he certainly does not promote it either, as we can see in his *Hemingway: The Paris Years* (New York: Blackwell, 1989): "There is no evidence that Hemingway found homosexual advances attractive, or that he ever encouraged them, but neither did he necessarily rage in the presence of homosexual men" (129).

4. Mark Spilka, *Hemingway's Quarrel With Androgyny* (Lincoln: University of Nebraska Press, 1990), 5.

5. Ibid., 3.

6. Nancy R. Comley and Robert Scholes, *Hemingway's Genders: Rereading the Hemingway Text* (New Haven: Yale University Press, 1994), 143–44.

7. Debra A. Moddelmog, *Reading Desire: In Pursuit of Ernest Hemingway* (Ithaca: Cornell University Press, 1999), 2. She sees the current state of Hemingway scholarship as divided between those critics who would reconstruct Hemingway's psyche and those his intellect to account for the rather uncharacteristic material encountered in his posthumous works.

8. Ibid., 4.

9. Ibid., 7, 92. Moddelmog argues that Hemingway's publishers have been at the heart of the push to maintain the macho image of the writer, evidenced in the censoring of sensitive pages in *The Garden of Eden*.

10. Carl P. Eby, *Hemingway's Fetishism: Psychoanalysis and the Mirror of Manhood* (New York: State University of New York Press, 1999), 39.

11. Ibid., 171.

12. Ibid., 3–4.

13. Ibid., 4.

14. Stephen P. Clifford, *Beyond the Heroic "I": Reading Lawrence, Hemingway, and "Masculinity"* (Lewisburg: Bucknell University Press, 1998), 39.

15. Thomas Strychacz, *Hemingway's Theaters of Masculinity* (Baton Rouge: Louisiana State University Press, 2003), 74.

16. Ibid., 4, his emphasis.

17. Ibid.

18. Ibid.

19. Ibid.

20. This is Leonard Leff's term for those figures, including publishers, admen, Hollywood producers, and literary critics, who have all contributed to constructing and maintaining the Hemingway myth in American literary tradition. As Leff writes,

Between 1923 and 1933, Hemingway rose from obscurity to prominence not only because he had talent and personality but because he was adopted and championed by publishers as well as reprint houses, reporters, photographers, and especially movie companies. He knew that the literary marketplace of the 1920s could be both rewarding and dangerous. He also knew what the magnifying glass of the new media could do to and for his reputation. He was nonetheless interested in the sale and promotion of his books and—more important—the accoutrements of a literary career and the blandishments of a culture of celebrity. (xviii)

See his *Hemingway and His Conspirators: Hollywood, Scribners, and the Making of American Celebrity Culture* (Lanham: Rowman & Littlefield, 1997).

21. Comley and Scholes discuss these last three stories at length in chapter 4, "Toros, Cojones, y Maricones," of their *Hemingway's Genders*.

22. Given the narrator's own suspected homosexuality (he is perhaps more than simply a member of the bullfighter's *cuadrilla*), it is more probable that he is cursing the bullfighter's penurious habits that included not paying him his six hundred pesos or leasing his mother's grave in perpetuity than he is attacking his sexual nature. At the same time, homosexuality and frugality combine to produce one type of bullfighter Hemingway describes in his definition of a *maricón* in *Death in the Afternoon* (DA 417–18).

23. We should read into Hemingway's language for references to gay slang, such as his repeated use of the terms "straight" to imply honesty and heterosexuality, "gay" to mean happy and homosexuality, as well as gay code words like "punk" or "wolf." No matter how we understand Hemingway's sexual nature itself, he was extremely well versed in gay argot long before the heterosexual world knew it existed.

24. Nina Schwartz, "Lovers' Discourse in *The Sun Also Rises*: A Cock and Bull Story," *Criticism: A Quarterly Journal for Literature and the Arts* 26.1 (Winter 1984): 49–69; Ira Elliott, "Performance Art: Jake Barnes and 'Masculine' Signification in *The Sun Also Rises*," *American Literature* 67.1 (Mar. 1995): 77–94; Gregory Woods, "The Injured Sex: Hemingway's Voice of Masculine Anxiety," *Textuality and Sexuality: Reading Theories and Practices*, eds. Judith Still and Michael Worton (Manchester: Manchester University Press, 1993), 160–72; Michael S. Reynolds, The Sun Also Rises: *A Novel of the Twenties* (Boston: Twayne, 1988); Cary Wolfe, "Fathers, Lovers, and Friend Killers: Rearticulating Gender and Race via Species in Hemingway," *boundary 2* 29.1 (Spring 2002): 223–57; Linda Wagner-Martin, "Racial and Sexual Coding in Hemingway's *The Sun Also Rises*," *The Hemingway Review* 10.2 (Spring 1991): 39–41; Peter L. Hays, "Catullus and *The Sun Also Rises*," *The Hemingway Review* 12.2 (Spring 1993): 15–23; Axel Nissen, "Outing Jake Barnes: *The Sun Also Rises* and the Gay World," *American Studies in Scandinavia* 31.2 (1999): 42–57; and Wolfgang E. H. Rudat, "Hemingway's *The Sun Also Rises*: Masculinity, Feminism, and Gender-Role Reversal," *American Imago* 47.1 (Spring 1990): 43–68. Though his ideas are repeated ad nauseum, see also Rudat, *A Rotten Way to be Wounded: The Tragicomedy of* The Sun Also Rises (New York: Peter Lang, 1990); Alchemy in The Sun Also Rises: *Hidden Gold In Hemingway's Narrative* (Lewiston: Edwin Mellon, 1992); "Hemingway's Jake and Milton's Adam: Sexual Envy and Vicariousness in *The Sun Also Rises*," *Journal of Evolutionary Psychology* 9.1–2 (Mar. 1988): 109–19; "Hemingway on Sexual Otherness: What's Really Funny in *The Sun Also Rises*," *Hemingway Repossessed*, ed. Kenneth Rosen (Westport CT: Greenwood, 1994), 169–79; and "Jake's Wound and Hemingway's War Trauma Once More: Allusion to *Tristram Shandy* and Other Jokes in *The Sun Also Rises*," *Journal of Evolutionary Psychology* 12.3–4 (Aug. 1991): 188–206.

25. In addition to Ira Elliott, see Arnold E. and Cathy N. Davidson's "Decoding the Hemingway Hero in *The Sun Also Rises*," New Essays on The Sun Also Rises, ed. Linda Wagner-Martin (Cambridge: Cambridge University Press, 1987), where they write that "Jake relies upon their homosexuality to define his manhood (at least his

desire is in the *right place*), but that definition is tested even as it is formulated by the joint presence of Georgette and Brett . . ." (92, my emphasis).

26. See, in addition to Moddelmog, Axel Nissen, where he argues both that the novel is a "remarkable time capsule through which to view the sexual politics of the 1920s" (42) and that *all* of its male characters save Cohn are gay. See also Rudat's "Hemingway on Sexual Otherness," where he writes, "By this I do not mean that at the conclusion . . . Jake Barnes turns gay, but I do believe that Hemingway wanted the more adventurously speculative among his readers to at least consider such a possibility" (175).

27. In *Ernest Hemingway: A Reconsideration* (University Park: Penn State University Press, 1966), Philip Young writes "we have come full circle" (86); and in *Hemingway's Craft* (Carbondale: University of Southern Illinois Press, 1973), Sheldon Norman Grebstein writes that the book's "thematic movement is circular and at the end of the novel the protagonists are headed back to where they started" (37).

28. Robert W. Cochran, for instance, in "Circularity in *The Sun Also Rises*," *Modern Fiction Studies* 14.3 (1968), finds the novel to be "far less bitter" (298) than others have contended. Stanley Wertheim, in "The Conclusion of Hemingway's *The Sun Also Rises*," *Literature and Psychology* 17.1 (1967), even notes that this is "perhaps the only instance in his fiction where phallic symbolism is utilized to achieve a mood of ironic poignancy . . ." (56). See also Mark Spilka, "The Death of Love in *The Sun Also Rises*," *Hemingway: A Collection of Critical Essays*, ed. Robert P. Weeks (Englewood Cliffs, NJ: Prentice-Hall, 1962), 127–38, where he first identifies the significance of the policeman and his baton but does not exploit its sexual symbolism: "he stands for the war and the society which made it, for the force which stops the lovers' car, and which robs them of their normal sexual roles" (137). For a rereading of the ending in light of Jake's irony, see the following: Arthur Waldhorn, *A Reader's Guide to Ernest Hemingway* (New York: Octagon, 1975), where he notes that his irony is "a determined rejection of the last shred of illusion" (111); Donald A. Daiker, "The Affirmative Conclusion of *The Sun Also Rises*," *Modern American Fiction: Form and Function*, ed. Thomas Daniel Young (Baton Rouge: Louisiana State University Press, 1989), 39–56, where he argues that in the end Brett is helping Jake to cope; Robert E. Jungman, "A Note on the Ending of *The Sun Also Rises*," *Fitzgerald/Hemingway Annual* (1977), where he finds the end "brings us full circle to the opening passages of the novel" (214); and Carole Gottlieb Vopat, "The End of *The Sun Also Rises*: A New Beginning," *Fitzgerald/Hemingway Annual* (1972): 245–55, where she argues that, though he "seems condemned to go around in circles" (93), Jake finally "breaks the circle" (55) in the end with his uncharacteristic "pretty" comment to Brett.

29. In thoroughly documenting the difficulties these two scenes posed for Hemingway when he revised the first draft during the winter of 1925/1926 in Austria, Frederic Joseph Svoboda lends credence to the popular theory that the novel's essential point is found uniquely in the juxtaposition of these two episodes. See his study of the manuscripts of the novel in *Hemingway & The Sun Also Rises: The Crafting of a Style* (Lawrence: University Press of Kansas, 1983), 45–50 and 92–95.

30. Interestingly enough, the young boy in Hemingway's story, nearly the same age as Williams's narrator in "Three Players of a Summer Game," is homosexual and wishes to be castrated so as to eliminate his "sinful" desires. When the doctor refuses to castrate the boy and tells him instead that it is "a natural thing. It's the way you are supposed to be and later on you will think you are very fortunate" (*CSS* 300), the boy incorrectly amputates his penis in the belief that if he castrates himself he will not longer feel his homosexual desires. See Ernest Hemingway, *The Complete Short Stories of Ernest Hemingway: The Finca Vigía Edition* (New York: Scribner's Sons, 1987). Unless otherwise

noted, all references to Hemingway's stories in this study come from this edition and are hereafter cited parenthetically in the text and abbreviated *CSS*.

31. Ernest Hemingway, *Selected Letters, 1917–1961*, ed. Carlos Baker (New York: Simon and Schuster, 2003), 745. Unless otherwise noted, all further references to Hemingway's letter in this study come from this edition and are hereafter cited parenthetically in the text and abbreviated *SL*. See also George Plimpton, "An Interview with Ernest Hemingway," *Ernest Hemingway's* The Sun Also Rises: *A Casebook*, ed. Linda Wagner-Martin (Oxford: Oxford University Press, 2002), where Hemingway told him, "Who ever said that Jake was 'emasculated precisely as a steer'? Actually he had been wounded in quite a different way and his testicles were intact and not damaged. Thus he was capable of all normal feelings as a *man* but incapable of consummating them. The important distinction is that his wound was physical and not psychological and that he was not emasculated" (25). Like Stendhal in *Armance*, Hemingway never informs his reader that his hero in impotent. For more on this, see James Ellis, "Hemingway's *The Sun Also Rises*," *Explicator* 36.3 (1978): 24.

32. Carlos Baker, *Hemingway: The Writer as Artist*, 4th ed. (Princeton: Princeton University Press, 1972), 92.

33. See Linda Wagner-Martin, "Racial and Sexual Coding in Hemingway's *The Sun Also Rises*," 39–41, and James Hinkle, "What's Funny in *The Sun Also Rises*," *The Hemingway Review* 4 (Spring 1985): 31–41, where he unveils "about sixty submerged jokes" in the novel. See also Darryl Hattenhauer, "More Humor in *The Sun Also Rises*," *The Hemingway Review* 10.2 (Spring 1991): 56–57; and Scott Donaldson, "Humor in *The Sun Also Rises*," in *New Essays on* The Sun Also Rises, 19–43.

34. There have been around a hundred or so penis jokes documented in the novel thus far, including Pedro being Spanish for *peter*, the double entendre of "You're cock-eyed" (*S* 122, 123), and the frequent play-on-words with Brett's comments to Jake like "Hardly" (*S* 29), "I've never let you down" (*S* 29), or "I say, you are slow on the up-take" (*S* 33).

35. Basing his interpretations on Hemingway's esoteric use of the word "funny" in the novel and other subtextual references here, Rudat convincingly argues that the impotent Count serves as Jake's sexual teacher. Leon Seltzer and William Kerrigan, however, had arrived at this conclusion long before Rudat. See their respective essays, "The Opportunity of Impotence: Count Mippipopolous in *The Sun Also Rises*," *Renascence* 31.1 (Autumn 1978): 3–14, and "Something Funny about Hemingway's Count," *American Literature* 46.1 (Mar. 1974): 87–93.

36. Robert Fleming has recognized the fun Hemingway has with the Greek Duke Zizi. See his note "The Fun Also Rises: A Tribute to Jim Hinkle," *The Hemingway Review* 13.1 (Fall 1993): 90–91. Though Fleming demonstrates that it "comically inverts the postwar concern with sterility and impotence" (91), he fails to exploit the pun fully. Even the standard French version of *The Sun Also Rises* from NRF, *Le Soleil se lève aussi* (trans. Maurice Edgar Coindreau [Paris: Gallimard, 1949]), does not recognize the many double-entendres in this passage alone, for it maintains the name "Zizi" without irony and fails to translate the puns in "rather hard" and "He gives me the willys": "*plutôt gênant*" and "*Il me crispe*" (66). Hemingway frequently makes use of French puns, such as when Jake repeats the phrase "pipe down" after Mike's drunken outburst of "Tell him bulls have no balls!" (*S* 176). *Un pipe*, a slang term in French for fallatio, again mocks Jake's impotence. Here, the NRF translation maintains the phrase in English, but only to keep its Englishness (as it does with the repeated use of the English "Hello" in the translation), giving at the bottom of the page its entirely *un*ironic translation, "*ferme ça*." A thorough study of how *The Sun Also Rises* has been translated through the years into French and into Spanish would contribute much to our understanding of

the novel and of Hemingway since many of Hemingway's puns are played out in both languages.

37. Stephen Clifford comes closest to my point when he writes, ". . . understanding the extent of Jake's physical injury and *how* it complicates his relationship with Brett, *and his own identification of himself and his very masculine problem,* is crucial to an understanding of Brett's complex position in the narrative" (190, his emphasis). He does not see Jake's problem in existential terms, however, and nor do I focus as extensively as he does on Brett's relationship to that anxiety in Jake.

38. See especially John Killinger, *Hemingway and the Dead Gods* (Lexington: University of Kentucky Press, 1960); Wayne C. Holcombe, "The Motive of the Motif: Some Thoughts on Hemingway's Existentialism," *The Hemingway Review* 3.1 (Fall 1983): 18–27; and Nina Schwartz, "Lovers' Discourse in *The Sun Also Rises*: A Cock and Bull Story," 49–69. Though both contain rather superficial analyses of Hemingway's existentialism, see also Uma K. Alladi, "Existentialism in the Novels of Hemingway and Camus," *Literary Half Yearly* 21.2 (1980): 43–51; and Joseph Petite, "Hemingway and Existential Education," *Journal of Evolutionary Psychology* 12.1–2 (Mar. 1991): 152–64.

39. Killinger, *Dead Gods*, i.

40. Jean-Paul Sartre, "American Novelists in French Eyes," *Atlantic Monthly* 78.2 (August 1946): 114.

41. Jean-Paul Sartre, *Being and Nothingness*, trans. Hazel E. Barnes (New York: Washington Square Press, 1992), 15. All references to *Being and Nothingness* noted in this study come from this edition and are hereafter cited parenthetically in the text and abbreviated *BN*.

42. Killinger, *Dead Gods*, 98.

43. Ibid., 39. Although Holcombe believes that "Hemingway is some kind of an existentialist" (26), he disagrees with Killinger's analysis and does not find any of Hemingway's characters to be existential, save Jake Barnes, because their approaches to confronting life's absurdities (that is, to "not think about it") run counter to the existential doctrine, which suggests that we cannot escape consciousness, and attempting to do so is to live in bad faith.

44. Ira Elliott's astute "gender" reading of the novel in 1995 has already explored paths that this essay proposes to follow. He queries "the ways in which Jake Barnes's male identity is called into question by the genital wound he suffered during the First World War, and the ways in which his fractured sense of self functions in relation to homosexuality and the homosexual men he observes at a *bal musette* in the company of Brett Ashley" (78). Though I use many of the same theoretical tools as Elliott and focus on some of the same passages from the novel, my analysis leads me to different, often opposite conclusions.

45. The same cannot be said of any other character in the novel whose sexual identity is or can be constructed through their performativity. In fact, the sexual identities of all of the characters in the novel save Jake (and maybe the Count) are defined more by how society perceives what they do or choose to do—be it boxing, fishing, killing bulls, or sleeping with the men who do any of these—than by how their appearances engender them.

46. Judith Butler, *Gender Trouble*, 2nd ed. (London: Routledge, 1999), 23. All references to *Gender Trouble* cited in the study come from this edition and are hereafter cited parenthetically in the text and abbreviated *GT*.

47. Elliott, "Performance Art," 79–80.

48. Or Cohn and Romero, who are heteromasculine because one is divorced but has three children, while the other kills bulls—both socially accepted signs, rightly or wrongly, of their assumed heterosexuality.

49. Significantly, this is said by an Italian, who, ever since classical times, has considered the *gallus*, or a castrated priest of the Mother Goddess Cybele, to be perhaps "the ultimate scare-figure of Roman masculinity" (128). See Craig A. Williams, *Roman Homosexuality: Ideologies of Masculinity in Classical Antiquity* (Oxford: Oxford University Press, 1999). See also Peter L. Hays, "Catullus and *The Sun Also Rises*," where he links the classical allusions to scatology, social satires, impotence, and castration in the novel to Catullus's *Carmina*.

50. As Thomas Strychacz writes, in *Hemingway's Theaters* Jake is fully aware of this audience in his observational role in narrating *The Sun Also Rises*, and his "watching reads as a compensatory mechanism operating within an economy of lack" (77).

51. Schwartz, "Lovers' Discourse," 49; and Seltzer, "Opportunity of Impotence," 13. Schwartz's linking of Jake's existentialism to his impotence approaches the line of thinking I am promoting here. Yet her inquiry remains heterosexual and self-reflexive in its gaze. See also John M. McLellan, "The Unrising Sun: The Theme of Castration in Hemingway's *The Sun Also Rises*," *Studies in English Literature and Linguistics* 18 (May 1992): 51–61.

52. Schwartz, "Lovers' Discourse," 54.

53. Seltzer argues in "Opportunity of Impotence" for the contrary when he finds that "Impotence in *The Sun Also Rises* . . . describes, paradoxically, not man's deficiency but his amazing potentiality" (13).

54. Martin, "Brett Ashley," 51.

55. The point I am making here is that if Jake lost any other limb during the war, his problems would be of an entirely different nature and (to some extent) socially easier to overcome since at least others could see the injury, which would also, ironically, signify his masculinity (if only for a time) for them whether he would want it to or not. I develop this point later in this chapter.

56. Louise R. Achuff, "'Nice' and 'Pleasant' in *The Sun*," *The Hemingway Review* 10.2 (Spring 1991): 42–46. See Frederic Joseph Svoboda in *Crafting of a Style* for a thorough documentation of the several changes from "nice as hell" to "pretty" (93–95).

57. Wolfgang Rudat, "Gender-Reversal" 60–61; and Mimi Reisel Gladstein, *The Indestructible Woman in Faulkner, Hemingway, and Steinbeck*, Studies in Modern Literature, No. 45 (Ann Arbor: University Microfilms International, 1986), 62.

58. Eve Kosofsky Sedgwick, *Epistemology of the Closet* (1990; London: Penguin, 1994), 47.

59. Annemarie Jagose, *Queer Theory: An Introduction* (Washington Square: New York University Press, 1996), 19.

60. Eve Sedgwick, *Epistemology of the Closet*, 186.

61. Donald Yacovone, "Abolitionists and the 'Language of Fraternal Love,'" *Meanings for Manhood: Constructions of Masculinity in Victorian America*, eds. Mark C. Carnes and Clyde Griffen (Chicago and London: University of Chicago Press, 1990), 86.

62. Yacovone, "Abolitionists," 94.

63. E. Anthony Rotundo, *American Manhood: Transformations in Masculinity from the Revolution to the Modern Era* (New York: Basic Books, 1993), 263.

64. Hinkle, "What's Funny," 37; and Wagner-Martin, "Racial and Sexual Coding," 40–41.

65. Philip Young, "*The Sun Also Rises*: A Commentary," *The Merrill Studies in "The Sun Also Rises*," ed. William White (Columbus: Merrill, 1969), 90.

66. See Gilles Barbedette and Michel Carassou, *Paris Gay 1925* (Paris: Presses de la Renaissance, 1981), 20–25; and John Leland, *A Guide to Hemingway's Paris* (Chapel Hill: Algonquin, 1989), 9.

67. Michael S. Reynolds, *Hemingway: The Paris Years*, 33–34, 24.

68. Michael S. Reynolds, *Hemingway Reading, 1910–1940: An Inventory* (Princeton: Princeton University Press, 1981), 121. See also James D. Brasch and Joseph Sigman, *Hemingway's Library: A Composite Record* (New York: Garland, 1981), 113; and Hemingway *SL* 447.

69. Havelock Ellis (co-authored with John Addington Symonds), *Studies in the Psychology of Sex*, Vol. I: *Sexual Inversion* (London: The University Press, Watford, 1897), 23–24.

70. George Chauncey, Jr., "From Sexual Inversion to Homosexuality: Medicine and the Changing Conceptualization of Female Deviance," *Salmagundi* 58–59 (Fall 1982–Winter 1983): 114–16.

71. Rotundo, *American Manhood*, 278–79.

72. George Chauncey, Jr., "Christian Brotherhood or Sexual Perversion? Homosexual Identities and the Construction of Sexual Boundaries in the World War I Era," *Hidden from History: Reclaiming the Gay & Lesbian Past*, eds. Martin Bauml Duberman, Martha Vicinus, and George Chauncey, Jr. (New York: New American Library, 1989), 317, 304.

73. George Chauncey, Jr., *Gay New York: Gender, Urban Culture, and the Making of the Gay Male World, 1890–1940* (New York: Basic Books, 1994), 99.

74. J. Brooks Atkinson, "The Play . . . Tragedy from the French," *New York Times*, Sept. 30, 1926: 23, partially cited in Jonathan Katz, *Gay American History: Lesbians and Gay Men in the U.S.A.* (New York: Crowell, 1976), 82–91.

75. Kaier Curtin, *"We Can Always Call Them Bulgarians": The Emergence of Lesbians and Gay Men on the American Stage* (Boston: Alyson, 1987), 84. See also Richard Helfer, "*The Drag:* Mae West and the Gay World," *Journal of American Drama and Theater* 8.1 (Winter 1996): 50–66; and John S. Bak, "'May I have a drag . . . ?': Mae West, Tennessee Williams, and the Politics of Gay Identification," *Journal of American Drama and Theater* 18.1 (Winter 2006): 5–32.

76. See Jeffrey Weeks, "Inverts, Perverts, and Mary-Annes: Male Prostitution and the Regulation of Homosexuality in England in the Nineteenth and Early Twentieth Centuries" in Duberman, Vicinus, and Chauncey, Jr., 195–211; and James D. Steakley, *The Homosexual Emancipation Movement in Germany* (1975; Salem, NH: Ayer, 1982).

77. Qtd. in Jonathan Katz, *Gay American History*, 388. The author of the charter describes later how, while serving in the Army of Occupation in Germany after World War I, he had "subscribed to German homophile magazines and made several trips to Berlin. . . . I had always bitterly felt the injustice with which my own American society accused the homosexual of "immoral acts." I hated this society which allowed the majority, frequently corrupt itself, to persecute those who deviated from the established norms in sexual matters" (qtd. in Katz 388).

78. Ellis, *Sexual Inversion*, 53. Before its revolution, France not only criminalized but "generally expressed disgust" for homosexuality (19). Cambacérès (a well-known homosexual) deserves credit for having any reference to homosexual acts in private omitted from the *Code civile*, though he had no part in the drafting of the *Code pénale* under Napoleon in 1791, where "repressive language was introduced" (24), especially in Article 330 against public indecency on which a large number of homosexuals were charged. See Antony Copley, *Sexual Moralities in France, 1780–1980: New Ideas on the Family, Divorce, and Homosexuality* (London: Routledge, 1989). Wayne R. Dynes, in *Homosexuality: A Research Guide* (New York: Garland, 1987), also attributes French tolerance toward homosexuality to its Enlightenment thinkers, who "decriminalized sodomy—the first accomplishment of this goal in any European country" (112–13). See François Porche, *L'Amour qui n'ose pas dire son nom* (Paris: Grasset, 1927), for an "advanced and tolerant text for the period, written by a heterosexual" (Dynes 120). And in explaining

Europe's rather lax legal attitude toward homosexuality, David Greenberg notes that "[c]onquests brought the French law to many other European and Latin countries, extending the decriminalization of homosexuality quite widely—" (352). In fact, Greenberg adds, by the early twentieth century, Belgium, France, Italy, Luxembourg, Monaco, Portugal, Romania, Spain, and the Netherlands had no criminal prohibition of consensual homosexual acts in private between consenting adults. Even in countries that still found homosexuality a penal offence, such as Germany (with the notorious Prussian Penal Code Paragraph 143, which would become Paragraph 175 after the Prussians annexed Hanover in 1866), Austria, Russia, and England (Criminal Law Amendment Act of 1885), prosecution was notoriously lax: "Even though male homosexuality was illegal under Paragraph 175 of the criminal code, German homosexuals were able to organize such a movement because traditional tolerance of the Berlin police, dating back to the eighteenth century, had permitted homosexual bars to operate; by 1914 the city had forty, with clientele drawn primarily from the middle class" (410).

However one looks at the issue, France was widely more tolerant toward homosexuality in the closing decades of the nineteenth and the opening decades of the twentieth centuries than America was, which could also account for why the term a "French artist" was used among the gay community of New York then to designate someone who was gay. See David F. Greenberg, *The Construction of Homosexuality* (Chicago: University of Chicago Press, 1998), 391. See also George Chauncey, Jr., "Christian Brotherhood or Sexual Perversion?," 300.

79. Barbedette and Carassou, *Paris Gay 1925*, 94.

80. The "Café des Deux Magots" episode in chapter 15 recounts the story the narrator tells the Old Lady he had heard once from a newspaperman while having lunch with him in Paris. Two men, one older than the other, were having a fight in the hotel room next to the newspaperman's. The fight, which concluded when the young man said he was going to kill himself, was apparently about the younger man's unwillingness to engage in homosexual activity with the older man, who was obviously his friend and protector. The young man did not know that, in agreeing to accompany the older man to Europe at his expense, he was obliged to perform sexual favors for him in return. When the newspaperman intervenes and offers to help, the young man refuses. The next day, the newspaperman saw them both again at breakfast outside the Café de la Paix, and the narrator tells the Old Lady that since then both can be seen daily at the Café des Deux Magots, "wearing well-tailored clothes, looking clean cut as ever, except that the younger of the two, the one who had said he would kill himself rather than go back in that room, had his hair hennaed" (*DA* 182). This story was first narrated in a different form in Hemingway's story "There's One in Every Town" to suggest how being in gay Paris in the 1920s made one susceptible to developing homosexual tendencies. See Comely and Scholes, *Hemingway's Genders*, 121–122 and 125–29.

81. Shari Benstock, "Paris Lesbianism and the Politics of reaction, 1900–1940," in Duberman, Vicinus, and Chauncey, Jr., 334.

82. Ernest Hemingway, *A Moveable Feast* (1964; New York: Simon and Schuster, 1996), 18. All references to *A Moveable Feast* cited in the study come from this edition and are hereafter cited parenthetically in the text and abbreviated *MF*. A "wolf" was a gay code word for an older pederast, as George Chauncey, Jr. notes in *Gay New York*, 88–89.

83. Gertrude Stein, *The Autobiography of Alice B. Toklas* (New York: Random House, 1933), 216, 218, 220, and 216. Hemingway responded by attacking Stein in several other works, most notably *For Whom the Bell Tolls*.

84. Ernest Hemingway, *Islands in the Stream* (New York: Simon and Schuster, 1970), 248. All further references to *Islands in the Stream* noted in this study come from this edition and are hereafter cited parenthetically in the text and abbreviated *IS*.

85. A few chapters later, Hemingway expounds on this digression: "My imagination was not great enough to picture the Informer when he was a Masai moran before his corruption by the great backward noble lord and the bwanas . . ." (*UK* 385).

86. Greenberg, *Construction*, 391n225.

87. Elliott, "Performance Art," 80. He later adds, "The source of his rage is in part his frustration at being unable to categorize the homosexual within the male/female binary. That these men represent and enact gender nonconformity violates the cultural boundaries established to demarcate appropriate social and sexual behaviors. Any attempted remapping of these culturally agreed upon borders exposes the arbitrariness of their frontiers, which in turn calls for a rethinking of the ontological groundwork of sex/gender itself" (83).

88. Davidson and Davidson, "Decoding," 92.

89. On this point, Nina Schwartz argues that Jake's rage is "not resentment over the homosexual's willing abnegation of the conventional male sexuality Jake has been forced to sacrifice. Rather, it results from the serious threat the homosexual might pose to Jake's privileged relation to Brett" (58–59). While she reads Jake's animosity as his fear that the homosexuals might become better "lovers" for Brett because their refusal to make love to her would stem from a physical inability to desire her and thus defuse any notion of unconsummated sexual arousal, Ira Elliott posits that the problems are much more profound since "Jake's sexual inadequacy and the homosexual's gender transgression are therefore conjoined: neither can properly signify 'masculinity'" (82).

90. Judith Butler insists that performative gender cannot be voluntary; sexual identity can only be constituted based on what a person cannot choose to do, or be, through the act. Thus, gender should not be defined by some cultural privileging of a sex act, despite the fact that heterosexual society inevitably does. See her *Bodies That Matter: On the Discursive Limits of "Sex"* (New York: Routledge, 1993), 95.

91. Elliott, "Performing Art," 86.

92. Jagose, *Queer Theory*, 56.

93. Mellow, *A Life*, 312.

94. Leslie A. Fiedler, "Come Back to the Raft Ag'in, Huck Honey!," *The Fiedler Reader* (New York: Stein & Day, 1977), 5, 4.

95. Eve Kosofsky Sedgwick, *Between Men: English Literature and Male Homosocial Desire* (New York: Columbia University Press, 1985), 1–2.

96. Comley and Scholes, *Hemingway's Genders*, 132.

97. *True at First Light* maintains this passage but substitutes "being homosexual" (*TFL* 68) for "homosexuality."

98. Ernest Hemingway, *The Dangerous Summer* (1960; New York: Scribner's Sons, 1985), 51–52.

99. In addition to the YMCA (founded in 1866), The Benevolent and Protective Order of Elks was founded in 1868 by the Englishman Charles Algernon Sidney Vivian under the precept of fellowship. The Loyal Order of Moose for men was also a fraternal order, founded in 1888 in Louisville, then reorganized in 1906. Father Michael J. McGivney founded the Knights of Columbus in 1882, which was based initially on unity and charity but later added fraternity and patriotism.

100. Michael Kimmel, *Manhood in America: A Cultural History* (New York: Free Press, 1996), 171; Mark C. Carnes, "Middle-Class Men and the Solace of Fraternal Ritual," *Meanings for Manhood: Constructions of Masculinity in Victorian America*, eds. Mark C. Carnes and Clyde Griffen (Chicago: University of Chicago Press, 1990), 38. In 1901, as the Plecks note, "five and a half million American men belonged to lodges, about five times the number of union members" (27). See Elizabeth Pleck and Joseph Pleck, eds., *The American Man* (Englewood Cliffs, NJ: Prentice-Hall, 1980).

101. Kimmel, *Manhood* 172.

102. Qtd. in Leff, *Hemingway and His Conspirators*, 65. Leff adds: "Invoking the Rough Rider, he [Fitzgerald] also showed Hemingway how masculine excess could be turned to ridicule" (66). And yet, Maxwell Perkins, Hemingway's editor at Scribner's, suggested to Hemingway that what "'the flapper idea' had done for Fitzgerald, 'the masculine idea' could do for Hemingway . . .'" (qtd. in Leff 67).

103. Theodore Roosevelt, "The Manly Virtues and Practical Politics," *The Forum* 17 (July 1894), in *Works* 13:32. He would repeat these sentiments of the "cult of masculinity" nearly two decades later, when he considered running again for the Presidency in 1912. In his rhetorically chauvinistic treatise of America at war, *The Great Adventure: Present-Day Studies in American Nationalism* (New York: Scribner's Sons, 1919), Roosevelt addressed equally the question of woman's suffrage (which he supported here, as long as women also served in the war effort with the men), the threat of spreading socialism, and the displacement of men in the workplace upon their return home as potential threats to masculinity. All of the significant Hemingway biographers of late — from Reynolds to Meyers to Lynn — have discussed Roosevelt's influence on the young Hemingway, with Suzanne Clark even examining closely that relationship and how Hemingway ultimately critiqued in his literature what he re-enacted in his life, namely the Rough Rider's heteromasculine image. See her *Cold Warriors: Manliness on Trial in the Rhetoric of the West* (Carbondale: Southern Illinois University Press, 2000), 59–96.

104. See Arnaldo Testi, "The Gender of Reform Politics: Theodore Roosevelt and the Culture of Masculinity," *Journal of American History* 81 (Mar. 1995): 1509–33.

105. Kimmel, *Manhood*, 181.

106. Theodore Roosevelt, *The Strenuous Life: Essays and Addresses* (New York: Century, 1900), 257.

107. With the transference of economic competition onto sports competition, the American male became preoccupied with the body and his health. "The male body moved to the center of man's gender concerns . . . and competitive impulses were transformed into male virtues" (Rotundo, *American Manhood*, 222). "Muscular Christianity," which matched the cult of masculinity's bodybuilding craze at the century's end, also became a way for men to re-appropriate the church from woman and to make Christ the American self-made man's-man once again (Kimmel, *Manhood*, 176–81).

108. Daniel Carter Beard, The Boy Scouts of America, Fourth Annual Report, *Scouting*, (n.c.: The Boy Scouts of America Publication, 1914), 109. Unlike his British counterpart, the American Scout took an oath "To keep [him]self physically strong, mentally awake, and morally straight"; whereas R. S. S. Baden-Powell had hoped to create soldiers, Ernest Thompson Seton had hoped to create men, combining the British model youth with the Native American to produce a cultured savage akin to hero worshipping of the fictive Natty Bumppo or the real Daniel Boone or Davy Crockett.

109. Jeffrey P. Hantover, "The Boy Scouts and the Validation of Masculinity," *The American Man*, eds. Elizabeth H. Pleck and Joseph H. Pleck (Englewood Cliffs, NJ: Prentice-Hall, 1980), 287.

110. Ibid., 287, 296.

111. For an excellent contextualization of homosexual culture within heterosexual America during the opening years of the twentieth century through to the Jazz Age, see, in addition to George Chauncey, Jr.'s "Christian Brotherhood or Sexual Perversion?," Eric Garber, "A Spectacle in Color: The Lesbian and Gay Subculture of Jazz Age Harlem," *Hidden from History: Reclaiming the Gay & Lesbian Past*, eds. Martin Bauml Duberman, Martha Vicinus, and George Chauncey, Jr. (New York: New American Library, 1989), 318–31. See also Henry Abelove, "Freud, Male Homosexuality, and the Americans," *The Lesbian and Gay Studies Reader*, eds. Henry Abelove, Michèle Aina

Barale, and David M. Halperin (New York: Routledge, 1993), 381–93; and Angus McLaren, *The Trials of Masculinity: Policing Sexual Boundaries, 1870–1930* (Chicago: University of Chicago Press, 1997).

112. Nissen, "Outing Jake," 54–56. Nissen gives all too "queer" a reading of Jake, Mike, the Count, and Bill, finding all of them representatives of the "queer" masculine gay world in contrast to the feminine "fairies" who arrive with Brett at the *bal musette*. I disagree with his "outing of Jake" here for essentially two reason: first, much of his evidence, though provocative enough, is either taken entirely out of context or is read into too closely (e.g., Jake and the Count, and the Burguete episode); and second, he assumes too narrowly that any phallus reference used in the book must unconditionally support a homosexual subtext rather than simply underpinning the seriocomic irony that constructs the novel and Hemingway's own view of the 1920s. If every penis joke were to carry a homosexual subtext, there would hardly be a heterosexual man alive today. A more astute reading of this passage can be found in Georges-Michel Sarotte: "In *The Sun Also Rises* the fishing party was a symbol of a rich love between comrades, in contrast to the deleterious and impure life of the city. . . . Hemingway is the most striking example we have in American letters of the (almost) *perfect sublimation of the homosexuality instinct*" (275–76). See his *Like a Brother, Like a Lover: Male Homosexuality in the American Novel and Theatre from Herman Melville to James Baldwin*, trans. Richard Miller (Garden City: Anchor, 1978).

113. Moddelmog, *Reading Desire*, 97.
114. Chauncey, Jr., *Gay New York*, 99.
115. Ibid., 48.
116. Ibid., 99.
117. Ibid., 100.
118. Ibid., 100.
119. Ibid., 101.
120. Ibid., 103.
121. Qtd. in Mellow, *A Life*, 312.
122. Ibid.

123. Particularly appropriate for Jake and his relationship to homosexuality here is that he rediscovers his true self in San Sebastián, where Saint Sebastian iconography has carried a gay signification since the Renaissance. For instance, when Wilde emerged from Reading Gaol, he adopted the name Sebastian Melmoth (Melmoth from the title character of his great-uncle Charles Maturin's gothic novel, *Melmoth the Wanderer*, with gothic literature itself being a haven for gay and camp themes). Tennessee Williams is certainly nodding to Wilde later with his gay poet Sebastian in *Suddenly Last Summer*, whose cruising for young boys in Cabeza de Lobo in Spain takes him to the La Playa de San Sebastián in Sitges, just outside of Barcelona. In Hemingway's *Islands in the Stream*, the novel's hero, Thomas Hudson, describes his second houseboy's "faintly fairy, half Saint Sebastian, sly, crafty, and long-suffering look" (*IS* 228). See Kenneth Lynn, *Hemingway*, 319–23; Jeffrey Meyers, *Hemingway*, 201–2; and Comley and Scholes, *Hemingway's Genders*, 119 for more on this point. See also Brian Parker, "Tennessee Williams and the Legends of St. Sebastian," *University of Toronto Quarterly* 69.3 (Summer 2000): 634–59.

124. Rena Sanderson, "Hemingway and Gender History," *The Cambridge Companion to Ernest Hemingway*, ed. Scott Donaldson (Cambridge: Cambridge University Press, 1996), 178. See also, Dana Fore, "Life Unworthy of Life?: Masculinity, Disability, and Guilt in *The Sun Also Rises*," *The Hemingway Review* 26.2 (Spring 2007): 74–88, where she reads the novel via disability studies and offers "a re-evaluation of Hemingway's attitudes towards wounds and masculinity" and explains Jake's vulnerability "to a new

range of sexual stereotypes and cultural assumptions—and especially to the idea that disability 'turns' men into homosexuals or childlike, asexual beings" (76).

125. Michael C. C. Adams, *The Great Adventure: Male Desire and the Coming of World War I* (Bloomington: University of Indiana Press, 1990), 15.

126. Kimmel, *Manhood*, 192.

127. Joanna Bourke, *Dismembering the Male: Men's Bodies, Britain and the Great War* (Chicago: University of Chicago Press, 1996), 25. In terms of shell-shock and *The Sun Also Rises*, see Wendy Martin, "Brett Ashley," 49.

128. Bourke, *Dismembering*, 16.

129. Ibid., 31.

130. Ibid., 58, 56.

131. Ibid., 60.

132. Rotundo, *American Manhood*, 188, 191. See his subchapter, "The Cultural Meaning of Male Neurasthenia," in *American Manhood*, 185–93.

133. McLaren, *Trials*, 233.

134. Jacques Lacan, "The Meaning of the Phallus," *Feminine Sexuality: Jacques Lacan and the école freudienne*, eds. Juliet Mitchell and Jacqueline Rose, trans. Jacqueline Rose (New York: Norton, 1982), 79–80.

135. Ibid., 83.

136. Ibid., 81.

137. Ibid., 83–84.

138. Ibid., 84, my emphasis.

139. See Martin, "Brett Ashley," 65–82.

140. Lacan, "The Meaning of the Phallus," 84–85.

141. Ibid., 85.

142. Schwartz, "Lovers' Discourse," 51–52.

143. Hemingway punningly prepares for this exchange just a page earlier when, in response to Jake's query about the latest literary craze of irony and pity, asking "Who got it up?" (*S* 114), Bill's response is poignantly ironic: "Everybody"—everyone, that is, except for Henry James and Jake Barnes.

144. In *A Rotten Way to Be Wounded*, Wolfgang Rudat uncovers how the word "pedal" in Bill's comment to Jake about how "you don't pedal" (*S* 116) a plane or a tricycle is a subverted erect-penis jokes connected to the idea of how a joystick is used in both modes of transportation (166–68). Rudat, however, misses the point that *"un pédale"* is also a derogatory term in French for someone who is gay (*un pédé*), something Hemingway takes delight in playing upon here, especially given the mystery surrounding Henry James's suspected homosexuality and his self-constructed myth about the injury to justify his bachelorhood. The pun is again used later in the novel when Jake meets the French cycle team who say the Spaniards "do not know how to pedal" (*S* 236).

145. For a clearer understanding of macho Spanish bullfighting culture per Hemingway, see his *Death in the Afternoon*. For a study of how bullfighting and homoerotics intertwine in Hemingway's canon, including the role of the *maricón*, see Comley and Scholes, in particular their chapter entitled "Toros, Cojones, y Maricones" (107–44). Keneth Kinnamon concludes his essay on Hemingway's relation to the *corrida*:

> One of the articles of Goya's faith, Hemingway asserts [in *Death in the Afternoon*], was a belief in his own *cojones*. Why, one wonders, would not the words "heart" or "guts" describe this concept just as well? The answer is not only that Hemingway wanted to stress the quality of masculinity as a major component of courage, but also that he had come to formulate his basic attitudes in Spanish terms; indeed, his attitudes from 1922–1932 were becoming progressively more Hispanicized. According to Spanish folklore, which Hemingway accepts in this respect, human courage resides in the *cojones*. (136)

In existential terms, then, Hemingway saw "*cojones* as man's defense against *nada*" (136). See Kinnamon, "Hemingway, the *Corrida*, and Spain," in Linda Wagner-Martin, *A Casebook*, 125–38.

146. What becomes apparent, then, is that Jake's earlier jab at Paris's gay glitterati was not intrinsically homophobic per se, since Jake had already known Montoya and was accepted among the aficionados. Rather, it is embittered by the fact that their effeminate, campy mannerisms tainted the macho homoerotics he (and Hemingway) admired in Spanish bullfighting culture by becoming *the* image of the homosexual in modern heterosexual epistemology and parlance, in America and Europe alike.

147. Rudat, "Gender-Reversal," 59. See also his first chapter of *A Rotten Way to be Wounded*, and his fourth chapter of *Alchemy in* The Sun Also Rises.

148. Jake uses the word "pretty" earlier in novel—"I was pretty well through with the subject" (*S* 27)—to signify his acceptance of his wound for himself, or at least the reality of the unattainable dream of masculinity that the phallus represented for him. Using the word here shows us a similar sense of that resignation.

149. Jagose, *Queer Theory*, 97.

150. Davidson and Davidson, "Decoding," 92–95.

151. That Hemingway uses bullfighting as a metaphor for sexual potency is implicit throughout the novel. Thus, after the bull has been killed and the mules carry it from the ring, Hemingway continues his visual phallic punning, for the bull is dragged out "one horn up" (*S* 169), after which Brett (as if in post-coitus) says, "I'm limp as a rag" (*S* 169). That Brett is limp *after* the (mock-sexual) experience contrasts sharply with Jake's being "limp" *during* the bullfight; limpness is again referenced later when Bill keeps buying bootshinings for Mike, and the bootblack asks if he would like another: "Limpia botas?" (*S* 173).

152. Killinger, *Dead Gods*, 18, 29, and 97–98; Schwartz, "Lovers' Discourse," 60–67.

153. Eve Sedgwick provides the anecdote of an ACT University Press T-shirt that echoes Descartes's *cogito, ergo sum*, which reads, "I am out, therefore I am." See her *Epistemology of the Closet*, 4.

154. In a letter of November 24, 1926, to F. Scott Fitzgerald, Hemingway jokingly subtitled the novel "THE SUN ALSO RISES (LIKE YOUR COCK IF YOU HAVE ONE)" (*SL* 231). See also Meyers, *Hemingway*, 190; Rudat, *A Rotten Way to Be Wounded*, 98, 175–76; and Fleming, "The Fun," 91.

155. Moddelmog, *Reading Desire*, 99.

Chapter 3. "A Dying Gaul"

1. In an entry dated July 29, 1951 of his personal notebook, Williams describes having completed a first draft of a story that would become "Three Players of a Summer Game." At the time of that draft's completion, Williams was reading Hemingway's *A Farewell to Arms*: "Am continuing 'Farewell to Arms'—The writing is good but the book superficial. The man seems brutal and stupid, or false. In a way, I prefer H's last book. Still this one is very readable. I'm glad to have it right now, anyway" (*NB* 525; cf. 521). Margaret Bradham Thornton suggests that the previous Hemingway book to which Williams was referring was the 1940 novel, *For Whom the Bell Tolls*, which Williams had read back in 1941 (*NB* 221). Given his Venice setting while completing "Three Players," to say nothing of the decade that had elapsed since Williams had apparently last read *For Whom the Bell Tolls*, Williams was likely referring to Hemingway's more recent novel, *Across the River and Into the Trees* (1950), which is set in Venice. In

his essay "A Writer's Quest for a Parnassus," published August 13, 1950, in the *New York Times Magazine*, Williams had this to say about *Across the River and Into the Trees*:

> I could not go to Venice, now, without hearing the haunting cadences of Hemingway's new novel. It is the saddest novel in the world about the saddest city, and when I say I think it is the best and most honest work that Hemingway has done, you may think me crazy. It will probably be a popular book. The critics may treat it pretty roughly. But its hauntingly tired cadences are the direct speech of a man's heart who is speaking that directly for the first time, and that makes it, for me, the finest thing Hemingway has done. (*WIL* 57)

    2. Brian Parker, "A Preliminary Stemma for the Drafts and Revisions of Tennessee Williams's *Cat on a Hot Tin Roof* (1955)," *Papers of the Bibliographical Society of America* 90.4 (Dec. 1996): 481. Williams confirms this in a March 21, 1954 letter to Audrey Wood: "I'm also pulling together a short-long play based on the characters in 'Three Players' which I started last summer in Rome . . ." (*SL II* 521).
    3. See Charles E. May, "Brick Pollitt as Homo Ludens: 'Three Players of a Summer Game' and *Cat on a Hot Tin Roof*," *Tennessee Williams: A Tribute*, ed. Jac Tharpe (Jackson: University Press of Mississippi, 1977), 277–91; Dennis Vannatta, *Tennessee Williams: A Study of the Short Fiction* (Boston: Twayne, 1988); and Tom Stokes Reck, "The First *Cat on a Hot Tin Roof*: Williams' 'Three Players,'" *University Review* 34.3 (Spring 1968): 187–92.
    4. Though May and Vannatta recognize the narrator's presence in the story, both fail to discern how, in recounting Brick's story, the narrator recalls his own sexual awakening. Perhaps more a product of his time, Reck does not even find any homosexual overtones in the story, stating that "the usual Williams intrigue with homosexuality" (191) only entered the plot when the story evolved into *Cat*. Parker does acknowledge that the "preliminary 'background material'" includes Brick's "making homosexual advances to his mulatto chauffeur" ("A Preliminary Stemma" 479). Though the play exhumes this background material and excises most of the story's plot and characters, it shows that homosexuality was still an early element that Williams wanted to include in the story but decided against doing so through Brick.
    5. Brenda Murphy, "Brick Pollitt Agonistes: The Game in 'Three Players of a Summer Game' and *Cat on a Hot Tin Roof*," *Southern Quarterly* 38.1 (Fall 1999): 42.
    6. Ibid., 39. While her declaration of the narrator's apparent homosexuality seems justified in light of textual evidence, her conclusion that he acquires his sexual bent from observing the agonistic game between the "closet lesbian" Margaret (39) and the homosexual Brick (40, 42, 44) is tenuous at best since nothing in the story can support (and, if anything, frequently counters) the contention that either are themselves gay, closeted or otherwise, or that they export homosexual tendencies, directly or indirectly, to the impressionable young narrator. The narrator's homosexual awakening is much more complex, as I argue in this chapter.
    7. Tennessee Williams, *Collected Stories* (New York: Ballantine, 1986), 322. Unless otherwise noted, all references to "Three Players of a Summer Game" in this study come from this edition and are hereafter cited parenthetically in the text and abbreviated *CS*.
    8. Freud's intricate working out of the castration theory, and the Oedipus complex from which it derived, took place between the years 1909, with his case study entitled "Little Hans," and 1925, with his essay "Some Psychical Consequences of the Anatomical Distinction between the Sexes." The castration complex can be found principally in his *Leonardo da Vinci and a Memory of his Childhood* (1910), *Totem and Taboo* (1913), *On Narcissism: An Introduction* (1914), *Introductory Lectures on Psycho-Analysis* (1915–1917), *From the History of an Infantile Neurosis* (1917–1918), *The Ego and the Id*

(1923), and "The Dissolution of the Oedipus Complex" (1924). See James Strachey, ed. and trans., *The Standard Edition of the Complete Psychological Works of Sigmund Freud*, 23 vols. (London: Hogarth, 1961).

9. See K. J. Dover, *Greek Homosexuality* (London: Duckworth, 1978), and Craig A. Williams, *Roman Homosexuality: Ideologies of Masculinity in Classical Antiquity* (Oxford: Oxford University Press, 1999).

10. The Renaissance marked one such seismic movement in the sex/gender binary. See Alan Bray, *Homosexuality in Renaissance England* (London: Gay Men's Press, 1982), Jonathan Goldberg, ed., *Queering the Renaissance* (Durham, NC: Duke University Press, 1994), and his *Sodometries: Renaissance Texts, Modern Sexualitites* (Stanford: Stanford University Press, 1992).

11. See E. Anthony Rotundo, *American Manhood: Transformations in Masculinity from the Revolution to the Modern Era* (New York: Basic Books, 1993), 262, 279, and Michael Kimmel, *Manhood in America: A Cultural History* (New York: Free Press, 1996), 119–20. Both posit in the opening chapters of their respective studies that American masculinity underwent a noticeable paradigm shift from the Republican era's self-made man to the Gilded Age's self-minded drone. For other studies that put forward a similar thesis, see Peter Filene, *Him/Her/Self: Sex Roles in Modern America*, 3rd ed. (Baltimore: Johns Hopkins University Press, 1998); Joseph Pleck, *The Myth of Masculinity* (Cambridge, MA: MIT Press, 1981); Joe Dubbert, *A Man's Place: Masculinity in Transition* (Englewood Cliffs: Prentice-Hall, 1979); Elizabeth Pleck and Joseph Pleck, eds., *The American Man* (Englewood Cliffs: Prentice-Hall, 1980); Elaine Frantz Parsons, *Manhood Lost: Drink, Gender, and Self in the Nineteenth-Century United States* (Baltimore: Johns Hopkins University Press, 2000); and Angus McLaren, *Trials of Masculinity: Policing Sexual Boundaries, 1870–1930* (Chicago: University of Chicago Press, 1997).

12. Rictor Norton, in *The Myth of the Modern Homosexual: Queer History and the Search for Cultural Unity* (London: Cassell, 1997), categorically denies "this era as the time when men *first* 'began to define themselves in opposition to all that was "soft" and "womanlike,"' since as early as 1720 pamphlets were being written in America about the "danger of boys being softened by their effeminate upbringing" (92). Both Chauncey (*Gay New York*) and Rotundo agree that the denouncing of male effeminacy was not unique to fin de siècle gender politics but argue that it was undeniably more pronounced. Surely there were other crises of masculinity throughout the world and throughout time, as Norton rightly asserts, but none had so much documented evidence an effect on its society as that perceived in America at the turn of the century.

13. Exploring the fin de siècle crisis of masculinity in Western culture in general, Angus McLaren argues that doctors, sexologists, magistrates, and sex reformers during this period "exploited the stereotype of a virile, heterosexual, and aggressive masculinity," having selected and "declared preeminent one particular model of masculinity from an existing range of male gender roles" (2). For specific treatments of homosexual scandals in England and in Germany at the turn of the century on par with that in Victorian America, see Jeffrey Weeks's "Inverts, Perverts, and Mary-Annes: Male Prostitution and the Regulation of Homosexuality in England in the Nineteenth and Early Twentieth Centuries," and James D. Steakley's "Iconography of a Scandal; Political Cartoons and the Eulenburg Affair in Wilhelmin Germany," both in *Hidden from History: Reclaiming the Gay & Lesbian Past*, eds. Martin Bauml Duberman, Martha Vicinus, and George Chauncey, Jr. (New York: New American Library, 1989), 195–211 and 233–63, respectively.

14. Rotundo, *American Manhood*, 263. See also his chapter, "The Roots of Change: The Woman Without and the Woman Within," and Kimmel's chapter, "Muscles, Money, and the M-F Test: Measuring Masculinity between the Wars." As Chauncey,

Jr. describes in "From Sexual Inversion to Homosexuality: Medicine and the Changing Conceptualization of Female Deviance," *Salmagundi* 58–59 (Fall 1982–Winter 1983): "the changing focus of medical inquiry into sexual deviance . . . can be analyzed as a response to particular changes in and challenges to the Victorian sex/gender system such as the women's movement, the growing visibility of urban gay male subcultures, and the changing gender structure of the economy" (114–16).

15. For a contemporary treatment of the third-sex debate of sexual inversion as described in Karl Heinrich Ulrichs's *Der mannmännlichen Liebe* (1864), Richard von Krafft-Ebing's *Psychopathia Sexualis* (1866), and Karl Friedrich Otto Westphal's "Die Konträre Sexlempfindung" (1869), see Michel Foucault, *History of Sexuality*, Vol. I: *An Introduction*, trans. Robert Hurley (New York: Pantheon, 1978), 42–45. For two historical summaries, see Havelock Ellis (co-authored with John Addington Symonds), *Studies in the Psychology of Sex*, Vol. I: *Sexual Inversion* (London: The University Press, Watford, 1897), 28–35; and Alfred C. Kinsey, Wardell B. Pomeroy, and Clyde E. Martin, *Sexual Behavior in the Human Male* (Philadelphia: W. B. Saunders, 1948), 617–22.

16. See John D'Emilio, *Sexual Politics, Sexual Communities: The Making of a Homosexual Minority in the United States, 1940–1970*, 2nd ed. (Chicago: University of Chicago Press, 1998), and chapter 4 of Chauncey, Jr.'s *Gay New York: Gender, Urban Culture, and the Making of the Gay Male World, 1890–1949* (New York: Basic Books, 1994).

17. Rotundo, *American Manhood*, 278.

18. For research on Victorian masculinity's relationship to social/fraternal orders, see William D. Moore, *Structures of Masculinity: Masonic Temples, Material Culture, and Ritual Gender Archetypes in New York State, 1870–1930* (Boston: Boston University Press, 1999); and Mark C. Carnes, "Middle-Class Men and the Solace of Fraternal Ritual," *Meanings for Manhood: Constructions of Masculinity in Victorian America*, eds. Mark C. Carnes and Clyde Griffen (Chicago: University of Chicago Press, 1990), 37–52; to Muscular Christianity, see Dubbert, *Man's Place*, 136–140; Rotundo, *American Manhood*, 223–24; and Kimmel, *Manhood*, 177–181; and to the Rough Riders, see Kimmel, *Manhood*, 181–88; and Filene, *Him/Her/Self*, 76–77. See also chapter 2 of this study.

19. For research on Victorian masculinity's relationship to Scouting, see Jeffrey P. Hantover, "The Boy Scouts and the Validation of Masculinity," *The American Man*, eds. Elizabeth Pleck and Joseph Pleck (Englewood Cliffs, NJ: Prentice-Hall, 1980), 285–301; and to sports, see Rotundo, *American Manhood*, 222–24; and Kimmel, *Manhood*, 117 ff.

20. For more on the shell-shock debate and Freud's introduction to American medical science, see Nathan G. Hale, Jr., *The Rise and Crisis of Psychoanalysis in the United States: Freud and the Americans, 1917–1985*, Vol. II (New York: Oxford University Press, 1995), 13–24.

21. David F. Greenberg, *The Construction of Homosexuality* (Chicago: University of Chicago Press, 1998), 426–27.

22. For further commentary on how Freud's thoughts on sex entered mainstream America, see Frederick J. Hoffman, *The 20s: American Writing in the Postwar Decade*, rev. ed. (New York: Free Press, 1965), 231–34; and Nathan G. Hale, Jr., *Rise and Crisis*, 57–73.

23. Greenberg, *Construction*, 428.

24. With women constantly being told by doctors during the Victorian times that they had no sexual drives equivalent to men, it is easy to see why Freud, who had argued convincingly that women in fact did, became so popular in America, especially in the 1920s, when women's liberation and the flapper movement strengthened their sexual visibility. See Charles E. Rosenberg, "Sexuality, Class and Role in 19th-Century America," in the Plecks, *The American Man*, 219–54.

25. Pleck and Pleck, *The American Man*, 30.

26. For the impact Freud (and Ford) had on small-town sexuality, see Robert Lynd and Helen Lynd, *Middletown: A Study in American Culture* (1929; New York: Free Press, 1955), and Robert Lynd and Helen Lynd, *Middletown in Transition: A Study in Cultural Conflicts* (1937; New York: Free Press, 1966).

27. D'Emilio, *Sexual Politics*, 19.

28. Hale, Jr., *Rise and Crisis*, 46–47.

29. McLaren, *Trials*, 9. McLaren later concludes:

> Intellectually the conflict, which had been entered into with much macho talk of "playing the game," gave birth to a culture of resignation and introspection. The bloodletting was taken by many as a sign of the end of an age of reason. Those male cultural rebels of the prewar period, such as Wilde, Proust, and Gide, who had embraced hedonism and castigated the repressive morality of the Victorians, were hailed by the progressives of the 1920s as prophets. And sophisticated readers living in a time in which repression seemed out of fashion and sexual experimentation in vogue necessarily turned for advice to seasoned explorers of the unconscious such as Freud. (235)

Gradually, the "pure" ideas of sexologists from Ulrichs to Moll, from Krafft-Ebing to Ellis, and from Carl Westphal to Magnus Hirschfeld had become vulgarized through the modern sexological knowledge by Dr. Jean Fauconney, pen named "Dr. Jaf" or, anagrammatically, "Dr. Caufeynon" (148).

30. Sigmund Freud, *Three Essays on the Theory of Sexuality*, trans. and ed., James Strachey (1905; New York: Basic Books, 1962), 11n.

31. Ibid., 7.

32. Qtd. in Henry Abelove, "Freud, Male Homosexuality, and the Americans," *The Lesbian and Gay Studies Reader*, eds. Henry Abelove, Michèle Aina Barale, and David M. Halperin (New York: Routledge, 1993), 381.

33. Ibid., 385, 387.

34. Brett, it is worth recalling, tells Jake that Romero demanded she grow out her short hair because "He said it would make me more womanly" (*S* 280). If Jeffrey Loomis sees Margaret as being "perhaps even lesbian" (93), Brenda Murphy finds her to be a "self-assured lesbian" ("Brick Pollitt Agonistes" 37) who desires Brick as "a possession but not as an object of desire" (42). While the latter is certainly true, little convincing proof for the former is provided in the story, and what evidence is given seems more appropriate in declaring Margaret a sexually-liberated flapper than as a lesbian, closeted or otherwise. Though a certain number of mannish New Women were lesbian and various emasculated men were gay, as sexologists from Krafft-Ebing to Ellis to Carpenter widely detailed in the closing years of the nineteenth century, they represented more the minority in early twentieth-century America than they did the norm; and for those who did openly celebrate their sexual antipathy to heteronormative standards frequently did so from afar, as in Paris or Berlin, and generally not in sexually conservative southern cities like Meridian, Mississippi. See Jeffrey B. Loomis, "Four Characters in Search of a Company: Williams, Pirandello, and the *Cat on a Hot Tin Roof* Manuscripts," *Magical Muse: Millennial Essays on Tennessee Williams*, ed. Ralph F. Voss (Tuscaloosa: University of Alabama Press, 2002), 91–110. See also Carroll Smith-Rosenberg, "Discourses of Sexuality and Subjectivity: The New Woman, 1870–1936," and Esther Newton, "The Mythic Mannish Lesbian: Radclyffe Hall and the New Woman," both in *Hidden from History: Reclaiming the Gay & Lesbian Past*, 264–80 and 281–93, respectively.

35. All that Brick himself (via the narrator) finally reveals to us about his past is

this: "'Whatever I do, I do it without any shame, and I've got a right to do it. I've been through a hell of a lot that nobody knows'" (*CS* 328–29).

36. Ford did more than "democratize" the automobile; he helped signify it as a distinction of class and masculinity. Like anything that became fodder for the masses, elite and expensive models gave the moneyed classes the opportunity to distinguish themselves from the herd, and since very few women in the 1920s possessed a fortune that was not attached to a husband or a father, the touring car was effectively a masculine signifier. With this in mind, Brick's Pierce Arrow, synonymous with luxury for its success in the Glidden Tours and in its choice as the car for the White House up to the Depression, is contrasted nicely with Margaret's "runabout," which is very likely an electric since the Baker Electric runabout was the choice of many women because it did not require the strength of cranking to get it started.

37. Hazel Kramer's grandmother, Old Mrs. Kramer, drove a "glossy new 'electric'" (*M* 15) around St. Louis in the 1920s. Williams later adds in his *Memoirs* that "Mrs. Kramer, *grand'mère*, had an 'electric' automobile and the pretentious old lady loved to sit in its square glass box tooling sedately among the more fashionable residential sections of the city. She doted on Hazel and she would sometimes allow Hazel to take me for rides. The electric only went at a speed of about twenty miles an hour, at the most" (*M* 29).

38. Murphy rightly calls it a "symbol of his masculinity" ("Brick Pollitt Agonistes" 37).

39. On Macomber's "unmasculine" fear of his wife and sudden bout of courage to stand the buffalo's charge, Williams noted this in a journal entry, dated March 23, 1943: "Hemingway is mistaken about fear. At least afterwards it is an aphrodisiac. And I think even during it might be" (*NB* 359).

40. As Murphy has already noticed, "Sexual prowess and strategic control come together in this final orgasmic resolution to the game" ("Brick Pollitt Agonistes" 37). While she reads the game of croquet in the story as a metaphor for the "escape from sexuality" rather than the "sexual pursuit itself" ("Brick Pollitt Agonistes" 43), as in *Cat on a Hot Tin Roof*, I read it more as precisely that pursuit itself, a sexually-charged discourse on how to win back one's sexual identity.

41. With this letter, Williams enclosed news magazine clippings of two bullfighters, Pepe Luis Vázques ("This one is my favorite") and Alphonso Reyes Lira (*TWLDW* 174). Five years later, in the summer of 1950, Williams again wrote Windham about spending "a week or so in Spain to see the bull-fights" (*TWLDW* 259). He later confessed to Margo Jones that he was "crazy about the bull-fights . . ." (*SL II* 11). And finally, Williams's writes in a notebook entry for July 18, 1953: "We went to the 'Toros' but I left after the first half as blood made me sickish and for the first time the spectacle offended me. No doubt the bad figures of the matadors has something to do with that. Spanish men are not beauties, at least not in this province" (*NB* 577; cf. *NB* 579, 639, 651, 679, 683, 685, and 723). In short, Williams began attending bullfights as early as 1945 during a trip to Mexico, and perhaps even earlier in 1940 when he first visited Mexico City; it would remain a passion for him for the rest of his life.

42. Murphy, "Brick Pollitt Agonistes," 42.

43. Williams was himself sixteen years old, and Hazel Kramer, on whom Mary Louise was modeled, was fourteen, when similar events transpired in their lives together (*M* 15).

44. Though Murphy interprets this comment as proof of the young narrator's awakening to his homosexuality, I will argue in this section that it is instead his initiation into transgenerational sex/gender types, which, upon failing him later in life to properly adjust to societal notions of masculinity or heterosexuality, teaches him to face his sexual identity in ways different from Brick or Brick's generation.

45. Jacques Lacan, *The Seminar of Jacques Lacan*, Book I: *Freud's Papers on Technique, 1953–54*, trans. John Forrester (New York: Norton, 1988), 288.

46. Williams's *Memoirs* recalls Hazel's "plumpness" in real life (*M* 15).

47. Hazel's "breasts developed early" as well (*M* 15).

48. Just as the museum curators had added the leaf as a form of puritan censorship, so too did the editors at *New Yorker* censor the penis here when they blue-penned this scene from the story before its publication. Significantly, Williams would later restore the scene when "Three Players" was reprinted in his queer short story collection, *Hard Candy*.

49. Steven Bruhm, "On Stephen King's Phallus, or The Postmodern Gothic," *American Gothic: New Interventions in a National Narrative*, eds. Robert K. Martin and Eric Savoy (Iowa City: University of Iowa Press, 1998), 77.

50. Jacques Lacan, *Écrits: A Selection*, trans. Alan Sheridan (New York: Norton, 1977), 147.

51. Ibid., 285.

52. In his *Memoirs*, Williams's description of his act of retelling his life story echoes very closely that of the narrator's in "Three Players":

> Do you think that I have told you my life story?
> I have told you the events of my life, and described it as best I could. . . .
> But life is made up of moment-to-moment occurrences in the nerves and the perceptions, and try as you may, you can't commit them to the actualities of your own history.
> The work of a fine painter, committed only to vision, abstract and allusive as he pleases, is better able to create for you his moments in intensely perceptive being. Jackson Pollock could paint ecstasy as it could not be written. Van Gogh could capture for you moments of beauty, indescribable as descent into madness.
> And those who painted and sculpted the sensuous and the sensual of naked life in its moments of glory made them palpable to you as we can never feel with our fingertips and the erogenous parts of our flesh. (*M* 250)

Many of Williams's early stories, more closely autobiographical than his drama, explore personal issues that are only universalized when they are later developed into material for a play.

53. Cf. Charles E. May, "Homo Ludens," who argues that the "irony and seeming contradiction of trying to prove one's masculinity by learning to play what Brick himself calls the 'sissy' game of croquet should be hint enough that Brick's problem is not emasculation and impotence in the psychosexual sense in which we usually understand the term" (282).

54. As Murphy writes in "Brick Pollitt Agonistes," the narrator is a "boy who doesn't know what his penis is like, and finds Brick's body far more interesting sexually than either Mary Louise's or Isabel's" since they give him a "repulsive image of female sexuality" (40).

55. Lacan, *Écrits*, 289.

56. Ibid., 323–24.

57. Jacques Lacan, "The Meaning of the Phallus," *Feminine Sexuality: Jacques Lacan and the école freudienne*, eds. Juliet Mitchell and Jacqueline Rose, trans. Jacqueline Rose (New York: Norton, 1982), 83–84.

58. Lacan, *Écrits*, 322. Judith Butler is critical of Freud's shift from the Oedipal complex to a primary bisexuality theory in explaining homosexuality: "That the boy usually chooses the heterosexual would, then, be the result, not of the fear of castration by the father, but of the fear of castration—that is, the fear of 'feminization' associated within heterosexual culture with male homosexuality. In effect, it is not primarily the

heterosexual lust for the mother that must be punished and sublimated, but the homosexual cathexis that must be subordinated to a culturally sanctioned heterosexuality" (*GT* 76).

59. Lacan, *Écrits*, 322.

60. Not only are Brick's masculine signifiers appropriated, so too is his real voice (and those of Isabel's and Mary Louise's), since the narrator must *recreate* what Brick had actually said that one summer day outside the Grey mansion.

61. Such an explanation, I feel, provides a more theoretical explanation to Brenda Murphy's intuited conclusion that Brick "is both the object of the boy's awakening sexual desire and the model for his awakening sexual identity" ("Brick Pollitt Agonistes" 40).

62. What is most significant here is the fact that, while the conclusion to the story appeared in the original version published in the *New Yorker*, the art museum scene did not, effectively neutering the story of its *Dying Gaul* signifier. In his *Memoirs*, Williams bitterly notes that the *New Yorker* "cut it out of the story, that incident of the fig leaf[,]" because they regarded it as being too blue for their readers and not because they found it covertly homosexual (*M* 29). Charles E. May, one of Williams's most sensitive early critics to discuss homosexuality in *Cat*, also fails to detect this scene's homoeroticism, finding instead that "the added incident has nothing directly to do with the problem of Brick" (287).

63. Further evidence that Williams was able to subvert his heterosexual text with homosexual overtones is found in this unexpurgated ending, which closely echoes, in image and in language, Gaveston's obsequious reply to his King in Christopher Marlowe's notorious (though then-relatively unknown) queer tragedy, *Edward II*:

> It shall suffice me to enjoy your love,
> Which whiles I have I think myself as great
> As Caesar riding in the Roman street
> With captive kings at his triumphant car.
>
> (I.i.171–74)

Williams knew the Marlowe play and was perhaps even reading it along with Sartre in the spring of 1949 (*NB* 499). See *The Complete Works of Christopher Marlowe*, ed. Fredson Bowers (Cambridge: Cambridge University Press, 1981), 20.

64. Lewis Terman and Catherine Cox Miles, *Sex and Personality* (New York: Russell and Russell, 1936); Michael Kimmel, *Manhood*, 209.

65. D'Emilio writes that the "medical model played only a minor role in society's understanding of homosexuality until the 1940s. Before then, it was elaborated upon primarily in the pages of specialized journals. However, psychiatric screening of inductees ordered by the federal government during World War II catapulted the psychiatric profession into the lives of millions of Americans" (17).

66. Kinsey, Pomeroy, and Martin, *Sexual Behavior*, 168.

67. Ibid., 171.

68. Ibid.

69. Williams finally did meet Kinsey in November 1950. Though Devlin and Tischler contend that Williams "declined to give his own sexual history" during that November meeting (*SL II* 286n), one can only wonder what else they might have talked about during their "four and a half hour talk" (*SL II* 535).

70. By no small coincidence, Hemingway also had a copy of the Kinsey report in his library, which may have influenced his own revisions on *The Garden of Eden* from May 20 to September 11, 1957. See John Leonard, "*The Garden of Eden*: A Question of Dates," *The Hemingway Review* 22.2 (Spring 2003): 63–85. See also James D. Brasch

and Joseph Sigman, *Hemingway's Library: A Composite Record* (New York: Garland, 1981), 200.

71. This fact no doubt played a significant role in Williams's decision to relocate Brick and Maggie's marital crisis to the 1950s. While female sexual emancipation was the dominant trend of the 1920s, homosexual emancipation, of the kind that *Cat on a Hot Tin Roof* flirts with, would have to wait another thirty years before reaching the public's attention.

72. Hazel's widowed mother, Miss Florence, was the model for Isabel Grey (*M* 15–16).

73. See also the *Memoirs*, where Williams recounts his hesitancy with heterosexuality and with Hazel and his projected homosexuality on the *Homeric* (*M* 14–20), and for his factual account of the incident at the art museum (*M* 28–29). See also Dakin Williams and Shepherd Mead, *Tennessee Williams: An Intimate Biography* (New York: Arbor, 1983), 20–21.

74. D. A. Miller's term in *The Novel and the Police* (Berkeley: University of California Press, 1988) for the glass closet that certain gay celebrities lived in—never acknowledging their homosexuality but never hiding it either (207). See also chapter 4 of this study.

Chapter 4. "Sneakin' an' spyin'" from Broadway to the Beltway

1. Two days prior to writing this letter, Williams jotted down in his notebook the gist of his argument to Kazan: "Things are not always explained. Situations are not always resolved. Characters don't always 'progress'. But I shall, of course, try to arrive at another compromise with him" (*NB* 663). If Kazan was never convinced of Brick's paralysis, or of Williams's explanation for it, it may have been due to the fact that Kazan was battling his own identity politics before HUAC and needed clarity and resolution in Brick, as he did in himself.

2. Walter Kerr, "A Secret Is Half-Told in Fountains of Words," *New York Herald Tribune*, Apr. 3, 1955, sec. 4: 1. Concerning Brick's problem, Kerr asks, "Is he a homosexual? At one moment he is denouncing 'queers,' at another describing the way he clasps his friend's hand going to bed at night. . . . Listening, we work at the play in an earnest effort to unlock its ultimate dramatic meaning. But the key has been mislaid, or deliberately hidden" (4: 1).

3. Arthur B. Waters, "Tennessee Williams: ten years later," *Theatre Arts*, July 1955: 73. Ironically, Williams wrote the editors of *Theatre Arts* in the fall of 1955, complaining to them that he never said what Waters's quoted him as having said: "It is true that the interview took place; it took place very dimly, almost unconsciously, during the dreadful last week before the New York opening of my play *Cat*. But even considering the conditions under which I had this interview, I am not able to believe that I actually said the things that I am directly quoted as having said . . . My article in the [New York] *Herald Tribune* deals accurately with my attitude toward Brick's sexual nature, not the one given in quotes in this interview" (*SL II* 589–90).

4. In addition to Kerr, see Brenda Murphy, "Seeking direction," *The Cambridge Companion to Tennessee Williams*, ed. Matthew C. Roudané (Cambridge: Cambridge University Press, 1997), 189–203; her *Tennessee Williams and Elia Kazan: A Collaboration in the Theatre* (Cambridge: Cambridge University Press, 1992), 98–108, 126–30; and Marian Price, "*Cat on a Hot Tin Roof*: The Uneasy Marriage of Success and Idealism," *Modern Drama* 38 (1995): 324–35.

5. See David Savran's comment noted earlier in the introduction to this study about *Cat* being a "bold rejoinder to the violently homophobic discourses and social practices that prevailed during the so-called domestic revival of the 1950s" ("'By coming into a room that I thought was empty'" 57). In his *Cowboys, Communists, and Queers: The Politics of Masculinity in the Works of Arthur Miller and Tennessee Williams* (Minneapolis: University of Minnesota Press, 1992), 99–110, and 84–88, Savran equally reminds us that anti-homophobic movements like Henry Hay's Mattachine Society, founded in 1951 to secure political rights for homosexuals, and its mouthpiece *ONE* did attempt to counter these witch hunts around the time that Williams was writing *Cat*, but Williams chose (subversively or collaboratively) to bury his politics in consumerist and conservative entertainment rather than vocalize it in leftist rhetoric. See also Steven Bruhm, "Blackmailed by Sex: Tennessee Williams and the Economics of Desire," *Modern Drama* 34.4 (Dec. 1991): 528–37, where he identifies Williams as having been a "threat to national security" for McCarthy because, being a homosexual, "he harbors a secret which is linked to economic imbalance, and which makes his behavior transgressive" (529).

6. For a discussion of plays with homosexual characters or themes before *Cat*, see Nicholas de Jongh, *Not in Front of the Audience: Homosexuality on Stage* (London: Routledge, 1992), and Kaier Curtin, *"We Can Always Call Them Bulgarians": The Emergence of Lesbians and Gay Men on the American Stage* (Boston: Alyson, 1987).

7. James Gilbert has recently argued that Brick's "purported homosexuality" in *Cat* "does not matter" because Williams was more concerned with "unmask[ing] the meaning of manhood by asserting, in his strongest language, that it is a truth based upon a lie" (188). While I agree that questions of masculinity haunt Brick and *Cat*—more in the story than in the play, however—I will argue that they do so precisely in connection with Brick's sexual epistemology, and thus the two cannot be so casually divorced from his character. Brick's problem in the play, unlike his namesake's in the story, is one of sexual, and not of gender, identity and the existential feeling that accompanies it. See James Gilbert, *Men in the Middle: Searching for Masculinity in the 1950s* (Chicago: University of Chicago Press, 2005).

8. When Williams revised *Cat on a Hot Tin Roof* for the American Shakespeare Theatre's 1974 revival, he could have made Brick less latently homosexual if he had so wished: the theater by then was already used to seeing gay characters onstage, he was himself out of the closet, and his explicit *Memoirs* were but a year shy from publicizing that fact more widely. I believe that, after having lived through the identity politics of the Cold War, and seeing them repeated to a certain extent during the Vietnam War, Williams began to understand more clearly the political and social significance behind Brick's asexual nature, not only to others but also, and perhaps more so, to himself.

9. Williams recalls in his *Memoirs* having met "quite a lot of artists" in Paris that summer of 1948 but was "most interested in meeting Jean-Paul Sartre, whose existential philosophy appealed to [him] strongly, as did his play *Huit* [*sic*] *Clos*" (*M* 149). In a 1953 letter to J. Brooks Atkinson, Williams expounds upon this anecdote: "Apparently he has no use for me. In the summer of 1948 I gave a cocktail party for theatrical friends in Paris and sent him a long wire, inviting him, to which he didn't respond, and during the party I heard he was in a bar nearby and dispatched a French writer to bring him over. He assured the writer he would come, but a short while later he strolled by my hotel without even looking up" (*SL II* 487). Apparently, out of hostility for having been snubbed by Sartre in Paris, Williams said in a 1965 interview with John Gruen: "Perhaps we all understood existentialism before Sartre did" (*CTW* 121).

Sartre's impression of Williams was equally a paradoxical mixture of respect for the artist but suspicion for the man, as he made clear in a 1961 interview with English theater critic Kenneth Tynan:

Tynan. Are there any English or American playwrights who appeal to you?
Sartre. Arthur Miller, certainly. And Tennessee Williams clearly has something, although his world is very different from mine, and his work is permeated with subjective myths. (308)

See Kenneth Tynan, *Right and Left* (London: Longmans, 1967).

10. Williams finally met Sartre, accompanied by Simone de Beauvoir, in Havana in late October 1960 (*M* 68–69). As Philip C. Kolin notes, "A story in the Cuban magazine *Bohemia,* for Nov. 20, 1960, reported that Williams was visiting the island and having a drink with Jean-Paul Sartre. The playwright discounted warnings from the American State Department not to go to Cuba because Cubans were killing Americans; he was there only as a tourist enjoying his daiquiris ('Un Misterio [Llamado Tennessee]')" (90). Sartre and Beauvoir had traveled to Brazil for two months during the fall of 1960 and stopped-over in Havana during the week of October 21–28 before heading back to France. Williams and Marion Vaccaro were apparently drunk that morning at the hotel when they disrupted an interview in progress with Humberto Arenal, a reporter for the weekly magazine, *Lunes de Revolución*. *Bohemia* reproduced a photograph that had just appeared that November in the chapter "Testimonio gráfico" of the book, *Sartre Visita a Cuba* (La Habana: Ediciones Revolucionarias, 1960). See Kolin's essay "Tennessee Williams's *A Streetcar Named Desire* in Havana: Modesto Centeno's Cuban *Streetcars,* 1948–1965," *South Atlantic Review* 60.4 (Nov. 1995): 89–110. Though Robert Bray suggests that "Williams met Jean Paul Sartre [*sic*]" at the Hotel Costa Verde in Acapulco, Mexico, in 1940, where "the two spent long hours in conversation discussing, among other topics, suicide" (169; cf. 288), it is more than likely that Williams spoke with Andrew Gunn and not with Sartre (cf. *TWLDW* 16). See Bray's entry for *The Night of the Iguana* in *The Tennessee Williams Encyclopedia* (Westport, CT: Greenwood Press, 2004), 169–74. See also Michel Contat and Michel Rybalka, eds., *The Writings of Jean-Paul Sartre* (Evanston, IL: Northwestern University Press, 1973), 376.

11. See Esther Merle Jackson, *The Broken World of Tennessee Williams* (Madison: University of Wisconsin Press, 1966), where she writes, "Williams finds, then, considerable support for his vision of humanity from Christian theology and existential philosophy, as well as from the modern arts" (74).

12. Though not published in English until 1956, Sartre's *Being and Nothingness* had been excerpted, with translations of various key passages appearing in such works like *Existential Psychoanalysis* (New York: Philosophical Library, 1953), which is where Williams may have acquired his informal knowledge of the theory. In his personal notebooks, Williams often spoke about his reading Sartre. In one entry dated May 23, 1949, for example, Williams writes: "I read Sartre & Cris. Marlowe. Odd pair. . . . Now bed again with Time and my Sartre" (*NB* 499).

13. For two studies that treat existentialism in Williams, see Deborah Marie Long, "The Existential Quest: Family and Form in Selected American Plays," Diss., University of Oregon, 1986, which only considers generalized existential ideas in *Cat,* and Rita Mary Colanzi, "'A flame burning nothing': Tennessee Williams' Existential Drama," Diss., Temple University, 1990, which reads his canon in light of Sartrean tenets. For a distillation of Colanzi's dissertation on Williams's specific use of Sartrean bad faith, see her article "Caged Birds: Bad Faith in Tennessee Williams's Drama," *Modern Drama* 35.3 (Sept. 1992): 451–65.

14. For another critic in addition to Deborah Marie Long who has studied existentialism in *Cat,* see Charles E. May, "Brick Pollitt as Homo Ludens: 'Three Players of a Summer Game' and *Cat on a Hot Tin Roof,*" *Tennessee Williams: A Tribute,* ed. Jac Tharpe (Jackson: University Press of Mississippi, 1977), 279–91. Though maintaining that Brick's problem in the play is essentially metaphysical, May acknowledges how Brick's

flesh/spirit dialectic also assumes an existential nature akin to Hemingway's sense of the *nada* in "A Clean Well-Lighted Place": "we are given no clues as to the nature of Brick's problem via an objectification of a possible solution or even, as in Hemingway's stories, a possible palliative" (281).

15. George W. Crandell refuses to see Brick's problem as an "existential condition," because that would suggest that his condition is untreatable; he instead qualifies Brick as suffering from a "narcissistic personality" as defined by the American Psychiatric Association (428). See George W. Crandell, "'Echo Spring': Reflecting the Gaze of Narcissus in Tennessee Williams's *Cat on a Hot Tin Roof,*" *Modern Drama* 42.3 (Fall 1999): 427–41.

16. Responding to an earlier version of this chapter published in *Theatre Journal*, Douglas Arrell writes that he finds my analysis of Brick's problem "singularly unconvincing": "The existentialist hero faces the truth with unflinching honesty; he or she acts freely and decisively, rejecting the inauthentic life of comforting illusions and conformity with social norms. Brick is someone who cannot face the truth, about himself, his relationship with Skipper, and his responsibility for Skipper's death. . . . 'Moral paralysis' is surely the opposite of the existential decisiveness Bak attributes to Brick" (62). My use of the term "existentialism" in this article, as well as throughout this chapter, is not textbook Sartre per se. Rather, it is based on the theoretical application of his and Simone de Beauvoir's philosophical theories on sociosexual identification in terms of how masculinity and, by extension, sexuality worked to construct and police sexed identities in America during the 1950s. See his essay "Homosexual Panic in *Cat on a Hot Tin Roof,*" *Modern Drama* 51.1 (2008): 60–72.

17. "Truth is the bird we hope to catch in 'this thing,' and it can be better approached through my life story than an account of my career. Jesus, career, it's never been that to me, it has just been 'doing my thing' with a fury to do it the best that I am able" (*M* 173).

18. John Clum offers a convincing argument about the nature of Brick's mysterious homosexuality when he compares Williams's use of the word "mystery" in *Cat* with another "peculiar rejoinder" (154) in the story "Hard Candy." Unlike with Brick, there is more obfuscation concerning Mr. Krupper's homosexuality than there is ambiguity, yet Williams still felt the need to shroud the character's sexual nature in "mystery": "When I say that there was a *certain mystery* in the life of Mr. Krupper, *I am beginning to approach those things in the only way possible without a head-on violence that would disgust and destroy and which would only falsify the story.* To have hatred and contempt for a person . . . calls for the assumption that you know practically everything of any significance about him. If you admit that he is a *mystery*, you admit that the hostility may be unjust" (qtd. in Clum 154, his emphasis and ellipses). See John M. Clum, "'Something Cloudy, Something Clear': Homophobic Discourse in Tennessee Williams," *Displacing Homophobia: Gay Male Perspectives in Literature and Culture*, eds. Ronald R. Butters, John. M. Clum, and Michael Moon (Durham, NC: Duke University Press, 1989), 149–67.

19. Robert J. Corber, *Homosexuality in Cold War America: Resistance and the Crisis of Masculinity* (Durham, NC: Duke University Press, 1997); Suzanne Clark, *Cold Warriors: Manliness on Trial in the Rhetoric of the West* (Carbondale: Southern Illinois University Press, 2000); Arthur M. Schlesinger, Jr., "The Crisis of American Masculinity," *The Politics of Hope* (Boston: Houghton-Mifflin, 1963), 237–46; and *Look*'s 1958 series in *Look, The Decline of the American Male* (New York: Random House, [1958]). In her article, "Cherchez la Femme: *The Searchers, Vertigo,* and Masculinity in Post-Kinsey America," *Journal of American Culture* 21.2 (1998): 73–87, Wendy Chapman Peek adds to the *Look* series a list of other magazine articles that demonstrate how the crisis of masculinity in Cold War America had reached endemic proportions: "Fragile Male"

(*Today's Health*), "Impotent Male" (*Newsweek*), "Our Men Are Killing Themselves" (*Saturday Evening Post*), "What's Wrong with American Men?" (*Reader's Digest*), "Uncertain Hero: the paradox of the American male" (*Women's Home Companion*), and "The New Burdens of Masculinity" (*Marriage and Family Living*). It is not coincidental, then, how *Look* featured a macho, big-game hunting Hemingway in its pages throughout the 1950s to counter this trend. For more on this, see Debra A. Moddelmog, *Reading Desire: In Pursuit of Ernest Hemingway* (Ithaca: Cornell University Press, 1999), 49, 113–16.

20. Corber, *Cold War*, 117.

21. Metaphors of disease and gender deviants fill the discourses of Cold War politicians. See Geoffrey S. Smith, "National Security and Personal Isolation: Sex, Gender, and Disease in the Cold-War United States," *International History Review* 14 (May 1992): 307–37. Analyzing Cold War-era scandal magazines, Barbara Epstein, in her "Anti-Communism, Homophobia, and the Construction of Masculinity in the Postwar U.S.," *Critical Sociology* 20.3 (1994): 21–44, shows how parallels were made between Communists and homosexuals.

22. Smith, "National Security," 318. See also, D'Ann Campbell, *Women at War with America: Private Lives in a Patriotic Era* (Cambridge, MA: Harvard University Press, 1984).

23. Kyle A. Cuordileone, "Politics in an Age of Anxiety: Cold War Political Culture and the Crisis American Masculinity, 1949–1960," *The Journal of American History* 87.2 (Sept. 2000) <http://www.historycooperative.org/journals/jah/87.2/cuordileone.html>: par 16. This article, distilled from his Ph.D. dissertation, was later reworked into the monograph, *Manhood and American Political Culture in the Cold War* (London: Routledge: 2005). See also Arthur M. Schlesinger, Jr., *Vital Center: Our Purposes and Perils on the Tightrope of American Liberalism* (1949; Cambridge, MA: Riverside Press, 1962).

24. Clark, *Cold Warriors*, 25. For examples of governmental phallogocentric rhetoric, see Frank Costigliola, "'Unceasing Pressure for Penetration:' Gender, Pathology, and Emotion in George Kennan's Formation of the Cold War," *Journal of American History* 83.4 (Mar. 1997): 1309–39.

25. Williams wrote to Carson McCullers on March 1, 1948, that he had just met Gore Vidal for the first time while in Rome but that he found his "new book 'The City and the Pillar' . . . not [to be] a good book" but one that "is absorbing": "There is not a really distinguishing line in the book and yet a great deal of it has a curiously life-like quality. The end is trashy, alas, a murder and suicide both" (*SL II* 171).

26. For popular literature, certainly several protagonists of the noir genre reflect this masculine/feminine duality, such as Mickey Spillane's Mike Hammer, Dashiell Hammett's Sam Spade, or Jim Thompson's and Raymond Chandler's subversive antiheroes. For other literary authors of the period, consider the antiheroes of Flannery O'Connor, James Baldwin, Bernard Malamud, John Hawkes, John Barth, John Updike, Joseph Heller, Gore Vidal, and Norman Mailer, to name but a few.

27. Clark, *Cold Warriors*, 1.

28. This is not to say that homosexuality was fully accepted in America before the Industrial Age, which of course it was not. The point I am trying to make here, one that I expound upon in chapter 2, is that homosexuality entered mainstream discourse more broadly at the end of the nineteenth century, while remaining essentially hidden in the legal annals of pre-industrial America. For more on this, see Jonathan Katz's *Gay American History: Lesbians and Gay Men in the U.S.A.* (New York: Crowell, 1976).

29. Richard Vowles, "Tennessee Williams: The World of His Imagery," *Tulane Drama Review* 3 (Dec. 1958), 54. Though Vowles's reading of *Cat* is similar to mine, he lacks the theory and Cold War context to defend it. Paul J. Hurley, in "Tennessee Wil-

liams: The Playwright as Social Critic," *The Critical Response to Tennessee Williams*, ed. George W. Crandell (Westport, CT: Greenwood, 1996), 126–39, too approaches my line of reasoning when he writes that "Brick's problem is not a question of whether he is homosexual or whether he may be cured. His problem is how an individual who has come to respect and understand individual differences may come to terms with a society which refuses to accept such differences" (135). Clearly, though, Brick has not accepted those differences in the play, and Hurley seems to be talking more about Big Daddy here, who has.

30. Jeffrey B. Loomis, "Four Characters in Search of a Company: Williams, Pirandello, and the *Cat on a Hot Tin Roof* Manuscripts," *Magical Muse: Millennial Essays on Tennessee Williams*, ed. Ralph F. Voss (Tuscaloosa: University of Alabama Press, 2002), 96.

31. Simone de Beauvoir, *The Second Sex*, trans. and ed. H. M. Parshley (1949; London: Vintage, 1997), 295. All references to *The Second Sex* noted in this study come from this edition and are hereafter cited parenthetically in the text and abbreviated *SS*.

32. As de Beauvoir is obliged to argue, if she wishes to remain loyal to Sartre's existential theory, "The truth is that there is never a single determining factor" in defining a woman's sexual identity. It is always "a matter of choice, arrived at in a complex total situation and based upon a free decision; no sexual fate governs the life of the individual woman. . . . Environmental circumstances, however, have a considerable influence on the choice" (*SS* 437).

33. Despite its ubiquity in the play (even in the Broadway version of act 3), Williams has Big Daddy deliver his elephant joke about the "excitin' odor of female fertility!" [*C* 3:205], which complements his earlier comment about Gooper's "pregnant-lookin' envelope"), fertility is categorically denounced, for all of the Pollitt "pregnancies" have produced undesirable "children": Mae's "no-neck monsters," all given "dawgs' names" (*C* 3:37); Big Daddy's plantation, which is "completely out of hand" (*C* 3.81); Big Mama's besotted Brick; and Maggie's lie. Only the gay couple, Straw and Ochello, is portrayed as having experienced a blissful partnership, in spite of—or because of—the sterility of their relationship. For these reasons, it is only fitting that the play should both begin and end with references to children, as they frame Brick's present sterility and bring into question his masculinity and sexuality. This "pedaphobic" rhetoric, of course, also reflects Williams's subtle attack against those who criticize homosexual relationships for their sterility.

34. See Murphy, *Tennessee Williams and Elia Kazan*, 100–1.

35. In a very early manuscript version of *Cat*, subtitled *A Place of Stone*, Williams had already envisioned Big Daddy's use of the phrase, "Wouldn't it be funny it that was true" (61).

36. Tennessee Williams, "Revisions to Act III of *Cat on a Hot Tin Roof*," box 8, folder 9, Papers of Tennessee Williams, Harry Ransom Humanities Research Center, The University of Texas at Austin. In another fragment, Brick repeats this more ardently: "I might be *impotent*, Maggie." See "*Cat* draft fragments," box 9, folder 1, Papers of Tennessee Williams, Harry Ransom Humanities Research Center, The University of Texas at Austin.

37. Loomis, "Four Characters," 94.

38. In spite of its bone-dry scientific flavor, the Kinsey report sold an astounding 275,000 copies, remained for nearly seven months on the *New York Times* best-seller list, and became the topic of mainstream discussion.

39. Joking to fellow journalist-novelist Harvey Breit in July 1950, Hemingway wrote, "Black Dog [one of his pets at the *finca* in Cuba] has gone to sleep now happy that I am writing. He doesn't know what but he loves to hear those keys go. He is a big

Springer and a good retriever. I love him and he loves me and Dr. Kinsey can have that for free" (*SL* 701).

40. Alfred C. Kinsey, Wardell B. Pomeroy, and Clyde E. Martin, *Sexual Behavior in the Human Male* (Philadelphia: W. B. Saunders, 1948), 650.

41. Ibid., 610, my emphasis. A 1950 study of collegiate males later confirmed Kinsey's numbers, and, as Michael Paller writes, "no study done in that era would ever claim to refute his findings" (120). See his *Gentleman Callers: Tennessee Williams, Homosexuality, and Mid-Twentieth Century Drama* (New York: Palgrave Macmillan, 2005).

42. The body of scholastic work devoted to the study of Victorian masculinity in America is exhaustive. See chapters 2 and 3 of this study for more on this crisis.

43. Kinsey, Pomeroy, and Martin, *Sexual Behavior*, 617.

44. Beth Baily, *From Front Porch to Back Seat: Courtship in Twentieth-Century America* (Baltimore: Johns Hopkins University Press, 1988), 102.

45. As I note at the end of chapter 3, when Alfred Kinsey and his research team published *Sexual Behavior in the Human Male* in 1948, Tennessee Williams was already thirty-seven years old. Though Williams certainly did not need any scientific research to prove to him that he was gay, the study no doubt would have supported Williams's natural sense of his sexual identity at a time when society and politics were growing increasingly vituperative in their homophobic discourse. At the dawn of entering into what would be his only sustained relationship with a partner, Williams could have drawn comfort from Kinsey's study, whose popularity or notoriety (depending on the point of view) seemingly provided scientific justification for a sexual practice deemed immoral, dirty, wrong, and, eventually, unAmerican. For more on Kinsey and Williams, see Michael Paller, "The Couch and Tennessee," *The Tennessee Williams Annual Review* 3 (2000): 40–42.

46. As I have already established in chapter 3, while Williams was drafting what would become his intended third act for *Cat on a Hot Tin Roof* in the summer of 1954 he wrote a letter to Cheryl Crawford about his and Kinsey's "four and a half hour talk" (*SL II* 535), which shows that Kinsey's study was on his mind during this crucial summer of composition.

47. James Gilbert states that Brick "embod[ies] nothing less than the male continuity that Kinsey described in his sexology" (165).

48. Georges-Michel Sarotte, *Like a Brother, Like a Lover: Male Homosexuality in the American Novel and Theatre from Herman Melville to James Baldwin*, trans. Richard Miller (Garden City: Anchor, 1978), 113.

49. See Corber, *Cold War*, and Murphy, *Congressional Theatre: Dramatizing McCarthyism on Stage, Film, and Television* (Cambridge: Cambridge University Press, 1999). Both scholars study Brick within a McCarthyist context. While Murphy fails to find any anti-McCarthy rhetoric in *Cat on a Hot Tin Roof*, arguing the opposite in fact when she says that Williams preferred avoiding controversy in the 1950s by writing apolitical psychodrama instead, Corber at least recognizes Williams's political agenda in how he "treated homosexuality as a subversive form of identity that had the potential to disrupt the system of representation underpinning the Cold War consensus" and, in effect, "contributed to the dismantling of the signifying practices that naturalized the production of gender and sexual identity in the postwar period" (3). Yet Corber, too, views Brick singularly as a closeted homosexual willing to sleep with Maggie in the end (which he does not in Williams's original ending to the play) "not because he has undergone a moral transformation and is no longer homosexual but because he refuses to relinquish the protection afforded by the closet" (132).

50. Therefore, Brick's rejoinder to Maggie, who claims his and Skipper's desire "had to be kept on ice" (*C* 3:58) should not be read as his incapability to utter the word

"homosexual" but more his inability to assimilate his and society's various (and at times contradictory) definitions of what homosexuality entails. It is worth noting, though, that Brick fails to say the "h" word twice in the play: "I married you, Maggie. Why would I marry you, Maggie, if I was—?" (*C* 3:58), and "How many others thought Skipper and I were—" (*C* 3:115).

51. Citing the *Iliad* and Williams's probable familiarity with it as his evidence, Myles Raymond Hurd argues that the ideal relationship between Greek heroes Achilles and Patroclus is similar to "the equally ambiguous parallel relationship between Brick and Skipper" (63). See his "Cats and Catamites: Achilles, Patroclus, and Williams's *Cat on a Hot Tin Roof*," *Notes on Mississippi Writers* 23.2 (June 1991): 63–66. Alan Bray finds an equivalent expression of "the masculine friend" during the Renaissance, wherein even sharing a bed meant intimate Platonic love more so than homoerotic attachment, but he is quick to underline the "difficulty the Elizabethans had in drawing a dividing line between those gestures of closeness among men that they desired so much and those they feared" (54). See his "Homosexuality and the Signs of Male Friendship in Elizabethan England," *Queering the Renaissance*, ed. Jonathan Goldberg (Durham, NC: Duke University Press, 1994), 40–61.

52. Brick is not distinguishing his brand of masculine homosexuality from the typical "fairy's" effeminate one, as George Chauncey, Jr. has contended certain queer males had done. Such a conclusion would render Brick determinably gay and thus depoliticize Williams's polemic in *Cat* against asserting collective truths about someone's sexual identity. See Chauncey, Jr.'s chapter, "The Forging of Queer Identities and the Emergence of Heterosexuality in Middle-Class Culture," in his *Gay New York: Gender, Urban Culture, and the Making of the Gay Male World, 1890–1949* (New York: Basic Books, 1994), 98–127.

53. Paller, *Gentlemen Callers*, 105.

54. Eve Kosofsky Sedgwick, *Epistemology of the Closet* (1990; London: Penguin, 1994), 47. See also David Halperin, *One Hundred Years of Homosexuality* (New York: Routledge, 1990), where he writes that while sex remains an incontestable fact of nature, "sexual identities are not 'given' by nature but are culturally constituted or produced" (10). Jeffrey Weeks concurs, and posits that anyone who affirms his sexual identity must recognize that that identity "is provisional, ever precarious, dependent upon, and constantly challenged by, an unstable relation of unconscious forces, changing social and personal meanings, and historical contingencies..." (187). See his *Sexuality and its Discontents: Meanings, Myths & Modern Sexualities* (London: Routledge, 1985).

55. Sedgwick, *Epistemology of the Closet*, 145.

56. Chauncey, Jr., *Gay New York*, 103.

57. See Gayle Rubin, "The Traffic in Women: Notes on the 'Political Economy' of Sex," *Toward an Anthropology of Women*, ed. Rayna R. Reiter (New York: Monthly Review, 1975), 180–83; and Eve Kosofsky Sedgwick, *Between Men: English Literature and Male Homosocial Desire* (New York: Columbia University Press, 1985), where she argues that "patriarchy structurally *requires* homophobia" (4), though the homophiliac patriarch Big Daddy seems to contradict this notion.

58. Alan Bray and Jonathan Goldberg, following Foucault's characterization of sodomy as "that utterly confused category," have shown how even sodomy has historically failed as a determiner of one's sexual identity. See Bray, *Homosexuality in Renaissance England* (London: Gay Men's Press, 1982), 13–32; and Goldberg, *Sodometries: Renaissance Texts, Modern Sexualities* (Stanford: Stanford University Press, 1992).

59. Big Daddy's distaste for his son's homophobia, as well as for men's clubs, shows an alternative view to homosocial and homosexual activities. Noting Big Daddy's sensitive respect for the gay scene (Robert Corber, John Clum, and Michael P. Bibler all

argue that Big Daddy is gay or engaged in homosexual activities with one or both of his landlords), Dean Shackelford writes: "Not only is *Cat on a Hot Tin Roof* a plea for tolerance of the gay lifestyle, the play also demonstrates the extent to which society dehumanizes men through its overt homophobia. As such, the play largely demonstrates that a homosocially-oriented social structure is responsible for problematizing homosexuality" (105). Interestingly, Big Daddy says that he spent time not only in the gay-signified "railroad Y[MCA]s", but also in "hobo jungles" (*C* 3:115), which George Chauncey, Jr. signifies as hotbeds of homosexual activity: "Indeed, homosexual relationships appear to have been so widespread among seamen and hoboes that historians need to recognize the desire to live in a social milieu in which such relationships were relatively common and accepted—or to escape the pressure to marry in a more family oriented milieu—as one of the motives that sent men on the road or to the sea" (*Gay New York* 91n). Jeffrey Loomis even reproduced one of Big Daddy's confessional speeches in the earlier drafts of the play: "Who loved me? Big Mama and Peter Ochello!—Ha ha ha ha ha ha! Big Mama and—Peter—Ochello, that ole—bitch . . . dead now! Hunh!—Sup with him in Hell or—Heaven. . . . (Wherever good old aunties go!)" (104–5).

60. As Kinsey notes, "The highest incidences of the homosexual, however, are in the group which often verbalizes its disapproval of such activity. . . . These are the males who most often condemn the homosexual, most often ridicule and express disgust for such activity, and most often punish other males for their homosexuality. And yet, this is the group which has the largest amount of overt homosexual activity" (384).

61. George Chauncey, Jr. adds in *Gay New York*, "Even as queer men began to define their difference from other men on the basis of their homosexuality, 'normal' men began to define their difference from queers on the basis of their renunciation of any sentiments or behavior that might be marked as homosexual. Only when they did so did 'normal men' become 'heterosexual men'" (100).

62. Judith Butler insists that performative gender cannot be voluntary and that sexual identity can only be constituted based on what a person cannot choose to do, or be, through the act. Thus, gender should not be defined by some cultural privileging of a sex act, despite the fact that heterosexual society inevitably does. See her *Bodies That Matter: On the Discursive Limits of "Sex"* (New York: Routledge, 1993), 95.

63. Hemingway's second African safari—underwritten by *Look* magazine (which had its own agenda for invigorating a languorous American masculinity, as we have seen)—began on September 1, 1953, and ended, twice, in subsequent plane crashes on January 23 and 24, 1954 (which precipitated his premature obituary to be published around the world). It would provide the material for what would eventually be published as *True at First Light/Under Kilimanjaro*, just as his first safari had been captured in *Green Hills of Africa*. *Under Kilimanjaro*'s editors, Robert Lewis and Robert Fleming, note in their introduction to the memoir that Hemingway wrote most of it from "October 1954 to the spring of 1956" (*UK* vii), then left it idle for a while, turning his attention instead to the film project of *The Old Man and the Sea* and to completing other manuscripts, which included *The Garden of Eden* and *A Moveable Feast*. Hemingway had, by late February 1956, written some 856 pages (some typed, some still handwritten) of the "African book," which, Michael S. Reynolds suggests in *Hemingway: The Final Years* (New York: Norton, 1999), he took up again for a short time from October to December 1957 (367). Though I make no claims that Hemingway was consciously reproducing Brick's dilemma here in his own troubles with Arap Meina, he may have well been influenced somewhat by it given that it was possible for him to have known of Williams's play at the time. He had certainly known Williams and the play by 1959 when they finally met in Cuba.

64. Though Williams could have been on Hemingway's mind when he wrote this, there were any number of gay playwrights that Hemingway had known over the years (he had just won the 1953 Pulitzer Prize for fiction with *The Old Man and the Sea* along side of William Inge, whose *Picnic* won the Prize for drama). Several chapters later, he even cites Noel Coward (*UK* 398).

65. As a gay man who lived his homosexual life openly during the 1950s, Williams never dared to present any of his gay characters as being psychosexually sound until well into the 1970s (and even then, they are few and far between). Given that Williams began seeking psychoanalytical help around the time of *Cat*'s rehearsals, Michael Paller suggests that we might rightly assume Williams himself could not fully rationalize his sexuality either. See his article "The Couch and Tennessee" and his book *Gentlemen Callers*.

66. As Peter Filene notes in *Him/Her/Self: Sex Roles in Modern America*, "Members of the class of '44 . . . produced more children within ten years than the class of 1921 had borne within twenty-five" (178). Brick, potentially one of those alumni, would have belied these cultural facts with Maggie, whereas his brother would have fit these numbers exactly. Thus, pregnancy during the 1950s was viewed as strong evidence of a performative act of heterosexuality. See his *Him/Her/Self: Sex Roles in Modern America*, 3rd ed. (Baltimore: Johns Hopkins University Press, 1998).

67. What is also significant here, which research has consistently shown, is that the lower classes have less antagonism toward homosexuality than bourgeois society does. As Kinsey writes, "the fewest objections to the homosexual are found in the very lowest of the social levels, in the best educated groups, and in top society. At the lowest social levels sex, whether it be heterosexual or homosexual, is more or less accepted as inevitable" (383). Both Big Daddy and Maggie, who generally have a more healthy response to homosexuality (so long as it does not include Brick, on whom they are relying to fulfill their patriarchal and financial needs), come from lower social classes and have fought their way into the American bourgeois family. Brick, however, was born into that bourgeois class and has adopted its Protestant ethics that presumably neither Big Daddy nor Maggie were raised with—Maggie acknowledges this when she calls Brick "an ass-achin' Puritan" (*C* 3.23)—and thus cannot accept homosexuality as they do.

68. Robert F. Gross, examining the play's erotica in "The Pleasures of Brick: Eros and the Gay Spectator in *Cat on a Hot Tin Roof*," *Journal of American Drama and Theater* 9.1 (Winter 1997): 1–25, notes that "Maggie lays down the law, and in so doing, gives male bonding a guilty conscience. Made forever anxious about the motives behind the motives, men are barred from the retrospectively constructed innocence of the male homo-Imaginary. Maggie, armed with Freudian discourse of latency and the unconscious, provokes a crisis of male identity, something that even Brick's gay fraternity brother was unable to elicit" (21).

See also Savran's eloquent passage about the psychology of castration and impotence in "Mapping the Closet" in *Cowboys, Communists, and Queers*, 102–10, where he writes of Maggie: "In her case, however, the absent Phallus becomes reinscribed in her body and so allows her to be produced as the one who 'is' the Phallus" (107). It is worth noting that Maggie says to Brick that she tried to make love to Skipper (given her now 'masculine' role to Skipper's 'feminized' one) because "it made both of us feel a little bit closer to you" (*C* 3:55); yet, like Jake with respect to Brett, Skipper proved to be impotent—"he made that pitiful, ineffectual little attempt to prove that what I had said wasn't true. . . ." (*C* 3:59, Williams's ellipses)—another similarity that Hemingway's and Williams's texts share.

69. Hemingway writes about the "doings" of Senator McCarthy thus:

In the last shipment of books we had received two books on the Senator and G.C. and I had tried to understand him and the problem that he presented. Pop [a character whom Hemingway admires in the book] had refused to read the books after a quick look through them and had dismissed the problem saying, "No—like that can exist for long." He had been slightly more pungent about the Senator and then dismissed the problem and the Senator. Miss Mary had refused to read about the Senator and would not have him discussed in her presence. (*UK* 364; cf. 197 and 411)

70. Though directed toward anti-communist collectivism, this was also Arthur Miller's controlling argument in *The Crucible,* which appeared on Broadway two years before *Cat.* Williams's anti-McCarthyist diatribe here, just as in the second act of his *Red Devil Battery Sign* (1975) years later, should be read as the gay complement to Miller's politicized play. Corber makes this point too, but his intention is to paint a Milleresque version of Williams (as opposed to a gay playwright trying to capture as best he could the sociopolitical unrest and uncertainty of his times) as wanting "to critique the emergence of the national-security state," in particularly "those who had cooperated with HUAC" (133), as his director Kazan had done (which is why, Corber argues, Kazan really wanted Williams to change the ending). Though I agree with Corber that "Williams's oblique references to the national-security state simultaneously reveal and conceal his criticisms of those who, like Kazan, had betrayed former friends and colleagues in order to protect their career" (133), I feel Williams's scope with *Cat* was much broader in its intent, extending beyond that context of the Cold War consensus to encompass much of the history of sexual identification in America throughout the twentieth century.

71. Williams does not waste the opportunity in pointing this out either, for when Maggie says to Mae, who declares before everyone that it was Maggie who had bought Big Daddy his cashmere robe and not Brick, "Sister Woman! Your talents are wasted as a housewife and mother, you really ought to be with the FBI or—" (*C* 3:71), the audience too is being implicated in what amounts to its intelligence-gathering role as voyeur.

72. Judith Butler, *Bodies That Matter,* 224–25. For Butler, performativity is not the action (or inaction, as the case may be) one does, but the process through which one is constituted by the action. Here, Brick's inaction constitutes one identity that could be countered or confirmed by the action of accepting or rejecting to uphold Maggie's declaration.

73. As John Clum concludes about the significance of this curtain-line,

> Love is not an operative term for the men in *Cat on a Hot Tin Roof.* It is a word used only by Maggie and Big Mama—the men can only wonder, "Wouldn't it be funny if it were true?" Not able to accept the love of women, neither can the men accept the unspoken option of sexual male/male love. Nor can Williams convincingly offer that option. The tenderness Williams sees as the clear side of his vision here exists only in a stage direction: the cloudiness of homosexuality remains an object of terror, not of the act, but of public disclosure. (161–62)

74. Michael P. Bibler also examines the paradox behind Brick's decision/indecision in sleeping with Maggie and argues that "[i]f Brick sleeps with Maggie, he only compounds the problem of his sexual identity because both options—sleeping with her or not sleeping with her—produce both possibilities of identity at the same time":

> If he sleeps with her, he proves his heterosexuality even as he enters into a homosexual economy with Skipper and Straw and Ochello. If he doesn't sleep with her, he avoids linking himself physically with those men and preserves sanctity of his heterosexuality; but he also appears to concede that he has no interest in a heterosexual union and that his sexual desires might indeed be reserved for other men like Skipper. Whatever he does, Brick's body thus becomes the site on which the contradictory forces of the plantation play themselves out. Just as his action will

define his identity as both and neither at the same time, his status as the future patriarch simultaneously attests to both the plantation's inherent privileging of sameness for white males in a homosocial and patrilineal economy, as well as its privileging of sexual *difference* in its demand that the patriarch produce his heir through heterosexual reproduction. (400)

See his essay, "'A Tenderness which was Uncommon': Homosexuality, Narrative, and the Southern Plantation in Tennessee Williams's *Cat on a Hot Tin Roof*," *Mississippi Quarterly* 55.3 (Summer 2002): 381–400.

75. By restoring the original ending for the New Directions re-release, Williams decidedly strengthened his resolve toward maintaining Brick's sexual "mystery."

76. Another Williams variation on this line reads: "Skipper and Brick would rather die than live with" any acknowledgment of mutual homosexual desire (*WIL* 77).

77. Clum, "Something Cloudy," 161. While it is easy to hold Williams accountable for his *seemingly* apolitical theater during these politically-charged Cold War years, when we consider that even the Kinsey Institute for Sex Research lost most of its funding in 1954, can we honestly justify such revisionist attacks against him?

78. See, for example, Caleb Crain *American Sympathy: Men, Friendship, and Literature in the New Nation* (New Haven: Yale University Press, 2000).

79. Steven Bruhm has argued a similar point about Williams's relationship to the audience with *Suddenly Last Summer*, though he approaches it from an economic angle:

> By writing the dissolution of these boundaries, Williams writes a play which is much more subversive than its critics have allowed. Clearly, in this play, they who pay the money make the rules: both on political and libidinal grounds. But Williams has written a play for an audience, a *paying* audience, which has paid to hear a story about paying not to hear a story. In short, he implicates his audience in an economic complicity that allows sexual behavior while at the same time demanding that the story of that behavior be silenced. ("Blackmailed" 535)

Though he is not speaking about *Cat* here, Bruhm obviously sees its application to the play, for in an earlier footnote, he writes: "It is my contention here that *Suddenly Last Summer* and *Cat on a Hot Tin Roof* are, among other things, indictments of the social structures that regulate homosexual behavior" ("Blackmailed" 537).

Chapter 5. The Impotence of Being Ernest

1. Like Broadway, the West End also had a complicated history with liberating homosexuality from the Lord Chamberlain's blue pen prior to the Theatres Act of 1968. Though the Lord Chamberlain had a decade earlier begun loosening his veto powers over plays that had homosexual content, marked advances were made by Noel Coward, Shelagh Delaney, Joe Orton, John Osborne, Peter Shaffer and Christopher Hampton, to name but a few playwrights. But because the two nations responded differently to censorship of homosexuality onstage (despite the ineffectual Wales-Padlock Law of 1927 or the moral code demands of Hays in 1930, the United States had no equivalent to the Lord Chamberlain), I only want to concentrate on Broadway. For more on the development of the gay play and gay theater, see Michael Paller, *Gentlemen Callers: Tennessee Williams, Homosexuality, and Mid-Twentieth Century Drama* (New York: Palgrave Macmillan, 2005), 158–62.

2. Eve Sedgwick describe the artistic production of the queer thus:

> It is with *homo*-style homosexuality, and *not* with inversion, pederasty, or sodomy (least of all, of course, with cross-gender sexuality) that an erotic language, an erotic discourse comes into

existence that makes available a continuing possibility for symbolizing slippages between identification and desire. It concomitantly makes available new possibilities for the camouflage and concealment, or the very selective or pointed display, of proscribed or resisted erotic relation and avowal through chains of vicariation—through the mechanisms that, I argue, cluster under the stigmatizing name "sentimentality." (159)

See her *Epistemology of the Closet* (1990; London: Penguin, 1994).

3. Stanley Kauffmann, "Homosexual Drama And Its Disguises," *New York Times*, Jan. 23, 1966, sec. 2: 1.

4. Ibid., 1.

5. Ibid., 1.

6. Paller, *Gentlemen Callers*, 160.

7. Kaier Curtin notes in *"We Can Always Call Them Bulgarians": The Emergence of Lesbians and Gay Men on the American Stage* (Boston: Alyson, 1987) that "eighty-four plays with either gay characters or gay themes were seen on New York stages" in the 1970s (328).

8. Others include Clive Barnes, Mel Gussow, John Simon, Douglas Watt, and Robert Brustein. *Life* magazine's article of June 13, 1969, for example, declared Williams a dead playwright (10), and *Time* wrote that *In the Bar of a Tokyo Hotel* was "more deserving of a coroner's report than a review" (May 23, 1969: 75). Williams repeatedly took these attacks personally, as he told Don Lee Keith: "There have been times when I have been truly crushed, humiliated, over the unkind remarks of critics. Some playwrights say they pay no attention to reviews, but I guess I'm not that strong, because the bad ones hurt me. Really hurt. Yet, I don't feel confident enough, actually, to answer a critic, even if I were invited to, which, of course, I never have been and never will be" (*CTW* 157; cf. 15, 163, 190, 236). See also Jacqueline O'Connor, "*The Strangest Kind of Romance:* Tennessee Williams and his Broadway Critics," *The Cambridge Companion to Tennessee Williams*, ed. Matthew C. Roudané (Cambridge: Cambridge University Press, 1997), 255–64.

9. The Albertine strategy—the "writing of stories about homosexual love in the imagery of heterosexual love" by "simply metamorphizing a boy with whom the male protagonist is involved with into a girl" (2)—was popularized by critic Stanley Edgar Hyman in his essay "Some Trends in the Novel," *College English*, 20.1 (Oct. 1958): 1–9. See also his earlier essay "Some Notes on the Albertine Strategy," *Hudson Review* 6 (Autumn 1953): 418, where he cites Blanche DuBois and *Streetcar* as a case in point. Eve Sedgwick expounds upon Hyman's "unattractive" trend in modern literature:

> To begin with: while the spectacle of M. de Charlus is ostentatiously that of *a closet* with *a homosexual* concealed, with riveting inefficiency, in its supposed interior, it is on the other hand notoriously hard to located *a homosexual* anywhere in the fluctuous privacy surrounding Albertine. With all their plurality of interpretive paths, there is no way to read the Albertine volumes without finding same-sex desire *somewhere*; at the same time, that specificity of desire, in the Albertine plot, notoriously refuses to remain fixed to a single character type, to a single character, or even to a single ontological level of the text. (*Epistemology* 231)

10. In an interview with Rex Reed for *Esquire* in 1971, Williams voiced his concern over this type of reading: "I've read things that say Blanche was a drag queen. Blanche DuBois, ya know . . . that George and Martha in *Who's Afraid of Virginia Woolf* by Albee were a pair of homosexuals . . . these charges are ridiculous!" (*CTW* 189, Williams's ellipses). Two years later in his confessional essay "Let Me Hang It All Out" (whose idiomatic reference to the exposed penis here is particularly relevant), Williams adds: "Some people who remember *Cat* only for its more sensational aspects think it was a

play about homosexuality just as some people, probably more or less the same bunch, persist in claiming that Blanche DuBois in *Streetcar* was really a drag queen. Well, such people pay the same price of admission to a play and are entitled to exercise their triviality of interpretation, if they so choose. It is not to anyone's detriment but their own." (*WIL* 172)

Strangely enough, the same charge against Williams would later be used by members of the gay community to attack Williams for his apparent lack of concern over the gay cause. Andrew Dvorsin, in a negative review of Williams's *Memoirs* for the *Gay Sunshine Review*, even complained that Williams's female characters were just men in drag: "What had once been a staple of homophobic and right-wing critics' and reviewers' attacks now became a weapon in the arsenal of intolerant left-wing gay liberationists" (qtd. in Paller, *Gentlemen Callers*, 212).

11. Williams "came out" on the David Frost Show in 1970 when, in responding to Frost's rather gossip-mongering approach to extracting facts from his personal life, said, "I don't want to be involved in some sort of scandal, but I've covered the waterfront" (*CTW* 146). Williams would often later admit to having come out publicly at that moment (cf. *CTW* 198, 232), though later in a 1979 interview with John Hicks he would change his story: "Strangely enough it was not I who first announced that I was homosexual. It was a news magazine" (*CTW* 322). It is important to add, however, that despite where and when Williams emerged from the closet, he was never really in it. The problem with taking Williams at his word revolves around the fact that he often fabricated certain details of his life, dating back to when he lied about his age to compete in the under twenty-five play competition for the Group Theatre back in December 1938, or he simply remembered them differently from how they really happened.

12. "Lee Barton," "Why Do Homosexual Playwrights Hide Their Homosexuality?," *New York Times*, Jan. 23, 1972, sec. 2: 1.

13. "Lee Barton," "Homosexual Playwrights," 3.

14. Paller, *Gentlemen Callers*, 157. Paller adds:

Many lesbians and gay men who came of age in the 1960s experienced their sexuality differently than people of Williams's generation had and this new era of gay theatre artists was reflected by the differences in their work. Many more were able to embrace their homosexuality proudly and publicly. They often identified themselves as gay men or women, or as gay writers; and those involved in the gay theatre that emerged in the 1960s and bloomed in the 1970s and early 1980s were likely to view theatre as a useful tool for community-building and for disseminating sexual and politically positive images of themselves. It was inevitable that they and Williams would misunderstand each other. (158)

Paller argues that Williams's career plummeted after *The Night of the Iguana* only in part because of his alcohol and drug addiction; rather, it was because he was out of step with the emerging gay theatre and was moving too far from the tastes of the middle and upper-middle classes who populated the Broadway theaters.

15. Paller has noticed this similarity as well, though he sees Williams as now shifting positions per Brick's sexuality: "Perhaps Williams had always thought that Brick was gay, and now, for the first time, felt comfortable about saying it publicly" (*Gentlemen Callers*, 213).

16. Williams also knew that a "gay" play, despite the financial and critical success that plays like *The Boys in the Band* had enjoyed, would not give him the comeback he so much desired in the 1970s. Even if it seemed that "society in the Western world is presumed to have discarded it prejudices" toward gays and the gay community, Williams wrote in his *Memoirs*, his feeling was "that the prejudices have simply gone underground" (*M* 204).

17. George Whitmore, "George Whitmore interviews Tennessee Williams," *Gay Sunshine Interviews*, Vol. I, ed. Winston Leyland (San Francisco: Gay Sunshine Press, 1978), 315, 320.

18. Tennessee Williams, *Moise and the World of Reason* (New York: Simon and Schuster, 1975), 139.

19. *Confessional*, a one-act play later expanded into *Small Craft Warnings*, was written in 1967, two years before Stonewall, but it was only first performed in 1971 in Bar Harbor, Maine, safe from the revealing lights of Broadway. Williams had written several other gay plays during the 1970s and 1980s, such as *Kirche, Küche, Kinder* (1979), *Steps Must Be Gentle* (1980), *A House Not Meant to Stand* (1980/1982), *Now the Cats with Jeweled Claws* (1981), *The Traveling Companion* (1981), and *The Remarkable Rooming-House of Mme. Le Monde* (published 1984). He had also written several non-gay (and apparently non-queer ones as well) with *Demolition Downtown* (1971) and a host of one-acts like *Lifeboat Drill* (1979) and *This is the Peaceable Kingdom; Or, Good Luck, God* (1979). Future research into these plays, I am willing to venture, may very well prove me wrong.

20. Paller, *Gentlemen Callers*, 164–65.

21. Even before writing his *Memoirs*, Williams frequently talked about his homosexuality in interviews: with Don Lee Keith in 1970; with Tom Buckley for *Atlantic Monthly* in 1970 (which he hated and against which he wrote a detraction); with Rex Reed for *Esquire* in 1971; and with C. Robert Jennings for *Playboy* in 1973.

22. Whitmore, "George Whitmore interviews," 315, 313.

23. Ibid., 316.

24. In his *Memoirs*, Williams describes in detail his sexual encounters with both men and women until turning exclusively toward men after college. For him, it was not solely a matter of destiny but also one of choice.

25. Linda Dorff argues that Williams began drafting *Clothes for a Summer Hotel* as late as 1977 or 1978. See her "Collapsing Resurrection Mythologies: Theatricalist Discourses of Fire and Ash in *Clothes for a Summer Hotel*," *Tennessee Williams: A Casebook*, ed. Robert F. Gross (New York: Routledge, 2002), 157.

26. Interestingly enough, Paller does not include *Clothes for a Summer Hotel* among the plays that deal with homosexuality, openly or not.

27. Williams was a gossip hound, particularly concerning gay gossip, as he confessed once to Elia Kazan in a letter about the recent gay bashings in Key West, which were sparked by the murder of a New York queen visiting there in March 1950: "I thought this would give you a laugh, but please forget that I told you about it, please! You and I both love gossip. At heart I'm a back-fence biddy. . . ." (*SL II* 524; cf. 296).

28. John Simon, "Damsels Inducing Distress," *New York*, Apr. 7, 1980: 82, 84.

29. Jackson Bryer, "'Entitled to Write About Her Life': Tennessee Williams and F. Scott and Zelda Fitzgerald," *Magical Muse: Millennial Essays on Tennessee Williams*, ed. Ralph F. Voss (Tuscaloosa: University of Alabama Press, 2002), 163–77. Alycia Smith-Howard and Greta Heintzelman have also noted that the "scholarly assessment of *Clothes for a Summer Hotel* has been surprisingly limited" (67), adding, "Much of the commentary is focused on an oversimplified notion that Williams was writing about his sister, Rose Williams, in the guise of Zelda Fitzgerald. This superficial reading of the play illustrates a reluctance to engage Williams's artistic license as a dramatist" (67). See their *Critical Companion to Tennessee Williams: A Literary Reference to His Life and Work* (New York: Facts On File, 2005).

30. See Thomas P. Adler, "When Ghosts Supplant Memories: Tennessee Williams' *Clothes for a Summer Hotel*," *Southern Literary Journal* 19.2 (Spring 1987): 5–19. Adler sees the play less as biographical drama and more, like *Vieux Carré* before it in 1978, as

autobiographical drama, with it emerging, just as *The Glass Menagerie* had, as a "play of guilt, spawned by the author's betrayal of the person closest to him" (6).

31. Elliott Martin, the play's Broadway producer, suggested this from the beginning when he told Donald Spoto, "... it's a play with a certain transferred paranoia—from the situation of Rose to that of Williams himself who ... was blaming the critics and media for his own failures" (384). See Donald Spoto, *The Kindness of Strangers: The Life of Tennessee Williams* (New York: Ballantine, 1986).

32. Jack Kroll, "Slender is the Night," *Newsweek*, Apr. 7, 1980: 95; and Richard Sandomir, "Tennessee Williams: On Age and Annoyance," *New York Sunday News*, Mar. 23, 1980, Leisure Section: 5, 12.

33. Clive Barnes, "'Clothes' needs some tailoring," *New York Post*, Mar. 27, 1980: 1.

34. The theatre critics were typically scathing. Robert Daniels called *Clothes* "ill-fitting" (2); Michiko Kakutani called it "[e]lliptical in structure, layered in meaning and almost devoid of plot ..." (26); Walter Kerr called it "wasteful," the result of "Tennessee Williams holding his tongue" (15); and Clive Barnes wrote that it "needs some tailoring" since it "seems more smoke than summer" (1). See Robert L. Daniels, "Still Exciting 'Sweeney Todd'—But a Dismal 'Clothes,'" *The Week Ahead*, Apr. 9, 1980: 1–2; Michiko Kakutani, "The Building of Williams's 'Summer Hotel,'" *New York Times*, Mar. 23, 1980: D 1, 26; Walter Kerr, "The Stage: 'Clothes for a Summer Hotel,'" *New York Times*, Mar. 27, 1980: D 15; and Clive Barnes, "'Clothes' needs some tailoring."

35. A sixth article on *Clothes for a Summer Hotel*, published after Bryer's essay, is Christopher Wixson's "'A Very Carefully Orchestrated Life': Dramatic Representations of and by Zelda Fitzgerald," *American Drama* 11.1 (Winter 2002): 32–57. Because Wixson's aim is to study Zelda's play *Scandalabra* more than her representation in *Clothes for a Summer Hotel*, the commentary on Williams's play here is more descriptive than analytical.

36. Paller even suggests that gay theater in general could be considered postmodern given that it "bumped comedy against tragedy, quoted works from literature, comic books and film, could be heavily ironic, was aware of itself as theatre and made its theatricality part of its subject-matter" (*Gentlemen Callers* 161).

37. Dorff, "Collapsing Resurrection Mythologies," 157, 158.

38. George W. Crandell, "'I Can't Imagine Tomorrow': Tennessee Williams and the Representations of Time in *Clothes for a Summer Hotel*," *The Undiscovered Country: The Later Plays of Tennessee Williams*, ed. Philip C. Kolin (New York: Peter Lang, 2002), 170. Crandell reads the play as Williams's postmodern "critique of realism's and modernism's great faith in the future to remedy or cure the present" (171).

39. Norma Jenckes, "'Let's Face the Music and Dance': Resurgent Romanticism in Tennessee Williams's *Camino Real* and *Clothes for a Summer Hotel*" in *The Undiscovered Country*, ed. Philip C. Kolin, 189.

40. As Jean-François Lyotard writes, "A postmodern artist or writer is in the position of a philosopher: the text he writes, the work he produces are not in principle governed by preestablished rules, and they cannot be judged according to a determining judgment, by applying familiar categories to the text or to the work. Those rules and categories are what the work of art it looking for. The artist and the writer, then, are working without rules in order to formulate the rules of what *will have been done*" (*PC* 81). See his "Answering the Question: What Is Postmodernism?," *The Postmodern Condition: A Report on Knowledge*, trans. Geoff Bennington and Brian Massumi (1979; Minneapolis: University of Minnesota Press, 1984), 81. All references to *The Postmodern Condition* cited in the article come from this edition and are hereafter cited parenthetically in the text and abbreviated *PC*.

Fredric Jameson equally notes in *Postmodernism, or, The Cultural Logic of Late Capital-*

ism (Durham, NC: Duke University Press, 1991) that the "point is that we are *within* the culture of postmodernism to the point where its facile repudiation is as impossible as any equally facile celebration of it is complacent and corrupt. Ideological judgment on postmodernism today necessarily implies, one would think, a judgment on ourselves as well as on the artifacts in question" (P 62). All references to *Postmodernism, or, The Cultural Logic of Late Capitalism* cited in the article come from this edition and are hereafter cited parenthetically in the text and abbreviated *P*.

41. See, for instance, two excellent studies on Williams's postmodern affinities: Annette J. Saddik, *The Politics of Reputation: The Critical Reception of Tennessee Williams' Late Plays* (Madison, NJ: Fairleigh Dickinson University Press, 1999); and Nicholas Pagan, *Rethinking Literary Biography: A Postmodern Approach to Tennessee Williams* (Rutherford: Fairleigh Dickinson University Press, 1993).

42. Similarly, Williams was probably not familiar with K. J. Dover's *Greek Homosexuality* or Michel Foucault's *History of Sexuality*, both published in 1978 around the time that *Clothes for a Summer Hotel* was taking shape, but we can certainly find echoes of their findings and theories in Williams's play. In an excellent essay, William Kleb describes how "Williams's work [was] a kind of imaginative prefiguration of Foucault's theory—an exploration of the common points of perception between the two can still be illuminating and rewarding" (27). See his "Marginalia: *Streetcar*, Williams, and Foucault," *Confronting Tennessee Williams's* A Streetcar Named Desire: *Essays in Critical Pluralism*, ed. Philip C. Kolin (Westport, CT: Greenwood Press, 1993), 27–43.

43. This is precisely what Nicholas Pagan pursues in his postmodern literary biography of Williams.

44. See, for instance, W. J. Weatherby, "Scott and Zelda Relive the Jazz Age," *London Sunday Times*, Mar. 30, 1980: 38. Thomas Adler explores this relationship more closely. Jackson Bryer, after a useful summary of *Clothes for a Summer Hotel* criticism and the relationship between Williams and Fitzgerald, pushes this reading even further in his intertextual study of *The Great Gatsby* and *A Streetcar Named Desire*.

45. Peter L. Hays, "Tennessee Williams 'Outs' Scott and Ernest," *The Author as Character: Representing Historical Writers in Western Literature*, eds. Paul Franssen and Ton Hoenselaars (Madison, NJ: Fairleigh Dickinson University Press, 1999). Hays argues, perhaps a bit haphazardly, that "Williams makes Fitzgerald and Hemingway homosexuals like himself, thereby forming a bond with two of America's canonical writers, bolstering his own image as a writer in the process" (253).

46. The same could be said of Williams's two other biographical plays, *I Rise in Flame, Cried the Phoenix* (1941) about D. H. Lawrence and *Steps Must Be Gentle* (1947) about Hart Crane. The difference here, perhaps, is that Williams does not only just color the facts of their biographies but he also pastiches the sources themselves, as I will argue later.

47. Tennessee Williams, *The Theatre of Tennessee Williams*, 8 vols. (New York: New Directions, 1971–1992), 8:n.p. All references to *Clothes for a Summer Hotel* cited in this study come from this edition and are hereafter cited parenthetically in the text and abbreviated *CSH*.

48. In *True at First Light/Under Kilimanjaro*, Hemingway argues with Miss Mary about the writer's responsibility in telling the truth. Earlier in the fictional memoir, Hemingway had already established his position that a "man who writes a novel or a short story is a liar ipso facto" and that "he makes the truth as he invents it truer than it would be" (*UK* 113). With Miss Mary, Hemingway adds "that certain lies were truer than the truth" (*UK* 282).

49. Michel Foucault, *History of Sexuality*, Vol. I: *The Will of Knowledge*, trans. Robert Hurley (1976; New York: Pantheon, 1978), 37. John D'Emilio and David Greenberg

have both advanced this reading that the transition away from the household family-based economy to a fully-developed free labor economy is in part responsible for the coalescing of homosexualities. See John D'Emilio, *Sexual Politics, Sexual Communities: The Making of a Homosexual Minority in the United States, 1940–1970*, 2nd ed. (Chicago: University of Chicago Press, 1998); and David Greenberg, *The Construction of Homosexuality* (Chicago: University of Chicago Press, 1998), where he adds, "Capitalism reorganized the family, sharpened gender stereotypes, created and disseminated new ideologies of love and sex, and established new methods of socializing children. All these developments had an impact on social responses to homosexuality" (369–70).

50. Jonathan Katz, *Gay American History: Lesbians and Gay Men in the U.S.A.* (New York: Crowell, 1976). For other challenges to the sexuality metanarrative, see K. J. Dover, *Greek Homosexuality* (London: Duckworth, 1978); John Boswell, *Christianity, Social Tolerance, and Homosexuality: Gay People in Western Europe from the Beginning of the Christian Era to the Fourteenth Century* (Chicago: University of Chicago Press, 1980); and Jeffrey Weeks, *Sexuality and its Discontents: Meanings, Myths & Modern Sexualities* (London: Routledge, 1985).

51. Some recent criticism of Butler's work has noted that, like Lyotard in his efforts to achieve paralogy in *The Postmodern Condition*, she has created her own metanarrative around the notion of performativity.

52. Butler adds: "The univocity of sex, the internal coherence of gender, and the binary framework for both sex and gender are considered throughout as regulatory fictions that consolidate and naturalize the convergent power regimes of masculine and heterosexist oppression" (*GT* 44).

53. Simon, "Damsels," 84; and Douglas Watt, "Williams' Ghost Play Shrouds New Insights into Fitzgeralds," *New York Daily News*, Mar. 27, 1980. Watt writes that Williams's play offers "no more about the Fitzgeralds and their companions than we might have picked up from stray accounts over the years without ever having cracked one of the novels or books about the pair" (107).

54. Alcohol is of course Jake Barnes's way of dealing with his sexual existentialism, just as it was for Brick in both "Three Players of a Summer Game" and *Cat on a Hot Tin Roof*. It is also worth noting that Scott echoes Maggie's comment about Brick and alcohol (Maggie says, "You're the only drinkin' man I know that it never seems t' put fat on" [*C* 3:29]) and how he has not lost his good looks yet: "Hasn't put fat on me yet—but there's time. Hemingway's still in good shape and drinks more than me" (*CSH* 8:233). Later in their conversation, Zelda admits to being "desperate" as a result of her relationship with Scott, just as Maggie is as desperate as *"a cat on a hot tin roof!"* (*C* 3:39) because of the way Brick is treating her.

55. Williams's substitutive use of "gender" here for "sexuality" is consistent with the sexual lexis of the day; it should therefore not be analyzed to mean anything else.

56. Though many feminists and members of the gay community, Williams included, oppose drag as being demeaning to women, Butler contends that its purpose is not to mimic but, rather, to subvert "the distinction between inner and outer psychic space" and to mock "both the expressive model of gender and the notion of a true gender identity" (*GT* 174). See also Esther Newton, *Mother Camp: Female Impersonators in America* (Chicago: University of Chicago Press, 1972).

57. Nancy Milford, *Zelda*, (1970; New York: HarperCollins, 1992), 122, 152. All references to *Zelda* cited in this study come from this edition and are hereafter cited parenthetically in the text and abbreviated *Z*.

58. In a letter to Arthur Mizener, Hemingway wrote, "Zelda really ruined Scott . . . she told him A.) That he had never given her physical satisfaction. B.) That it was because his sexual organ was too small" (287). See Michael S. Reynolds, *Hemingway: The Paris Years* (1989; New York: Norton, 1999).

59. Norma Jenckes has already noted the similarities between Brick and Skipper and Hemingway and Scott but does little else with them.

60. Again, Williams's term "gender" here should be understood as a "sexed identity." Williams is, of course, describing himself since he frequently spoke later in his life, especially in his interviews, of his own androgynous nature as having been a necessity in creating his believable male and female characters. See also Peter Hays, "Tennessee Williams 'Outs,'" 256; and Hilton Anderson, "Tennessee Williams' *Clothes for a Summer Hotel:* Feminine Sensibilities and the Artist," *Publications of the Mississippi Philological Association* (1988): 1–9.

61. Linda Hutcheon, *The Politics of Postmodernism*, 2nd ed. (London: Routledge, 2002), 67.

62. Dotson Rader, *Tennessee: Cry of the Heart* (New York: Doubleday, 1985), 312. Rader adds: "He had begun to write a play about Hemingway and Fitzgerald . . . , was reading every book he could find on the two men, and considered himself an expert" (308).

63. See Adler, "When Ghosts," 12–15; and Bryer, "Entitled to Write," 166, where both establish this point more profoundly.

64. In his 1979 interview with John Hicks about the play, Williams even echoes Milford's thesis that Zelda's life was Scott's material (*CTW* 322).

65. Several people within the Fitzgerald circle had alluded to his homosexuality after their marriage began declining in 1926, prompting Fitzgerald to address the rumor in the letter to Maxwell Perkins. By 1929, when their marriage was finally over, Zelda was among those suggesting that Scott was homosexual, saying that he had never satisfied her in bed. Though Ronald Berman, in *Fitzgerald, Hemingway, and the Twenties* (Tuscaloosa: University of Alabama Press, 2001), examines the connection between "the work of Fitzgerald and Hemingway to the loss of certainty" (2) that defined the social tenor of the Jazz Age, he fails to push that inquiry to its sexual boundaries, which a study still needs to do.

66. Hutcheon's response to Jameson in *The Politics of Postmodernism* that parody, and not pastiche, is the quintessential postmodern aesthetic is well known. While she agrees with Jameson that there is an irony central to both parody and pastiche, she does not accept his definition that parody must necessarily be humorous nor that it is "ahistorical or dehistoricizing": "it does not wrest past art from its historical context and reassemble it into some sort of presentist spectacle. Instead, through a double process of installing and ironizing, parody signals how present representations come from the past ones and what ideological consequences derive from both continuity and difference" (89). In other words, "Postmodern parody is both deconstructively critical and constructively creative, paradoxically making us aware of both the limits and the powers of representation—in any medium" (94). While her argument is as convincing as it is different from Jameson's, I have chosen to adopt Jameson's notion of the pastiche for this study as it forms an essential part of his overall argument about cultural schizophrenia as the logic of late capitalism.

67. Hutcheon's point, on the contrary, is that all postmodern texts take as their goal to "de-doxify" history and its cultural representations, while never losing sight that it is part of the system of meaning it has produced; in other words, postmodernism "critiques" the socio-economic havoc created by postmodernism as it "replicates, reinforces, and intensifies" it, all the while "never pretending to be able to operate outside them" (25).

68. In Hutcheon's terms, postmodern is "where documentary historical actuality meets formalist self-reflexivity and parody" (7).

69. For more on this, see Kenneth Lynn, *Hemingway* (New York: Simon & Schuster,

1987), 242–44 and 284–89; and Debra A. Moddelmog, "Reconstructing Hemingway's Identity: Sexual Politics, the Author, and the Multicultural Classroom," *Narrative* 1 (Oct. 1993): 187–206. Judith Butler explains how disavowed homosexuality is a common cause for melancholic men of strong heteromasculinist gender:

> If the heterosexual denial of homosexuality results in melancholia and if melancholia operates through incorporation, then the disavowed homosexual love is preserved through the cultivation of an oppositionally defined gender identity. In other words, disavowed male homosexuality culminates in a heightened or consolidated masculinity, one which maintains the feminine as the unthinkable or unnameable. . . . But here it becomes clear that the heterosexual refusal to acknowledge the primary homosexual attachment is culturally enforced by a prohibition on homosexuality which is in no way paralleled in the case of the melancholic homosexual. In other words, heterosexual melancholy is culturally instituted and maintained as the price of stable gender identities related through oppositional desires. (*GT* 88–89)

70. What sounds like an admission of having had homosexual contact (physical or otherwise) is then quickly twisted to infer something else: "The excessive praise on the one side and the—envious other" (*CSH* 8:261). Ambiguity is left to linger in Williams's Hemingway.

71. Ernest Hemingway, *The Garden of Eden* (New York: Simon and Schuster, 1986), 15. All further references to *The Garden of Eden* noted in this study come from this edition and are hereafter cited parenthetically in the text and abbreviated *GE*.

72. Williams reportedly told Dotson Rader in their 1981 interview for *The Paris Review*: "You know what he said about Fitzgerald? Hemingway said that, 'Fitzgerald was pretty. He had a mouth that troubled you when you first met him, and troubled you more later'" (*CTW* 347).

73. It is perhaps telling that, in recalling this same first meeting between Hemingway and Fitzgerald, Hemingway biographer Michael S. Reynolds describes Scott's "delicate, blond features" as being "handsome" and not pretty (283). Reading Reynolds's account against Hemingway's is a good litmus test to measure, if not the truth of certain events he describes in *A Moveable Feast*, then at least the tone and style in which he recalls them, which influenced Williams perhaps as much, if not more, than the facts themselves. Also worth noting is the fact that Hemingway described the fire-eater whom he met in Lyon as having "a fine dark face that glowed and shone" (*MF* 158). Since the fire-eater story is obviously used to distinguish Fitzgerald from Hemingway (who saw hack writers abusing their métier just as the fire-eater says certain "False fire-eaters" in his trade "would continue to ruin it wherever they were allowed to practice" (*MF* 158), the descriptions of the two men's facial features help signify not just their masculinity but their work ethic as well.

74. Much could be said about the similarities between the white boxer Ad and the black giant/nurse Bugs and Williams's Anthony Burns and the giant black masseur in "Desire and the Black Masseur." Also, Nick's meeting Bugs and Ad at a hobo camp, which George Chauncey, Jr. has identified as a "social milieu" where homosexual relationships were "relatively common and accepted" (91n), recalls Big Daddy's confession to his son Brick in *Cat on a Hot Tin Roof* that he had "knocked around" in his time "bumming this country" and sleeping in "hobo jungles and railroad Y's and flophouses in all cities . . ." (*C* 3:115). See Chauncey, Jr., *Gay New York. Gender, Urban Culture, and the Making of the Gay Male World, 1890–1949* (New York: Basic Books, 1994).

75. Curiously, Williams refers to Hemingway throughout the play by his surname, though he calls Fitzgerald "Scott." This could suggest both his respect for and trepidation of the man-cum-legend.

76. Though John Simon criticized Williams's "typical gossip-mongering approach"

(84) here, Williams retorted that the scene was "an integral part of the play because each was a central figure in the life of the other. I thought the confrontation between them indispensable" (*CTW* 359).

77. Refer to my list at the beginning of chapter 2 of Hemingway's stories, novels, and nonfiction that deal with homosexuality or include homosexual themes.

78. According to George Monteiro, "Tennessee Williams Misremembers Hemingway," *The Hemingway Review* 10.1 (Fall 1990): 71, Williams confused Hemingway's story "The Sea Change," about a man whose wife confesses her lesbianism, pushing the husband into recognizing his "homosexual" role now in their failed marriage, with a passage from Hemingway's *Death in the Afternoon* (*DA* 180–82) which "takes place in a Paris hotel rather than on ship." That Hemingway here should describe the relationship between the two men as "something funny" (*DA* 181) is also very telling apropos Jake's frequent use of the word "funny" as a signifier for "something not quite right" in *The Sun Also Rises*. No doubt Williams also encountered Hemingway's caustic definition of the Spanish *maricón*, or sodomite, in the glossary to *Death in the Afternoon* (*DA* 417–18).

79. Maria St. Just describes in her journal for the summer of 1954 that "Tenn thinks Hemingway is really queer as he has an unnatural concern about queens—and, Tenn says, writes uninterestingly about women" (96). See *Five O'Clock Angel: Letters of Tennessee Williams to Maria St. Just, 1948–1982* (New York: Knopf, 1990).

80. The same conclusion has also frequently been applied to Hemingway's father, whose troubled life with an emasculating wife ended in suicide.

81. See also *CTW* 245–46.

82. Hutcheon, *Politics of Postmodernism*, 77. Though she is talking about a scene from E. L. Doctorow's *Ragtime*, where Freud and Jung take a ride "through the Coney Island tunnel of love" (77), this quote could readily be applied to Williams's effort to put Fitzgerald and Hemingway on that ride as well.

83. More forcefully than Jameson, Hutcheon argues that postmodern representations are "unavoidably political" (1): "Postmodern art cannot but be political, at least in the sense that its representations—its images and stories—are anything but neutral, however "aestheticized" they may appear to be in their parodic self-reflexivity. While the postmodern has no effective theory of agency that enables a move into political *action*, it does work to turn its inevitable ideological grounding into a site of de-naturalizing critique" (3).

84. Fredric Jameson, "Postmodernism and Consumer Society," *The Anti-Aesthetic: Essays on Postmodern Culture*, ed. Hal Foster (Seattle: Bay Press, 1983), 119.

85. Williams frequently recalled similar experiences he had had with his sister Rose while she was living at Stony Lodge in Ossining, New York. See, for example, *CTW* 328.

86. Jameson, "Postmodernism and Consumer Society," 125.

87. As I note in chapter 2, Jeffrey Meyers writes in *Hemingway: A Biography* (New York: Harper & Row, 1985) that "Hemingway has been suspected and even accused of being a covert homosexual because of his aggressive masculinity, his preference for exclusively male company, his occasional impotence, his sexual boasts and his hostility to inverts. . . . Despite all the theorizing, there is not a shred of real evidence to suggest that Hemingway ever had any covert homosexual desires or overt homosexual relations" (202).

88. Hutcheon, *Politics of Postmodernism*, 97.

89. Gilles Deleuze and Félix Guattari, *Anti-Oedipus: Capitalism and Schizophrenia*, trans. Robert Hurley, Mark Seem, and Helen R. Lane (1972; Minneapolis: University of Minnesota Press, 1983), 296, 295.

90. Deleuze and Guattari, *Anti-Oedipus*, 59. "This something in common," they add,

"the great Phallus, the Lack with two nonsuperimposable sides, is purely mythical; it is like the One in negative theology, it introduces lack into desire and causes exclusive series to emanate, to which it attributes a goal, an origin, and a path of resignation" (60).

91. Deleuze and Guattari, *Anti-Oedipus*, 67. In terms of homosexuality via schizoanalysis, they add,

> everyone is bisexual, everyone has two sexes, but partitioned, noncommunicating; the man is merely the one in whom the male part, and the woman the one in whom the female part, dominates statistically. . . . We are statistically or morally heterosexual, but personally homosexual, without knowing it or being fully aware of it, and finally we are transsexual in an elemental, molecular sense. That is why Proust, the first to deny all oedipalizing interpretations of his own interpretations, contrasts two kinds of homosexuality, or rather two regions only one of which is Oedipal, exclusive, and depressive, the other being anoedipal schizoid, included, and inclusive. (69–70)

Williams often discussed humankind's bisexual androgyny, which I will discuss a bit later on in this chapter.

92. Deleuze and Guattari, *Anti-Oedipus*, 122.

93. Artaud used the term for theater actors to transcend the meaning of a play's text, performance or reception. "Theatre of Cruelty" is Arnaud's treatise on the obligation of the actor to provide a performance unique with regards to the play, so that the actors create a new dramatic voice—sounds, voices, languages and gestures—though actions that are not rehearsed but have to be produced anew each time.

94. Deleuze and Guattari, *Anti-Oedipus*, 8, 1. Though perhaps not faithful to Deleuze and Guattari's original concept of the Body without Organs, which "has nothing whatsoever to do with the body itself" (8), its postmodern conceptualization of castration used here does recall much of their political program as it is espoused in their two works and, therefore, I feel captures the essence of their anti-establishmentarian stance on the phallic economy.

95. In addition to the androgynous and homoerotic opening of Hemingway's *The Garden of Eden* already discussed, see Mark Spilka, *Hemingway's Quarrel With Androgyny* (Lincoln: University of Nebraska Press, 1990), where he argues that Hemingway's engendering by his mother was strictly androgynous in nature: "Her twinship experiments, in which she tried to match Ernest with his sister Marcelline, his elder by a year, have long been misunderstood as attempts to feminize or sissify her son after the popular notion of Fauntleroy. But androgynous dollhood comes closer to her apparent intention. Ernest and Marcelline were her twin Dutch dollies, boy and girl, and the Dutch length of their hair and their matching dresses were androgynous features" (46). See also Donald Junkins, "Myth-making, Androgyny and the Creative Process, Answering Mark Spilka," *Hemingway Repossessed*, ed. Kenneth H. Rosen (Westport, CT: Greenwood, 1993), 57–67; and Cary Wolfe, "Fathers, Lovers, and Friend Killers: Rearticulating Gender and Race via Species in Hemingway," *boundary 2* 29.1 (Spring 2002): 223–57.

96. In her 1971 interview "Meeting with Tennessee Williams," Jeanne Fayard asked if his work was "a quest of the androgynous" (*CTW* 209). Williams agreed, but replied that it could never be achieved. For a detailed explanation of Williams's esoteric use of the word *androgyny* here and elsewhere in his canon that goes beyond Foucault's description of a homosexual's "hermaphroditism of the soul" (43), see my dissertation, "Tennessee Williams and the Southern Dialectic: In Search of Androgyny" (Ball State University, 1993). See also Lee Quinby, "Tennessee Williams' Hermaphroditic Symbolism in *The Rose Tattoo, Orpheus Descending, The Night of the Iguana,* and *Kingdom of*

Earth," Tennessee Williams Newsletter 1 (Fall 1979): 12–14, where he argues that Williams believed in the power of the sexual life force in his early plays and thus employed hermaphroditic symbols like the rose, which reinforces the "union of opposites" since it represents both spiritual and physical love (12). Williams viewed these symbols, Quinby maintains, as manifestations of the androgynous because they exhibit "a unity involving the fusion and balance of the masculine and the feminine, the spiritual and the physical within the individual's psyche" (12). See also Harry Alexander Kinney's 1983 dissertation, "Tennessee Williams and the Fugitive Kind" (*DAI* 44.8 [Feb. 1983]: 2294A, University of California–Berkeley), where he uses "several paradigms from the literature of androgyny as focal points for Williams' approach to characterization and dramatic form," positing that "Williams' recurrent theme of the individual's need for completion has its basic antecedent in the myth of the androgynes," as told by Plato in his *Symposium* (189D) (2294A). For an application of the term toward Williams's antimimetic realism (involving the destruction of theatrical representation binaries), see Thomas P. Adler, "Tennessee Williams's 'Personal Lyricism': Toward an Androgynous Form," *Realism and the American Dramatic Tradition*, ed. William W. Demastes (Tuscaloosa: University of Alabama Press, 1996), 172–78.

97. Kari Weil, *Androgyny and the Denial of Difference* (Charlottesville: University Press of Virginia, 1992), 11.

98. Ibid., 11.

99. Ibid., 47.

100. Roland Barthes, *S/Z: An Essay*, trans Richard Miller (1974; New York: Noonday, 1988), 35. For Barthes, Balzac's *Sarrasine*, like Williams's *Clothes for a Summer Hotel*, is not built structurally on biological categories of sex but rather on relationships of characters to castration: "of *castrating/castrated, active/passive*" (36). Here, Zelda certainly is the active castrator of Fitzgerald and Hemingway (and we may even add Hemingway too as an active castrator of Fitzgerald), though perhaps only Scott remains passive to her attempts.

101. Roland Barthes, *S/Z*, 95. He adds later: "The proper name enables the person to exist outside the semes, whose sum nonetheless constitutes it entirely. As soon as a Name exists (even a pronoun) to flow toward and fasten onto, the semes become predicates, inductors of truth, and the Name becomes a subject: we can say that what is proper to narrative is not action but the character as Proper Name: the semic raw material (corresponding to a certain moment of or history of the narrative) *completes* what is proper to being, *fills* the name with adjectives" (191).

102. Barthes, *S/Z*, 164.

103. Hutcheon, *Politics of Postmodernism*, 68.

104. In *Reading Desire: In Pursuit of Ernest Hemingway* (Ithaca: Cornell University Press, 1999), Debra A. Moddelmog suggests that Scribner's helped to "promote the popular image of Hemingway as unquestionably masculine and heterosexual in order to retain Hemingway's commodity value in the marketplace" (7). Leonard Leff devotes an entire to book to the construction of Hemingway's image by Scribner's, Hollywood, and magazines like *Look* and *Life*. See his *Hemingway and His Conspirators: Hollywood, Scribners, and the Making of American Celebrity Culture* (Lanham: Rowman & Littlefield, 1997). Specifically in terms of safe-guarding Hemingway's masculine image, his family has taken over the task of editing his posthumous manuscripts—in particular *The Garden of Eden* and *True at First Light*—often censoring material that could appear as damaging to the novelist's heteromasculine image. For more on the scholarly task of restoring nearly two hundred pages that Patrick Hemingway originally edited out of *True at First Light*, see Robert W. Lewis, "The Making of *Under Kilimanjaro*," *The Hemingway Review* 25.2 (2006): 87–90.

105. The entire quote from his 1979 interview with John Hicks reads: "I think that society has imposed upon homosexuals a feeling of guilt that makes them somewhat neurotic, that makes all of us somewhat neurotic" (*CTW* 322).
106. Paller, *Gentlemen Callers* 189.
107. Whitmore, "George Whitmore interviews," 315.
108. See Chauncey, Jr., *Gay New York*, especially his fourth chapter entitled "The Forging of Queer Identities and the Emergence of Heterosexuality in Middle-Class Culture."
109. Whitmore, "George Whitmore interviews," 312. Williams's 1979 absurdist play *Kirche, Küche, Kinder* is often discussed as Williams's sardonic commentary on the gay movement.
110. Williams had professed this idea even as early as 1947, when Blanche in *A Streetcar Named Desire* describes her gay husband Allan Grey (echoed later in Isabel Grey's name in "Three Players of a Summer Game") as not having had visible signs that foretold of his homosexuality: "There was something different about the boy, a nervousness, a softness and tenderness which wasn't like a man's, although he wasn't the least bit effeminate looking . . ." (1:354).
111. *Love in Earnest: Sonnets, Ballads, and Lyrics* (1892) — to which Wilde covertly alluded in the title of his queer play, *The Importance of Being Earnest* — was a collection of poems about homosexual love, with "earnest" subsequently becoming a code word for homosexuality in the late Victorian period. See Timothy D'Arch Smith, *Love in Earnest: Some Notes on the Lives and Writings of English 'Uranian' Poets from 1889 to 1930* (London: Routledge & K. Paul, 1970).

Conclusion

1. Hemingway owned a copy of Williams's novel *The Roman Spring of Mrs. Stone* and the published film script to *Baby Doll*, which suggests that his personal indifference to Williams at least did not extend to his professional judgment of him. See James D. Brasch and Joseph Sigman, *Hemingway's Library: A Composite Record* (New York: Garland, 1981), 401. He also owned a copy of Alfred C. Kinsey's *Sexual Behavior in the Human Male* and Havelock Ellis's *Studies in the Psychology of Sex*, Vol. 1: *Sexual Inversion*, which further suggests that Hemingway's interest in homosexuality might also have brought him to regard Williams's work on sexual politics in the manner we have only been discovering of late. See also Brasch and Sigman 113, 200, and Michael S. Reynolds, *Hemingway Reading, 1910–1940: An Inventory* (Princeton: Princeton University Press, 1981), 121.

Williams's collection of Hemingway's work at his Key West home, now housed in the Rare Book and Manuscript Library of the Columbia University Library, was even more impressive: *Across the River and Into the Trees* (on the inside back cover and facing the flyleaf is written some stanzas, of which the first is: "The key turns holy / as though a god moved / through it, / wanderingly, / alone, unknowing, unknown"); *Death in the Afternoon; Islands in the Stream, Men without Women;* and *To Have and Have Not* (on the front flyleaf is written: "Literature is composed / of exageration [*sic*], and so / is life. / T.W." Also on the inside back cover are a phone number, a couple of addresses and names and times).

2. See also Margaret Bradham Thornton, "Journals," *The Tennessee Williams Encyclopedia*, ed. Philip C. Kolin (Westport, CT: Greenwood, 2004), 105. As Thornton notes in her introduction to the *Notebooks*, "Unlike his letters, where he modulated his tone and style to suit the recipient, the journals reveal Williams' authentic voice — genuine

and unadorned" (*NB* ix). Thus, Williams's comment in his personal notebooks that Hemingway's "great quality, aside from his prose style, is this fearless expression of brute nature" (*NB* xi, 649) should be understood in light of his unqualified admiration for Hemingway's work.

3. For various writers who have written about Williams's and Hemingway's first and only meeting, see my introduction to this book.

4. This novel, left incomplete in 1950–1951 though published by Scribner's Sons in 1970, was particularly influential in Williams's understanding and appreciation of Hemingway. See *CTW* 245–46.

5. The extent to which Williams fully understood French existentialism as a theory is contentious, but, as I argue in chapter 3 on *Cat on a Hot Tin Roof*, he certainly admired it and knew its general principles.

6. Williams even appreciated Hemingway's discerning tastes and ability to capture it on paper. As he writes in his *Memoirs* of various meals he ate with Anna Magnani, "Every meal was a feast which it would take Ernest Hemingway with his gourmet appreciation to describe with justice" (*M* 164).

7. Tennessee Williams, "A Report On Four Writers Of The Modern Psychological School," box 10, folder 12, College papers, 1930–1938, n.d., Papers of Tennessee Williams, Harry Ransom Humanities Research Center, The University of Texas at Austin, 7–9, all *sic*.

8. Tennessee Williams, "Authors and Critics Appraise Works," *New York Times*, July 3, 1961: 6.

9. Yet another reference to Hemingway by Williams can be found in his 1973 interview for *Playboy*, where he told C. Robert Jennings that "Hemingway was, without any question, the greatest; he had a poet's feeling for words, economy. Fitzgerald's early books I thought were shit—I couldn't finish *Gatsby*—but I read *Tender Is the Night* several times. There are very few authors I can stand" (*CTW* 245–46).

10. Even as early as 1941, Williams expressed his affiliations with Hemingway. In an unmailed letter to Laurence Langner, dated February 1941, Williams wrote about his problems in rewriting *Battle of Angels*: "I have written about seven different endings in search of the right one. I hate to spend so much time on one play—but after all Hemingway spent three years on 'For Whom the Bell Tolls'" (qtd. in *NB* 220n373). Thornton adds that Audrey Wood mailed Williams a clipping from *American Mercury* in September 1941 that describes the young author as a "sort of D. H. Lawrence and Hemingway and Wolfe rolled into one . . ." (*NB* 220n373).

11. The term is used by Jeff Johnson to describe the attractive male characters in William Inge's plays who elicit desires from both gay and straight audience members. See his *William Inge and the Subversion of Gender: Rewriting Stereotypes in the Plays, Novels, and Screenplays* (New York: McFarland, 2005).

12. Lyle Leverich, *Tom: The Unknown Tennessee Williams* (London: Hodder & Stoughton, 1995), 288.

13. Tennessee Williams, *The Selected Letters of Tennessee Williams*, Vol. I: *1920–1945*, eds. Albert J. Devlin and Nancy M. Tischler (New York: New Directions, 2000), 342. All letters noted in this study taken from this volume are hereafter cited parenthetically in the text and abbreviated *SL I*. In the notes to an earlier 1941 letter to Bigelow, Williams writes, "It was really a frightful sad sort of thing. Queens! Oh, God, what a mess it all is!" (*SL I* 334).

14. George Whitmore, "George Whitmore interviews Tennessee Williams," *Gay Sunshine Interviews*, Vol. I, ed. Winston Leyland (San Francisco: Gay Sunshine Press, 1978), 312.

15. Dotson Rader, *Tennessee Williams: Cry of the Heart* (New York: Doubleday, 1985), 311.

16. For a more candid, if not semi- or entirely fictional account of this conversation, see Dotson Rader, *Cry of the Heart*, 308–14, where he fills in much of the gaps left out of the original interview.

17. As Leff writes,

> Novels like *The Sun Also Rises* were routinely optioned and occasionally adapted for the stage. . . . Early on, two producers William Brad Jr. and Dwight Deere Winman had expressed interest in a stage version of *The Sun Also Rises*. There were certainly stage and movie possibilities in the fiesta novel, Perkins wrote Hemingway. Like Broadway, though, which would use the novel more as a blueprint than bible, Hollywood "would require, I should think, such a revision to make a movie story, that you might hesitate." (63–64)

See his *Hemingway and His Conspirators: Hollywood, Scribners, and the Making of American Celebrity Culture* (Lanham: Rowman & Littlefield, 1997). Carlos Baker even points out in *A Life Story* that Hemingway "Had long considered writing a play, without going any further than "Today is Friday," that tasteless little account of the aftermath of the Crucifixion. As early as 1927, he had broached the subject of playwriting to Perkins, saying that he knew nothing about working for the stage, though it might be fun to try" (488). Though his play *The Fifth Column* was optioned by the Theatre Guild in 1938, the problems Hemingway faced in getting it onstage in a form he found acceptable had made him "completely disgusted with plays, playwrights, producers, and even with life itself" (Baker 514). It was finally produced on Broadway in March 1940 to mixed reviews.

18. Leverich, *Tom*, 90–91.

19. Tom Williams, "A Festival Night in Paris," *U. City Pep* 9.9 (Mar. 5, 1929): 2; reprt. in *WIL* 232–33.

20. Tennessee Williams, "~~12~~ 13 Golden (?) Rules for New Playwrights," typescript, collection 492, box 1–2, Tennessee Williams Papers, 1930–1970, Charles E. Young Research Library, Department of Special Collections, UCLA: [2, my emphasis]. The original title of the typed manuscript with holograph corrections and deletions reads "SOME MAXIMS FOR NEW PLAYWRIGHTS." It was signed "T Williams" and dated "Acapulco, August, '59."

Bibliography

Abelove, Henry. "Freud, Male Homosexuality, and the Americans." In *The Lesbian and Gay Studies Reader*. Eds. Henry Abelove, Michèle Aina Barale, and David M. Halperin. New York: Routledge, 1993.

Achuff, Louise R. "'Nice' and 'Pleasant' in *The Sun*." *The Hemingway Review* 10.2 (Spring 1991): 42–46.

Adams, Michael C. C. *The Great Adventure: Male Desire and the Coming of World War I.* Bloomington: University of Indiana Press, 1990.

Adler, Thomas P. "Tennessee Williams's 'Personal Lyricism': Toward an Androgynous Form." In *Realism and the American Dramatic Tradition*. Ed. William W. Demastes. Tuscaloosa: University of Alabama Press, 1996.

———. "When Ghosts Supplant Memories: Tennessee Williams' *Clothes for a Summer Hotel*." *Southern Literary Journal* 19.2 (Spring 1987): 5–19.

Alladi, Uma K. "Existentialism in the Novels of Hemingway and Camus." *Literary Half Yearly* 21.2 (1980): 43–51.

Allen, Dennis W. "Homosexuality and Artifice in *Cat on a Hot Tin Roof*." *Coup de Théâtre* 5 (Dec. 1985): 71–78.

Anderson, Hilton. "Tennessee Williams' *Clothes for a Summer Hotel*: Feminine Sensibilities and the Artist." *Publications of the Mississippi Philological Association* (1988): 1–9.

Arrell, Douglas. "Homosexual Panic in *Cat on a Hot Tin Roof*." *Modern Drama* 51.1 (2008): 60–72.

Atkinson, J. Brooks. "The Play . . . Tragedy from the French," *New York Times* Sept. 30, 1926: 23.

Baily, Beth. *From Front Porch to Back Seat: Courtship in Twentieth-Century America*. Baltimore: Johns Hopkins University Press, 1988.

Bak, John S. "'A Dying Gaul': The Signifying Phallus in Tennessee Williams's 'Three Players of a Summer Game.'" *Mississippi Quarterly* 58.1–2 (Winter 2004–5 and Spring 2005): 41–73.

———. "'May I have a drag . . . ?': Mae West, Tennessee Williams, and the Politics of Gay Identification." *Journal of American Drama and Theater* 18.1 (Winter 2006): 5–32.

———. "'sneakin' and spyin' from Broadway to the Beltway: Cold War Masculinity, Brick, and Homosexual Existentialism." *Theatre Journal* 56 (May 2004): 225–49.

———. "Tennessee Williams and the Southern Dialectic: In Search of Androgyny." Diss. Ball State University, 1993.

Baker, Carlos. *Ernest Hemingway: A Life Story*. [1969]. London: Penguin, 1972.

———. *Hemingway: The Writer as Artist*. 4th ed. Princeton: Princeton University Press, 1972.

Barbedette, Gilles, and Michel Carassou. *Paris Gay 1925*. Paris: Presses de la Renaissance, 1981.

Barnes, Clive. "'Clothes' needs some tailoring." *New York Post*, Mar. 27, 1980: 1.

Barthes, Roland. *S/Z: An Essay*. [1974]. Trans Richard Miller. New York: Noonday, 1988.

Beard, Daniel Carter. *Scouting*. n.c.: The Boy Scouts of America Publication, 1914.

Benstock, Shari. "Paris Lesbianism and the Politics of reaction, 1900–1940." In Duberman, Vicinus, and Chauncey, Jr., *Hidden from History*, 332–46.

Berman, Ronald. *Fitzgerald, Hemingway, and the Twenties*. Tuscaloosa: University of Alabama Press, 2001.

Bibler, Michael P. "'A Tenderness which was Uncommon': Homosexuality, Narrative, and the Southern Plantation in Tennessee Williams's *Cat on a Hot Tin Roof*." *Mississippi Quarterly* 55.3 (Summer 2002): 381–400.

Bigsby, Christopher W. E. *A Critical Introduction to Twentieth-Century American Drama*. Vol. II: *Williams, Miller, Albee*. Cambridge: Cambridge University Press, 1984.

Boswell, John. *Christianity, Social Tolerance, and Homosexuality: Gay People in Western Europe from the Beginning of the Christian Era to the Fourteenth Century*. Chicago: University of Chicago Press, 1980.

Bourke, Joanna. *Dismembering the Male: Men's Bodies, Britain and the Great War*. Chicago: University of Chicago Press, 1996.

Brasch James D., and Joseph Sigman. *Hemingway's Library: A Composite Record*. New York: Garland, 1981.

Bray, Allan. *Homosexuality in Renaissance England*. London: Gay Men's Press, 1982.

———. "Homosexuality and the Signs of Male Friendship in Elizabethan England." In Goldberg, *Queering the Renaissance*, 40–61.

Brenton, Myron. *The American Male*. New York: Coward-McCann, 1966.

Bruhm, Steven. "Blackmailed by Sex: Tennessee Williams and the Economics of Desire." *Modern Drama* 34.4 (Dec. 1991): 528–37.

———. "On Stephen King's Phallus, or The Postmodern Gothic." In *American Gothic: New Interventions in a National Narrative*. Eds. Robert K. Martin and Eric Savoy. Iowa City: University of Iowa Press, 1998.

Bryer, Jackson. "'Entitled to Write About Her Life': Tennessee Williams and F. Scott and Zelda Fitzgerald." In Voss, *Magical Muse*, 163–77.

Butler, Judith. *Bodies That Matter: On the Discursive Limits of "Sex."* New York: Routledge, 1993.

———. *Gender Trouble*. 2nd ed. London: Routledge, 1999.

Campbell, D'Ann. *Women at War with America: Private Lives in a Patriotic Era*. Cambridge, MA: Harvard University Press, 1984.

Carnes, Mark C., and Clyde Griffen, eds. *Meanings for Manhood: Constructions of Masculinity in Victorian America*. Chicago: University of Chicago Press, 1990.

Carr, Virginia Spenser. *The Lonely Hunter: A Biography of Carson McCullers*. Garden City, NY: Doubleday, 1975.

Chauncey, Jr., George. "Christian Brotherhood or Sexual Perversion? Homosexual Identities and the Construction of Sexual Boundaries in the World War I Era." In Duberman, Vicinus, and Chauncey, Jr., *Hidden from History*, 294–317.

———. "From Sexual Inversion to Homosexuality: Medicine and the Changing Conceptualization of Female Deviance." *Salmagundi* 58–59 (Fall 1982–Winter 1983): 114–16.

———. *Gay New York: Gender, Urban Culture, and the Making of the Gay Male World, 1890–1949.* New York: Basic Books, 1994.

Chesler, S. Alan. "Tennessee Williams: Reassessment and Assessment." In Tharpe, *A Tribute*, 848–80.

Clark, Suzanne. *Cold Warriors: Manliness on Trial in the Rhetoric of the West.* Carbondale: Southern Illinois University Press, 2000.

Clifford, Stephen P. *Beyond the Heroic "I": Reading Lawrence, Hemingway, and "Masculinity."* Lewisburg: Bucknell University Press, 1998.

Clum, John M. "'Something Cloudy, Something Clear': Homophobic Discourse in Tennessee Williams." In *Displacing Homophobia: Gay Male Perspectives in Literature and Culture.* Eds. Ronald R. Butters, John. M. Clum, and Michael Moon. Durham, NC: Duke University Press, 1989.

Cochran, Robert W. "Circularity in *The Sun Also Rises.*" *Modern Fiction Studies* 14.3 (1968): 297–305.

Colanzi, Rita Mary. "Caged Birds: Bad Faith in Tennessee Williams's Drama." *Modern Drama* 35.3 (Sept. 1992): 451–65.

———. "'A flame burning nothing': Tennessee Williams' Existential Drama." Diss. Temple University, 1990.

Comley, Nancy R., and Robert Scholes, *Hemingway's Genders: Rereading the Hemingway Text.* New Haven: Yale University Press, 1994.

Contat, Michel, and Michel Rybalka, eds. *The Writings of Jean-Paul Sartre.* Evanston, IL: Northwestern University Press, 1973.

Copley, Antony. *Sexual Moralities in France, 1780–1980: New Ideas on the Family, Divorce, and Homosexuality.* London: Routledge, 1989.

Corber, Robert J. *Homosexuality in Cold War America: Resistance and the Crisis of Masculinity.* Durham, NC: Duke University Press, 1997.

Costigliola, Frank. "'Unceasing Pressure for Penetration:' Gender, Pathology, and Emotion in George Kennan's Formation of the Cold War." *Journal of American History* 83.4 (Mar. 1997): 1309–39.

Crain, Caleb. *American Sympathy: Men, Friendship, and Literature in the New Nation.* New Haven: Yale University Press, 2000.

Crandell, George W. "*Cat on a Hot Tin Roof.*" In Kolin, *Tennessee Williams: A Guide to Research and Performance,* 109–25.

———, ed. *The Critical Response to Tennessee Williams.* Westport, CT: Greenwood, 1996.

———. "'Echo Spring': Reflecting the Gaze of Narcissus in Tennessee Williams's *Cat on a Hot Tin Roof.*" *Modern Drama* 42.3 (Fall 1999): 427–41.

———. "'I Can't Imagine Tomorrow': Tennessee Williams and the Representations of Time in *Clothes for a Summer Hotel.*" In Kolin, *The Undiscovered Country,* 168–80.

Cuordileone, Kyle A. "Politics in an Age of Anxiety: Cold War Political Culture and the Crisis American Masculinity, 1949–1960." *The Journal of American History* 87.2 (Sept. 2000) <http://www.historycooperative.org/journals/jah/87.2/cuordileone.html> (June 28, 2001).

———. *Manhood and American Political Culture in the Cold War.* London: Routledge: 2005.

Curtin, Kaier. *"We Can Always Call Them Bulgarians": The Emergence of Lesbians and Gay Men on the American Stage.* Boston: Alyson, 1987.

Daiker, Donald A. "The Affirmative Conclusion of *The Sun Also Rises.*" In *Modern Ameri-*

can Fiction: Form and Functions. Ed. Thomas Daniel Young. Baton Rouge: Louisiana State University Press, 1989.

Daniels, Robert L. "Still Exciting 'Sweeney Todd'—But a Dismal 'Clothes.'" *The Week Ahead*, Apr. 9, 1980: 1–2.

Davidson, Arnold E., and Cathy N. Davidson. "Decoding the Hemingway Hero in *The Sun Also Rises*." In Wagner-Martin, *New Essays*, 83–108.

de Beauvoir, Simone. *The Second Sex*. [1949]. Trans. and ed. H. M. Parshley. London: Vintage, 1997.

de Jongh, Nicholas. *Not in Front of the Audience: Homosexuality on Stage*. London: Routledge, 1992.

Deleuze, Gilles, and Félix Guattari. *Anti-Oedipus: Capitalism and Schizophrenia*. [1972]. Trans. Robert Hurley, Mark Seem, and Helen R. Lane. Minneapolis: University of Minnesota Press, 1983.

D'Emilio, John. *Sexual Politics, Sexual Communities: The Making of a Homosexual Minority in the United States, 1940–1970*. 2nd ed. Chicago: University of Chicago Press, 1998.

Donaldson, Scott. "Humor in *The Sun Also Rises*." In Wagner-Martin, *New Essays*, 19–41.

Dover, K. J. *Greek Homosexuality*. London: Duckworth, 1978.

Dorff, Linda. "Collapsing Resurrection Mythologies: Theatricalist Discourses of Fire and Ash in *Clothes for a Summer Hotel*." In Gross, *Tennessee Williams: A Casebook*, 153–72.

Dubbert, Joe L. *A Man's Place: Masculinity in Transition*. Englewood Cliffs: Prentice-Hall, 1979.

Duberman, Martin Bauml, Martha Vicinus, and George Chauncey, Jr., eds. *Hidden from History: Reclaiming the Gay & Lesbian Past*. New York: New American Library, 1989.

Dundy, Elaine. *Life Itself!* New ed. London: Virgo, 2002.

Dynes, Wayne R. *Homosexuality: A Research Guide*. New York: Garland, 1987.

Eby, Carl P. *Hemingway's Fetishism: Psychoanalysis and the Mirror of Manhood*. New York: State University of New York Press, 1999.

Elliott, Ira. "Performance Art: Jake Barnes and 'Masculine' Signification in *The Sun Also Rises*." *American Literature* 67.1 (Mar. 1995): 77–94.

Ellis, Havelock (co-authored with John Addington Symonds). *Studies in the Psychology of Sex*. Vol. I: *Sexual Inversion*. London: The University Press, Watford, 1897.

Ellis, James. "Hemingway's *The Sun Also Rises*." *Explicator* 36.3 (1978): 24.

Epstein, Barbara. "Anti-Communism, Homophobia, and the Construction of Masculinity in the Postwar U.S." *Critical Sociology* 20.3 (1994): 21–44.

Falk, Signi Lenea. *Tennessee Williams*. New York: Twayne, 1961.

Fasteau, Marc. *The Male Machine*. New York: McGraw-Hill, 1974.

Fielder, Leslie A. *The Fiedler Reader*. New York: Stein & Day, 1977.

Filene, Peter. *Him/Her/Self: Sex Roles in Modern America*. 3rd ed. Baltimore: Johns Hopkins University Press, 1998.

Fleming, Robert. "The Fun Also Rises: A Tribute to Jim Hinkle." *The Hemingway Review* 13.1 (Fall 1993): 90–91.

Fore, Dana. "Life Unworthy of Life?: Masculinity, Disability, and Guilt in *The Sun Also Rises*." *The Hemingway Review* 26.2 (Spring 2007): 74–88.

Foucault, Michel. *History of Sexuality.* Vol. I: *An Introduction.* Trans. Robert Hurley. New York: Pantheon, 1978.

Freud, Sigmund. *The Standard Edition of the Complete Psychological Works of Sigmund Freud.* Trans. and ed. James Strachey. 23 vols. London: Hogarth, 1961.

———. *Three Essays on the Theory of Sexuality.* [1905]. Trans. and ed. James Strachey. New York: Basic Books, 1962.

Garber, Eric. "A Spectacle in Color: The Lesbian and Gay Subculture of Jazz Age Harlem." In Duberman, Vicinus, and Chauncey, Jr., *Hidden from History,* 318–31.

Gerbaud, Collette. "Famille et homosexualité dans *Cat on a Hot Tin Roof* de Tennessee Williams." *Coup de Théâtre* 5 (Dec. 1985): 55–70.

Gilbert, James. *Men in the Middle: Searching for Masculinity in the 1950s.* Chicago: University of Chicago Press, 2005.

Gladstein, Mimi Reisel. *The Indestructible Woman in Faulkner, Hemingway, and Steinbeck.* Studies in Modern Literature, No. 45. Ann Arbor: University Microfilm International, 1986.

Goldberg, Jonathan, ed. *Queering the Renaissance.* Durham, NC: Duke University Press, 1994.

———. *Sodometries: Renaissance Texts, Modern Sexualities.* Stanford: Stanford University Press, 1992.

Grebstein, Sheldon Norman. *Hemingway's Craft.* Carbondale: University of Southern Illinois Press, 1973.

Greenberg, David. *The Construction of Homosexuality.* Chicago: University of Chicago Press, 1998.

Griffen, Clyde. "Reconstructing Masculinity from the Evangelical Revival to the Waning of Progressivism: A Speculative Synthesis." In Carnes and Griffen, *Meanings for Manhood,* 183–204.

Gross, Robert F., ed. *Tennessee Williams: A Casebook.* New York, London: Routledge, 2002.

———. "The Pleasures of Brick: Eros and the Gay Spectator in *Cat on a Hot Tin Roof.*" *Journal of American Drama and Theater* 9.1 (Winter 1997): 1–25.

Hale, Jr., Nathan G. *The Rise and Crisis of Psychoanalysis in the United States: Freud and the Americans, 1917–1985.* 2 vols. New York: Oxford University Press, 1995.

Halperin, David. *One Hundred Years of Homosexuality.* New York: Routledge, 1990.

Hantover, Jeffrey P. "The Boy Scouts and the Validation of Masculinity." In Pleck and Pleck, *The American Man,* 285–302.

Hattenhauer, Darryl. "More Humor in *The Sun Also Rises.*" *The Hemingway Review* 10.2 (Spring 1991): 56–57.

Hayman, Ronald. *Tennessee Williams: Everyone Else Is an Audience.* New Haven: Yale University Press, 1993.

Hays, Peter L. "Catullus and *The Sun Also Rises.*" *The Hemingway Review* 12.2 (Spring 1993): 15–23.

———. "Tennessee Williams 'Outs' Scott and Ernest." In *The Author as Character: Representing Historical Writers in Western Literature.* Eds. Paul Franssen and Ton Hoenselaars. Madison, NJ: Fairleigh Dickinson University Press, 1999.

Heasley, Robert. "Queer Masculinities of Straight Men: A Typology." *Men and Masculinities* 7 (Jan. 2005): 310–20.

Helfer, Richard. "*The Drag:* Mae West and the Gay World." *Journal of American Drama and Theater* 8.1 (Winter 1996): 50–66.

Hemingway, Ernest. *The Complete Short Stories of Ernest Hemingway: The Finca Vigía Edition.* New York: Scribner's Sons, 1987.

———. *The Dangerous Summer.* New York: Simon and Schuster, 1985.

———. *Death in the Afternoon.* [1932]. New York: Simon and Schuster, 1996.

———. *The Garden of Eden.* New York: Simon and Schuster, 1986.

———. *Islands in the Stream.* New York: Simon and Schuster, 1970.

———. *A Moveable Feast.* [1964]. New York: Simon and Schuster, 1996.

———. *Selected Letters, 1917–1961.* Ed. Carlos Baker. New York: Simon and Schuster, 2003.

———. *Le Soleil se lève aussi.* Trans. Maurice Edgar Coindreau. Paris: Gallimard, 1949.

———. *The Sun Also Rises.* [1926]. New York: Scribner's Sons, 1954.

———. *True at First Light.* New York: Simon and Schuster, 1999.

———. *Under Kilimanjaro.* Eds. Robert W. Lewis and Robert E. Fleming. Canton, OH: Kent State University Press, 2005.

Hewes, Henry. "A Streetcar Named Mendacity." *Saturday Review,* Apr. 9, 1955: 32–33.

Hicks, John. "Bard of Duncan Street: Scene Four." In Devlin, *Conversations with Tennessee Williams,* 318–24.

Hinkle, James. "What's Funny in *The Sun Also Rises.*" *The Hemingway Review* 4 (Spring 1985): 31–41.

Hirsch, Foster. *A Portrait of the Artist: The Plays of Tennessee Williams.* Port Washington, NY: Associated Faculty, 1979.

Hoffman, Frederick J. *The 20s: American Writing in the Postwar Decade.* Rev. ed. New York: Free Press, 1965.

Holcombe, Wayne C. "The Motive of the Motif: Some Thoughts on Hemingway's Existentialism." *The Hemingway Review* 3.1 (Fall 1983): 18–27.

Hurd, Myles Raymond. "Cats and Catamites: Achilles, Patroclus, and Williams's *Cat on a Hot Tin Roof.*" *Notes on Mississippi Writers* 23.2 (June 1991): 63–66.

Hurley, Paul J. "Tennessee Williams: The Playwright as Social Critic." In Crandell, *The Critical Response to Tennessee Williams,* 126–39.

Hutcheon, Linda. *The Politics of Postmodernism.* 2nd ed. London and New York: Routledge, 2002.

Hyman, Stanley Edgar. "Some Notes on the Albertine Strategy." *Hudson Review* 6 (Autumn 1953): 417–22.

———. "Some Trends in the Novel." *College English* 20.1 (Oct. 1958): 1–9.

Jackson, Esther Merle. *The Broken World of Tennessee Williams.* Madison: University of Wisconsin Press, 1966.

Jagose, Annemarie. *Queer Theory: An Introduction.* Washington Square: New York University Press, 1996.

Jameson, Fredric. "Postmodernism and Consumer Society." In *The Anti-Aesthetic: Essays on Postmodern Culture.* Ed. Hal Foster. Seattle: Bay Press, 1983.

———. *Postmodernism, or, The Cultural Logic of Late Capitalism.* Durham, NC: Duke University Press, 1991.

Jenckes, Norma. "'Let's Face the Music and Dance': Resurgent Romanticism in Tennessee Williams's *Camino Real* and *Clothes for a Summer Hotel*." In Kolin, *The Undiscovered Country*, 181–93.

Johnson, David K. *The Lavender Scare: The Cold War Persecution of Gays and Lesbians in the Federal Government*. Chicago: University of Chicago Press, 2003.

Johnson, James Weldon. *The Autobiography of an Ex-Colored Man*. [1912]. Ontario: Dover, 1995.

Johnson, Jeff. *William Inge and the Subversion of Gender: Rewriting Stereotypes in the Plays, Novels, and Screenplays*. New York: McFarland, 2005.

Jungman, Robert. "A Note on the Ending of *The Sun Also Rises*." *Fitzgerald/Hemingway Annual* (1977): 214.

Junkins, Donald. "Myth-making, Androgyny and the Creative Process, Answering Mark Spilka." In Rosen, *Hemingway Repossessed*, 57–67.

Kakutani, Michiko. "The Building of Williams's 'Summer Hotel.'" *New York Times*, Mar. 23, 1980: D 1, 26.

Katz, Jonathan Ned. *Gay American History: Lesbians and Gay Men in the U.S.A.* New York: Crowell, 1976.

———. *The Invention of Heterosexuality*. New York: Plume, 1995.

Kauffmann, Stanley. "Homosexual Drama And Its Disguises." *New York Times*, Jan. 23, 1966, sec. 2: 1

Kazan, Elia. *A Life*. New York: Knopf, 1988.

Kerr, Walter. "A Secret Is Half-Told in Fountains of Words." *New York Herald Tribune*, Apr. 3, 1955, sec. 4: 1.

———. "The Stage: 'Clothes for a Summer Hotel.'" *New York Times*, Mar. 27, 1980: D 15.

Kerrigan, William. "Something Funny about Hemingway's Count." *American Literature* 46.1 (Mar. 1974): 87–93.

Killinger, John. *Hemingway and the Dead Gods*. Lexington: University of Kentucky Press, 1960.

Kimmel, Michael. *Changing Men: New Directions in Research on Men and Masculinity*. Newbury Park, CA: Sage, 1987.

———. *Manhood in America: A Cultural History*. New York: Free Press, 1996.

Kinnamon, Keneth. "Hemingway, the *Corrida*, and Spain." In Wagner-Martin, *A Casebook*, 125–38.

Kinney, Harry Alexander. "Tennessee Williams and the Fugitive Kind." Diss. University of California–Berkeley, 1983.

Kinsey, Alfred C., Wardell B. Pomeroy, and Clyde E. Martin. *Sexual Behavior in the Human Male*. Philadelphia: W. B. Saunders, 1948.

Kleb, William. "Marginalia: *Streetcar*, Williams, and Foucault." In Kolin, *Confronting Tennessee Williams's* A Streetcar Named Desire, 27–43.

Kolin, Philip C., ed. *Confronting Tennessee Williams's* A Streetcar Named Desire: *Essays in Critical Pluralism*. Westport, CT: Greenwood Press, 1993.

———, ed. *The Tennessee Williams Encyclopedia*. Westport, CT: Greenwood Press, 2004.

———. "Tennessee Williams, Ernest Hemingway, and Fidel Castro." *Notes on Contemporary Literature* 26.1 (Jan. 1996): 6–7.

———. *Tennessee Williams: A Guide to Research and Performance*. Westport, CT: Greenwood, 1998.

——. "Tennessee Williams's *A Streetcar Named Desire* in Havana: Modesto Centeno's Cuban *Streetcars*, 1948–1965." *South Atlantic Review* 60.4 (Nov. 1995): 89–110.

——, ed. *The Undiscovered Country: The Later Plays of Tennessee Williams*. New York: Peter Lang, 2002.

Kroll, Jack. "Slender is the Night." *Newsweek*, Apr. 7, 1980: 95.

Lacan, Jacques. *Écrits: A Selection*. Trans. Alan Sheridan. New York: Norton, 1977.

——. "The Meaning of the Phallus." In *Feminine Sexuality: Jacques Lacan and the école freudienne*. Eds. Juliet Mitchell and Jacqueline Rose. Trans. Jacqueline Rose. New York: Norton, 1982.

——. *The Seminar of Jacques Lacan*. Book I: *Freud's Papers on Technique, 1953–54*. Trans. John Forrester. New York: Norton, 1988.

"Lee Barton." "Why Do Homosexual Playwrights Hide Their Homosexuality." *New York Times*, 23 Jan. 1972, sec. 2: 1.

Leff, Leonard. *Hemingway and His Conspirators: Hollywood, Scribners, and the Making of American Celebrity Culture*. Lanham: Rowman & Littlefield, 1997.

Leland, John. *A Guide to Hemingway's Paris*. Chapel Hill: Algonquin, 1989.

Leonard, John. "*The Garden of Eden*: A Question of Dates." *The Hemingway Review* 22.2 (Spring 2003): 63–85.

Leverich, Lyle. *Tom: The Unknown Tennessee Williams*. London: Hodder & Stoughton, 1995.

Lewis, Robert W. "The Making of *Under Kilimanjaro*." *The Hemingway Review* 25.2 (2006): 87–90.

Long, Deborah Marie. "The Existential Quest: Family and Form in Selected American Plays." Diss. University of Oregon, 1986.

Look, The Decline of the American Male. New York: Random House, [1958].

Loomis, Jeffrey B. "Four Characters in Search of a Company: Williams, Pirandello, and the *Cat on a Hot Tin Roof* Manuscripts." In Voss, *Magical Muse*, 91–110.

Lynd, Robert, and Helen Lynd. *Middletown: A Study in American Culture*. [1929]. New York: Free Press, 1955.

——. *Middletown in Transition: A Study in Cultural Conflicts*. [1937]. New York: Free Press, 1966.

Lynn, Kenneth. *Hemingway*. New York: Simon & Schuster, 1987.

Lyotard, Jean-François. *The Postmodern Condition: A Report on Knowledge*. [1979]. Trans. Geoff Bennington and Brian Massumi. Minneapolis: University of Minnesota Press, 1984.

Mandel, Miriam. "Truer than the Truth." *The Hemingway Review* 25.2 (2006): 95–100.

Mansur, R. M. "The Two 'Cats' on the Tin Roof: A Study of Tennessee Williams's *Cat on a Hot Tin Roof*." *Journal of the Karnatak University: Humanities* 14 (1970): 150–58.

Marlowe, Christopher. *The Complete Works of Christopher Marlowe*. Ed. Fredson Bowers. Cambridge: Cambridge University Press, 1981.

Martin, Wendy. "Brett Ashley as New Woman in *The Sun Also Rises*." In Wagner-Martin, *New Essays*, 65–82.

May, Charles E. "Brick Pollitt as Homo Ludens: 'Three Players of a Summer Game' and *Cat on a Hot Tin Roof*." In *Tennessee Williams: A Tribute*. Ed. Jac Tharpe. Jackson: University Press of Mississippi, 1977.

McLaren, Angus. *Trials of Masculinity: Policing Sexual Boundaries, 1870–1930*. Chicago: University of Chicago Press, 1997.

McLellan, John M. "The Unrising Sun: The Theme of Castration in Hemingway's *The Sun Also Rises*." *Studies in English Literature and Linguistics* 18 (May 1992): 51–61.

Mellow, James. *A Life without Consequence: Hemingway.* Boston: Houghton Mifflin, 1992.

Meyers, Jeffrey. *Hemingway: A Biography.* New York: Harper & Row, 1985.

Milford, Nancy. *Zelda.* [1970]. New York: HarperCollins, 1992.

Miller, D. A. *The Novel and the Police.* Berkeley: University of California Press, 1988.

Moddelmog, Debra A. *Reading Desire: In Pursuit of Ernest Hemingway.* Ithaca: Cornell University Press, 1999.

―――. "Reconstructing Hemingway's Identity: Sexual Politics, the Author, and the Multicultural Classroom." *Narrative* 1 (Oct. 1993): 187–206.

Monteiro, George. "Tennessee Williams Misremembers Hemingway." *The Hemingway Review* 10.1 (Fall 1990): 71.

Moore, William D. *Structures of Masculinity: Masonic Temples, Material Culture, and Ritual Gender Archetypes in New York State, 1870–1930.* Boston: Boston University Press, 1999.

Murphy, Brenda. "Brick Pollitt Agonistes: The Game in 'Three Players of a Summer Game' and *Cat on a Hot Tin Roof.*" *Southern Quarterly* 38.1 (Fall 1999): 36–44.

―――. *Congressional Theatre: Dramatizing McCarthyism on Stage, Film, and Television.* Cambridge: Cambridge University Press, 1999.

―――. "Seeking direction." In Roudané, *The Cambridge Companion to Tennessee Williams,* 189–203.

―――. *Tennessee Williams and Elia Kazan: A Collaboration in the Theatre.* Cambridge: Cambridge University Press, 1992.

Nelson, Benjamin. *Tennessee Williams: The Man and His Work.* New York: Ivan Obolensky, 1961.

Newton, Esther. *Mother Camp: Female Impersonators in America.* Chicago: University of Chicago Press, 1972.

―――. "The Mythic Mannish Lesbian: Radclyffe Hall and the New Woman." In Duberman, Vicinus, and Chauncey, Jr., *Hidden from History,* 281–93.

Nissen, Axel. "Outing Jake Barnes: *The Sun Also Rises* and the Gay World." *American Studies in Scandinavia* 31.2 (1999): 42–57.

Norton, Rictor. *The Myth of the Modern Homosexual: Queer History and the Search for Cultural Unity.* London: Cassell, 1997.

O'Connor, Jacqueline. "*The Strangest Kind of Romance:* Tennessee Williams and his Broadway Critics." In Roudané, *The Cambridge Companion to Tennessee Williams,* 255–64.

Pagan, Nicholas. *Rethinking Literary Biography: A Postmodern Approach to Tennessee Williams.* Rutherford, NJ: Fairleigh Dickinson University Press, 1993.

Paller, Michael. "The Couch and Tennessee." *The Tennessee Williams Annual Review* 3 (2000): 40–42.

―――. *Gentlemen Callers: Tennessee Williams, Homosexuality, and Mid-Twentieth-Century Drama.* New York: Palgrave Macmillan, 2005.

Parker, Brian. "Bringing Back Big Daddy." *The Tennessee Williams Annual Review* 3 (2000): 91–99.

―――. "A Preliminary Stemma for the Drafts and Revisions of Tennessee Williams's *Cat on a Hot Tin Roof* (1955)." *Papers of the Bibliographical Society of America* 90.4 (Dec. 1996): 475–96.

———. "Tennessee Williams and the Legends of St. Sebastian." *University of Toronto Quarterly* 69.3 (Summer 2000): 634–59.

Parsons, Elaine Frantz. *Manhood Lost: Drink, Gender, and Self in the Nineteenth-Century United States.* Baltimore: Johns Hopkins University Press, 2000.

Peek, Wendy Chapman. "Cherchez la Femme: *The Searchers, Vertigo*, and Masculinity in Post-Kinsey America." *Journal of American Culture* 21.2 (1998): 73–87.

Peterson, William. "Williams, Kazan, and the Two Cats." *New Theatre Magazine* 7.3 (Summer 1967): 14–20.

Petite, Joseph. "Hemingway and Existential Education." *Journal of Evolutionary Psychology* 12.1–2 (Mar. 1991): 152–64.

Pipkin, Turk. *The Old Man and the Tee: How I Took Ten Strokes Off My Game and Learned to Love Golf All Over Again.* New York: St. Martin's, 2004.

Pleck, Elizabeth, Joseph Pleck, eds. *The American Man.* Englewood Cliffs, NJ: Prentice-Hall, 1980.

Pleck, Joseph. *The Myth of Masculinity.* Cambridge, MA: MIT Press, 1981.

Plimpton, George. "An Interview with Ernest Hemingway." In Wagner-Martin, *A Casebook*, 15–32.

Porche, François. *L'Amour qui n'ose pas dire son nom.* Paris: Grasset, 1927.

Price, Marian. "*Cat on a Hot Tin Roof*: The Uneasy Marriage of Success and Idealism." *Modern Drama* 38 (1995): 324–35.

Quinby, Lee. "Tennessee Williams' Hermaphroditic Symbolism in *The Rose Tattoo, Orpheus Descending, The Night of the Iguana,* and *Kingdom of Earth.*" *Tennessee Williams Newsletter* 1 (Fall 1979): 12–14.

Rader, Dotson. *Tennessee: Cry of the Heart.* New York: Doubleday, 1985.

Reck, Tom S. "The First *Cat on a Hot Tin Roof*: Williams' 'Three Players.'" *University Review* 34.3 (Spring 1968): 187–92.

Reynolds, Michael S. *Hemingway: The Final Years.* New York: Norton, 1999.

———. *Hemingway: The Paris Years.* New York: Norton, 1989.

———. *Hemingway Reading, 1910–1940: An Inventory.* Princeton: Princeton University Press, 1981.

———. *The Sun Also Rises: A Novel of the Twenties.* Boston: Twayne, 1988.

Rich, Frank. "Turner and Durning in 'Cat on a Hot Tin Roof.'" *New York Times,* Mar. 22, 1990, sec. 3: 22.

Roosevelt, Theodore. *The Great Adventure: Present-Day Studies in American Nationalism* New York: Scribner's Sons, 1919.

———. "The Manly Virtues and Practical Politics." *The Forum* 17 (July 1894). Rptd. in *The Works of Theodore Roosevelt.* Vol. XIII. Ed. Hermann Hagedorn. New York: National Edition, 1926..

———. *The Strenuous Life: Essays and Addresses.* New York: Century, 1900.

Rosen, Kenneth H., ed. *Hemingway Repossessed.* Westport, CT: Greenwood, 1993.

Rotundo, E. Anthony. *American Manhood: Transformations in Masculinity from the Revolution to the Modern Era.* New York: Basic Books, 1993.

Roudané, Matthew C., ed. *The Cambridge Companion to Tennessee Williams.* Cambridge: Cambridge University Press, 1997.

Rubin, Gayle. "The Traffic in Women: Notes on the 'Political Economy' of Sex." In *Toward an Anthropology of Women.* Ed. Rayna R. Reiter. New York: Monthly Review, 1975.

Rudat, Wolfgang E. H. "Hemingway's Jake and Milton's Adam: Sexual Envy and Vicariousness in *The Sun Also Rises.*" *Journal of Evolutionary Psychology* 9.1–2 (Mar. 1988): 109–19.

———. "Hemingway on Sexual Otherness: What's Really Funny in *The Sun Also Rises.*" In Rosen, *Hemingway Repossessed*, 169–79.

———. "Hemingway's *The Sun Also Rises*: Masculinity, Feminism, and Gender-Role Reversal." *American Imago* 47.1 (Spring 1990): 43–68.

———. "Jake's Wound and Hemingway's War Trauma Once More: Allusion to *Tristram Shandy* and Jake's Other Jokes in *The Sun Also Rises.*" *Journal of Evolutionary Psychology* 12.3–4 (Aug. 1991): 188–206.

———. *A Rotten Way to be Wounded: The Tragicomedy of* The Sun Also Rises. New York: Peter Lang, 1990.

———. "Sexual Dilemmas in *The Sun Also Rises*: Hemingway's Count and the Education of Jacob Barnes.' *The Hemingway Review* 8.2 (Spring 1989): 2–13.

Russo, Vito. *The Celluloid Closet: Homosexuality in the Movies*. Rev. ed. New York: Harper & Row, 1985.

Sacksteder, William. "The Three Cats: A Study in Dramatic Structure." *Drama Survey* 5.3 (Winter 1967): 252–66.

Saddik, Annette J. *The Politics of Reputation: The Critical Reception of Tennessee Williams' Late Plays*. Madison, NJ: Fairleigh Dickinson University Press, 1999.

Sanderson, Rena. "Hemingway and Gender History." In *The Cambridge Companion to Ernest Hemingway*. Ed. Scott Donaldson. Cambridge: Cambridge University Press, 1996.

Sandomir, Richard. "Tennessee Williams: On Age and Annoyance." *New York Sunday News*, Mar. 23, 1980, Leisure Section: 5, 12.

Sarotte, Georges-Michel. *Like a Brother, Like a Lover: Male Homosexuality in the American Novel and Theatre from Herman Melville to James Baldwin*. Trans. Richard Miller. Garden City: Anchor, 1978.

Sartre, Jean-Paul. "American Novelists in French Eyes." *Atlantic Monthly* 78.2 (Aug. 1946): 114–18.

———. *Being and Nothingness*. [1943]. Trans. Hazel E. Barnes. New York: Washington Square Press, 1992.

———. *Sartre Visita a Cuba*. La Habana: Ediciones Revolucionarias, 1960.

Savran, David. "'By coming into a room that I thought was empty': Mapping the Closet with Tennessee Williams." *Studies in the Literary Imagination* 24.2 (Fall 1991): 57–74.

———. *Cowboys, Communists, and Queers: The Politics of Masculinity in the Works of Arthur Miller and Tennessee Williams*. Minneapolis: University of Minnesota Press, 1992.

Schlesinger, Jr., Arthur M. *The Politics of Hope*. Boston: Houghton-Mifflin, 1963.

———. *Vital Center: Our Purposes and Perils on the Tightrope of American Liberalism*. [1949]. Cambridge, MA: Riverside Press, 1962.

Schonhorn, Manuel. "*The Sun Also Rises:* I. The Jacob Allusion. II. Parody of Meaning." *Ball State University Forum* 16.2 (1975): 49–55.

Schwartz, Nina. "Lovers' Discourse in *The Sun Also Rises:* A Cock and Bull Story." *Criticism: A Quarterly Journal for Literature and the Arts* 26.1 (Winter 1984): 49–69.

Sedgwick, Eve Kosofsky. *Between Men: English Literature and Male Homosocial Desire*. New York: Columbia University Press, 1985.

———. *Epistemology of the Closet*. London: Penguin, 1990, 1994.

Seltzer, Leon. "The Opportunity of Impotence: Count Mippipopolous in *The Sun Also Rises*." *Renascence* 31.1 (Autumn 1978): 3–14.

Shackelford, Dean. "The Truth That Must Be Told: Gay Subjectivity, Homophobia, and the Social History in *Cat on a Hot Tin Roof*." *The Tennessee Williams Annual Review* Premiere Issue (1998): 103–18.

Simon, John. "Damsels Inducing Distress." *New York*, Apr. 7, 1980: 82, 84.

Smith, Geoffrey S. "National Security and Personal Isolation: Sex, Gender, and Disease in the Cold-War United States." *International History Review* 14 (May 1992): 307–37.

Smith, Timothy D'Arch. *Love in Earnest: Some Notes on the Lives and Writings of English 'Uranian' Poets from 1889 to 1930*. London: Routledge & K. Paul, 1970.

Smith-Howard, Alycia, and Greta Heintzelman, eds. *Critical Companion to Tennessee Williams: A Literary Reference to His Life and Work*. New York: Facts On File, 2005.

Smith-Rosenberg, Carroll. "Discourses of Sexuality and Subjectivity: The New Woman, 1870–1936." In Duberman, Vicinus, and Chauncey, Jr., *Hidden from History*, 264–80.

Spilka, Mark. "The Death of Love in *The Sun Also Rises*." In *Hemingway: A Collection of Critical Essays*. Ed. Robert P. Weeks. Englewood Cliffs, NJ: Prentice-Hall, 1962.

———. *Hemingway's Quarrel With Androgyny*. Lincoln: University of Nebraska Press, 1990.

Spoto, Donald. *The Kindness of Strangers: The Life of Tennessee Williams*. New York: Ballantine, 1986.

Steakley, James D. *The Homosexual Emancipation Movement in Germany*. [1975]. Salem, NH: Ayer, 1982.

———. "Iconography of a Scandal: Political Cartoons and the Eulenburg Affair in Wilhelmin Germany." In Duberman, Vicinus, and Chauncey, Jr., *Hidden from History*, 233–63.

Stein, Gertrude. *The Autobiography of Alice B. Toklas*. New York: Random House, 1933.

Steinke, Jim. "Brett and Jake in Spain: Hemingway's Ending for *The Sun Also Rises*." *Spectrum* 27.1–2 (1985): 131–41.

Strychacz, Thomas. *Hemingway's Theaters of Masculinity*. Baton Rouge: Louisiana State University Press, 2003.

Svoboda, Frederic Joseph. *Hemingway & The Sun Also Rises: The Crafting of a Style*. Lawrence: University Press of Kansas, 1983.

Tamke, Alexander. "Jacob Barnes's 'Biblical Name': Central Irony in *The Sun Also Rises*." *English Record* 18.2 (1967): 2–7.

Terman, Lewis, and Catherine Cox Miles. *Sex and Personality*. New York: Russell and Russell, 1936.

Testi, Arnaldo. "The Gender of Reform Politics: Theodore Roosevelt and the Culture of Masculinity," *Journal of American History* 81 (Mar. 1995): 1509–33.

Tharpe, Jac, ed. *Tennessee Williams: A Tribute*. Jackson: University Press of Mississippi, 1977.

Tischler, Nancy. *Tennessee Williams: Rebellious Puritan*. New York: Citadel, 1961.

Traister, Bryce. "Academic Viagra: The Rise of American Masculinity Studies." *American Quarterly* 52.2 (2000): 298–99.

Tynan, Kenneth. "Papa and the Playwright." *Playboy* XI (May 1964): 138–41.

———. *Right and Left*. London: Longmans, 1967.

———. *Sweet Bird of Youth* [review]. *The New Yorker,* Mar. 21, 1959: 98.

———. "A Visit to Havana." *Holiday* 27 (Feb. 1960): 50–58.

Vannatta, Dennis. *Tennessee Williams: A Study of the Short Fiction.* Boston: Twayne, 1988.

Vopat, Carole Gottlieb. "The End of *The Sun Also Rises:* A New Beginning." *Fitzgerald/Hemingway Annual* (1972): 245–55.

Voss, Ralph F., ed. *Magical Muse: Millennial Essays on Tennessee Williams.* Tuscaloosa and London: University of Alabama Press, 2002.

Vowles, Richard. "Tennessee Williams: The World of His Imagery." *Tulane Drama Review* 3 (Dec. 1958): 51–56.

Wagner-Martin, Linda, ed. *Ernest Hemingway's* The Sun Also Rises*: A Casebook.* Oxford: Oxford University Press, 2002.

———, ed. *New Essays on* The Sun Also Rises. Cambridge: Cambridge University Press, 1987.

———. "Racial and Sexual Coding in Hemingway's *The Sun Also Rises.*" *The Hemingway Review* 10.2 (Spring 1991): 39–41.

Waldhorn, Arthur. *A Reader's Guide to Ernest Hemingway.* New York: Octagon, 1975.

Waters, Arthur B. "Tennessee Williams: *ten years later.*" *Theatre Arts* July 1955: 72–73, 96.

Watt, Douglas. "Williams' Ghost Play Shrouds New Insights into Fitzgeralds." *New York Daily News,* Mar. 27, 1980: 107.

Weatherby, W. J. "Scott and Zelda Relive the Jazz Age." *London Sunday Times,* Mar. 30, 1980: 38.

Weeks, Jeffrey. "Inverts, Perverts, and Mary-Annes: Male Prostitution and the Regulation of Homosexuality in England in the Nineteenth and Early Twentieth Centuries." In Duberman, Vicinus, and Chauncey, Jr., *Hidden from History,* 195–211.

———. *Sexuality and its Discontents: Meanings, Myths & Modern Sexualities.* London: Routledge, 1985.

Weil, Kari. *Androgyny and the Denial of Difference.* Charlottesville: University Press of Virginia, 1992.

Wertheim, Stanley. "The Conclusion of Hemingway's *The Sun Also Rises.*" *Literature and Psychology* 17.1 (1967): 55–56.

Whitmore, George. "George Whitmore interviews Tennessee Williams." *Gay Sunshine Interviews.* Vol. I. Ed. Winston Leyland. San Francisco: Gay Sunshine Press, 1978.

Williams, Craig A. *Roman Homosexuality: Ideologies of Masculinity in Classical Antiquity.* Oxford: Oxford University Press, 1999.

Williams, Dakin, and Shepherd Mead. *Tennessee Williams: An Intimate Biography.* New York: Arbor, 1983.

Williams, Edwina, and Lucy Freeman. *Remember Me to Tom.* St. Louis: Sunrise, 1963.

Williams, Tennessee. "Authors and Critics Appraise Works." *New York Times,* July 3, 1961: 6.

———. "*Cat* draft fragments." Box 9, folder 1. Papers of Tennessee Williams. Harry Ransom Humanities Research Center. The University of Texas at Austin.

———. "*Cat on a* [Hot] *Tin Roof*"; or, "*A Place of Stone.*" Box 8, folder 3. Papers of Tennessee Williams. Harry Ransom Humanities Research Center. The University of Texas at Austin.

———. *Cat on a Hot Tin Roof.* [1955]. New York: New Directions, 1975.

———. *Cat on a Hot Tin Roof.* [1955]. New York: Samuel French, 1986.

———. *Collected Stories*. New York: Ballantine, 1986.

———. *Conversations with Tennessee Williams*. Ed. Albert J. Devlin. Jackson: University Press of Mississippi, 1986.

——— [as Tom Williams]. "A Festival Night in Paris." *U. City Pep* 9.9 (Mar. 5, 1929): 2.

———. *Five O'Clock Angel: Letters of Tennessee Williams to Maria St. Just, 1948–1982*. Ed. Maria St. Just. New York: Knopf, 1990.

———. *Memoirs*. Garden City: Doubleday, 1975.

———. *Moise and the World of Reason*. New York: Simon and Schuster, 1975.

———. *New Selected Essays: Where I Live*. Ed. John S. Bak. New York: New Directions, 2009.

———. *Notebooks*. Ed. Margaret Bradham Thornton. New Haven and London: Yale University Press, 2006.

———. "A Report On Four Writers Of The Modern Psychological School." Box 10, folder 12. College papers, 1930–1938, n.d. Papers of Tennessee Williams. Harry Ransom Humanities Research Center. The University of Texas at Austin.

———. "Revisions to Act III of *Cat on a Hot Tin Roof*." Box 8, folder 9. Papers of Tennessee Williams. Harry Ransom Humanities Research Center. The University of Texas at Austin.

———. *The Selected Letters of Tennessee Williams*. Vol. I: *1920–1945*. Eds. Albert J. Devlin and Nancy M. Tischler. New York: New Directions, 2000.

———. *The Selected Letters of Tennessee Williams*. Vol. II: *1945–1957*. Eds. Albert J. Devlin and Nancy M. Tischler. New York: New Directions, 2004.

———. *The Theatre of Tennessee Williams*. 8 vols. New York: New Directions, 1971–1992.

———. "~~12~~ 13 Golden (?) Rules for New Playwrights." Typescript, collection 492, box 1–2. Tennessee Williams Papers, 1930–1970. Charles E. Young Research Library. Department of Special Collections, UCLA.

———. *The Traveling Companion & Other Plays*. Ed. Annette J. Saddik. New York: New Directions, 2008.

Winchell, Mark Royden. "Come Back to the Locker Room Ag'in, Brick Honey!" *Mississippi Quarterly* 48.4 (Fall 1995): 701–12.

Windham, Donald, ed. *Tennessee Williams' Letters to Donald Windham, 1940–1965*. New York: Holt, Rinehart, and Winston, 1972.

Wixson, Christopher. "'A Very Carefully Orchestrated Life': Dramatic Representations of and by Zelda Fitzgerald." *American Drama* 11.1 (Winter 2002): 32–57.

Wolfe, Cary. "Fathers, Lovers, and Friend Killers: Rearticulating Gender and Race via Species in Hemingway." *boundary 2* 29.1 (Spring 2002): 223–57.

Woods, Gregory. "The Injured Sex: Hemingway's Voice of Masculine Anxiety." In *Textuality and Sexuality: Reading Theories and Practices*. Eds. Judith Still and Michael Worton. Manchester: Manchester University Press, 1993.

Wright, Les. "Introduction to 'Queer' Masculinities." *Men and Masculinities* 7 (Jan. 2005): 243–47.

Yacovone, Donald. "Abolitionists and the 'Language of Fraternal Love.'" In Carnes and Griffen, *Meanings for Manhood*, 85–95.

Young, Philip. *Ernest Hemingway: A Reconsideration*. University Park: Penn State University Press, 1966.

———. "*The Sun Also Rises*: A Commentary." *The Merrill Studies in "The Sun Also Rises."* Ed. William White. Columbus: Merrill, 1969.

Index

Abelove, Henry, 108, 250 n. 32
Adler, Alfred, 143
Adler, Thomas P., 174, 268–69 n. 30, 270 n. 44, 272 n. 63, 277 n. 96
Aesthete, the, 60, 71, 105
Albee, Edward, 161, 266 n. 10
Albertine strategy, the, 163, 232 n. 50, 266 n. 9. *See also* Proust, Marcel; Hyman, Stanley Edgar
Allen, Dennis, 38
Althusser, Louis, 68
American Mercury (magazine), 278
American Shakespeare Theatre, 35, 166, 222, 255 n. 8
Anderson, Hilton, 272 n. 60
Anderson, Sherwood, 209
Arenal, Humberto, 256 n. 10
Arrell, Douglas, 228 n. 13, 257 n. 16
Artaud, Antonin, 200, 300, 275 n. 93; the "Theatre of Cruelty," 200, 275 n
Atkinson, J. Brooks, 34, 73, 138, 240 n. 74
Atlantic Monthly (magazine), 268 n. 21

Baden-Powell, Lord Robert, 84, 243 n. 108
Baily, Beth, 260 n. 44
Bak, John S., 240 n. 75, 257 n. 16, 275 n. 96
Baker, Carlos, 5, 19, 20, 70, 71, 224 n. 5, 225 nn. 38–39, 237 nn. 31–32, 279 n. 17
Baker Electric, the (car), 251 n. 36
Baker, Josephine, 40
Baldwin, James, 141, 258 n. 26; *Giovanni's Room*, 141
Ballard, J. G., 176
Bankhead, Tallulah, 113
Barbedette, Gilles, 74, 239 n. 66, 241 n. 79
Barnes, Clive, 168, 266 n. 8, 269 n. 33
Barnes Hospital, the, 173
Barnes, Djuna, 74

Barney, Nathalie, 51
Barth, John, 258 n. 26
Barthes, Roland, 56, 201–2, 276 n. 100–102; "Death of the Author," 56; *S/Z*, 201–2, 276 nn. 100–102
"Barton, Lee", 162, 267 n. 12–13
Batista, Fulgencio, 22
Baudrillard, Jean, 168, 170
Beard, Daniel Carter, 84, 243 n. 108; *Hardly a Man Is Now Alive*, 84
Beech, Sylvia, 51, 71
Belmonte, Juan, 113
Benstock, Shari, 74, 241 n. 81
Bibler, Michael, 38, 228 n. 15, 261–62 n. 59, 264–65 n. 74
Bigelow, Paul, 217, 218, 278 n. 13
Bigsby, Christopher W. E., 229 n. 22
Bledsoe, Thomas, 60
Body without Organs (BwO), 200, 275 n. 94. *See also* Deleuze, Gilles; Guatarri, Félix
Bohemia (Cuban magazine), 256 n. 10
Bordelon, Eloi, 218
Bourdet, Edouard, 73; *La Prisonnière*, 73, 99
Bourke, Joanna, 90, 245 nn. 127–31
Boy Scouts of America, the, 82, 84, 106, 243 n. 109–10, 249 n. 19
Boyce, William D., 84
Brando, Marlon, 131, 141
Bray, Alan, 248 n. 10, 261 n. 51
Bray, Robert, 256 n. 10
Brenton, Myron, 45, 231 nn. 35 and 37
Brockden Brown, Charles, 158
Brooks, Richard, 36
Bruhm, Steven, 132, 252 n. 49, 255 n. 5
Brustein, Robert, 266 n. 8
Bryer, Jackson, 168, 268 n. 29, 269 n. 35, 270 n. 44
Burroughs, William, 51
Butler, Judith, 53, 64–67, 128, 153, 157,

INDEX

160, 177–83, 192, 199, 204, 238 n. 46, 242 n. 90, 252–53 n. 58, 262 n. 62, 264 n. 72, 271 nn. 51, 52, and 56, 273 n. 69; *Bodies That Matter, On the Discursive Limits of "Sex,"* 53, 242 n. 90, 262 n. 62, 264 n. 72; *Gender Trouble,* 66, 160, 177–79, 204, 213, 238 n. 46, 252–53 n. 58, 271 nn. 52 and 56, 273 n. 69

Caffe Cino, 161
Camus, Albert, 61, 67, 238 n. 38
Capote, Truman, 102 (illustration)
Captive, The. See *La Prisonnière*
Carassou, Michel, 74, 239 n. 66, 241 n. 79
Carnes, Mark C., 242 n. 100, 249 n. 18
Carpenter, Edward, 106, 108, 250 n. 34
Carr, Virginia Spenser, 27, 226 n. 43
Castro, Fidal, 17–19, 22, 25, 28, 208, 209, 224 n. 2, 225 n. 15, 226 nn. 45 and 47
Cather, Willa, 42; *One of Ours,* 42
Catullus, 235 n. 24, 239 n. 49; *Carmina,* 239 n. 49
Cendrars, Blaise, 92
Chandler, Raymond, 258 n. 26
Chauncey, Jr., George, 46, 48, 72, 86, 150–53, 230 n. 31, 231 n. 43, 232 n. 52, 240 nn. 70 and 72–73, 240–41 n. 78, 241 n. 82, 243–44 n. 111, 244 nn. 114–20, 248 nn. 12, 248–49 n. 14, 249 n. 16, 261 nn. 52 and 56, 261–62 n. 59, 262 n. 61, 273 n. 74, 277 n. 108
Chekhov, Anton, 212
Chicago Society for Human Rights, the, 73
Christian Muscularity, 82
Clark, Suzanne, 139–41, 243 n. 103, 258 nn. 24 and 27
Cleveland Street (sex scandal), 43
Clifford, Stephen, 56, 234 n. 14, 238 n. 37
Clift, Montgomery, 140
Clum, John, 158, 229 n. 17, 257 n. 18, 261–62 n. 59, 264 n. 73, 265 n. 77
Cocteau, Jean, 81
Cohn, Roy, 37
Colanzi, Rita Mary, 256 n. 13
Cold War, the, 29–30, 39–40, 130, 133–34, 140, 147–51, 154–55, 161, 165, 170, 174, 197, 203, 212–14, 229 n.18, 229–30 n. 27, 243 n. 103, 255 n. 8, 257–58 n. 19, 258 nn. 20–24, and 27, 258–59 n. 29, 260 n. 49, 264 n. 70, 265 n. 77

Comley, Nancy, 54–55, 231–32 n. 45, 234 n. 6, 235 n. 21, 241 n. 80, 242 n. 96, 244 n. 123, 245 n. 145
Copley, Anthony, 240 n. 78
Corber, Robert, 39, 139, 229 n. 18, 257–58 n. 19, 258 n. 20, 260 n. 49, 261–62 n. 59, 264 n. 70
Coward, Noel, 265 n. 1
Crain, Caleb, 265 n. 78
Crandell, George, 168, 228 n. 9, 229 n. 17, 257 n. 15, 269 n. 38
Crane, Hart, 212, 270 n. 46
Crane, Stephen, 210
Crawford, Cheryl, 113, 128, 260 n. 46
Crowley, Mart, 160; *The Boys in the Band,* 160, 163, 267 n. 16
cult of masculinity, the, 42, 44, 46, 78, 82, 103, 243 n. 107
cultural schizophrenia, 196–206, 272 n. 66, 274 n. 89, 274–75 n. 90, 275 nn. 91–92, and 94
cummings, e. e., 42; *The Enormous Room,* 42
Cuordileone, Kyle A., 258 n. 23
Curtin, Kaier, 73, 232 n. 53, 240 n. 75, 255 n. 6, 266 n. 7

D'Arch Smith, Timothy, 277 n. 111
D'Emilio, John, 48, 107, 230 n. 30, 232 n. 52, 249 n. 16, 250 n. 27, 253 n. 65, 270–71 n. 49
da Vinci, Leonardo, 130, 247 n. 8
Davidson, Arnold, 77, 98, 235–36 n. 25, 242 n. 88, 246 n. 150
Davidson, Cathy, 77, 98, 235–36 n. 25, 242 n. 88, 246 n. 150
Davies, Howard, 228 n. 10
de Beauvoir, Simone, 134 (photo), 135, 142–46, 148, 150, 158, 177, 256 n. 10, 257 n. 16, 259 n. 31; *The Second Sex,* 142–46, 259 n. 31
de Saussure, Ferdinand, 66, 68, 91, 119
Dean, James, 141
Delaney, Shelagh, 265 n. 1
Deleuze, Gilles, 199–200, 274 n. 89, 274–75 n. 90, 275 nn. 91–92, and 94
DeLillo, Don, 176
Devlin, Albert J., 253 n. 69
Dictionnaire historique de la langue francaise, le, 61
Doctorow, E. L., 176, 274 n. 82

Doolittle, Hilda ("H.D."), 74
Dorff, Linda, 168, 268 n. 25, 269 n. 37
Dos Passos, John, 42, 50; *Three Soldiers*, 42
Dover, K. J., 248 n. 9, 270 n. 42, 271 n. 50
Dubbert, Joe, 45, 231 n. 35, 248 n. 11, 249 n. 18
Dundy, Elaine, 22–25, 47, 49, 225 nn. 18–28, 30, and 35–37, 232 n. 47
Dvorsin, Andrew, 267 n. 10

Eagles, the, 82
Eastman, Max, 53
Eby, Carl, 55–56, 231–32 n. 45, 234 n. 10
Eliot, T. S., 42, 57, 101; *The Confidential Clerk*, 101; *The Waste Land*, 42
Eliot, The (Washington University student literary magazine), 18
Elks, the, 82, 149, 242 n. 99
Elliott, Ira, 58, 65, 77–78, 235–36 n. 25, 238 nn. 44 and 47, 242 nn. 87, 89, and 91
Ellis, James, 237 n. 31
Ellis, Havelock, 47, 69, 71, 74, 81, 105, 108, 176, 212, 240 n. 69, 240–41 n. 78, 249 n. 15, 250 nn. 29, 34, 277 n. 1; *Studies in the Psychology of Sex*, 71, 240 n. 69, 240–41 n. 78, 249 n. 15, 277 n. 1
Esquire (magazine), 266 n. 10, 268 n. 21
existentialism, 30, 50, 53, 59, 61–67, 79, 87–89, 91–100, 104, 109, 115, 126, 128, 130, 133–39, 141, 142–46, 148, 151–52, 153–57, 158, 166, 201, 207, 209, 212, 213, 215, 219, 221, 238 nn. 37–39, and 43, 245–46 n. 145, 255 n. 7, 255–56 n. 9, 256 nn. 11–12, 256–57 n. 13, 257 nn. 14–16, 259 n. 32, 271 n. 54, 278 n. 5

Fasteau, Marc, 45, 231 n. 35
Faulkner, William, 21
Fayard, Jeanne, 275 n. 96
Fiedler, Leslie, 80, 242 n. 94
Filene, Peter, 45, 231 n. 35
Fitzgerald, F. Scott, 50, 83, 166, 173–75, 179–86, 188–98, 202–6, 218–19, 243 n. 102, 246 n. 154, 268 n. 29, 270 n. 44, 271 n. 53, 272 nn. 62 and 65, 273 nn. 72–73, and 75, 274 n. 82, 276 n. 100, 278 n. 9; *Tender Is the Night*, 278 n. 9; *The Great Gatsby*, 278 n. 9
Fitzgerald, Zelda, 53, 166, 173, 180–95,

197–98, 204, 268 n. 29, 269 n. 35, 271 n. 53, 272 nn. 64 and 65, 276 n. 100
flappers, the, 29, 42, 85, 94, 107–8, 118, 126, 215, 243 n. 102, 249 n. 24, 250 n. 34
Fleming, Robert E., 232 n. 49, 237 n. 36, 246 n. 154, 262 n. 63
Floridita Bar, El (or La or The), 4, 6, 12, 16, 18–20, 22, 24, 25–26, 27 (photo)
Ford, Ford Maddox, 92
Ford, Henry, 41, 49, 109, 250 n. 26, 251 n. 36
Fore, Dana, 89, 244–45 n. 124
Foucault, Michel, 43, 49, 68, 176–78, 230 n. 28–29, 232 n. 54, 249 n. 15, 261 n. 58, 270 n. 42; *History of Sexuality*, 43, 49, 176, 230 n. 29, 232 n. 54, 249 n. 15, 270 n. 42
Freud, Sigmund, 40, 49, 66, 70, 71, 81, 85, 91–97, 103–9, 111–12, 115–17, 119–22, 123–24, 143, 176–77, 199–200, 212, 243–44 n. 111, 247–48 n. 8, 249 nn. 20, 22, and 24, 250 nn. 26 and 29–32, 251 n. 45, 252–53 n. 58, 263 n. 68, 274 n. 82; *Three Essays on the Theory of Sexuality*, 85, 141, 142, 251
Friedan, Betty, 231 n. 35
Frost, David, 164, 267

Gaines, Jim, 34, 209
Gay Sunshine (magazine), 163, 206, 218, 267 n. 10, 268 n. 17, 278 n. 14. *See also* Whitmore, George
Gide, André, 217, 250 n. 29; *Corydon*, 217
Gilbert, James, 36, 37, 228 nn. 11 and 14, 255 n. 7, 260 n. 47
Ginsberg, Allan, 51
Gladstein, Mimi Reisel, 68, 239 n. 57
Glaser, Benjamin, 225 n. 38
Glidden Tours, the, 251 n. 36
Goldberg, Jonathan, 248 n. 10, 261 n. 58
Gonzalez, Amado Rodriguez y (Pancho), 208
Greco, El (Domínikos Theotokópoulos), 130
Greenberg, David, 76–77, 106, 230 nn. 29 and 30, 240–41 n. 78, 242 n. 86, 249 nn. 21 and 23, 270–71 n. 49
Grenfell, Natasha, 27
Griffen, Clyde, 231 n. 39
Gross, Robert F., 51, 233 n. 62, 263 n. 68
Group Theatre, the, 267 n. 11

Gruen, John, 209, 255 n. 9
Guattari, Félix, 199–200, 274 n. 89, 274–75 n. 90, 275 nn. 91–92 and 94
Gunn, Andrew, 256 n. 10
Gussow, Mel, 266 n. 8

Habermas, Jürgen, 169
Hale, Jr., Nathan G., 249 n. 22, 250 n. 28
Hall, G. Stanley, 106, 212
Halperin, David, 230 n. 30, 261 n. 54
Hammett, Dashiell, 258 n. 26
Hampton, Christopher, 265 n. 1
Hansberry, Lorraine, 222; *A Raisin in the Sun*, 222
Hantover, Jeffrey P., 84, 243 n. 109, 249 n. 19
Hari, Mata (Margaretha Geertruida "Grietje" Zelle), 40
Harper's Bazaar (magazine), 113
Havana, Cuba, 18–22, 25, 26–28, 31, 47, 49–50, 113, 134, 222, 224 nn. 2–3, and 7, 225 n. 17, 226 n. 44, 256 n. 10
Hawkes, John, 258 n. 26
Hay, Henry, 255 n. 5. *See also* the Mattachine Society
Hayman, Ronald, 226 n. 47
Hays Code, the, 48, 232 n. 53, 265 n. 1
Hays, Peter, 58, 173, 235 n. 24, 239 n. 49, 270 n. 45, 272 n. 60
Hazen, Joe, 217
Heasley, Robert, 231 n. 44
Heidegger, Martin, 61, 134
Heller, Joseph, 258 n. 26
Hemingway, Ernest, and Africa, 47, 76, 153–54, 210, 232 nn. 49–51, 262 n. 63, 270 n. 48; and androgyny, 54, 56, 67, 192, 234 nn. 4–6, 275 n. 95; and bullfights and matadors, 20–21, 24–25, 31, 49, 55, 57, 81–82, 98, 99, 112, 130, 208, 224 n. 11, 233 n. 64, 235 n. 22, 242 n. 98, 245–46 n. 145, 246 n. 151; on camp, 216–17; criticism on his sexual obsessions, 53–57, 234 nn. 1–19, 234–35 n.20, 335 n. 21; and the Cuban revolution, 21–22, 31; and existentialism, 61–63, 238 nn. 38–39 and 42–43, 257 n. 14; on Fitzgerald, 190–91, 271 n. 58, 273 n. 72–73, 276 n. 100; on Henry James, 66, 96, 137, 210, 245 n. 143; on Joseph McCarthy, 263–64 n. 69; judgment of Williams's plays, 25, 262 n. 63; homosexuality in his writing, 57–59, 74–76, 77, 81–82; 232–33 n. 49, 235 nn. 21–24, 235–36 n. 25, 237 n. 33, 238 nn. 37 and 44, 241 n. 80, 242 nn. 85 and 89, 245 nn. 143–44, 245–46 n. 145, 246 n. 146; and homosexuality, 46–47, 49, 70–71, 73, 74–75, 81, 226 n. 41, 241 n. 80, 244 n. 123, 245 n. 144, 274 n. 78; and masculine education, 46, 82–85, 89, 231–32 n. 45, 234–35 n. 20, 243 nn. 102–3, 244 n. 112, 276 n. 104; on meeting Williams, 18–25, 224 nn. 2 and 7; and playwrights, 154, 263 n. 64, 279 n. 17; on reading Kinsey, 253–54 n. 70, 259–60 n. 39; on reading Williams, 262 n. 63, 277 n. 1; on sexual experimentation, 24, 47–48; similarities with Williams, 23; and Theodore Roosevelt, 70, 83, 243 nn. 102–3; in Williams criticism, 26–28
—Works of short fiction, "The Battler," 191; "Che Ti Dice La Patria," 57, 74, 216; "God Rest You Merry, Gentlemen," 57, 60, 74; "A Lack of Passion" 57, 74; "The Last Good Country," 57; "The Light of the World," 57, 216; "The Mother of a Queen," 57, 74, 216; "Mr. and Mrs. Elliot," 57, 74, 189; "Portrait of Three or the Paella," 57, 81; "A Pursuit Race," 57, 216; "The Sea Change," 57, 74, 75, 189, 192, 274 n. 78; "The Short Happy Life of Francis Macomber," 111, 251 n. 39; "A Simple Enquiry," 57, 74, 192; "There's One in Every Town," 57, 74, 241 n. 80
—Works of fiction, *Across the River and Into the Trees*, 246–47 n. 1, 277 n. 1; *A Farewell to Arms*, 58, 101, 191, 210, 246 n. 1; *The Fifth Column*, 25, 160, 279 n. 17; *For Whom the Bell Tolls*, 58, 241 n. 83, 246 n. 1, 278 n. 10, *The Garden of Eden*, 17, 24, 30, 47, 50, 54, 58, 188–89, 193, 197, 202, 216, 220, 232 n. 49, 234 n. 9, 253 n. 70, 262 n. 63, 273 n. 71, 275 n. 95, 276 n. 104; *In Our Time*, 42; *Islands in the Stream*, 30, 50, 54, 58, 76, 101, 186, 188, 189–90, 193, 197, 204, 209, 216–17, 219, 226 n. 49, 241 n. 84, 244 n. 123, 277 n. 1; *Men without Women*, 277 n. 1; *The Old Man and the Sea*, 262 n. 63; *The Sun Also Rises*, 29, 30, 47, 50–51, 53–

100, 113, 114, 118, 138, 151, 157, 159, 178, 181, 190, 210, 211–16, 221–22, 233 nn. 59, 64, and 66, 236 nn. 28–29, 237 nn. 31, 33, and 35, 237–38 n. 36, 238 n. 38, 239 nn. 49–57, and 65, 244 n. 112, 244–45 n. 124, 245 n. 127, 246 nn. 147 and 154, 274 n. 78, 279 n. 17 (androgyny in, 54; the Broadway production of, 221–22, 279 n. 17; and *Cat on a Hot Tin Roof*, 50–52, 100, 138, 151, 157, 181, 212, 214–15, 221–22, 233 nn. 64 and 66, 263 n. 64, 271 n. 54; and *Clothes for a Summer Hotel*, 178, 181, 190–91, 221; the "cult of masculinity in," 78–88, 96–97; [sexual] existentialism in, 61–68, 79, 88, 89, 92–94, 99–100, 159, 238 nn. 37–38 and 43–45, 239 nn. 51–53; gender questions in, 64–67, 68, 76–78, 85, 87–88, 94, 96–97, 98, 178, 212–13, 215, 235 nn. 21–24, 235–36 n. 25, 236 nn. 26 and 30, 237 n. 33, 244–45 n. 124, 112–13, and 123, 246 nn. 146–48, 150–51, and 154; homophobia in, 68–78, 79, 86–87, 151, 216; homoeroticism in, 80–81, 97–98, 244 nn. 112 and 123, 244–45 n. 24, 245 nn. 144–45; homosexual panic in, 65–66, 70–71, 76–78, 80–81, 86–87, 151, 216; homosociality in, 58–59, 70–71, 74–76, 80–85, 86–87, 96–98, 244 n. 112; [phallic] humor in, 60–61, 237 n. 34–35, 237–38 n. 36, 245 n. 144, 274 n. 78; impotence and phallic lack in, 60–61, 66, 77–78, 93–96, 159, 214, 237 n. 35, 239 nn. 49, 51, and 55; irony in, 29, 50–52, 59–60, 61, 63, 87–88, 98, 114, 157, 181–82, 190–91, 212–13, 216, 221–22, 236 n. 26, 237–38 n. 36, 239 n. 55, 244 n. 112, 245 n. 143; and the "pretty" ending, 29–30, 50–52, 59–60, 69, 88, 98, 157, 181, 180–81, 221–22, 236 n. 28; and "Three Players of a Summer Game," 112–14, 116, 118, 250 n. 34; war wounds in, 89–93, 237 n. 31, 244–45 n. 124, 245 nn. 127–31; Williams's reading of, 233 n. 64; the writing of, 70, 73, 86, 210, 236 n. 29); *The Torrents of Spring*, 323 52; *To Have and Have Not*, 58, 277 n. 1; *True at First Light*, 30, 47, 54, 58, 76, 153, 156, 188, 226 n. 49, 232 nn. 49–50, 242 n. 97, 262 n. 63, 270 n. 48, 276 n. 104; *Under Kilimanjaro*, 30, 32, 47, 54, 58, 76, 81, 153, 156, 188, 226 n. 49, 232 nn. 49–50, 262 n. 63, 270 n. 48, 276 n. 104
—Works of nonfiction, *The Dangerous Summer*, 82, 226 n. 49, 242 n. 98; *Death in the Afternoon*, 58, 74, 76, 130, 216, 224 n. 11, 233 nn. 64 and 66, 235 n. 22, 245 n. 145, 274 n. 78, 277 n. 1 ("Café des Deux Magots," 74, 216, 241 n. 80); *Green Hills of Africa*, 52, 209, 232 n. 51, 233 n. 64, 262 n. 63; *A Moveable Feast*, 58, 74, 75, 76, 92, 180, 181, 186, 189–95, 198, 202, 216–17, 219, 226 n. 49, 241 n. 82, 262 n. 63, 273 n. 73

Hemingway, Grace (Hall), 54
Hemingway, Mary (Welsh), 18, 27, 47, 54, 153–54, 232 n. 51, 263–64 n. 69, 270 n. 48
Hemingway, Pauline (Pfeiffer), 21, 28, 222, 224 n. 13, 232 n. 51
Hicks, John, 22, 225 n. 16, 267 n. 11, 272 n. 64, 277 n. 105
Hinkle, James, 60, 71, 237 n. 36, 239 n. 64
Hirsch, Foster, 38, 229 n. 20
Hirschfeld, Al, 102
Hirschfeld, Magnus, 105, 108, 176, 250 n. 29
Holiday (magazine), 20, 22, 224 n. 7
Homo americanus, 40, 59, 158, 166, 201, 215, 219
homosexual existentialism, 30, 148, 151, 157–58
homosexuality, 19–20, 24, 29, 30, 31, 32, 34, 36–42, 43–45, 46–50, 52, 53–55, 57–58, 65–66, 68–78, 80–82, 85–87, 97–103, 105–8, 115–16, 118, 125–29, 131–33, 135–37, 139, 141, 144, 146–59, 160–67, 174, 176–77, 179–86, 188–90, 192–95, 198–99, 201, 204–6, 212–21, 226 nn. 41 and 48, 228 nn. 11, and 13–15, 228–29 n. 16, 229 nn. 17–18, and 22, 230 nn. 28–31, 232 n. 53, 234 nn. 3–19, 235 nn. 22–24, 235–26 n. 25, 236–37 n. 30, 238 n. 44, 239 n. 49, 240 nn. 69–77, 240–41 n. 78, 241 nn. 79–81, 242 nn. 87–91, and 97, 243–44 n. 111, 244–45 nn. 112, and 123–24, 245 nn. 140–45, 246 nn. 146–55, 247 nn. 4 and 6, 248 nn. 9–13, 248–49 n. 14, 249 nn. 15–16, and 21, 250 n. 32, 251 n. 44, 252–53 n. 58,

253 nn. 59, and 62–69, 254 nn. 71 and 73–74, 254 n. 2, 255 nn. 5–8, 257 nn. 16–18, 257–58 n. 19, 258 nn. 21 and 28, 259 n. 33, 260 nn. 40, and 48–49, 260–61 n. 50, 261 nn. 51–58, 261–62 n. 59, 262 nn. 60–63, 263 nn. 64–68, 264 n. 73, 264–65 n. 74, 265 nn. 75–79, 265 n. 1, 265–66 n. 2, 266 nn. 3–9, 266–87 n. 10, 267 nn. 11–16, 268 nn. 17–24, and 26, 270–nn. 42 and 45, 270–71 n 49, 271 n. 50, 272 n. 65, 272–73 n. 69, 273 nn. 70 and 74, 274 nn. 77–78, and 87, 275 n. 91, 275–76 n. 96, 277 n. 105
Hoover, J. Edgar, 37, 140
Hotchner, Ed, 18
Hotel Nacional, the, 19, 23, 134, 134 (photo), 224 n. 3
House on UnAmerican Activities (HUAC), the, 141, 153, 155–56, 254 n. 1, 264 n. 70
Hurd, Myles Raymond, 261 n. 51
Hutcheon, Linda, 170, 185, 203, 272 nn. 61 and 66–68, 274 nn. 82, 83, and 88, 276 n. 103
Hyman, Stanley Edgar, 232 n. 50, 266 n. 9

Iliad, the, 261 n. 51
impotence, 35, 42, 54, 60–61, 63, 67–68, 76, 77, 86, 88, 89, 95–96, 99, 112, 114, 115, 126, 129, 135, 145–46, 155, 157, 159, 181, 186, 198–99, 201, 221, 237 nn. 31 and 35–36, 239 nn. 49, 51, and 53, 252 n. 53, 257–58 n. 19, 259 n. 36, 263 n. 68, 274 n. 87
Inge, William, 161, 263 n. 64, 278 n. 11; *Picnic*, 263 n. 64
Irigaray, Luce, 101, 177

Jackson, Esther Merle, 256 n. 11
Jagose, Annemarie, 239 n. 59, 242 n. 92, 246 n. 149
James, Henry, 66, 85, 96, 137
James, William, 69
Jameson, Fredric, 170, 187–88, 194, 196–97, 199, 202, 203, 216, 269–70 n. 40, 272 n. 66, 274 n. 83; *Postmodernism, or, The Cultural Logic of Late Capitalism*, 187–88, 269–70 n. 40
Jaspers, Karl, 61, 134, 135
Jazz Age, the, 40, 42, 50, 73, 85, 107, 180, 243 n. 111, 270 n. 44, 272 n. 65

Jenckes, Norma, 168, 269 n. 39
Jennings, C. Robert, 164, 268 n. 21, 278 n. 9
Johnson, David K., 229–30 n. 27
Johnson, James Weldon, 49, 232 n. 56; *The Autobiography of an Ex-Colored Man*, 49, 232 n. 56
Johnson, Jeff, 278 n. 11
Jones, Margo, 251 n. 41
Judson Poets' Theatre, 161
Jung, Carl Gustav, 274n

Katz, Jonathan, 45, 177, 231 n. 36, 240 nn. 74 and 77, 258 n. 28, 271 n. 50; *Gay American History*, 45, 177, 231 n. 36, 240 nn. 74 and 77, 258 n. 28, 271 n. 50
Kauffmann, Stanley, 161–62, 266 n. 82
Kazan, Elia, 25, 33–35, 37, 132, 226 n. 1, 227 nn. 2–4, 229 n. 23, 233–34 n. 67, 254 n. 1, 264 n. 70, 268 n. 27; on Brick's "mystery," 132, 229 n. 23, 254 n. 1; *A Life*, 33, 227 n. 3; on the third-act revisions for *Cat on a Hot Tin Roof*, 33–35, 37, 227 n. 2, 233–34 n. 67, 264 n. 70
Keith, Don Lee, 209, 266 n. 8, 268 n. 21
Kennan, George F., 140
Kerr, Walter, 36–37, 40, 52, 131–32, 156, 163, 165, 174, 213, 228 n. 16, 254 nn. 2 and 4, 269 n. 34
Kerrigan, William, 237 n. 35
Kertbeny, Károly Mária, 230 n. 28
Key West, 18, 21–23, 26, 222, 268 n. 27
Kierkegaard, Søren, 61, 133, 135
Killinger, John, 61, 63, 68, 99, 238 nn. 38–39, and 42–43, 246 n. 152
Kimmel, Michael, 44, 45, 83, 89, 105, 126, 231 n. 33, 242 n. 100, 243 nn. 101, 105, and 107, 245 n. 126, 248 nn. 11 and 14, 249 nn. 18–19, 253 n. 64
Kinnamon, Keneth, 245–46 n. 145
Kinsey, Alfred, 47, 49–50, 101, 127–28, 129, 133, 146–48, 150, 152, 176, 233 n. 58, 249 n. 15, 253 nn. 66–70, 259 n. 38, 259–60 n. 39, 260 nn. 40–41, 43, 45–46, and 47, 262 n. 60, 263 n. 67, 265 n. 77, 277 n. 1; first meeting Williams, 101, 127–28, 253 n. 69, 260 n. 45–46; Hemingway reading, 47, 260n; *Sexual Behavior in the Human Male*, 127, 133, 146–48, 176, 253 nn. 66–70, 259 n. 38, 259–60 n.

39, 260 nn. 40–41, 43, and 45, 262 n. 60, 263 n. 67, 277 n. 1
Knights of Columbus, the, 82, 242 n. 99
Kolin, Philip C., 27–28, 226 n. 47, 256 n. 10
Kramer, Hazel, 121, 129, 251 n. 43, 252 nn. 46–47, 254 n. 72
Kristeva, Julia, 177
Kroll, Jack, 269 n. 32

La Mama, 161
Lacan, Jacques, 40, 66, 68, 91, 93–96, 98, 115–17, 119–20, 122–24, 128–29, 177, 196, 198, 245 nn. 134–38 and 140–41, 251 n. 45, 252 nn. 50–51 and 55–57, 252–53 n. 58, 253 n. 59; *Écrits*, 119–20, 123–24, "The Meaning of the Phallus," 91, 124, 245 nn. 134–38 and 140–41, 252 n. 57
Latham, Aaron, 55
Lawrence, D. H., 168, 212, 270 n. 46, 278 n. 10
Leff, Leonard, 221, 234–35 n. 20, 243 n. 102, 276 n. 104, 279 n. 17
Leverich, Lyle, 217, 278 n. 12
Lewis, Robert W., 232 n. 49, 262 n. 63, 276 n. 104
Life (magazine), 266 n. 8, 276 n. 104
Lira, Alphonso Reyes, 251 n. 41
Long, Deborah Marie, 256 n. 13
Look (magazine), 46, 139, 257–58 n. 19, 262 n. 63, 276 n. 104
Loomis, Jeffrey, 141, 146, 227 nn. 3 and 8, 250 n. 34, 259 nn. 30 and 37, 262 n. 59
Lunes de Revolución (Cuban magazine), 256 n. 10
Lynd, Helen, 49, 232–33 n. 57, 250 n. 26
Lynd, Robert, 49, 232–33 n. 57, 250 n. 26
Lynn, Kenneth S., 26, 53, 225 n. 40, 234 n. 1, 243 n. 103, 244 n. 123, 272–73 n. 69
Lyotard, Jean–François, 169–72, 174–77, 179, 196, 199, 216, 269 n. 40, 271 n. 51; *The Postmodern Condition*, 169–72, 269 n. 40, 271 n. 51

MacGregor, Robert, 113
Magnani, Anna, 278 n. 6
Mailer, Norman, 258 n. 26
Malamud, Bernard, 258 n. 26
male neurasthenia, 90, 245 n. 132
Mandel, Miriam, 226 n. 49

Mann, Thomas, 210
Manolete (Manuel Laureano Rodríguez Sánchez), 113
Marcel, Gabriel, 134
Marlowe, Christopher, 253 n. 63, 256 n. 12; *Edward II*, 253 n. 63
Martin, Elliott, 173, 269 n. 31
Martin, Wendy, 69, 245 nn. 127 and 139
Marvell, Andrew, 75
masculine existentialism, 30, 87, 104, 109, 215
masculinity, 30, 40–46, 48–52, 54–58, 65–66, 68–69, 72, 81–85, 89, 91–92, 97–98, 99, 101, 103–9, 111–15, 116–17, 120–23, 125, 126, 128, 129, 130, 133, 139–41, 147, 149–51, 153–54, 167, 181–82, 188, 192, 205, 212, 214, 212, 228 nn. 11 and 15, 229 nn. 18 and 22, 230 nn. 31 and 33, 231 nn. 35, 38–40, and 42–44, 231–32 n. 45, 235 n. 24, 238 nn. 37 and 48, 239 nn. 49, 55, 61, and 63, 242 nn. 89 and 100, 243 nn. 101–8, 244 nn. 111–12 and 124, 245 n. 145, 246 n. 148, 248 nn. 9, 11–13, 248–49 n. 14, 247 nn. 18–19, 251 nn. 36, 38–39, and 44, 253 n. 60, 255 nn. 5 and 7, 257 n. 16, 257–58 n. 19, 258 nn. 21, 23, and 26, 259 n. 33, 260 n. 42, 261 nn. 51–52, 262 n. 63, 263 n. 68, 271 n. 52, 273 nn. 69 and 73, 274 n. 87, 276 nn. 96 and 104
Masons, the, 149
Mattachine Society, the, 177, 255 n. 5
Maturin, Charles, 244 n. 123
May, Charles E., 36, 39, 51, 157, 228 n. 10, 229 n. 19, 233 n. 60, 247 nn. 3–4, 252 n. 53, 253 n. 62, 256–57 n. 14
McAlmon, Robert, 184
McCarthy, Joseph, 37, 41, 140, 153, 156, 255 n. 6, 260 n. 49, 263–64 n. 69, 264 n. 70
McCullers, Carson, 26–27, 134, 208, 258 n. 25; *Reflections in a Golden Eye*, 134
McLaren, Angus, 91, 107, 230 n. 31, 244 n. 111, 245 n. 133, 248 nn. 11 and 13, 250 n. 29
Mellow, James R., 26, 53–54, 79–80, 225 n. 40, 234 n. 2, 242 n. 93, 244 n. 121
Melmoth, Sebastian. *See* Wilde, Oscar
Merlo, Frank, 34, 139, 209
Meyers, Jeffrey, 26, 54, 225–26 n. 41, 234 n. 3, 243 n. 103, 244 n. 123, 246 n. 154, 274 n. 87

INDEX

Middletown (the Lynds' studies), 49, 232–33 n. 57, 250 n. 26
Miles, Catherine Cox, 126, 253 n. 64
Milford, Nancy, 180, 183–84, 186–87, 204, 271 n. 57, 272 n. 64
Milk, Harvey, 164
Miller, Arthur, 256 n. 9, 264 n. 70
Miller, D. A., 254 n. 74
Mizener, Arthur, 271 n. 58
Moddelmog, Debra A., 47, 55, 86, 99, 232 n. 46, 234 nn. 7–9, 236 n. 26, 244 n. 113, 246 n. 155, 258 n. 19, 273 n. 69, 276 n. 104
Moll, Albert, 250 n. 29
Monroe Doctrine, the, 141
Monteiro, George, 274 n. 78
Moose, the, 82, 242 n. 99
Morosco Theatre, 34
Moscone, George, 224
Murphy, Brenda, 34, 39, 51, 102–3, 116, 123, 126, 227 nn. 3–4, 233 n. 61, 247 nn. 5–6, 250 n. 34, 251 nn. 38, 40, 42, and 44, 252 n. 54, 253 n. 61, 254 n. 4, 259 n. 34, 260 n. 49
Murphy, Gerald, 182, 185, 191
Murphy, Sara, 182, 185, 191

Nelson, Benjamin, 229 n. 19
New Directions, 34, 39, 173, 226 n. 1, 233 n. 67, 265 n. 75
New Orleans, 18, 218
New Orleans Athletic Club, the, 218
Newton, Esther, 250 n. 34
New York, 23, 48, 73, 85–87, 163, 225 n. 38, 241 n. 82, 254 n. 3, 266 n. 7, 268 n. 27, 274 n. 85
New York (newspaper), 167, 268 n. 28
New York Daily News (newspaper), 271 n. 53
New York Drama Critics' Circle Award, the, 211
New York Herald Tribune (newspaper), 131, 228 n. 12, 254 nn. 2–3
New York Post (newspaper), 168, 269
New York Star (newspaper), 155
New York Sunday News (newspaper), 269 n. 32
New York Times (newspaper/magazine), 34, 55, 73, 113, 138, 161, 211, 228 n. 10, 240 n. 74, 246–47 n. 1, 259 n. 38, 266 n. 3, 267 nn. 12–13, 269 n. 34, 278 n. 8

New Yorker (magazine), 101, 113, 114, 116, 129, 224 n. 3, 252 n. 48, 253 n. 62
Nicholson, John Gambril Francis, 207; *Love in Earnest, Sonnets, Ballads, and Lyrics*, 207
Nissen, Axel, 58, 85, 235 n. 24, 236 n. 26
Nixon, Richard M., 140
Nobel Prize for Literature, the, 18, 211; Hemingway's, 18; Williams's denied, 211
Norton, Rictor, 230 n. 28, 231 n. 39, 248 n. 12

O'Connor, Flannery, 258 n. 26
O'Connor, Jacqueline, 266 n. 8
Ordóñez, Antonio, 20–21, 24, 25, 26 (photos), 82
Ordóñez, Cateyano (Nino de la Palma), 20
Ortiz, José, 57
Orton, Joe, 265 n. 1
Osborne, John, 265 n. 1

Pagan, Nicholas, 270 nn. 41 and 43
Paller, Michael, 38, 150, 163, 165, 206, 228 n. 15, 260 nn. 41 and 45, 261 n. 53, 263 n. 65, 265 n. 1, 266 n. 6, 267 nn. 10 and 14–15, 268 nn. 20 and 26, 269 n. 36, 277 n. 106
Paragraph 175, 241 n. 78
Paris, 47, 71, 73–74, 77, 79, 81, 85–86, 89, 96, 102, 134, 182, 221–22, 239 nn. 66–67, 241 nn. 79–81, 246 n. 146, 250 n. 34, 255 nn. 8–9, 274 n. 78, 279 n. 19
Paris Review, The (magazine), 60, 219, 273 n. 72
Parker, Brian, 101, 227 nn. 2, 3, and 7, 233 n. 67, 244 n. 123, 247 nn. 2 and 4
Parrot, Jim, 224 n. 13
Parsons, Elaine Frantz, 248 n. 11
pastiche, 187–90, 192–95, 196, 199, 202–4, 216, 218, 270 n. 46, 272 n. 66
Peek, Wendy Chapman, 257–58 n. 19
phallocriticism, 45
phallogocentrism, 106–7, 115, 117, 178, 198–200, 203, 258 n. 24
phallus, the, 40–42, 47, 64, 66–67, 88, 89, 91–95, 98, 101, 104–6, 108–9, 109–22, 111, 115–16, 119, 120–22, 123–25, 160, 176, 198–99, 200–202, 244 n. 112; Brick's lack of, 104, 109–10, 111,

115–17; Brick's signifying phallus, 108–22, 124–25; Jake's lack of, 41, 59, 60–61, 64, 66–67, 88, 89, 94–95, 246 n. 148; Jake's signifying phallus, 64, 66; and lack, 42, 59, 60–61, 66–67, 88, 89, 93–95, 104, 109–10, 111, 115–17, 122–23, 198–99; as signifier, 42, 64, 66–67, 91–95, 101, 104–6, 108–9, 117, 119, 120–22, 124–25, 198, 200–202
Pipkin, Turk, 225 n. 31
Playboy (magazine), 19, 20, 160, 164, 224 n. 7, 268 n. 21, 278 n. 9
Pleck, Elizabeth, 44–45, 107, 231 n. 34, 242 n. 100, 243 n. 109, 248 n. 11, 249 nn. 19 and 24–25
Pleck, Joseph, 44–45, 107, 231 n. 34, 242 n. 100, 243 n. 109, 248 n. 11, 249 nn. 19 and 24–25
Plimpton, George, 23, 24, 25, 60, 225 n. 17, 237 n. 31
Pollock, Jackson, 252 n. 52
Porche, François, 240 n. 78
postmodernism, 31, 166–67, 168–70, 171–76, 177–86, 186–203, 203–5, 216, 218, 221, 269–70 nn. 36, 38, and 40, 270 nn. 41 and 43, 272 nn. 66–68, 274 nn. 83–88, 275 n. 94; and Williams, 166–67, 168–70, 173–76, 180–86, 189–96, 197–98, 200–203, 216, 218, 269 nn. 36 and 38, 270 n. 43
Pound, Ezra, 42, 71
Price, Marian, 34, 227 n. 5, 254 n. 4
Proust, Marcel, 47, 85, 211, 250 n. 29, 275 n. 91; *Remembrance of Things Past*, 211
Provincetown Players, the, 162
Pulitzer Prize, the, 132, 263 n. 64, Hemingway's for *The Old Man and the Sea*, 263 n. 64; Williams's for *Cat on a Hot Tin Roof*, 132

queer masculinity, 43–46
Quinby, Lee, 275–76 n. 96

Rader, Dotson, 22, 186, 219, 272 n. 62, 273 n. 72, 278 n. 15, 279 n. 16
Reagan, Ronald, 174
Reed, Rex, 266 n. 10, 268 n. 21
Revolución (Cuban newspaper), 28, 224 n. 2
Reynolds, Michael S., 26, 58, 71, 224 n. 4, 225 n. 40, 232 n. 48, 234 n. 3, 235 n. 24, 239 n. 67, 240 n. 68, 243 n. 103, 262 n. 63, 271 n. 58, 273 n. 73, 277 n. 1
Roberts, Meade, 28
Roosevelt, Franklin D., 139, 197
Roosevelt, Theodore "Teddy," 41, 46, 70, 82–84, 106, 243 nn. 103 and 106
Rosenberg, Charles E., 249 n. 24
Rosenberg, Ethel, 40
Rotary Club, the, 149
Roth, Hy, 19 (illustration)
Rotundo, E. Anthony, 32, 44, 45, 72, 105–6, 231 n. 33, 239 n. 63, 240 n. 71, 243 n. 107, 245 n. 132, 248–49 nn. 11, 12, and 14, 249 nn. 17–19
Rough Riders, the, 59, 70, 82–83, 106, 243 n. 103, 249 n. 18
Rubin, Gayle, 151, 177
Rudat, Wolfgang, 58, 60, 68, 235–36 n. 24, 237 n. 35, 239 n. 57, 245 n. 144, 246 n. 147
Russo, Vito, 232 n. 53

Saddik, Annette J., 270 n. 41
Sanderson, Rena, 89, 244–45 n. 124
Sandomir, Richard, 269 n. 32
Sarotte, Georges-Michel, 148, 244 n. 122, 260 n. 48
Sartre, Jean-Paul, 61–63, 66, 133–39, 134 (photo), 141, 142–44, 148, 152, 209, 238 n. 40, 253 n. 63, 255–56 n. 9, 256 nn. 10 and 13, 257 n. 16, 259 n. 32; *Age of Reason*, 138; *Being and Nothingness*, 62, 135, 138, 238 n. 41, 256 n. 12; comparison to Southern Gothic writers, 134; *Huis Clos*, 255 n. 9; interests in Williams, 255–56 n. 9, 256 n. 10; on meeting Williams, 134, 255–56 n. 9, 256 n. 10; Williams's interests in, 133–34, 138, 209; Williams's reading of, 253 n. 63, 256 n. 12
Savran, David, 39, 132, 229 nn. 18 and 25, 255 n. 5, 263 n. 68
Schlesinger, Jr., Arthur, 130, 139, 257 n. 19, 258 n. 23
Scholes, Robert, 54–55, 231–32 n. 45, 234 n. 6, 235 n. 21, 241 n. 80, 242 n. 96, 244 n. 123, 245 n. 145
Schwartz, Nina, 58, 67, 96, 99, 235 n. 24, 238 n. 38, 239 nn. 51–52, 242 n. 89, 245 n. 142, 246 n. 152

INDEX

Sedgwick, Eve Kosofsky, 69, 80–81, 85, 150–52, 153, 239 nn. 58 and 60, 242 n. 95, 246 n. 153, 261 nn. 54–55, 57, 265–66 n. 2, 266 n. 9
Seltzer, Leon, 67, 237 n. 35, 239 nn. 51 and 53
Seton, Ernest Thompson, 243
sexual existentialism, 30, 53, 59, 66–67, 87–88, 89, 91, 95, 142–46, 148, 155, 201, 212–13, 271 n. 54
Shackelford, Dean, 38, 229 n. 21, 262 n. 59
Shaffer, Peter, 265 n. 1
Shakespeare and Co. bookstore, the, 51, 71. *See also* Beech, Sylvia
Shakespeare, William, 130
Shipman, Evan, 92
Show Boat (Jerome Kern and Oscar Hammerstein II), 221
Showalter, Elaine, 45
Simon, John, 167, 180, 266 n. 8, 268 n. 28, 271 n. 53, 273–74 n. 76
Smith, Geoffrey S., 140, 258 n. 21
Smith-Rosenberg, Caroll, 250 n. 34
Somme, la, 41, 63
Sons of the American Revolution, the, 82
Spilka, Mark, 54, 55, 234 n. 4, 236 n. 28, 275 n. 95
Spillane, Mickey, 258 n. 26
Sports Illustrated (magazine), 226 n. 49
Spoto, Donald, 27–28, 226 nn. 42, 44, 46, 269 n. 31
St. Just, Maria (Britneva), 27 (photo), 208, 233 n. 66, 274 n. 79
St. Sebastian (the gay myth of), 244 n. 123
Stage/West Theater, 35
Steakley, James, 73, 230 n. 31, 240 n. 76, 248 n. 13
Stein, Gertrude, 51, 53, 71, 74–76, 81, 188, 209–10, 216, 219, 241 n. 83; Hemingway on, 74–76, 81; Williams on, 209–10, 219; *The Autobiography of Alice B. Toklas*, 75, 209, 241 n. 83
Stewart, David, 101
Stonewall Riots, the, 29, 31, 160, 162, 164–67, 186, 188, 197, 200, 204, 206, 216, 220, 268 n. 19
Strindberg, August, 168
Strychacz, Thomas, 56–57, 231–32 n. 45, 234 nn. 15–19, 239 n. 50

Symonds, John Addington, 71, 240 n. 69, 249 n. 15

Terman, Lewis, 126, 253 n. 64
Terman-Miles "M–F test," the, 126–27
Testi, Arnaldo, 243 n. 104
Théâtre Femina, 73
Theatre Guild, the, 225 n. 38, 279 n. 17
Thornton, Margaret Bradham, 28, 208, 233 n. 64, 246 n. 1, 277–78 n. 2, 278 n. 10
Time (magazine), 211, 256 n. 12, 266 n. 8
Tischler, Nancy, 228–29 n. 16, 253 n. 69
Toklas, Alice B., 75
Tolstoy, Leo, 210
Traister, Bryce, 45–46, 231 n. 38
Triangle Club, the (Princeton), 180
Truman, Harry S., 139
Twain, Mark, 52, 211; *The Adventures of Huckleberry Finn*, 52, 211
Tynan, Kenneth, 17–22, 24–25, 26, 31, 112, 209, 224 nn. 7–10 and 12, 225 nn. 14, 15, 29, and 32, 225–26 n. 41, 226 nn. 47–48 and 50, 255–56 n. 9

U. City Pep (Williams's high school newspaper), 221–22, 279 n. 19
Ulrichs, Karl Heinrich, 176, 230 n. 28, 249 n. 15, 250 n. 29
Updike, John, 176, 258 n. 26

Vaccaro, Marion Black, 18–20, 27, 134 (photo), 226 n. 44, 256 n. 10
Van Gogh, Vincent, 252 n. 52
Vannatta, Dennis, 247 n. 4
Vázques, Pepe Luis, 251 n. 41
Verdun, 63
Vidal, Gore, 80, 141, 258 nn. 25 and 26; *The City and the Pillar*, 80, 141, 258 n. 25; and first meeting Williams, 258 n. 25; Williams's criticism of, 258 n. 25
von Krafft-Ebing, Richard, 176, 230 n. 28, 249 n. 15, 250 n. 29
Vosper, Frank, 27
Vowles, Richard, 141, 258 n. 29

Wagner-Martin, Linda, 58, 60, 71, 235–36 n. 25, 237 n. 33, 239 n. 64
Wales-Padlock Law, the, 48, 232 n. 53, 265 n. 1
Wallace, Henry, 156
Washington University, 18, 29, 209

Waters, Arthur, 132, 229 n. 23, 254 n. 3
Watt, Douglas, 180, 266 n. 8, 271 n. 53
Wayne, John, 140; *Big Jim McLain,* 140; *The Red Menace,* 140
Weeks, Jeffrey, 73, 230 n. 31, 240 n. 76, 248 n. 13, 261 n. 54, 271 n. 50
Weil, Kari, 200, 276 nn. 97–99
Wescott, Glenway, 81
West, Mae, 73, 240 n. 75; *The Drag,* 73, 240 n. 75
Westphal, Karl Friedrich Otto, 43, 230 n. 28, 249 n. 15, 250 n. 29; "Die Konträre Sexlempfindung," 43, 230 n. 28, 249 n. 15
Wharton, Edith, 42; *A Son at the Front,* 42
Whitmore, George, 163, 165, 166, 268 nn. 17 and 22, 277 nn. 107 and 109, 278 n. 14
Wilde, Oscar, 43, 70, 74, 207, 217, 244 n. 123, 250 n. 29, 277 n. 111; *The Importance of Being Earnest,* 207, 277 n. 111
Williams, Craig A., 239 n. 49, 248 n. 9
Williams, Edwina, 224 n. 1
Williams, Rose, 168, 173, 197, 268 n. 29, 269 n. 31, 274 n. 85
Williams, Taylor, 18
Williams, Tennessee, and androgyny, 182–83, 189, 192, 200–201, 272 n. 60, 275 nn. 91 and 95, 276 n. 96; and bullfights and matadors, 20–21, 24–25, 30, 31, 49, 113–14, 208, 222–23, 233 n. 66, 251 n. 41; on camp, 164, 216–18, 271 n. 56; on the Cuban revolution, 21–22, 31; and the fear of Hemingway, 20, 23–24, 226 n. 47; and gay liberation, 30–31, 162–65, 166, 167, 178, 205–7, 267 nn. 10 and 14–16, 268 nn. 18 and 21, 277 nn. 105 and 109, 278 n. 13; and the gay v. the queer play, 160–65, 166; and Hazel Kramer (his childhood sweetheart), 121, 129, 251 nn. 37 and 43, 254 n. 72; in Hemingway criticism, 25–26, 224 nn. 4–5, 225 nn. 17, and 38–40, 225–26 n. 41; on Hemingway, his novels and his nonfiction, 52, 189, 192–93, 209–12, 226 n. 48, 233 nn. 64–66, 236–37 n. 30; 246–47 n. 1, 251 n. 39, 273 nn. 72 and 75, 274 n. 78, 277 n. 1, 277–78 n. 2, 278 nn. 6 and 9–10; on Hemingway's death, 211, 278 n. 8, and Kazan, 25, 33–35, 37, 131, 132, 226 n. 1, 227 nn. 2–4, 229 n. 23, 233–34 n. 67, 254 n. 1, 264 n. 70, 268 n. 27; and Kinsey, 127–29, 146–48, 260 nn. 45–46; on meeting Kinsey, 101, 127–29, 253 n. 69, 260 n. 46; similarities with Hemingway, 23; on meeting Hemingway, 18–25, 224 nn. 1–12, 224–25 n. 13, 225 nn. 14–32; on the public v. private Hemingway, 48, 167, 192–96, 198, 201–3, 205, 212–13; reading Christopher Marlowe, 253 n. 7, 256 n. 12; on reading Sartre, 256 n. 12; and his theater critics, 36–37, 40, 53, 131–32, 156, 161–64, 165, 167, 168, 174, 213, 228 n. 12, 254 nn. 2–3, 266 n. 8, 266–67 n. 10, 267 nn. 11–13, 268 nn. 25, and 26–29, 269 nn. 30–34, and 38–39, 271 n. 53, 273–74 n. 76; and travels to Paris, 134, 221–22, 255 n. 9; and Wilde, 244, 277 n. 111; and his youthful writings, 209, 221–22, 233 n. 65, 278 n. 7, 279 n. 19
—Works of short fiction: "Miss Coynte of Green," 200; "Three Players of a Summer Game," 30, 39, 101–29, 227 n. 3, 228 n. 10, 236 n. 30, 246–47 n. 1, 247 nn. 2–7, 250 nn. 34–35, 251 nn. 36–40, 252 n. 52, 253 nn. 60–63, 254 n. 71 (autobiographical elements in, 121, 128–29, 251 nn. 37, 41, and 43–44, 252 nn. 46–47 and 52, 254 nn. 71–73; bullfighting in, 30, 112–14; castration and emasculation in, 104, 109–11, 115, 117–18, 122; and *Cat on a Hot Tin Roof,* 30, 39, 101, 102–4, 126, 128, 133, 159; and censorship, 118, 252 n. 52, 253 n. 62; the "cult of masculinity" in, 103–9; [sexual or masculine] existentialism in, 109, 257 n. 16, 271 n. 64; the Freudian phallus in, 109–12; and Hemingway, 112–14, 195, 236–37 n. 30; homosexuality in, 118–23, 125–26, 277 n. 110; the Lacanian Phallus in, 116–22, 123–25; masculine signification in, 109–12, 114–15, 122–23; and *The Sun Also Rises,* 112–14, 116, 118, 250 n. 34; the writing of, 30, 101–3, 246–47 n. 1, 247 n. 2); "Desire and the Black Masseur," 273 n. 74; *Eight Mortal Ladies Possessed,* 164
—Works of nonfiction: "~~12~~ 13 Golden (?) Rules for New Playwrights," 222, 279 n. 20; "A Festival Night in Paris,"

279 n. 19; "Let Me Hang It All Out," 166, 266 n. 10; *Memoirs*, 18, 21, 25, 129, 137, 164, 165, 174–75, 187, 218, 224 n. 6, 251 n. 37, 252 nn. 46–47, and 52, 253 n. 62, 254 n. 73, 255 nn. 8–9, 267 nn. 10 and 16, 268 nn. 21 and 24, 278 n. 6; *Notebooks*, 17, 25, 28, 113, 130, 158, 208, 211, 212, 225 n. 33, 226 n. 48, 233 n. 64, 233–34 n. 67, 256 n. 12, 277–78 n. 2 (Hemingway in, 226 n. 48, 233 n. 64, 277–78 n. 2; Sartre in, 256 n. 12); "Note of Explanation," 33, 35, 227 n. 3, 233–34 n. 67; "A Report On Four Writers Of The Modern Psychological School," 209, 233 n. 65, 278 n. 7; "Something Wild . . . ," 155

— Works of fiction: *Moise and the World of Reason*, 163, 164, 165, 200, 268 n. 18; *The Roman Spring of Mrs. Stone*, 277

— Works of the theater: *Battle of Angels*, 222, 224–25 n. 13, 278 n. 10; *Camino Real*, 201, 214; *Cat on a Hot Tin Roof*, 18, 22, 26, 29, 30, 32–40, 48, 50–52, 53, 64–65, 96, 100, 101, 102–4, 115, 118, 126, 128, 130–59, 162–64, 166–67, 174, 182, 184, 185–86, 189, 201, 203–5, 213, 214–15, 219–20, 221–22, 226 n. 48, 226 n. 1, 227 nn. 2–3, 5, and 7–8, 227–28 n. 9, 228 nn. 10, 13, and 15, 229 nn. 17, and 20–22, 233 n. 62, 233–34 n. 67, 247 nn. 2–5, 250 n. 34, 251 n. 40, 253 n. 62, 254 nn. 71(ch. 3) and 1–4, 255 nn. 6 and 8, 256 n. 13, 256–57 n. 14, 257 nn. 15–18, 258–59 n. 29, 259 nn. 30, and 33–37, 260 n. 46, 260–61 n. 50, 261 n. 52, 261–62 n. 59, 263 n. 68, 264 nn. 71 and 73, 264–65 n. 74, 265 nn. 75–77, and 79, 266–67 n. 10, 271 n. 54, 273 n. 74, 278 n. 5 (Brick's ironic curtain-line in, 33, 35, 36–39, 40; 48, 50, 52, 145, 157, 158, 221–22, 259 n. 35, 264 n. 73; and *Clothes for a Summer Hotel*, 166–67, 174, 182, 184, 185–86, 203–5, 219–21; as Cold War signifer, 135–42, 148, 149–51, 174; criticism of, 33–40; and "Three Players of a Summer Game," 30, 39, 101, 102–4, 126, 128, 133, 159; existentialism in, 133–39, 148, 256–57 n. 14, 278 n. 5; homophobia in 151–53, 255 nn. 5–8; homosexual existentialism in, 153–57; the homosexual question in, 48, 52, 64–65, 96, 115, 131–33, 157, 162–64, 219, 227–28 n. 9, 228 nn. 10–15, 228–29 n. 16, 229 nn. 17–22, 251 n. 40, 253 n. 62, 254 nn. 2–3, 255 nn. 5–8, 257 nn. 16–17, 261 nn. 51–52, 264 n. 73, 264–65 nn. 74, 273 n. 74; and HUAC, 155–56, 254 n. 1, 260 n. 49, 264 n. 70; and the Kinsey Report, 146–48; sexual existentialism in, 142–46; and *The Sun Also Rises*, 50–52, 100, 138, 151, 157, 181, 212, 214–15, 221–22, 233 nn. 64 and 66, 263 n. 68, 271 n. 54; the third acts of, 32–36, 50, 52, 100, 128, 131–32, 145–46, 158–59, 213, 214, 221–22, 226 n. 48, 226 n. 1, 227 n. 3, 227–28 n. 9, 228 nn.10 and 12, 233–34 n. 67, 259 n. 36, 260 n. 46; the writing and rewriting of, 35, 101, 128, 133, 141–42, 145–46, 158–59, 166, 222, 226 n. 48, 226–27 n. 1, 227 nn. 2–4, 233–34 n. 67, 247 n. 2, 250 n. 34, 255 n. 6, 259 nn. 30, 33, and 35–37, 260 n. 46, 261–62 n. 59); *Clothes for a Summer Hotel*, 20, 22, 31, 57, 160, 166–207, 211, 218, 219, 220, 221, 226 n. 48, 268 nn. 25–26 and 29, 268–69 n. 30, 269 nn. 31–35 and 38–39, 270 nn. 42, 44, and 47, 272 n. 60, 276 n. 100 (androgyny in, 180–82, 200–201; and *Cat on a Hot Tin Roof*, 166–67, 174, 182, 184, 185–86, 203–5, 219–21; criticism of, 167–69, 173, 180; cultural schizophrenia in, 196–203; the Fitzgeralds in, 180–84; Hemingway in, 57, 184–85, 191–92, 193, 194, 211, 226 n. 48; homoeroticism in, 191–92; as postmodern pastiche of Hemingway's *A Moveable Feast*, 186–96; as sexuality metanarrative, 176–86, 216, 218, 276 nn. 100–101; similarities with Lyotard's *The Postmodern Condition*, 169–76; and *The Sun Also Rises*, 178, 181, 190–91, 221; theater reviews of, 167–68, 180, 269 nn. 32–34, 270 n. 44, 273–74 n. 76; the writing of, 166, 168, 219, 268 n. 25, 270 n. 42); *Confessional*, 268 n. 19. See also *Small Craft Warnings*; *The Glass Menagerie*, 201, 214, 216, 268–69 n. 30; *A House Not Meant to Stand*, 268 n. 19; *I Can't Imagine Tomorrow*, 161, 269 n. 38; *In the Bar of a Tokyo Hotel*, 161, 266 n. 8; *Kirche, Küche, Kinder,*

268 n. 19; *Lifeboat Drill*, 268 n. 19; *A Lovely Sunday for Crève Cœur*, 166, 197; *The Milk Train Doesn't Stop Here Anymore*, 161; *The Night of the Iguana*, 211, 256 n. 10, 267 n. 14; *Now the Cats with Jeweled Claws*, 268 n. 19; *Out Cry*, 200, 203, 216. See also *The Two-Character Play*; *A Place of Stone*, 133, 158–59; *The Red Devil Battery Sign*, 166, 264; *The Remarkable Rooming-House of Mme. Le Monde*, 268 n. 19; *Slapstick Tragedy*, 161; *Small Craft Warnings*, 163–65, 268 n. 19; *Something Cloudy, Something Clear*, 203, 216; *Steps Must Be Gentle*, 268 n. 19; *A Streetcar Named Desire*, 25, 127–28, 214, 216, 218, 256 n. 10, 266 n. 9, 266–67 n. 10, 270 nn. 42 and 44, 277 n. 110; *Suddenly Last Summer*, 31, 48, 162, 164, 244 n. 123, 265 n. 79; *Summer and Smoke*, 201, 212, 214; *Sweet Bird of Youth*, 18, 222, 224 n. 3; *This is the Peaceable Kingdom; Or, Good Luck, God*, 268 n. 19; *The Two-Character Play*, 161; *Vieux Carré*, 163–165, 197, 268–69 n. 30
— Works of poetry: *Androgyne, Mon Amour*, 200

Winchell, Mark Royden, 35, 51, 227 n. 9, 228 n. 16, 233 n. 63
Windham, Donald, 101, 113, 128, 217, 224 n. 3, 251 n. 41
Wister, Owen, 41
Wittig, Monique, 66, 177
Wixson, Christopher, 269 n. 35
Wolfe, Cary, 58, 235 n. 24, 275 n. 95
Wolfe, Thomas, 210, 278 n. 10
Wood, Audrey, 34, 233 n. 67, 247 n. 2, 278 n. 10
Woolf, Virginia, 52, 216
Wright, Les, 46, 231 n. 42
Wyatt, Jane, 40

Yacovone, Donald, 239 n. 61
York Theatre, 167
Young, Philip, 60, 236 n. 27, 239 n. 65